Learning Disabilities:
Theoretical and Research Issues

LEARNING DISABILITIES:
Theoretical and Research Issues

Edited by

H. LEE SWANSON
UNIVERSITY OF BRITISH COLUMBIA
BARBARA KEOGH
UNIVERSITY OF CALIFORNIA, LOS ANGELES

LAWRENCE ERLBAUM ASSOCIATES, PUBLISHERS
1990   HILLSDALE, NEW JERSEY   HOVE AND LONDON

Copyright © 1990 by Lawrence Erlbaum Associates, Inc.
All rights reserved. No part of this book may be reproduced in
any form, by photostat, microform, retrieval system, or any other
means without the prior written permission of the publisher.

Lawrence Erlbaum Associates, Inc., Publishers
365 Broadway
Hillsdale, New Jersey 07642

Library of Congress Cataloging-in-Publication Data

Learning disabilities : theoretical and research issues / edited by
    H.L. Swanson, Barbara Keogh.
        p.   cm.
    ''The incentive for this text was the result of a 1988 conference
sponsored by the International Academy for Research in Learning
Disabilities, held at the University of California, Los Angeles''–
–Pref.
    Includes bibliographical references.
    ISBN 0-8058-0392-0
    1. Learning disabilities—Congresses.   I. Swanson, H. Lee, 1947–.   II Keogh, Barbara
K.   III. International Academy for Research in Learning Disabilities.
LC4704.L413   1990
371.9—dc20   89-37575
                                                                                  CIP

Printed in the United States of America
10 9 8 7 6 5 4 3 2 1

Contents

PART I: INTELLIGENCE AND LEARNING DISABILITIES

PART III: SUBTYPING RESEARCH

Preface

The purpose of this text is to provide a review and critique of the current state of research in the areas of intelligence, social cognition, and achievement as it relates to learning disabilities. Specific attention is also paid to developments in an area of subtyping research. The chapters are up to date with regard to theoretical and technical developments in the field of learning disabilities and yet readable for anyone with a reasonable scientific background. The incentive for this text was the result of a 1988 conference sponsored by the International Academy for Research in Learning Disabilities, held at the University of California at Los Angeles. The 3-day conference was organized primarily around symposium topics that focused on the areas of intelligence, motivation and social cognition, and methodological issues in subtyping research. Within each session, either three or four papers were presented. This was followed by an open discussion of conference participants and a predesignated discussant. The same organization that was used in the conference serves as the structure for the text. A separate section of individual papers devoted to issues related to achievement also merged as an area with emerging technical advances. A small number of these papers are included in this text. Although two of the papers in this latter section do not have an isolated focus on achievement, per se, we included them because of their important contribution to the literature.

Overview of Theoretical and Research Issues

OVERVIEW

As a beginning point in our discussion related to the symposium topics, we would like to suggest that major theoretical advances have occurred in our understanding of learning disabilities. The progress we see is reciprocal—in which practical issues of diagnosis and intervention are beginning to become tightly intertwined with theory. Individuals in cognitive science, for example, and learning disabilities, are beginning to profit from collaborative efforts. No doubt, this progress has occurred in the face of difficulties associated with defining and diagnosing learning disabilities. As suggested in the first chapter by Keogh, this is because the integration and evaluation of findings from diverse orientations is complicated considerably when researchers cannot determine whether inconsistent or contradictory results are due to the heterogeneity in the LD sample or to deficiencies in their theories. Given the substantial dilemmas posed by inexact, incomplete and overlapping definitions of learning disabilities, that progress has occurred might be surprising. The following chapters, however, suggest that a much closer connection between the formulations of theory and learning disabilities are occurring. These advances in our conceptions of theories about areas of cognition, and achievement, for example, will, we hope, lead to improved diagnostic practices, which in turn should result in refined subject selection criteria and further theoretical progress. With this as an introduction, we would like to summarize the salient points of each chapter.

In the first chapter, Keogh provides an overview of federal financial resources that have been allocated toward the research of learning disabilities. Unfortunately, research from the various funding agencies (e.g., National Institutes of

1

Health, U. S. Department of Education) has been motivated from psychological, neuropsychological, educational, or biomedical perspectives that have not been interactive with each other. One reason for this interative work on learning disabilities, especially when it comes to translations into clinical and educational applications, relates to such issues as identification, classification and the heterogeneity of the learning disabled population. In an attempt to enhance interactive efforts across various orientations, Keogh suggests that some common assumptions must be shared. Some of these assumptions are: (1) the locus of the learning disability is in the individual, (2) learning disabled individuals do not function at levels consistent with their intellectual potential, and (3) learning disabled individuals exhibit unexpected failures in specific academic or educational tasks. Keogh suggests that several steps are necessary if one is to encourage the integration of various approaches to learning disabilities. Some of these steps include (1) detailing the primary attributes that distinguish learning disabilities from other conditions, (2) providing a detailed and comprehensive taxonomy (also see chapters by Speece, Kavale, and Forness) of the heterogeneity within learning disabilities, (3) searching for viable aptitude-treatment interactions, (4) relating learning disabilities to the content and structure of learning tasks (also see Ceci, Pelligrino, and Goldman, this volume), (5) testing competing models of treatment, instruction or intervention, and (6) documenting the longitudinal course of learning problems. Unless progress is made in some of these areas there will be minimal cross over effects between various perspectives (psychological, neuropsychological, biomedical).

INTELLIGENCE

In the first section of the text, Swanson provides an introduction to the area of intelligence. Several issues are raised related to measuring intelligence, but the majority of those issues revolve around what is meant by a specific versus a general learning deficit. Differential approaches to understanding learning disabled children's intellectual deficits are criticized because (a) they provide global constellation of performances that are insensitive to the specific processes necessary for learning, and (b) isolated performance deficits are most likely related to "Matthew Effects." It is suggested that disabled children's intelligence may be best understood within a framework that focuses on the accessing of information and the monitoring or coordination of resources. While it is argued that "specific models" are critical to the field, and may in fact underlie monitoring or high order deficits, a focus on monitoring process that coordinate multiple resource pools is also an important area of research focus (see Ceci, this volume, for a related discussion). The contribution of information processing models to our understanding of intelligence was described in terms of knowledge representation, response consistency, domain expertise, intellectual competence, and subtle processing differences. Consistent with Keogh's discussion in Chapter 1, it is noted that integrative and reciprocal work is beginning to occur between researchers in the areas of intelligence and learning disabilities. The aims of the following 4 chapters on intelligence details the direction to this reciprocal process.

Pellegrino and Goldman provide an excellent discussion related to our understanding of learning disabilities and intelligence by directing our attention to the notion of cognitive competence. They begin by suggesting that the link of learning disabilities to the construct of intelligence is confusing. For example, on the surface the relationship between intelligence and learning disabilities seems related because they are linked into diagnostic practices and operational definitions. However, if one defines intelligence as the ability to learn, intelligence does not seem like a construct that would attach itself to children who are deficient in their ability to learn. This conceptual problem is redressed by considering the fact that intelligence is more than what a test measures; intelligence is composed of many elements that involve processes and content. Unfortunately, modern theories of intelligence, as they relate to learning disabilities, are vague and have yet to be translated into operational testing practices. Further, our tests of intelligence do not emanate from theories of intelligence and cognition and our current tests of achievement do not incorporate theories on the development of domain expertise (see chapter by Hall and Gerber, this volume, for a related discussion). Pellegrino and Goldman's chapter provides several suggestions about how cognitive theories of intelligence can enhance our understanding of learning disabilities. One way this can be done is to test the learner in terms of the processes they will need for learning. Thus, an analysis of cognitive competence would include a precise analytic description of what is to be learned. These descriptions would include a description of (a) the initial state of the learner in terms of their domain specific knowledge, (b) the conditions that foster the acquisition of competence (e.g., specific abilities and strategies), and (c) the assessment of the effects of instructional implementation.

Ceci takes a slightly different view of the problems of relating learning disabilities to the construct of intelligence. He focuses on the advantages of a multiple resource model. He begins his discussion with an overview of the processes that characterize intellectual behavior. He views the process used by various ability groups as *comparable,* but individual differences exist in terms of the efficiency to which they are used. To appreciate this position one must make a contrast to traditional models. It has been traditional to think of learning disabilities in terms of aptitude by x process interactions. That is, LD students are characterized in terms of the capabilities they bring to a task, as well as the processes that are evoked to perform the task. Ceci argues, however, that these two factors do not appear in a vacuum, but rely on an informational and motivational context. Another traditional position has been to think of intelligence as a single resource pool that permeates all abilities and that a deviation or breakdown is manifested into some underlying process that supports it. This position assumes that intelligence represents a common resource pool that underpins and energizes all purposeful behavior. Thus, when a child has an uneven profile, (e.g., deficit in reading or math), as with the learning disabled, but average intelligence, it is assumed that relevant processing cites are blocking accesses to a general pool of resources. Ceci argues, however, that it may be appropriate to view intelligence as analogous to a modular computational device which is made up of independent processing systems. This modular view suggests that there are many independent processing centers and thus the profile variations we see in LD children reflect problems attributed to *independent* resource pools. The implications of the modular view is that variations in knowledge about a particular domain influence performance independent of the overall IQ. He suggests that many children, because of biological constraints or because they lack certain information requirements, do not process information effectively. This ineffective processing cannot be described in terms of general intelligence, but rather in terms of the efficiency in which there are mental processes from a particular pool of resources that are used.

Richard Wagner and Janet Kistner focus on two types of intelligence: *academic* intelligence, which are intercorrelated competencies required for success in formal situations (of which IQ tests are indirect measures), and *practical* intelligence, which is a tacit knowledge or informal know-how. Of particular interest is their development of the practical knowledge in which they focus on two areas:

1. Achievement-related beliefs or informal theories about one's abilities.
2. How to informally do academic tasks—via some type of improvisation.

The authors tackle a major and messy paradox in the field of learning disabilities captured in the following quote: ''A specific learning disability is related to some generalized deficits.'' To address this paradox, they pose several questions. They ask first, ''Is academic intelligence at the heart of poor academic performance in LD children?'' The authors make the case that disabled readers perform poorly on tasks that are not directly related to specific deficits. They also address the flip side of the question: Does poor academic performance of LD children result in deficits in academic IQ? The answer is yes—one who profits from educational experience will enhance general cognitive abilities. That is, the primary problem (reading) has an influence on academic intelligence. (Dr. Siegel may agree since IQ is only indirectly related to academic intelligence.) In short, LD children have deficits in intelligence and this conclusion runs counter to our general assumptions that IQ is normal and difficulties occur in some specialized academic areas.

In the area of practical intelligence, the authors ask, ''Are deficits in practical intelligence responsible for poor academic performance?'' The authors provide evidence that normative deficits related to achievement related beliefs and strategies are related to LD student's academic performance. The literature suggests that strategies for acquiring specific academic intelligence may differ between ability groups thus placing demands on LD children's academic performance.

There is the flip side of the question. "Is the impaired academic performance the result of deficits in practical intelligence?" Yes, repeated failures and maladaptive achievement related beliefs leads to demands on practical intelligence. In short, the questions posed by the authors are all affirmative suggesting that a reciprocal relationship exists between achievement and academic and practical intelligence.

As an introduction to the chapter by Short, Cuddy, Friebert, and Schatschneider, it is important to note that problem solving is probably one of the most important constructs of intelligence. As stated by Short et al., problem solving appears to be a skill critical to both academic and social success. Despite this fact, problem solving measures are seldom used to assess LD children's functioning. For example, placement of LD children into special programs traditionally rely on IQ tests, even though the relationship between IQ measures and problem solving is questionable. Learning disabled children are characterized as not only being less efficient in problem solving, but are less flexible in their selection of strategies than their NLD counterparts. Short et al., report findings that suggest that LD samples differ in IQ. This finding is of interest in itself, in that the IQ measures are low for LD's, but their results also suggest a deficit in LD kids in a fundamental component of intelligence—problem solving. Their study is important in terms of the implications related to individual differences to instructions that influence problem solving, as well as supporting the generality of IQ deficits in LD children.

Dr. Siegel presents some striking data which address the question of whether IQ scores are irrelevant to an analysis of reading difficulty. She presents evidence suggesting that variations in IQ within ability groups *are not* adequate predictors of performance measures. Thus, low IQ scores do not necessarily mean a reading problem and high IQ scores within reading ability groups does not necessarily mean better readers. The implications of her findings are quite clear: There is little support for the argument that differences on any IQ level may require different types of remediation. Another interesting aspect of her data was that reading samples appear to be rather homogeneous groups (e.g., in terms of language and memory skill) when defined by word recognition difficulty. This latter finding is of particular interest when one considers the heterogeneity issue that emerges in a number of chapters in this volume.

SUBTYPING

The major purpose of subtype research is to reduce heterogeneous sample of LD youngsters into homogeneous subgroups. While this goal seems rather straightforward there are, according to Forness, two major problems (a) measures or variables used to subtype are unreliable, and fail to account for a significant amount of the variance, and (b) most subgroups have little predictive power to external measures. Further and most importantly, Forness has suggested that the subgrouping enterprise has not resulted in substantiated classroom applications.

In terms of the methodological issues related to subtyping, the chapter by Speece is both astute and directive in terms of application to future subtype research. Some vexing issues noted by Speece related to cluster analysis techniques are theory formulation, problems regarding subject definition, number of subjects required for cluster analysis, selection of variables, defining how subjects are similar or dissimilar, what is normal performance, and questions about the reliability of clusters. The issues may be classified according to theory and validity. For example, in terms of theory formulation, Speece indicates that subtype research has not been theory driven, thus, a comprehensive system of identification is unlikely. Not only is there a problem related to definition, one does not know how many subjects to include in a cluster analysis. Further, we still have not agreed upon methodology for determining the absolute number of clusters. There are notable differences in clustering procedures and the means by which those procedures can be reliably evaluated.

Kavale views LD subtyping research as multivariate in nature in which the aim is not one of dividing the population along a single dimension. Rather, the classification in LD is aimed at identifying subgroups along a variety of dimensions that may be used to describe the heterogenous nature of LD. There are some negative aspects to this kind of subtype research. For example, Kavale has noted that LD subtype research has produced subtypes that are directed by the measures used, rather than producing new concepts. Further, one-third of the subjects classified as LD show no major deficits and therefore cannot be generalized to the entire LD population. In addition, the subtypes that are produced are rather gross categorizations (Kavale call this a macrotaxonomy) and what now is required is a refinement at a microlevel. Kavale presents a framework of subtyping research in which the first goal is to form categories on the basis of common attributes. He suggests researchers involved in the subtyping research should pool their efforts into producing a single classification scheme for the field of LD. This upward classification would unify what appears to be independent subtyping research that produces more heterogeneity in the population than appears necessary.

SOCIAL COGNITION

Bryan and Bryan's excellent analysis on the chapters on social cognition indicated a number of interesting insights. First, the field is becoming more sophisticated in focusing on the interpersonal aspects of learning disabilities. Thompson and Kronenberger's chapter, focuses on the area of emotional disturbances,

Vaughn and Hagan's chapter and Pearl and Bryan's chapter focus on social cognitive skills. Second, there is a need for more complex models of social status than has occurred in the previous literature. The limitations of previous models is partly related to the use of multiple indices of social status, as well as the limited parameters related to social cognition. Bryan and Bryan suggest from their analysis that the existing data base provides strong support for continued research on the social factors in learning disabilities.

Pearl and Bryan provide a provocative chapter on the vulnerability of learning disabled adolescents. As in the Vaughn and Hogan chapter, learning disabled students are viewed as being less liked by their peers and suffering from social cognitive deficits. Thus, they suffer social rejection and isolation. In addition, linguistic and pragmatic limitations lessens their ability to deal effectively in social situations. For example, problems in language comprehension make it difficult for them to fend off invitations to engage in socially inappropriate behaviors. Thus, one would expect an overrepresentation of learning disabilities among delinquent youth. To test the notion that LD students are vulnerable to delinquency and victimization, several studies are reviewed. The conclusions of these studies were that (a) conformity is related to the peers they perceive to be friends, (b) learning students are vulnerable to being participants in undesirable activity, (c) learning disabled students do not appear to have different assumptions about going along with a peer's request to engage in undesirable behavior, and (d) learning disabled students are less able to determine deceptive statements. These findings suggest that learning disabled students are more vulnerable than nondisabled students to engage in inappropriate behaviors. Data also suggest that learning disabled students seem to lack the knowledge and skills that protect them from being victimized by an ostensible friendly peer.

Thompson and Kronenberger suggest that the study of behavior problems in learning disabled students has been hampered by an absence of an empirically identified classification system. Progress in identifying children with specific types of behavior patterns has been made along two lines of research: peer nominations, and parent and teacher checklists. Both types of research have extended the delineation of behavior problems in children with learning problems. Results have suggested that children with educational problems have higher levels of behavior problems when compared to controls, but the various subtypes of children with educational problems share similar behavior problems. For example, most types of studies indicate that there is some degree of personality and conduct problems. Children with learning disabilities demonstrate higher levels of behavior problems than normal control children, but differences between LD and mentally retarded children are mixed. One important area of work has focused on children's behavior problems in the context of chronic developmental and medical problems. Thompson and Kronenberger reported in their research that:

1. preschool children who are at risk for developmental problems are also at risk for behavioral problems,

2. clinic referred children who have poor school performance have a high frequency of behavior problems,

3. there is little difference in the behavior problems across LD and mildly retarded children or other children with poor school performance, and

4. children perceived competency and family support have a mediating influence on behavior problems.

Consistent with some points of Bryan and Bryan, Sharon Vaughn and Anne Hogan have indicated that the area of social competence has remained an illusive research area. They define social competence as including four areas: positive relations with others, appropriate social cognition, absence of maladaptive behaviors, and effective social behaviors. Based on their analysis, they found, for example, that high risk children in kindergarten, later identified as learning disabled, have lower peer acceptance rating when compared to controls. Two possible hypotheses can be used to interpret the existing literature: one which views social competence as reflective of academic functioning, the other as a correlate of academic functioning. The results appear to support the latter. Learning disabled children display problems in all four areas of social competence. They were more frequently rejected, less accepted, and received lower overall rating by their peers. They also tend to have inaccurate perceptions of academic success and peer perceptions.

ACHIEVEMENT

Hall and Gerber provide an excellent introduction to the area of cognition and academic performance. They characterize achievement in terms of cognitive competence (also see Pelligrino and Goldman, this volume). That is, achievement should not only reflect the correctness of performance, but also how performance comes to be "initiated, sustained, and completed by the learner." The basic premise of their chapter is that student errors are often systematic and the analysis of those errors provides diagnostic information that is specific to an academic domain. Hall and Gerber provide an overview of what they consider to be the advantages and limitation in the measurement of achievement. Some of the advantages relate to the documentation of child progress. For example, standardized tests are often used to determine a child's academic strengths and weaknesses and to establish whether performance in one or more academic areas warrants recommendation for remedial services. The limitations of achievement testing is that the results have little or no impact on instruction. In analyzing this comment, the authors analyze the roles of the school psychologist and the teacher. With specific reference to the teacher, they indicate that teachers must be able to generate models of efficient problem solving for all tasks to be taught. This problem-solving model allows for the creation of specific correction subroutines and general instruction plans that can accommodate incomplete skill development. The authors complete their chapter by demonstrating how competence is better understood by mapping performance to domain specific indicators of processing.

Bos and Anders provide initial support for an interactive model for teaching text-based concepts. Although strides have been made in learning strategy instruction, there has been a growing concern that such research must be broadened to content area subjects. While much of the learning strategies research has been based on cognitive training models, Bos and Anders call for a closer inspection of teaching strategies that emanate from schema theory, psycholinguistic, and concept models of the reading process. Schema are data structures that provide an organizational framework in which new information can be integrated. Instructional principles from this orientation include procedures that develop relationships between and among existing and new concepts. Psycholinguistic models of reading provide a focus on comprehension and the student's ability to strategically access graphophonic, syntactic, and semantic subsystems. Conceptual learning can be viewed as a subset of schema theory in which emphasis is placed on instruction that explicates a concept. The authors focus on the interactive nature of learning by centering on the dialogue of the teacher and student in sharing their prior knowledge about key concepts. To test the model, the authors focused on vocabulary instruction and compared one model (semantic feature analysis—a procedure that encourages students to predict and confirm text-based meanings and relationships among vocabulary words) and a dictionary method (write definition from dictionary). The results of their study lead to an initial support of the interactive model.

Reading comprehension ability is probably one of the most important academic skills to be mastered by LD youngsters. Joanne Carlisle discusses one technique, the sentence verification method, as a basis for understanding comprehension difficulties. The author contrasted other means of assessment but views the sentence verification task (SVT) as a means of tapping language comprehension abilities without requiring the use of sophisticated reasoning skills. A research project was devised that utilized the SVT as a means for separating children with low and high reading ability. The procedure was successful in the areas of reading, listening, and word recognition. The importance of this procedure is its ability to measure the level of language comprehension.

To read efficiently requires skills in phonological syntheses. For example, to make sense of the alphabetic system of writing, a child must have an awareness that words are composed of separate, reusable phonemic segments. Further, beginning to read involves blending activities. If children have difficulty acquiring blending skills during reading instruction, their initial progress in learning to read will be delayed. Given the importance of sound blending, Torgesen and Morgan address three issues related to phonological coding: the developmental course of sound blending, the relationship between attainment of sound blending and reading skills, and, the component skills that contribute to good performance on blending tasks. Their analysis of the literature suggest that sound blending (synthesis skills) improves gradually during most periods from preschool to later elementary grades, except for the period between the end of kindergarten and mid to latter 1st grade. During this period, there is an accelerated growth pattern. Sound blending, as measured by auditory blending tasks is related to proficiency in reading acquisition. Consistent with Siegel's analysis, Torgesen and Morgan view phonological coding tasks as largely independent of general measures of verbal intellectual ability. One possible component that underlies individual differences in phonological synthesis is phonological awareness. Thus, Torgesen raises the question of whether a distinction between phonological synthesis and "awareness" is useful. The distinction is useful to the extent to which blending enables readers to decode and awareness is represented as a rather inert form of knowledge.

Hagen and Kamberelis present a cognitive–social developmental model of learning disabilities which cuts across several diagnostic categories. A dimensional approach is advocated. The first dimension includes the diagnostic groups of learning disabilities, low academic achievement with no discernible learning disability, diabetes mellitus, and seizure disorders. The second dimension includes elements that cut across diagnostic factors such as etiology, intellectual and cognitive abilities, academic performance, motivation, self-concept, family environment, and socioeconomic status. The third dimension is the developmental level of the child. Their model is a functional, developmental characterization of strengths and weaknesses across cognitive, behavioral, and social variables. When their data were analyzed utilizing the dimensional approach, there were a number of similarities across diagnostic categories. For example, children with seizure disorders and children with learning disabilities were similar in aptitude, achievement, information processing, and self-esteem. These findings corroborate with recent work on the relationship between motivation, attribution, and academic achievement. The implication for the field of learning disabilities is that cognitive deficits are not entities in and of themselves. They are an integral part of the environmental and cultural context (see the chapter by Ceci).

Although the chapter by Forness and Sinclair appears out of context for this section of the text, there can be no doubt that depression as an emotional disorder can occur with learning disabilities. Forness and Sinclair provide a succinct analysis of the diagnostic and symptomatic patterns related to diagnosis. As with most diagnoses, the prevalence of the diagnosis depends on the choice of diagnostic criteria and instrumentation. Regardless, special education populations tend to have a higher prevalence of depression. Although the link between learning disabilities and depression is not clear, the preliminary data by Forness and Sinclair suggest some relationship. Future research will determine whether depression results from learning disabilities, is related to the onset of learning disabilities, or some combination of factors.

La Greca and Stone focus on the role of achievement on the social, personal, and behavioral functioning of children with learning disabilities. Their chapter highlights several conceptual issues and methodological concerns that have affected our understanding of learning disabilities. In particular, they discuss the tendency of investigators to confound LD social status with academic achievement. They also raise the issue about whether the social, personal, and behavioral difficulties that are reported among LD students are primarily explained by low academic achievement. In a comprehensive review of a study, they assess whether LD/NLD differences in social functioning are largely accounted for by achievement differences. In the preliminary analysis of the results they suggest that boys and girls in LD groups receive lower peer rating of acceptance than their same-sex NLD counterparts. When attempts were made, however, to restrict the NLD sample to students whose achievement is within the same range as the LD student, they found that the NLD group was more competent on a variety of social and behavioral measures. Thus, they argue that poor achievement alone does not appear to be an adequate explanation for the peer relationship problems that characterize LD students. On the other hand, the authors admit that it is not clear which factors do underlie LD/NLD social status differences. As they have highlighted in their chapter, significant proportions of LD students are either neglected or rejected, and there is good reason to believe that the correlates of these two peer status problems are quite different. The authors suggest the possibility that achievement may play a mediating role in social status, but its status will not be understood until we begin to examine subtypes of LD students (this point is also made in the chapters of Keogh, Speece, Kavale).

FINAL COMMENT

We wish to thank all presenters who participated in the conference. A number of individuals presented papers, but their chapters were not included because of page constraints, as well as the fact that their papers were not part of the topical areas represented by the symposium. This selection process in no way discounts the significance of these presentations since many of those papers will be published in reputable journals and texts.

H. Lee Swanson
Barbara K. Keogh

1 Definitional Assumptions and Research Issues

Barbara K. Keogh
University of California, Los Angeles

Learning disabilities represent a major educational/clinical enterprise and a substantive topic of scientific inquiry. Each is supported by extensive human and financial resources. According to the U.S. Department of Education's *Ninth Annual Report to Congress,* in 1985–86 almost 5% of school children nationally were identified as learning disabled and received special educational services. This figure is in contrast to the next most prevalent categories of handicap, speech impairment (2.86%) and mental retardation (1.86%). It should be emphasized that learning disabilities is the only handicapping condition that increased in prevalence over a 10-year period, the percentages of children identified and served growing from 1.79% in 1976 to 4.73% in 1986.

Mandates in PL 94-142 have resulted in a proliferation of programs, increased demands for trained personnel, and a heavy financial demand on school districts. Following the passage of PL 94-142 in 1975, financial expenditures for special education rose at a rate of 14% annually, a figure almost twice that for regular education (Stark, 1982). In the 1981 Rand Corporation study of the costs of special education, Kakalik, Furry, Thomas, and Carney (1981) reported that the cost of educating a learning disabled child averaged $2875 above that already expended for regular education, and they anticipated increasing additional costs in subsequent years. Based on both prevalence and costs, it is clear that special education in general, and learning disabilities in specific, represent practical educational problems of major importance.

Concern for learning disabilities as a topic of scientific study is evidenced also in the proliferation of published studies and in increased research support from funding agencies. In 1986 the National Institutes of Health and the U. S. Department of Education allocated over $40,000,000 to learning disabilities specific research and over $103,000,000 to learning disabilities related research (Interagency Committee on Learning Disabilities, 1987). This support covered a diverse range of topics, e.g. cognitive phenotypes in familial dyslexics, brain mechanisms in learning and memory, brain imaging, auditory and attentional functions, developmental agraphia, and dyslexia.

With some exceptions, research funded by the Department of Education has been directed at applied problems, at programmatic, organizational, and policy concerns (Interagency Committee *Report*, 1987). Topics addressed in recent years include identification, classification, and placement procedures, adherence to PL 94-142 requirements, prevalence of handicapping conditions, barriers to service, and policy related to the Regular Education Initiative. These are important questions, given the number of individuals with learning problems. However, policy and programmatic research sheds limited light on etiological and functional aspects of learning disabilities. Clearly both "basic" and "applied" efforts involving a number of disciplines are necessary if we are to understand learning disabilities and what to do about them. Somewhat paradoxically, it is the need for input from different disciplines that leads to inconsistencies and confusions. Findings from different perspectives do not necessarily translate well, and too often research efforts are parallel rather than integrated. Intervention techniques based on biomedical or neuropsychological models may lack validity within an educational context, and educationally important data may have little relevance for research on specific cognitive processing functions.

It should not surprise us that educational, psychological, and biomedical approaches to learning disabilities are often parallel rather than integrated, nor should we necessarily view this as a negative. As with other conditions that lack clear definition, our understanding of learning disabilities is both plagued and enhanced by the diversity of perspectives and by the range of indicators or symptoms presented by individuals identified as learning disabled. Historically, the search has been for a unified condition and a single encompassing definition. This has lead to long and often heated arguments, and to definitions that are so broad they do not differentiate among conditions or to definitions that are so narrow they lack coverage. Indeed, few operational definitions meet the Blashfield and Draguns (1976) criteria of reliability, coverage, descriptive validity, and predictive validity. The problem is partly because we do not deal with a single condition or syndrome, nor is there a single etiology. Reviewing the array of conditions or symptoms that have been used to describe learning disabilities, it is logical to argue for a multiple rather than a single syndrome approach.

If learning disabilities are viewed as a set of related but partially independent conditions with a number of possible etiologies, we can put aside the futile search for a single condition and respond in orderly fashion to a range of problems. Recognition that the term, learning disabilities, refers to a heterogeneous set of conditions or problems allows us to deal with a diversity of symptoms or attributes and the educational or clinical responses to them. The multiple syndrome approach is not novel, and there is increasing consensus that the diversity in any group of learning disabled individuals is not due just to errors in identification and classification, but rather represents real and legitimate variation. Part of the conceptual task is to impose order on the variation, and part of the applied task is to link differentiated and powerful clinical/educational responses.

COMMON ASSUMPTIONS

It should be emphasized that there are some commonly held assumptions which cut across the array of attributes associated with learning disabilities and which bring some consensus to the various conceptualizations or definitions. First, it is assumed that a learning disability is locused in the individual. The most prevalent early inference was that a learning disability was a direct consequence of neurological damage or central nervous system pathology, a view based primarily on clinical reports of medically diagnosed patients. The notion of minimal brain dysfunction, an extrapolation of the neural damage hypothesis, received major impetus from the work of Strauss, Kephart, Lehtinen, and their coworkers, and was explicitly tied to learning disabilities by Cruickshank (see Doris, 1986 for review). This tradition has been expanded and developed by work in the neurosciences and neuropsychology which has focused on identification of brain-behavior links (see Knights & Bakker, 1976; Obrzut & Hynd, 1986; and *School Psychology Review*, Volume 10, 1981). Recent work derived primarily from information processing paradigms also implicates a range of within-individual problems (Swanson, 1988) but emphasizes functional processing problems rather than structural ones. Despite differences in the nature of the causal hypotheses, however, the assumption of an individually based problem is fundamental, and leads to the incorporation of the troublesome "exclusionary criteria" (e.g., social or economic disadvantage, lack of educational opportunity) in most definitions.

A second common assumption is that learning disabled individuals do not function at levels consistent with their intellectual potential. The aptitude-achievement discrepancy has been operationalized with different formulae and different measures (see Cone & Wilson, 1981; Reynolds, 1984-1985). The discrepancy model has been analyzed, supported, and criticized, and a number of investigators have described inconsistencies in decision making related to the method of assessment, the formulae, or the statistics applied (Shepard, 1980, 1983; Ysseldyke, Algozzine, Richey, & Graden, 1982). There is also disagreement as to what and how much constitute a meaningful discrepancy. A large literature addresses these problems (see *Learning Disabilities Research*, Volume 3, number 1, 1987). However, the notion of a discrepancy between aptitude and achievement continues to be fundamental to most definitions of learning disabilities, and is one of the indicators that presumably differentiates learning disabled individuals from slow learners or retarded learners.

A third assumption has to do with specificity (Stanovich, 1986). Broadly stated, it is argued that learning disabled individuals exhibit unexpected failures in certain, but not all, academic or educational tasks (e.g., reading, arithmetic, spelling). Stanovich (1986) notes that the assumption of specificity ". . . is a necessary concomitant to the idea of a learning disability, because violation of the assumption undermines the utility of the label" (p. 232). If depressed performance or achievement were evident in all academic areas, the individual would more likely be considered a slow learner, mildly retarded, or lacking in motivation. A number of causal hypotheses have been proposed to explain the specific failure, most inferring some links between neural or cognitive functions and the demands of particular academic tasks. Thus, we might expect a specific deficit in short-term memory to present problems for certain kinds of tasks but not in others; similarly, we would expect short-term memory deficits to have different consequences than deficits in elaborative coding. The notion of specificity provides a way of differentiating the learning disabled poor achiever from other groups of poor achievers. It also provides direction for identification of qualitatively different types of learning disabilities.

CLASSIFICATION AND IDENTIFICATION

Critics quite rightly challenge both the conceptualizations and the operational definitions that have guided both research and practice in learning disabilities. Yet, lack of agreement is not necessarily bad; indeed premature consensus might lead to narrow and inequitable inferences. It is possible, too, that the challenges have been based on inappropriate evidence. A good deal of the controversy about definition relates to imprecise measurement and inadequate clinical/educational practices used to identify individuals as learning disabled. Definitions are derived or inferred from identified groups. The consequence is that the conceptualization of learning disabilities has been confused with the operational data of assessment. Too often classification and identification issues have been confounded, leading to faulty inferences and improper generalizations (Keogh, 1987). Farnham-Diggory (1986) summarized the research catch 22: "We are trying to find out what's wrong with children whom we won't be able to accurately identify until after we know what's wrong with them." (p. 155).

Closely related, there are possible and reasonable differences in definitional and operational criteria as a function of the purposes of classification (Keogh, 1983). Definitional criteria for delivery of services and for research on particular neuropsychological processes are quite different. Thus, we should expect some subject differences when identification is made for research or for clinical purposes, or when research is directed at different aspects of learning disabilities. These differences do not negate the validity of the problem condition. Indeed, a growing literature documents the reality of learning disabilities while at the same time acknowledging the inconsistencies and ambiguities that characterize the condition.

RESEARCH ISSUES

Looking to the future, several steps are necessary if we are to understand learning disabilities as a personal and educational problem. Many of these are addressed in subsequent chapters in this volume.

First, the primary criterial attributes which distinguish learning disabilities from other problem conditions must be specified and agreed upon. Critics have argued that learning disabled children are no different from slow learners or mildly retarded individuals. If so, there is no need for detailed diagnostic assessment or specialized instructional programs. Establishment of the validity and independence of the condition, thus, is a major and important challenge.

Second, it is necessary to organize and order the diversity captured in the learning disabilities rubric. The first point dealt with interproblem characteristics, the second with intraproblem attributes. A number of efforts toward organization have been attempted and many are currently in progress (McKinney, 1988). These efforts may well lead to an accepted taxonomy of learning disabilities which could improve diagnostic precision and clarify research findings.

The need for a detailed and comprehensive taxonomy or organization of the heterogeneity within learning disabilities is also apparent when applications to interventions are considered. Thus, a third consideration relates to the search for aptitude-treatment interactions. Historically this search has proved disappointing (Cronbach & Snow, 1977) but the effort seems promising in learning disabilities. Swanson (1988) has argued that past efforts have failed because of imprecisely defined and poorly operationalized psychological processes, nonspecific and inappropriate treatment strategies, and weak statistical analyses. If it is possible to specify legitimate and meaningful subgroups of learning disabilities, then it is possible to develop and test appropriate and powerful educational and clinical responses. It is clear that the aptitude-treatment interaction model is not effective for learning disabilities broadly defined, but rather, must be based on the specification of coherent and theoretically sound subgroups.

Fourth, and closely related, understanding learning disabilities requires understanding of the content and organization or structure of the tasks to be learned. From this perspective, learning disabilities do not exist in a vacuum, but rather are specific to particular demands or learnings, and are contextually based. Thus, disabilities in reading may differ from disabilities in mathematics, not just because the individuals differ in perceptual or cognitive abilities, but because the demands of the tasks differ. Even if we were able to agree upon precise sampling criteria, thus ensuring homogeneity of subjects, we should expect different expressions of problems as a function of the constraints in the learning tasks themselves. This perspective mandates research on the demands and constraints inherent in the content of schooling, including social and affective accomplishments. It also moves us beyond the historical notion of an exclusive in-child deficit (e.g. visual perceptual or auditory perceptual problems) as the basis of learning disabilities.

A fifth consideration relates to practice and concerns the need to test competing models. The literature on learning disabilities is filled with descriptions of particular programs and treatments. Many claim success, although the evidence in support is often limited in power and lacking in generalization. While many approaches claim some success, the *relative* success of programs is unknown. There are few reported efforts to compare program effectiveness or to test competing hypotheses about diagnosis or treatment. This question is of interest from a theoretical perspective, as comparative analyses may shed light on the nature of various subconditions subsumed by learning disabilities. The issue is important on a practical level given the extensive human and financial resources which go into clinical decision making and treatment. There is an incredible array of diagnostic techniques and treatment programs designed to remediate learning disabilities. Yet, we are uncertain if the time and cost of particular approaches lead to more insightful diagnosis and more powerful remediation than other simpler and less detailed efforts. As example, it is reasonable to ask if strategy training programs are more efficacious than applied behavioral techniques, if vision training is more effective than direct remedial instruction. Clinical experience suggests that almost any treatment or intervention has an effect, that some intervention is better than no intervention. However, global and unspecified effectiveness is not enough, from both theoretical and applied perspectives. The relative effectiveness of competing programs requires test.

Finally, there is increasing consensus that learning disabilities are expressed across a wide age range, and that problems are not limited to school age children. There is, however, little longitudinal evidence to document the developmental course of learning problems, and the mechanisms and dynamics which influence their expression are unspecified. Unraveling the developmental issues will necessitate consideration of both individual and contextual variables, and will also require the test of models from different disciplines.

ACKNOWLEDGMENTS

All correspondence should be sent to: Barbara K. Keogh, Ph.D., Graduate School of Education, 122 Moore Hall, UCLA, Los Angeles, CA, 90024. Preparation of this chapter was supported in part by the National Institute of Child Health and Human Development under a grant to the Socio-behavioral Group of the Mental Retardation Research Center, UCLA.

REFERENCES

Blashfield, R. K., & Draguns, J. G. (1976). Evaluative criteria for psychiatric classification. *Journal of Abnormal Psychology, 85* (2), 140–150.

Cone, T. E., & Wilson, L. R. (1981) Quantifying a severe discrepancy: A critical analysis *Learning Disability Quarterly, 4* (4), 359–371.

Cronbach, L. J., & Snow, R. E. (1977). *Aptitudes and instructional methods.* New York: Irvington.

Doris, J. (1986). Learning disabilities. In S. J. Ceci (ed.), *Handbook of cognitive, social, and neurological aspects of learning disabilities, Volume 1* (pp. 3–54). Hillsdale, NJ: Lawrence Erlbaum Associates.

Interagency Committee on Learning Disabilities. *A report to the U.S. Congress* (1987) .

Farnham-Diggory, S. (1986). Time, now, for a little serious complexity. In S. J. Ceci (Ed.), *Handbook of cognitive, social and neurological aspects of learning disabilities.* Hillsdale, NJ: Lawerence Erlbaum Associates.

Kakalik, J. S., Furry, W. S., Thomas, M. A., & Carney, M. F. (1981) . *The cost of special education.* Santa Monica, CA: The Rand Corporation.

Keogh, B. K. (1983) . Classification, compliance, and confusion. *Journal of Learning Disabilities, 16*(1), 25.

Keogh, B. K. (1987) . Learning disabilities: In defense of a construct. *Learning Disability Research, 3* (1), 4–9.

Keogh, B. K. (1988). Diversity in search of order. In M. Wang, M. Reynolds, & H. Walberg (Eds.), *Handbook of special education research and practice, Vol. 2.* Oxford, England: Pergamon Press.

Knights, R. M., & Bakker, D. J. (Eds.). (1976). *The neuropsychology of learning disorders.* Baltimore, MD: University Park Press.

Learning Disabilities Research (1987), *3* (1), 10–63.

McKinney, J. D. (1988). Research on conceptually and empirically derived subtypes of specific learning disabilities. In M. Wang, M. Reynolds, & H. Walberg (Eds.), *Handbook of special education research and practice.* Oxford, England: Pergamon Press.

Obrzut, J. E., & Hynd, G. W. (Eds.). 1986. *Child neurospychology, Volumes 1 & 2.* Orlando, FL: Academic Press.

Reynolds, C. R. (1984–1985). Critical measurement issues in learning disabilities. *The Journal of Special Education, 18* (4), 451–476.

School Psychology Review. (1981). Volume 10.

Shepard, L. (1980). An evaluation of the regression discrepancy method for identifying children with learning disabilities. *The Journal of Special Education, 14* (1), 79–91.

Shepard, L. A. (1983). The role of measurement in educational policy: Lessons from the identification of learning disabilities. *Educational Measurement: Issues and Practice, 2* (3), 4–8.

Stanovich, K. (1986). New beginning, old problems. In S. J. Ceci (Ed.), *Handbook of cognitive, social, and neurological aspects of learning disabilities, Volume 1* (pp. 3–54). Hillsdale, NJ: Lawrence Erlbaum Associates.

Stark, J. H. (1982). Tragic choices in special education: The effects of scarce resources on the implementation of Pub. L 94–142. *Connecticut Law Review, 14* (47), 477–493.

Swanson, H. L. (1988). Comments, counter comments, and new thoughts. *Journal of Learning Disabilities, 21* (5), 289–298.

United State Department of Education (1987). *Ninth Annual Report to Congress.*

Ysseldyke, J. E., Algozzine, B., Richey, L., & Graden, J. (1982). Declaring students eligible for disability services: Why bother with the data? *Learning Disability Quartorly, 5* (1), 37–43.

INTELLIGENCE AND LEARNING DISABILITIES

2 Intelligence and Learning Disabilities: An Introduction

H. Lee Swanson
University of Northern Colorado

A causal review of the research relating learning disabilities to intelligence indicates that the field has been plagued by vague conceptualizations and a lack of clear theoretical foundation (e.g., Farnham-Diggary, 1986). One approach to enhance conceptual clarity is to examine theoretical principles related to cognitive explanations of intelligence and to identify points of overlap with the field of LD (e.g., Day & Borkowski; 1987; Sternberg, 1987). The chapters in the next section offer an extension of current models of intelligence and add definitional clarity to our understanding of LD. These advances cover such topics as domain specific knowledge (Pellegrino and Goldman, Chapter 3), multiple resource models (Ceci, Chapter 4, & Short, Cuddy, Friebert, and Schatschneider, Chapter 6), practical intelligence and student attributions (Wagner and Kistner, Chapter 5, and IQ scores, Siegel, Chapter 7) to intellectual functioning of learning disabled students.

In order to provide an introduction to the difficulties in relating what we know about intelligence to learning disabilities, let us first focus on how one conceptualizes learning disabilities. The traditional account of learning disabilities is one that suggests there is a deficit in intellectual performance, but this deficit depresses only a limited aspect of contextually appropriate behavior. Traditionally, this depression of contextually appropriate behavior is described in terms of a discrepancy between some aspect of academic performance and intellectual behavior (e.g., Brown et al., 1986; Forness, Sinclair, & Guthrie, 1983). So, for example, a child may be identified as learning disabled if he or she displays reading performance 2 or more years below grade level, but nevertheless tests in the overall average IQ range. While this conception seems like one that would easily lend itself to operationalization there are immense conceptual problems with such an approach (see Kavale, 1987; Kavale & Forness, 1985, Siegel, Chapter 6 for a review).

To begin with, the term learning disabilities itself is somewhat of a misnomer, especially if one attempts to distinguish the learning disabled from other exceptional children, such as the mentally retarded (also see Sternberg, 1987, for a related discussion). For example, the difference between the learning disabled and the mentally retarded cannot be adequately described in terms of *mentality* or *learning* (or in terms of retardation or disabilities for that matter). Rather, the distinction between LD children and the mentally retarded is in terms of the *generality* of their performance deficit (see Stanovich, 1986; Sternberg, 1987; for a related discussion). Unfortunately, the generality of these performance deficits are also not easy to distinguish or conceptualize. For example, which aspects of learning disabilities are general to all or almost all environments, and which are limited to more specific environmental situations (see Wagner and Kistner, Chapter 5 for a related discussion)? In addition, how does one conceptualize a learning disability outside of the classroom context? We can, of course, skirt around these issues by focusing on contextual behavior (i.e., behavior in the classroom). However, even if the researcher limits him or herself to the study of the classroom context, several perplexing issues emerge. For example, what constitutes intelligent behavior when LD children's specific intellectual deficits are on tasks highly correlated with successful classroom functioning? Further, how can these children's intellectual functioning be specific when they perform poorly on a multitude of cognitive tasks? Answers to these fundamental questions in the literature are unclear. In fact, because of some of the aforementioned conceptual ambiguities, some researchers have begun to question the utility of intelligence (as measured by IQ tests) as an appropriate construct for the field of learning disabilities (e.g., Stanovich, 1986; Siegel, Chapter 7).

Assuming for a moment that the aforementioned issues can be put aside, one obvious strategy to begin operationalizing learning disabled children's intellectual functioning would be to combine all the relevant dimensions of their adaptive and nonadaptive behavior (for example, classroom functioning) into an overall test or index. No doubt, such a test would be somewhat arbitrary in the items selected, but in principle it might provide some device to separate LD from NLD children. Of course, this ideal is unattainable since many of the relevant dimensions of LD children's behavior, such as poor strategy use (e.g., Bauer & Emhert, 1984; Borkowski, Johnston & Reid, 1987) or metacognitive deficiencies, (e.g., Palincsar & Brown, 1987) are not standardized or even identified. Further, the poor adapting characteristics of the LD child would have to include not only measures of vocabulary, analogical reasoning, social judgments, and general information, but also creativity, flexibility, the learning of wit, and common sense. These later characteristics exhibit themselves only in practical or unique situations, and others cannot be evaluated except by observing this child over an extended period of time. Thus, the researcher is seemingly left with two possibilities in an attempt to conceptualize and ultimately assess the intellectual functioning of learning disabled students: to forget about measuring intelligence altogether (e.g., Siegel, Chapter 7) or to measure it inadequately. In relation to civil rights, economics, and social bias concerning who gets labeled LD (e.g., Shephard & Smith, 1983; Shephard, Smith, & Voijer, 1983; also see Ceci, Chapter 4), much could be said for the first alternative, but for various reasons the field has adopted the second. Because the second alternative characterizes the field of learning disabilities, it is critical that theoretical models of intelligence direct such practices. The position considered here is to direct the measurement of LD students' intelligence in terms of theoretical models based on cognitive science.

DIFFERENTIAL APPROACHES

Until recently, the measurement of LD children's intelligence has been predominately characterized by differential or psychometric approaches. Differential approaches are based on the assumption that latent sources of individual differences are related to mathematically derived factors (e.g., simultaneous and successive factors on the Kaufman ABC-test, verbal and performance factors on the WISC-R). While interpretations of factor analysis are equivocal (e.g., see Carroll, 1983), the goal of such procedures is to isolate global constellations of LD children's functioning. In a practical sense, this approach assumes that standardized intelligence tests assess individual differences along some continuum, and that the test items reflect some meaningful construct; otherwise, the test would be of little interest or value as a descriptive and/or predictive instrument. An important goal of the differential orientation is the accurate prediction of task performance. This is an important goal (however, see Pellegrino and Goldman, Chapter 3) in that appropriate placement of LD children constitutes a serious problem in public school assessment procedures (Shephard & Smith, 1983). Unfortunately for the field of learning disabilities, the differential approach tends to focus on a relatively narrow range of predictors, of which only the products of performance are measured (e.g., a battery of tests are given such as the WISC-R, and scores are recorded). In addition, the focus on such product (i.e., test-score) information, derived from measures of narrowly defined aptitudes (e.g., school success), are questionable (e.g., Messick, 1984). For example, rarely have the data from traditional psychometric products accounted for adequate amounts of variation in criterion-task performance (e.g., McCall, 1977). Further, children identified as learning disabled, via psychometric procedures, often may not be reliably distinguished from other low-achieving children (e.g., Kavale & Forness, 1984; Shephard, Smith, & Voijer, 1983; Ysseldyke, Thurlow, Graden, Wesson, Deno, & Algozzine, 1983). More importantly, there is some emerging data based that suggests that such an approach has difficulty (a) defining the mental processes necessary for effective learning, (b) identifying subprocesses required on school tests as well as global processes required for school learning, and (c) providing a link between cognitive-instructional theory and educational practices (see Wagner & Sternberg, 1984 for a review).

Perhaps, the most serious limitation of the differential approach, at least in terms of operationalizing the term learning disabilities, is that such an orientation obscures the *specific* learning disability we are trying to find (see Stanovich, 1986 for a related discussion). For example, several reviews (e.g., Brown & Campione, 1986; Stanovich, 1986; Ysseldyke et al., 1983) have suggested the LD children perform less well than nondisabled students on a multitude of psychometric measures. Recognizing this, practitioners to date (e.g., see Ysseldyke et al., 1983) focus on a differential deficit; that is, a greater deficit in one or more subtests than in others. Unfortunately, poor subtest performance does not necessarily represent a differential deficit in ability. It may instead reflect learning disabled children's generalized performance deficits (Stanovich, 1986, refers to these as "Matthew effects"), coupled with the fact that one or a combination of the subtest items better measure these generalized deficits than others. Thus, low scores on various test items cannot be interpreted as indicating a "specific" learning disability. In support of the earlier inferences, two arguments are brought to bear.

First, while these factor analyses indicate general abilities needed on these tests, they have not provided insight into LD students intellectual functioning. One reason for this state of affairs is that much of what may be called intelligent behavior is organized into problem-solving skills or cognitive strategies which are, in turn, composed of subskills and substrategies (see Chase & Ericsson, 1981; Borkowski, 1985; Borkowski, Carr, & Pressley, 1987; Greeno, Riley, & Gelman, 1984; Rozin, 1976; Simon, 1981; also see Short et al., Chapter 6). Therefore, the intellectual factors derived from psychometric measures are constructed from interrelated cognitive skills. The implication for understanding LD students' intellectual functioning is that much of their cognitive behavior reflects their ability to *access* various cognitive subroutines as well as apply strategies to an increasing range of tasks. Thus, an understanding of how LD children strategically access to tasks as related resources in integral to any theoretical, as well as practical, explanation of learning disabilities (see Ceci, Chapter 4; Brown & Campione, 1986; Palincsar & Brown, 1987; Pressley, Johnson, & Symons, 1987 for a review).

Second, psychometric research may be misdirected in its focus on specific psychological deficits. The assumption of many of these studies (standardized or curriculum related) is that specific, independent, and identifiable clusters of skills or abilities are involved in LD children's learning impairment (e.g., reading, math). However, even if such skills are identified, it may be argued that such skills do not represent isolated difficulties in specific skills or processes, but may reflect high-order cognitive difficulties that influence the coordination and monitoring of these processes. That is, several studies in the last few years have indicated that disabled children have difficulties on a number of general or global mental activities (see Stanovich, 1986; for a discussion related to the conceptual ambiguities related to these findings).

In support of this assumption, the research resource monitoring may be summarized as follows: LD children experience difficulty with such self-regulatory mechanisms as checking, planning, testing, revising, and evaluating during an attempt to learn or solve problems (e.g., Bos & Filip, 1982; Brown & Palinscar, 1982, 1988; Butkowsky & Willows, 1980; Palincsar & Brown, 1984, 1987; Pressley & Levin, 1987; Wong, 1978, 1979, 1982; Wong, Wong, Perry, & Sawatsky, 1986). Such children perform poorly on a variety of tasks that require the use of general control processes or strategies for solution (e.g., Bauer & Emhert, 1984; Dallego & Moeley, 1980; Deshler, Alley, Warner, & Schumaker, 1981; Englert, Raphael, Anderson, Anthony, Fear, & Gregg, in press; Garner & Reis, 1981). Under some conditions, well designed strategy training improves performance (e.g., Borkowski, Weyhing, & Carr, 1988; Duffy et al., 1986, 1987; Gelzheiser, 1984; Graham, 1985; Graves, 1986; Hallahan, Lloyd, Kosiewica, Kaufman, & Graves, 1979; Malamoth, 1979; Hasselborn & Korkel, 1986; Leon & Pepe, 1983; Torgesen, Murphy, & Ivey, 1979; Short & Ryan, 1984; Wong & Jones, 1982), while at other times some general cognitive constraints prevent the effective use of control processes (e.g., Baker, Ceci, & Herrmann, 1987; Shankweiler et al., 1979; Swanson, 1984b, 1987; Wong, Wong, & Foth, 1977; see Cooney & Swanson, 1988 for a review). However, when training of information processing components includes self-evaluation (e.g., predicting outcomes, organizing strategies, using various forms of trial and error), and attributions are related to effective strategy use (Licht, 1983; Licht, Kistner, Ozkaragoz, Shapiro, & Clausen, 1985; Oka & Paris, 1987; Pearl, Bryan, & Herzog, 1985) subprocesses are automatized (see Samuels, 1987; Pellegrino & Goldman, 1987; Kolligian & Sternberg, 1987; however, see Cheng, 1985), and training attempts are successful (e.g., Borkowski et al., 1988; Englert et al., in press; Graves, 1986; McLoone, Scruggs, & Mastropieri, & Zucker, 1986; Meichenbaum, 1982; Palinscar & Brown, 1984; Torgesen et al., 1979; Worden & Nakamura, 1983; Schumaker, Deschler, Alley, Warner, & Denton, 1982; Scruggs, Mastropieri, & Levin, 1987; Short & Ryan, 1984; Wong & Sawatsky, 1984).

Thus, research that primarily focuses on isolated deficiencies may not adequately capture the integrative or higher-order nature of LD children's intellectual and academic functioning (Stanovich, 1986). That is, learning disabilities may be the result of a unique coordination of multiple processes that include high order (as well as low order) activities rather than a specific type of processing deficiency isolated to a particular academic domain (see Ceci, Chapter 4 for a related discussion).

It is not the intent of the foregoing comments to suggest that the differential or domain-specific models of LD be abandoned, but rather put into perspective. While the "notion of specificity" is a critical assumption to the field of learning disabilities (Stanovich, 1986; e.g., a localized deficiency can be treated effectively if diagnosed properly), this orientation has generated too many competing hypotheses. Further, even if a specific deficit is isolated the problem is pervasive over time in its influence on cognition and the acquisition of knowledge. Without denying a specific etiology of LD, there are both theoretical and practical benefits on high-order processes when one attempts to understand such children's intellectual functioning (also see Paris & Oka, in press, for a related discussion).

In sum, previous intellectual frameworks on LD children's intellectual functioning may be rather limited, at least in the general sense because they fail to incorporate the research on LD children's general cognitive-monitoring abilities. The position suggested here is that additional theories must be considered in order to elaborate and mutually compliment current psychometric approaches in understanding LD students' intellectual functioning.

INFORMATION PROCESSING

In response to the previous limitations of research on learning disabilities and intelligence, the subsequent chapters attempt to sketch some major concepts that seem particularly relevant to our understanding of LD (also see Spear & Sternberg, 1987). The majority of these concepts are couched within the information-processing framework. Such a framework assumes that three general components underlie intellectual functioning:

(a). a constraint or structural component, akin to the hardware of a computer, which defines that parameter within which information can be processed at a particular stage (e.g., sensory storage, short-term memory, long-term memory),

(b) a control or strategy component, akin to the software of a computer system, which describes the operations of the various stages; and

(c) an executive process, by which the learner's activities (e.g., strategies) are overseen and monitored (see Campione, Brown, & Ferrara, 1982; for a related discussion).

It is assumed that the flow of information occurs in stages, and each stage operates on the information available to it. Thus, at a global level, information-processing theory consists of stages and components (see Campione, Brown, & Ferrara, 1982; Sternberg, 1984, for review). The role I see for information processing theories is not to overthrow differential models but to provide a more comprehensive and elaborate understanding of learning disabilities. I now delineate some applications of such a model.

KNOWLEDGE REPRESENTATION

One major contribution of information-processing theory to the understanding of intelligence is its focus on knowledge representation (Pellegrino & Goldman, Chapter 3). A knowledge representation may be defined as how a person organizes relationships among concepts. As Messick (1984) points out, knowledge representations are how we relate and organize information—how we understand information. As knowledge representations develop in children, it goes beyond the representation of simple facts to include complex systems of multiple relationships that are organized for interpretation and action.

In terms of a theoretical framework, several researchers (e.g., Anderson 1982, 1983) have described knowledge representations as having both a declarative and procedural form. Declarative knowledge is a network of facts represented as propositions, such as a series of facts about math or history. Procedural knowledge is a series of rules or principles that directs knowledge (Pellegrino & Goldman, Chapter 3). For novice learners in a particular domain (e.g., reading), acquired knowledge always starts out in the declarative form and, by means of general problem-solving abilities, is applied interpretatively. That is, the new learner relies on cues, prompts, verbal rehearsal, and other strategies to make factual information more understandable. However, with experience and practice in an academic domain, declarative knowledge (i.e., the reliance on facts) becomes replaced by procedures or specific cognitive routines that carry the function of knowledge with them.

ACCESSIBILITY

A second application related to how LD children represent knowledge (e.g., either declaratively or procedurally), is related to the accessibility of knowledge (Short et al., Chapter 6). Accessibility refers to the notion that the information necessary for task performance resides within the child. Some children are able to access this information flexibly, that is, a particular behavior is not delimited to a constrained set of circumstances (Campione, Brown, Ferrara, Jones, & Steinberg, 1985). In addition, some children are "aware" of these processes and are able to consciously describe and discuss their own cognitive activities that allow them to access information. Currently, a number of researchers in the field of learning disabilities have converged on the notion that learning disabled children's ability to access knowledge remains inert, unless they are explicitly prompted to use certain cognitive strategies (e.g., see Ferrara, Brown, & Campione, 1986 for a review). For example, LD children may be taught to (a) organize lists of pictures and words in common categories, (b) rehearse the category names during learning and (c) use the names as retrieval cues at the time of the test (e.g., see Cooney & Swanson, 1987 for a review). The data suggest that when LD children are explicitly encouraged to use such strategies on some tasks, their performance improves and thus the discrepancy between the general intellectual ability and contextually related deficits is lessened.

Based on these assumptions related to knowledge representation and accessibility, what insights are to be gleaned to enhance our understanding of some of the intellectual deficits noted in LD children and how can such insight compliment differential models of LD? I suggest three possibilities. These areas focus on discrepancies between general intellectual functioning and the depressions in certain isolated contextual behaviors, (e.g., the typical discrepancies between IQ and achievement).

A FRAMEWORK FOR COVARIATION

First, a focus on knowledge representations provides a basis for explaining covariation (response consistency or discrepancies) in intellectual test performance. Messick (1983, 1984) has recently argued that a major problem of test scores interpretation is in our accounting of response consistency. That is, the cognitive abilities of learning disabled children are not accurately revealed from standardized tests because of the tests inability to reliability account for variance. A medical analogue may explicate this idea. When we take a person's temperature and find that it is 103 F, we can reasonably assume that there is something discrepant in our expectation, because 103 F is much higher than 98.6, the expected temperature. From a medical perspective, the determination of the discrepancy (i.e., difference between expected and actual behavior) is not a difficult problem. However, in the psychological and educational domain the determination of a discrepancy between the actual and expected score is more difficult since the education instrument is subject to variation across time, setting, versions of the test, and so on. By contrast, variations across medical "tests," for example, thermometers, are minimal. The point is that the LD child's performance on intelligence tests cannot be interpreted at *face value* (see Siegel, Chapter 7 for a related discussion). The variance in performance across various measures emerge because the measures are not perfectly *reliable (as well as not perfectly correlated)*, and, thus some factions of the child's performance arise wholly or in part by chance (Bereiter, 1963, Chapman & Chapman, 1973; Thorndike, 1972).

One possible framework of explaining this covariation is to focus on the interaction between two forms of knowledge (Pellegrino & Goldman, Chapter 3). As stated earlier, one form of knowledge, the declarative form, focuses on *facts* (as possibly measured by intelligence tests). While the other form, procedural knowledge, represents how the child encodes knowledge as *rules* or procedures, not as an enumeration of the entire data base of facts. For example, the missed facts on a series of tests which LD students are having difficulty may reflect errors in declarative knowledge. However, to understand the discrepancy between tests, however, one must determine the *rules* that give rise to these errors. That is, the information processing perspective focuses on an *array of rules* that may account for the observed errors in child performance within or between standardized tests. My point is that one may argue that the covariations across various intellectual and achievement measures are not necessarily due to inadequate knowledge (i.e., declarative knowledge), as much as they are to inadequate or inappropriate assembly of control processes and/or ineffective mobilization or organization of complex relevant abilities (i.e., procedural knowledge). Of course, performance on certain subtests of intelligence measures in which LD children do not meet expectation includes a variety of acquired specific skills, such as the acquisition of mathematical facts. As Richard Snow (1980) states however, "achievement is as much an *organization function* as it is an acquisition function." Thus, what a LD student does on various tests embraces processes that are reflective of the transition between declarative and procedural forms of knowledge. Further, these processes are applied to various subject matter in order to interpret, remember, visualize, transform, evaluate, and think, both convergently and divergently about material.

To avoid, however, a post-hoc theorizing of the reasons why covariation (discrepanies) occurs across various intellectual measures for LD students, efforts need to be made toward restructuring current assessment instruments. This does not mean making intelligence tests used to determine LD children discrepancies progressively more difficult at low and intermediate levels, but rather one must construct test items that are sensitive to processes operative with the various forms of knowledge representations. One direct means to accomplish this is to fashion tests that capture the development of expertise in a particular domain (see Pellegrino & Goldman, Chapter 3; Ceci, Chapter 4; Short et al., Chapter 6).

Domain Expertise

Several studies are available that allow us to characterize, albeit tentatively, some of the complexities of developed knowledge that constitute the power of expertise (e.g., Chi, Feltovich, & Glaser, 1981; Messick, 1983; Pellegrino & Goldman, Chapter 3). It appears from recent work that experts (non LD's in this case) not only know more than novices (i.e., LD's) and have a vastly richer store of relevant knowledge in long-term memory (i.e., declarative knowledge), but they also structure and continually restructure their procedural knowledge in more complex ways. In particular, experts construct complex representations that combine some of the dimensions and simpler schemes used by novices into integrated functional patterns, while at the same time discarding as redundant or irrelevant some other dimensions that novices attend to. The challenge for assessing the performance discrepancies in LD children is to fashion assessment tasks that capture the functional dimensions of developing competence or expertise. These dimensions go beyond the traditional standard test measures of performance accuracy, speed and fluency in an academic domain, to include the measurement of the restructuring, fine tuning and the automatization of cognitive processes.

Determining Intellectual Competence

Second, a focus on knowledge accessibility would refine our understanding of performance discrepancies between competency and performance. The assessment of competence indicates what the child knows and can do under ideal circumstances, whereas performance refers to what may be done under existing circumstances. Competence embraces a child's knowledge representation, whereas performance subsumes the processes of accessing and utilizing those structures and a host of effective, motivational, attentional, and stylistic factors that influence the ultimate response (Wagner & Kistner, Chapter 5). Thus, a LD student's competence (in terms of IQ or achievement-performance) might not be revealed in test performance because of the personal or circumstantial factors that affect behavior (Wagner & Kistner, Chapter 5).

Enhancing Access.   In support of the above assumption, let us consider the earlier research by Ann Brown and her colleagues on the use of complex study strategies by children. In one seminal study by Brown and Smiley (1978), subjects from grades 5 to 12 were asked to learn passages approximately 400 words long. Each passage was read by the subject and then they were asked to recall the main ideas. After recall, the subjects were told they had some time to restudy the passage and they "could undertake any activity they wished to improve their recall" (Brown & Smiley, 1978, p. 1080). Only 6% of the 5th graders took notes spontaneously, compared to 12% and 50% of the junior and senior high school students. Older subjects also underlined more often than younger ones. Findings such as these on the developmental use of strategies has been generalized to the field of learning disabilities in which it is assumed that such children follow the same patterns as younger children (e.g., Cooney & Swanson, 1987). Learning disabled children are less likely to underline critical information in a passage, categorize information, suggest strategies for comprehending and remembering information, and so on, when compared to non-disabled children matched on IQ. However, the fact that LD children have normal intelligence means that they learn some information fairly well. Thus, a conceptual issue to be contended with is why then are there so many discrepancies, as noted in the literature, on how LD children perform compared to what other information suggests that they are capable of doing? From a cognitive perspective, I have argued that the problem is one of accessing an organized knowledge system rather than a "true" discrepancy in performance. If this is the case, what do methodology information processing frameworks have to offer for determining a true discrepancy? Consider one methodological application-dynamic assessment.

Dynamic Assessment. Brown and French (1979) consider the understanding of performance discrepancies as occurring when one attempts to improve performance. Utilizing Vygotsky's (1978) notion of the "zone of potential development," Brown and French make a distinction between a child's potential and actual level of performance (also see, Ferrara, Brown, & Campione, 1986). That is, a distinction is made between a child's actual level of performance, e.g., actual level as might be measured on a standardized test, and his potential level of performance, the degree of competence he or she can achieve with aid. In practical terms, dynamic assessment may include giving the child a test in a standardized fashion. If the child fails to determine a problem solution (answer) or concept, the examiner provides progressive cues to facilitate problem solution. The number of cues or promptings needed is considered the "width" of their zone potential. Another similar problem is given to the child, and the examiner makes note if fewer cues are needed. This transfer test is especially important in conceptualizing a performance discrepancy since it reflects the child's attempts to implement a strategy. The ability of the child to benefit from cues given by the examiner allows one to infer the child's competence. Within the context of learning disabilities, one can make the argument that a "large" difference is indicative of a "lesser" discrepancy (or disability). Children who have a wide zone of potential (competence) are those who have a reduction in the number of cues needed from problem to probelm and who show effective transfer to new solutions across similar problems (see Brown & French, 1979, p. 260).

Covert Discrepancies

Finally, since the focus of information processing is to determine *underlying* cognitive structures in performance, it is possible that subtle as well as more important "discrepancies" in intellectual functioning may exist when none have been identified on psychometric measures. One may argue that the traditional means or procedures for determining performance discrepancies in LD children may ignore "true underlying patterns of processing strengths and deficiencies." For example, two learners earning the same test scores may have very different information-processing strengths and weaknesses. Psychometric tasks may not separate LD and NLD children in terms of overt performance, yet actual processes used in such a task may be complex and the differences between ability groups subtle. That is, LD children use inefficient processes that would *not be expected* based upon their "normal" test scores. To illustrate this point, consider an information processing framework that views the human system as highly adaptive and that individuals have at their disposal a large number of alternative routes for achieving (normal) performance on any particular task (Newell, 1980).

Now suppose the LD and NLD child's task is to remember a short list of visually presented nouns that are orthographically and phonemically distinct. Some of these children might use primarily phonemic or semantic information, others might remember the global shapes of words and their referents, and still others might use a combination of strategies, yet the final levels of performance to obtain similar levels of performance are due to different processing strategies and hence subsets of resources that are quite distinct.

A recent study of learning disabled children's intellectual functioning (Swanson, 1988) illustrates the above point. The assumption tested was that learning disabled children do not rely on the same mental component processes as non-disabled children on subtests of the WISC-R in which their overt performance is comparable to NLD children. The results suggested that the two groups varied in the algorithms and heuristics used to solve the problems, even though task performance and the total number of mental processes used were comparable. Thus, clear discrepancies exist between ability groups in the means by which they access information.

Summary and Implications

In summary, I have sketched, and the following four chapters sketch, some ways that information-processing theory make application to the study of intelligence in LD disabled children. For example, I have suggested one way is to provide a framework for explaining covariation in test performance, another is to focus on competence rather than performance and finally to help us uncover processing discrepancies when overt performance is comparable to their normal counterparts. My own bias (Swanson, 1984a) is that proficient intellectual functioning reflects selecting from a repertoire of strategies (monitoring function) a plan of action (strategy) relevant to the problem. In addition, an intellectually proficient student must have the necessary information (knowledge base) and knowledge of cognitive resources (metacognition) to be able to transfer and efficiently refine (strategy abstraction) his or her learning processes. By inference, it is possible that LD children fail to integrate all these cognitive activities into one complex act for successful task performance on some isolated tasks (e.g., reading). Therefore, a learning disability may not be simply a deficiency in certain cognitive area or skill, per se but may also reflect some monitoring difficulties (as well as the poor automatization of skills, see Kolligian and Sternberg, 1987) of the cognitive components involved in information processing.

As a summary point in my discussion about intelligence, I would like to suggest that if theoretical advances are to continue to occur in our understanding of intelligence and learning disabilities, the progress must be reciprocal—in which practical issues of diagnosis and intervention are tightly entwined with theoretical insights about intelligence and learning disabilities. In this reciprocal process, research in both the areas of intelligence and learning disabilities profit from collaborative efforts. The aim of the following chapters is to provide direction to this reciprocal process.

REFERENCES

Anderson, J. R. (1982). Acquisition of cognitive skill. *Psychological Review, 89,* 369–406.

Anderson, J. R. (1983). *The architecture of cognition.* Cambridge, MA: Harvard University Press.

Baker, J. G., Ceci, S. J., & Hermann, N. D. (1987). Semantic structure and processing: Implications for the learning disabled child. In H. L. Swanson (Ed.), *Memory and learning disabilities* (pp. 83–110). Greenwich, CT: JAI Press.

Bauer, R. H., & Emhert, J. (1984). Information processing in reading-disabled and nondisabled children. *Journal of Experimental Child Psychology, 37,* 271–281.

Bereiter, C. (1963). Some persistent dilemmas in the measurement of change. In C. A. Harris (Ed.), *Problems in measuring change.* Madison: University of Wisconsin Press.

Borkowski, J. G. (1985). Signs of intelligence: Strategy generalization and metacognition. In S. Yussen (Ed.), *The growth of reflection in children* (pp. 105–144). Orlando, FL: Academic Press.

Borkowski, J. G., Carr, M., & Pressley, M. (1987). "Spontaneous" strategy use: Perspectives from metacognitive theory. *Intelligence, 11,* 61–75.

Borkowski, J. G., Johnston, M. B., & Reid, M. K. (1987). Metacognition, motivation, and controlled performance. In S. J. Ceci (Ed.), *Handbook of cognitive, social and neuropsychological aspects of learning disabilities* (pp. 147–174). Hillsdale, NJ: Lawrence Erlbaum Associates.

Borkowski, J. G., Weyhing, R. S., & Carr, M. (1988). Effects of attributional retraining on strategy-based reading comprehension in learning-disabled students. *Journal of Educational Psychology, 80,* 46–53.

Bos, C., & Filip, D. (1982). Comprehension monitoring skills in learning disabled and average students. *Topics in Learning and Learning Disabilities, 2,* 79–85.

Brown, A. L., Campione, J. C. (1986). Psychological theory and the study of learning disabilities. *American Psychologist, 41,* 1059–1068.

Brown, A., & French, L. (1979). The zone of potential development: Implications for intelligence in the year 2000. *Intelligence, 4,* 255–273.

Brown, A., & Palinscar, A. (1982). Inducing strategic learning from texts by means of informed, self-control training. *Topics in Learning and Learning Disabilities, 2,* 1–18.

Brown, A. L., & Palincsar, A. S. (1988). Reciprocal teaching of comprehension strategies: A natural history of one program for enhancing learning. In J. Borkowski & J. P. Das (Eds.), *Intelligence and cognition in special children: Comparative studies of giftedness, mental retardation, and learning disabilities.* Norwood, NJ: Ablex.

Brown, A., & Smiley, S. (1978). The development of strategies for studying texts. *Child Development, 49,* 1076–1088.

Brown, L. et al., Council for Learning Disabilities (1986). Use of discrepancy formulas in the identification of learning disabled individuals. *Learning Disability Quarterly, 9,* 245.

Butkowsky, I. S., & Willows, D. M. (1980). Cognitive-motivational characteristics of children varying in reading ability: Evidence for learned helplessness in poor readers. *Journal of Educational Psychology, 72,* 408–422.

Campione, J. C., Brown, A. L., & Ferrara, R. A. (1982). Mental retardation and intelligence. In R. J. Sternberg (Ed.), *Handbook of human intelligence* (pp. 392–473). New York: Cambridge University Press.

Campione, J. C., Brown, A. L., Ferrara, R. A., Jones, R. S., & Steinberg, E. (1985). Breakdown in flexible use of information: Intelligence-related differences in transfer following equivalent learning performance. *Intelligence, 9,* 297–315.

Carroll, J. B. (1983). Studying individual difference in cognitive abilities: Through and beyond factor analysis. In R. Dillon & R. Schneck (Eds.), *Individual differences in cognition* (pp. 1–28). New York: Academic Press.

Chapman, L. J., & Chapman, J. P. (1973). Problems in the measurement of cognitive deficit. *Psychological Bulletin, 79*, 380–385.

Chase, W. G., & Ericsson, K. A. (1981). Skilled memory. In J. R. Anderson (Ed.), *Cognitive skills and their acquisition* (pp. 73–96). Hillsdale, NJ: Lawrence Erlbaum Associates.

Cheng, P. W. (1985). Restructuring versus automaticity: Alternative accounts of skill acquisition. *Psychological Review, 92*, 414–423.

Chi, M. T. H., Feltovitch, P. J., & Glaser, R. (1981). Representation of physics knowledge by experts and novices. *Cognitive Science, 5*, 121–152.

Cooney, J. B., & Swanson, H. L. (1987). Memory and learning disabilities: An overview. In H. L. Swanson (Ed.), *Memory and learning disabilities* (pp. 1–40. Greenwich, CT: JAI Press.

Dallego, M., & Moeley, B. (1980). Free recall in boys of normal and poor reading levels as a function of task manipulations. *Journal of Experimental Child Psychology, 30*, 62–78.

Day, J. D., & Borkowski (Eds.) (1987). *Intelligence and exceptionality*. Norwood, NJ: Ablex.

Deshler, D. D., Alley, G. R., Warner, M. M., & Schumaker, J. B. (1981). Instructional practices for promoting skill acquisition and generalization in severely learning-disabled adolescents. *Learning Disability Quarterly, 4*, 415–421.

Duffy, G. G., Roehler, L. R., Meloth, M., Vavrus, L., Book, C., Putnam, J., & Wesselman, R. (1986). The relationship between explicit verbal explanation during reading skill instruction and student awareness and achievement: A study of reading teacher effects. *Reading Research Quarterly, 21*, 237–252.

Duffy, G. G., Roehler, L. R., Sivan, E., Rackliffe, G., Book, C., Meloth, M., Vavrus, L., Wesselman, R., Putnam, J., & Bassiri, D. (1987). The effects of explaining the reasoning associated with using reading strategies. *Reading Research Quarterly, 22*, 347–368.

Englert, C. S., Raphael, T. E., Anderson, L. M., Anthony, H., Fear, K., & Gregg, S. (in press). A case for writing instruction: Strategies for writing informational text. *Learning Disabilities Focus*.

Farnham-Diggory, S. (1986). Time, now, for a little serious complexity. In S. Ceci (Ed.), *Handbook of cognitive, social, and neuropsychological aspects of learning disabilities* (pp. 123–158). Hillsdale, NJ: Lawrence Erlbaum Associates.

Ferrara, R. A., Brown, A. L., & Campione, J. C. (1986). Children's learning and transfer of inductive reasoning rules: Studies of proximinal development. *Child Development, 57*, 1087–1089.

Forness, S. R., Sinclair, E., & Guthrie, D. (1983). Learning disabilities discrepancy formulas: Their use in actual practice. *Learning Disability Quarterly, 6*, 107–114.

Garner, R., & Reis, R. (1981). Monitoring and resolving comprehension obstacles: An investigation of spontaneous look backs among upper-grade good and poor comprehenders. *Reading Research Quarterly, 16*, 569–582.

Gelzheiser, L. M. (1984. Generalization from categorical memory tasks to prose in learning disabled adolescents. *Journal of Educational Psychology, 76*, 1128–1138.

Graham, S. (1985). Effects of direct instruction and metacomprehension on finding main ideas. *Learning Disability Research, 1*, 90–100.

Graves, A. (1986). Effects of direct instruction and metacomprehension on finding main ideas. *Learning Disability Research, 1*, 90–100.

Greeno, J. G., Riley, M. S., & Gelman, R. (1984). Conceptual competence and children's counting. *Cognitive Psychology, 16*, 94–143.

Hallahan, D. P., Lloyd, J., Kosiewica, M., Kaufman, J., & Graves, J. (1979). A self monitoring of attention as a treatment for learning disabled boy's off task behavior. *Learning Disability Quarterly, 2*, 24–32.

Hasselborn, M., & Korkel, J. (1986). Metacognitive versus traditional reading instructions: The mediating role of domain-specific knowledge on children's text processing. *Human Learning, 5,* 75–90.

Kavale, K. (1987). *Discrepancy Issue Learning Disabilities Researcher. 3.* (Whole Issue).

Kavale, K. A., & Forness, S. R. (1984). A meta-analysis of the validization of Wechsler Scale Profile and Recategorizations. *Learning Disability Quarterly, 7,* 136–156.

Kavale, K. A., & Forness, S. R. (1985). *The science of learning disabilities.* San Diego, CA: College-Hill Press.

Kolligian, J., & Sternberg, R. J. (1987). Intelligence, information processing, and specific learning disabilities: A triarchic synthesis. *Journal of Learning Disabilities, 20,* 8–17.

Leon, J. A., & Pepe, H. J. (1983). Self-instruction training: Cognitive behavioral modifications for remediating arithmetic deficits. *Exceptional Children, 50,* 54–60.

Licht, B. G. (1983). Cognitive-motivational factors that contribute to the achievement of learning disabled children. *Journal of Learning Disabilities, 16,* 483–490.

Licht, B. G., Kistner, J. A., Ozkaragoz, T., Shapiro, S., & Clausen, L. (1985). Causal attributions of learning disabled children: Individual differences and their implications for persistence. *Journal of Educational Psychology, 77,* 208–216.

Malamoth, Z. N. (1979). Self-management training for children with reading problems. Effects on reading performance and sustained attention. *Cognition Therapy and Research, 3,* 279–290.

McCall, R. F. (1977). Childhood IQ's as predictors of adult educational and occupational status. *Science, 197,* 482–283.

McLoone, B. B., Scruggs, T. E., Mastropieri, M. A., & Zucker, S. F. (1986). Memory strategy instruction and training with learning-disabled adolescents. *Learning Disability Research, 2,* 45–53.

Meichenbaum, D. (1982). *Teaching thinking: A cognitive behavioral approach.* Austin, TX: Society for Learning Disabilities and Remedial Education.

Messick, S. (1983). Abilities and knowledge in educational achievement testing: The assessment of dynamic cognitive structures. In B. Plake (Ed.), *Social and technical issues in testing: Implications for test construction and usage.* Hillsdale, NJ: Lawrence Erlbaum Associates.

Messick, S. (1984). The psychology of educational measurement. *Journal of Educational Measurement, 21,* 215–237.

Newell, A. (1980). Reasoning, problem solving and decision processes: The problem space as a fundamental category. In R. Nickerson (Ed.), *Attention and performance VIII.* Hillsdale, NJ: Lawrence Erlbaum Associates.

Oka, E. R., & Paris, S. A. (1987). Patterns of motivation and reading skills underachieving children. In S. J. Ceci (Ed.), *Handbook of cognitive, social, and neuropsychological aspects of learning disabilities* (pp. 115–145). Hillsdale, NJ: Lawrence Erlbaum Associates.

Palincsar, A. S., & Brown, A. L. (1984). Reciprocal teaching of comprehension-fostering and monitoring activities. *Cognition and Instruction, 1,* 117–175.

Palincsar, A., S., & Brown, A. (1987). Enhancing instructional time through attention to metacognition, *Journal of Learning Disabilities, 20,* 66–76.

Paris, S. G., & Oka, E. R. (in press). Strategies for comprehending text and coping with reading difficulties. *Learning Disability Quarterly.*

Pearl, R. A., Bryan, T., & Herzog, A. (1983). Learning disabled children's attributions for success and failure. *Learning Disability Quarterly, 6,* 67–74.

Pellegrino, J., & Goldman, S. (1987). Information processing and math. *Journal of Learning Disabilities, 20,* 23–34.

Pressley, M., Johnson, C. J., & Symons, S. (1987). Elaborating to learn and learning to elaborate. *Journal of Learning Disabilities, 20,* 76–91.

Pressley, M., & Levin, J. R. (1987). Elaborative learning strategies for the inefficient learner. In S. J. Ceci (Ed.), *Handbook of cognitive, social and neuropsychological aspects of learning disabilities* (Vol. 11). Hillsdale, NJ: Lawrence Erlbaum Associates.

Rozin, P. (1976). The evaluation of intelligence and access to the cognitive unconscious. In J. M. Sprague & A. Epstein (Eds.), *Progress in psychobiology and physiological psychology*. New York: Academic Press.

Samuels, S. J. (1987). Information processing and reading. *Journal of Learning Disabilities, 20,* 18–22.

Schumaker, J. B., Deshler, D. D., Alley, G. R., Warner, M. M., & Denton, P. H. (1982). Multipass; A learning strategy for improving reading comprehension. *Learning Disability Quarterly, 5* (3), 295–304.

Scruggs, T. E., Mastropieri, M. A., & Levin, J. R. (1987). Transformational mnemonic strategies for learning disabled students. In H. L. Swanson (Ed.), *Memory and Learning Disabilities* (pp. 225–244). Greenwich, CT: JAI Press.

Shankweiler, D., Liberman, I., Mark, L., Fowler, C., & Fisher, F. (1979). The speech code and learning to read. *Journal of Experimental Psychology: Human Learning and Memory, 5,* 531–545.

Shephard, L. A., & Smith, M. L. (1983). An evaluation of the identification of learning disabled students in Colorado. *Learning Disabilities Quarterly, 6* (2), 115–127.

Shephard, L. A., Smith, M. L., & Voijir, C. P. (1983). Characteristics of pupils identified as learning disabled. *American Educational Research Journal, 20* (3), 309–331.

Short, E. J., & Ryan, E. B. (1984). Metacognitive differences between skilled and less skilled readers: Remediating deficits through story grammar and attribution training. *Journal of Educational Psychology, 76,* 225–235.

Simon, H. A. (1981). Information processing model of cognition. *Journal of the American Society for Information Science, 32,* 364–375.

Snow, R. E. (1980). Aptitude and achievement. In W. B. Schrader (Ed.), *New directions for testing and measurement: Measuring achievement: Progress over a decade—Proceedings of the 1979 ETS Invitational Conference*. San Francisco: Jossey-Bass.

Spear, L. C., & Sternberg, R. J. (1987). An information-processing framework for understanding reading disability. In S. Ceci (Ed.), *Handbook of cognitive, social and neuropsychological aspects of learning disabilities* (pp. 3–32). Hillsdale, NJ: Lawrence Erlbaum Associates.

Stanovich, K. (1986). Matthew effects in reading: Some consequences of individual differences in the acquisition of literacy. *Reading Research Quarterly, 21,* 360–387.

Sternberg, R. (1984). Toward a triarchic theory of human intelligence. *Behavioral and Brain Sciences, 2,* 269–315.

Sternberg, R. M. (1987). A unified theory of intellectual exceptionality. In J. D. Day, & J. G. Borkowski (Eds.), *Intelligence and exceptionality: New directions for theory, assessment, and instructional practices* (pp. 135–172). Norwood, NJ: Ablex.

Swanson, H. L. (1984a). Process assessment of intelligence in learning disabled and mentally retarded children: A multidirectional model. *Educational Psychologist, 19,* 149–162.

Swanson, H. L. (1984b). Semantic and visual memory codes in learning disabled readers. *Journal of Experimental Child Psychology, 37* (1), 124–140.

Swanson, H. L. (1987). Verbal-coding deficits in the recall of pictorial information by learning disabled children: The influence of a lexical system for input operations. *American Educational Research Journal, 24,* 143–170.

Swanson, H. L. (1988). Learning disabled children's problem solving: Identifying mental processes underlying intelligent performance. *Intelligence, 12,* 261–278.

Thorndike, R. L. (1972). Dilemmas in diagnosis. In W. H. MacGinitie (Ed.), *Assessment problems in reading* (pp. 57–67). Newark, DE: International Reading Association.

Torgesen, J. K., Murphy, H., & Ivey, G. (1979). The effects of an orienting task on the memory performance of reading disabled children. *Journal of Learning Disabilities, 12,* 396–401.

Vygotsky, L. S. (1978). *Mind in society: The development of higher psychological processes.* (M. Cole, V. John-Steiner, S. Scribner, & E. Souberman, Eds. and Trans.). Cambridge, MA: Harvard University Press.

Wagner, R. K., & Sternberg, R. J. (1984). Alternative conceptions of intelligence and their implications for education. *Review of Educational Research, 72,* 32–38.

Wong, B. Y. L. (1978). The effects of directive cues on the organization of memory and recall in good and poor readers. *Journal of Educational Research, 72,* 179–223.

Wong, B. Y. L. (1979). Increasing retention of main ideas through questioning strategies. *Learning Disability Quarterly, 2,* 42–47.

Wong, B. Y. L. (1982). Strategic behaviors in selecting retrieval cues in gifted, normal achieving and learning disabled children. *Journal of Learning Disabilities, 15,* 33–37.

Wong, B. Y. L., & Jones, W. (1982). Increasing metacomprehension in learning-disabled and normally-achieving students through self-questioning training. *Learning Disability Quarterly, 5,* 228–240.

Wong, B. Y. L., & Sawatsky, D. (1984). Sentence elaboration and retention of good, average and poor readers. *Learning Disability Quarterly, 6–7,* 229–236.

Wong, B. Y. L., Wong, R., & Foth, D. (1977). Recall and clustering of verbal materials among normal and poor readers. *Bulletin of the Psychonomic Society, 10,* 375–378.

Wong, B. Y. L., Wong, R., Perry, N., & Sawatsky, D. (1986). The efficacy of a self-questioning summarization strategy for use by underachievers and learning-disabled adolescents. *Learning Disability Focus, 2,* 20–35.

Worden, P. E., & Nakamura, G. V. (1983). Story comprehension and recall in learning-disabled vs. normal college students. *Journal of Educational Psychology, 74,* 633–641.

Ysseldyke, J. E., Thurlow, M. L., Graden, J. L., Wesson, C., Deno, S. L., & Algozzine, B. (1983). Generalizations from five years of research on assessment and decision making. *Exceptional Education Quarterly, 4,* 75–93.

3 Cognitive Science Perspectives on Intelligence and Learning Disabilities

James W. Pellegrino
Susan R. Goldman
University of California, Santa Barbara

One goal of this volume is to consider some of the ways that contemporary views of intelligence can contribute to research and theory on learning disabilities. In this chapter we present some of the implications of contemporary work in the cognitive sciences for understanding interpretive issues associated with the terms intelligence and learning disabilities. Our emphasis, however, is not on the terms intelligence and learning disabilities per se but on the analysis and understanding of individual differences in cognitive competence. Implicit in the terms intelligence and learning disabilities is the idea of individual variation among learners. What has been problematic, however, is how to conceptualize such variation and what to do about it in the educational environment. The pragmatic solution has often been operational classification and categorization schemes that occur in the absence of any real understanding of individual cases. We feel that the real issues of significance have to do with going beyond global, and often poorly defined, constructs to detailed representations of individuals' knowledge and cognitive skill. Thus, a primary goal of this chapter is to illustrate how contemporary thinking can provide for a richer understanding and analysis of individual differences in cognitive competence and why that should be the focus of attention.

There are four parts to our chapter. The first part deals with some of the conceptual and definitional problems surrounding the constructs of intelligence and learning disabilities. The second part then considers what our goals and strategies should be in light of the previously considered conceptual and pragmatic issues. Part three focuses on potential contributions of work in the cognitive sciences and provides an illustrative example from a specific area of cognitive competence, the domain of elementary mathematics. The final section is a consideration of some future directions for research and theory on learning disabilities drawing upon work in the cognitive sciences.

SOME PROBLEMS OF DEFINITION

There seems to be an implicit assumption in the theme for this section of the volume that the concept of intelligence is (or, at least, should be) of particular relevance to the concept of learning disabilities. Theory and research on intelligence should inform theory and research on learning disabilities and vice versa. This seems a reasonable assumption on the surface, particularly because, historically, intelligence and learning disabilities have been inextricably tied together at the operational level. Unfortunately, illustrating the relationships between concepts and theories of intelligence and learning disabilities, rather than just their operational definitions, remains problematic. Consider first the conceptual level. It is a fact that people's conceptions of intelligence involve a variety of elements such as facility in reasoning and problem solving, verbal facility, and the ability to learn (e.g., Sternberg, Conway, Ketron, & Bernstein, 1981). At the same time a learning disability is conceptually and operationally defined as a discrepancy between achievement or school learning and measured intelligence (PL 94-142). It seems more than just a bit anomalous to conceptually, operationally, and/or legally define learning disabilities as a situation of normal intelligence but an inability to learn when intelligence is, at least partly, conceived of as the ability to learn.

The problem we have illustrated involves a conflict between poorly defined conceptual constructs such as intelligence and learning disabilities and operational definitions of those constructs. Particularly problematic is the lack of an adequate conceptual definition of intelligence apart from the standard operational definition that intelligence is "what the tests test." The operational definition of intelligence, not the conceptual definition, has become embedded in a further conceptual/operational definition, namely that of learning disabilities. These problems of relating conceptual and operational definitions within and across constructs seem inescapable and yet an awareness of them seems central to making further progress on issues of theory, research, and practice in the field of learning disabilities.

This conundrum regarding the concept and definition of learning disabilities can be traced to psychology's general failure to conceptually specify what is meant by the term intelligence, as opposed to providing an operational definition. To understand how we got to where we are now regarding conceptual and operational definitions of intelligence, it is useful to briefly consider some of the historical context. The operational definition of intelligence was partly the product of an "apparent failure" to achieve conceptual consensus at a famous symposium on the nature of intelligence published in 1921 in the Journal of Educational Psychology. The 1921 symposium brought together leading theorists and researchers on intelligence and posed to each participant two general questions: (1) What they conceived intelligence to be, and by what means it could best be measured by group tests? and (2) What were the most crucial next steps in research? Many interesting definitions were offered by individuals such as Thurstone, Terman, Thorndike, and others. Unfortunately, most of that theoretical and conceptual discussion was subsequently ignored in favor of the operational definition offered in 1923 by E. G. Boring, namely that intelligence was what the tests test.

Sixty-five years later, in 1986, a similar symposium was published presenting the views of two dozen theorists in response to the same two questions (Sternberg & Detterman, 1986). The respondents represented the gamut from traditional psychometrics (e.g., Anastasi and Eysenck), to cognitive psychology (e.g., Hunt and Estes), to developmental psychology (e.g., Baltes and Zigler), to artificial intelligence (e.g., Schank) to individuals associated with the field of learning disabilities (e.g., Brown, Campione, and Das). Just as in 1921 there was no consensus other than the fact that a unidimensional, unifactor view of intelligence was untenable. Table 3.1 is a list constructed by Sternberg and Berg (1986) showing the various attributes provided by the 1921 and 1986 theorists and the percent occurrence of each attribute at each point in time. The attributes are ordered by frequency of occurrence within the 1986 sample. There are some remarkable similarities as well as some interesting differences reflecting changing theoretical orientations. Most theorists in 1986 preferred a multidimensional, nonfactorial view emphasizing general and specific knowledge and cognitive processes applied within varying social contexts to achieve specific goals. The

TABLE 3.1
Attributes of Intelligence Mentioned in 1921 and 1986 Symposia

	% Mentioned	
	1986	1921
Higher level processes	50	57
What is valued by culture	29	0
Executive processes	25	7
Elementary processes	21	21
Knowledge	21	7
Effective/Successful responses	21	21
Metacognition	17	7
Process-Knowledge interaction	17	0
Ability to learn	17	29
Discrete abilities	17	7
g	17	14
Not easily defined, not one construct	17	14
Adaptation to environment	13	29
Speed of processing	13	14
Automated performance	13	0
Capacities prewired at birth	13	7
Physiological mechanisms	8	29
Real world manifestations	8	0
Restricted to academic/cognitive abilities	8	14

need to consider social context was partially reflected in the distinction between academic and practical intelligence. Furthermore, there seemed to be some discomfort with use of the term intelligence and some agreement that the term itself was dysfunctional. For some theorists there is so much excess baggage associated with the term, mostly as a result of the history of the uses and abuses of tests, that it is sometimes difficult to separate out issues of scientific theory from issues of social justice.

The results of the 1986 symposium reflect what has generally occurred in contemporary research and theory that has tried to grapple with issues concerning the nature and definition of intelligence (see for example, Kail & Pellegrino, 1985; Resnick, 1976; Sternberg, 1985). There seems to clear concensus that Boring was very wrong, intelligence is not just "what intelligence tests test." It is much more than the product of responses made to a limited set of items on a test. Such a conclusion has two major implications. The first implication is that a theory of intelligence must be composed of many elements and, most importantly, it must be grounded in a general theory of the nature of human cognition. The latter must be oriented toward process and content rather than factorial structures emanating solely from patterns of individual differences data.

The second implication is that we need not throw out the baby with the bathwater. Current tests of intelligence and aptitude need not be abandoned; they can provide potentially useful information about an individual's current levels of cognitive functioning. We need to better understand just what is being measured by conventional tests and then use that knowledge to help design better tests that are more useful for instructional decision making (e.g., Embretson, 1985; Glaser, 1976; Pellegrino, 1988). The latter issue is one we return to shortly.

If there is no concensus with respect to conceptualizing and defining the nature of human intelligence (or learning disabilities) then where does that leave individuals who would like to understand what it means to have children who score at or above the 50th percentile on conventional tests of intelligence and aptitude and who simultaneously score at the lowest percentile levels on conventional tests of achievement? Maybe we should ask whether we would be any better off in understanding this type of situation if we had better theories and definitions. An interpretive dilemma will always exist unless measures of an individual's cognitive competence are theory based, something that is not currently the case for most tests of either intelligence or academic achievement. The latter are the product of a technology designed to maximize measurement principles rather than content and construct validity. Furthermore, even though we have contemporary theories of intelligence, theories that are grounded in theories of cognition, we still have problems in dealing with the interpretive situation described above. Contemporary theories of intelligence are rather general, only vaguely address the issue of learning disabilities, e.g., Kolligian and Sternberg (1987) and Spear and Sternberg (1986), and have yet to be translated into operational testing procedures.

We can summarize much of our discussion regarding conceptual and operational definitions in terms of the following set of problems:

(a) our current tests of intelligence (the operational domain) are not theory based (the conceptual domain), i.e., they do not emanate from a theory of intelligence and cognition,

(b) our current tests of achievement (the operational domain) are only weakly diagnostic relative to theories of domain specific expertise (the conceptual domain), and

(c) current cognitive theories of general and specific abilities and domain specific knowledge (the conceptual domain) have yet to be translated into practical and prescriptive measurement devices (the operational domain).

WHAT DO WE WANT?—HOW DO WE GET THERE?

At issue is how contemporary cognitive theories and research can allow us to go beyond global concepts such as intelligence and learning disabilities and global test scores to get to an understanding of an individual's underlying cognitive competence. This is not a new idea, particularly as regards individual variation among learners vis-á-vis the goals of testing and assessment in the schools. "Teachers and schools need information on individuals that is oriented toward instructional decision rather than prediction. Tests in a helping society are not mere indexes which predict that the individual child will adjust to the school or which relieve the school from assisting the student to achieve as much as possible. The test and the instructional decision should be an integral event" (Glaser, 1981, p. 924). If tests are to be used to devise instruction for the individual, rather than the more traditional emphasis on placing an individual in the appropriate niche in a fixed instructional system, then how should we proceed? One position is that tests should be able

to describe the initial state of the learner in terms of processes involved in achieving competent performance. This would then allow us to influence learning in two ways: (a) to design instructional alternatives that adapt to these processes, and (b) to attempt to improve an individual's competence in these processes so that he is more likely to profit from the instructional resources available. (Glaser, 1976, p. 14)

The sentiments just expressed regarding testing seem to be highly consistent with the goals of contemporary research on learning disabilities, public policy actions such as PL 94-142, and recent judicial decisions regarding test use. What all of these efforts seem to be pursuing is a better way of understanding and assessing what individuals do and do not know, can and cannot do, and how to go about adapting to and modifying the cognitive competence of the individual learner. Pursuit of these goals is independent of the label attached to that learner, i.e., whether he or she is called learning disabled, EMR, gifted, mildly handicapped or normal. To do so, however, requires the existence of a body of knowledge that can serve as the foundation for Glaser's (1976) components of a psychology of instruction, the elements of a "science of instructional design."

There are four components specified by Glaser (1976) and these include: (a) the analysis of competent performance, (b) description of the initial state of the learner, (c) conditions that foster the acquisition of competence, and (d) assessment of the effects of instructional implementation. The analysis of competent performance is concerned with a precise analytic description of what it is to be learned. This requires detailed task analyses of the content domain as well as empirical and theoretical analyses of the elements of knowledge and skill that distinguish the "expert" from the "novice" within that domain and the transition from novice to expert. The domain can be reading, elementary mathematics, writing, physics problem solving etc.

The description of the initial state of the learner involves a number of features. One such feature is a description of the individual's current domain specific knowledge. Instruction begins with the initial state of the learner and proceeds from this point toward the development of competent performance. Thus, it is essential that we have specific knowledge of what a given individual knows and does not know at particular points in his or her learning. Another critical aspect of the initial state of the learner is knowledge of general and specific abilities and strategies that can affect how and how readily an individual learns.

The third component, conditions that foster the acquisition of competence, involves knowledge of procedures that assist learning and optimize instructional outcomes. This knowledge can include the effects of different modes of presenting material, optimal presentation sequences, and processing strategies internal or external to the learner that are beneficial to learning. Finally, instructional decision making and prescription obviously require detailed assessment of the effects of instructional implementation. In contrast to norm referenced assessment, what is needed is criterion referenced assessment. However, the criterion must be specified by a theory of competent performance and the assessment techniques must be diagnostic relative to that same theory.

CONTRIBUTIONS FROM COGNITIVE SCIENCE

We believe that contemporary theory and research in the cognitive sciences offer the conceptual and analytic tools for providing the body of knowledge prerequisite to developing a science of instructional design. Before providing a concrete illustration of the application to learning disabled students, it is useful to sketch out some of the general characteristics of this contemporary form of theorizing (see also Swanson, 1987a, 1987b). A primary characteristic is that cognition is understood in terms of the general idea of symbolic processing in which there is a complex interplay between a variety of specific processes operating on symbolic representations of information (e.g., Newell & Simon, 1972). Second, there are various forms of knowledge that can coexist within the same system and these different knowledge forms often serve different purposes (e.g., Anderson, 1983). Third, there are specifiable mechanisms governing the acquisition and representation of knowledge (e.g., Anderson, 1981, 1982, 1987). Fourth, knowledge is a constructive product resulting from the unique history of an individual's experience within a given environment, including the instructional environment (e.g., Siegler & Shrager, 1984). Fifth, theories can be instantiated computationally and formally tested for their sufficiency in modeling complex cognitive phenomena. One way to sum up what is at the heart of contemporary work in the cognitive sciences is that theory drives observation and measurement. This can be contrasted with measurement driving theory which heretofore has been the primary operational model for theory construction in the study of intelligence and individual differences.

As research and theory in cognitive science have matured there has been a decided shift away from modeling simple tasks and limited knowledge domains towards modeling the kinds of complex cognitive phenomena that are instructionally relevant and at the heart of the interpretive dilemma presented earlier. In addition, the assessment and modeling of performance have shifted from an emphasis solely on nomothetic or group level data to an equal, if not greater, emphasis on ideographic or individual level data and interpretive concerns. The theoretical models of performance and learning are robust enough to sustain methods of analysis that concentrate on the performance characteristics of individuals. The individuals can vary in age, developmental level, measured intelligence, aptitude, and/or achievement level. The performance domains need not be restricted to the simple perceptual, memorial and learning tasks traditionally found in the experimental psychologist's laboratory. Rather, the tasks are typically drawn from performance domains of greater social significance. Examples include the types of tasks, content and problems found on conventional tests of aptitude and intelligence, in the classroom and on tests of achievement.

There now exists an extensive body of cognitive science theory and research that is directly relevant to Glaser's four components of a psychology of instruction (see e.g., Glaser, 1978, 1982). It is well beyond this chapter to attempt a comprehensive review of that literature. Those interested in analyses of competent performance and the acquisition of competence in areas ranging from reading through mathematics and scientific reasoning should see articles and volumes such as Carpenter, Moser, and Romberg (1982), Gentner and Stevens (1983), Lesgold and Perfetti (1981), Lesh and Landau (1983), Schoenfeld (1985), and Samuels (1987). Much of the work on the analysis of competence also relates very directly to the analysis of the initial state of the learner as regards domain specific knowledge and skill. With respect to the analysis of the initial state of the learner, a great deal of work has also been done on the cognitive analysis of general and specific aptitudes for learning (see e.g., Kail & Pellegrino, 1985; Snow, Federico, & Montague, 1980; Sternberg, 1982, 1984, 1986). The general processes of learning, domain specific learning, and conditions that foster the acquisition of competence have also been the topic of considerable study (see e.g., Anderson, 1981, 1982, 1987; Segal, Chipman, & Glaser, 1985). Finally, issues of theory-based, diagnostic assessment have been considered extensively in recent work such as Embretson (1985), Fredericksen, Lesgold, Glaser, and Shafto (in press), and Lidz (1988).

Rather than continuing our discussion at a general level, we now provide a concrete illustration of how contemporary cognitive theory and research methods can contribute to theory based assessment and an understanding of the cognitive competence of learning disabled children. The area of our work is basic mathematics. One reason for being interested in this domain of knowledge and performance is that there is more than ample evidence that many children who fit the operational definition of learning disabilities are substantially less proficient than their peers in basic mathematical competencies such as computing the basic number "facts" of addition, subtraction, multiplication and division (see Goldman, Pellegrino, & Mertz, 1988; Pellegrino & Goldman, 1987).

We have spent considerable time trying to understand the addition performance of 19 such children all of whom fit the classic operational definition of learning disabilities. All 19 children had been previously identified as learning disabled on the basis of reading and as a result they were receiving resource room special services in the public schools. These children were drawn from a single, middle class district in Southern California. As shown in Table 3.2 these 19 children represented a wide range of ages and grades. Although the children were identified on the basis of reading, their mathematics achievement scores were also consistent with discrepancy based definitions of learning disabilities. As shown in the table, scores on aptitude measures, with one exception, are in the average range while mathematics achievement scores are typically quite low.

The performance of these children on basic addition facts such as $2+3$, $8+7$ etc. was assessed at two points in time. The first assessment was prior to a period of microcomputer based extended practice in basic addition facts. The second assessment was following the period of extended practice. One of our goals was to determine whether the performance of these children could be interpreted as representing a situation of developmental delay as opposed to developmental difference. Doing so requires the existence of adequate theory and data on the course of normal development in this domain. A second goal was to test for heterogeneity among these children with regard to the difference versus delay issue. Sensitivity to the individual differences issue requires that we consider the possibility that these children are differentiable among themselves. A third goal was to test whether instruction designed to correct or reduce developmental

TABLE 3.2
Child Characteristics

Gender	Grade	Age	Aptitude Score	Achievement Percentile
Male	6	12-01	WISCR-109	08
Female	5	12-01	PPVT-102	14
Female	5	10-07	LEITER-98	27
Female	5	10-07	WISCR-95	03
Male	4	10-03	(NA)	06
Male	4	10-00	(NA)	34
Female	4	9-08	(NA)	55
Male	3	10-04	WISCR-70	19
Male	3	9-11	PPVT-100	19
Male	3	9-08	WISCR-93	16
Male	3	9-04	(NA)	27
Male	3	9-01	WISCR-109	47
Male	3	8-11	WISCR-95	13
Female	3	8-05	CMMS-108	32
Female	2	8-08	WISCR-95	01
Female	2	8-02	PPVT-92	16
Male	2	8-11	McCarthy-Ave.	19
Male	2	7-07	WISCR-95	30

delays would produce for learning disabled children the types of performance changes typically manifest by normally achieving children.

Cognitive developmental models of the acquisition of addition skill assume that children move from a stage of slow, error prone and laborious computation of answers to a stage of fast, efficient and relatively effortless direct retrieval of answers (e.g., Ashcraft, 1987; Siegler, 1987; Siegler & Shrager, 1984). As children practice the basic addition facts and produce answers to these problems they are presumed to establish a table of associations between addends and sums. The stronger the association between the correct sum and the addends, the more likely it is that the answer will exceed a response certainty threshold and can then be read out of memory, i.e., directly retrieved. If there is no response strong enough to exceed the threshold then the child will be forced to engage in some computational method of solution. Table 3.3 provides a description of various strategies for problem solution, and Table 3.4 schematically illustrates the developmental sequence of strategy use and strategy mixture. Theory and data suggest that use of a count all strategy is developmentally prior to use of a more efficient counting strategy such as counting on from the minimum addend. The latter is developmentally prior to direct retrieval. Furthermore, for normal children there tends to be a mixture of strategies in any child's performance at any point in time. During early phases in the acquisition of addition skill there is a greater mixture of strategies than during later stages culminating in the situation of expert performance which represents highly efficient direct retrieval from memory. By late elementary school, i.e., 10–12 years-of-age, the performance of normally achieving children is similar to that of adults with all answers to basic

TABLE 3.3
Strategies for Answering Basic Addition Fact Problems

Strategy Label	Strategy Description
COUNT ALL (SUM)	Child counts out an amount equal to first addend then counts on an amount equal to the second addend
COUNT ON	Child sets counter to value of first addend then counts on an amount equal to the second addend
MIN COUNT ON	Child sets counter to value of larger addend then counts on an amount equal to the second addend
DIRECT RETRIEVAL	Child retrieves answer from associative memory

addition facts quickly retrieved from memory. For more detailed discussions of the cognitive and developmental literature on the analysis of basic mathematical competence and the acquisition of competence see Carpenter, Moser, and Romberg (1982), Ginsburg (1983), Goldman et al. (1988), Lesh and Landau (1983), Pellegrino and Goldman (1987), and Schoenfeld (1985).

The cognitive developmental theories and data that we have quickly summarized have important implications for conducting highly refined analyses of the performance of individual children (see Goldman et al., 1988). Some of the implications can be illustrated by considering prototypical performance patterns that would be observed in individual children's response latencies for individual addition problems. Such prototypical patterns are illustrated in Fig. 3.1. If we test a child on the basic addition facts ranging from $1+2$ to $8+9$ and measure the time to produce an answer for each problem then we will have a distribution of the child's response times. These distributions can be interpreted by comparing them to the prototypes illustrated in Fig. 3.1. If a child is always using a sum or count all strategy then the distribution of response times will look like that in panel a. If the child is always using a minimum addend count on strategy then the distribution will look that in panel b. If the child mixes use of a count all and minimum addend counting strategy then the distribution will look that in panel c.

TABLE 3.4
Developmental Changes in Addition Strategy Use

	Counting		Direct Retrieval
	Sum	Min	
Preschool	XXXX		
Kindergarten	XX	XX	X
Grade 1	X	XX	XX
Grade 2		XX	XXX
Grade 3		X	XXX
Grade 4+			XXXX

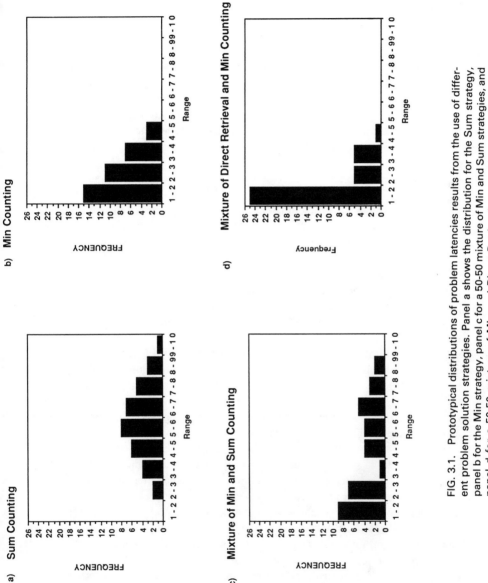

FIG. 3.1. Prototypical distributions of problem latencies results from the use of different problem solution strategies. Panel a shows the distribution for the Sum strategy, panel b for the Min strategy, panel c for a 50-50 mixture of Min and Sum strategies, and panel d for a 50-50 mixture of Min and Direct Retrieval strategies. From Goldman, Pellegrino, and Mertz (1988).

Finally, if the child is mixing use of a minimum addend counting strategy with direct retrieval then the distribution will look like panel d. In addition to distribution shape, the ordering of problems within time classes provides further information about probable strategy use and strategy mixture. These distributional data can be used together with results from quantitative model fitting to reach conclusions about a given child's strategy use and efficiency.

These methods of analysis were applied to performance data obtained from our 19 children. Consistent with general expectations, our children had initial response times considerably slower than normally achieving peers of comparable age. Of particular interest was the fact that the individual childrens' distributions of response latencies were interpretable relative to the prototypes illustrated in Fig. 3.1. In fact, the response time distributions suggested the existence of four identifiable subgroups of children, each of which differed in strategy use. A discriminant analysis using the first three moments of each child's response time distribution confirmed the existence of the four subgroups. Age and grade did not uniquely specify subgroup membership.

Figure 3.2 shows the problem latency distribution for one of the four groups of children. The children in this group had the fastest average response time. The top panel shows the latency distribution prior to the period of extended practice while the bottom panel shows the latency distribution at posttest. Both pretest and posttest data for these children suggest a mixture of direct retrieval with minimum addend counting for the problems with larger sums. The intervening practice seems to have increased the likelihood of direct retrieval which would be expected for children at this developmental stage in the acquisition of basic addition skill.

Figure 3.3 illustrates the other extreme with respect to performance. These data come from our fourth subgroup which consists of two children. Obviously, these children are very slow and their performance is idiosyncratic. It appears as if they retrieve the answers for some problems but have no systematic algorithm for determining answers when retrieval fails. Intervening practice improves performance but stability in strategy use has yet to be achieved.

We have very briefly illustrated some of the data obtained from these children. It is useful to summarize the major results of our study relative to the issues raised earlier. First, detailed cognitive developmental theories of mathematical competence and performance can be used as the basis for precise analyses of the performance of learning disabled as well as normal children. Second, when this is done, the majority of the children provide evidence of developmental delay rather than developmental difference. Third, precise knowledge of a child's developmental level (i.e., the initial or current state of the learner) has different implications for the expected effects of specific instructional interventions. In short, practice had predictably different effects given the developmental stage of children prior to practice. Fourth, gross categorization on the basis of aptitude and achievement scores and discrepancies between the two fails to provide any

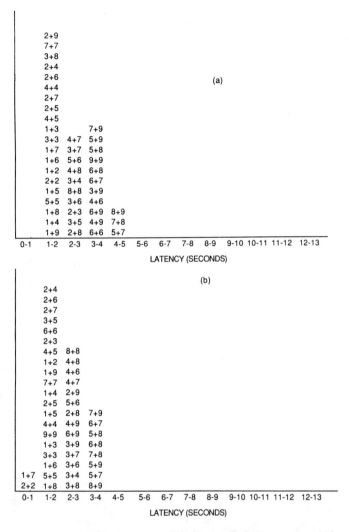

FIG. 3.2. Pretest (a) and posttest (b) histograms for one group of "fast responding" learning disabled children. Problems are ordered by ascending latency within each one second interval class. Plots are based on per problem mean correct latency, aggregated over individual subjects. From Goldman, Pellegrino, and Mertz (1988).

basis for further differentiation and grouping of children. The addition of age or grade information is only minimally helpful. In contrast, theory driven assessment seems to have a much better chance of identifying different performance profiles that are conceptually meaningful and prescriptively useful.

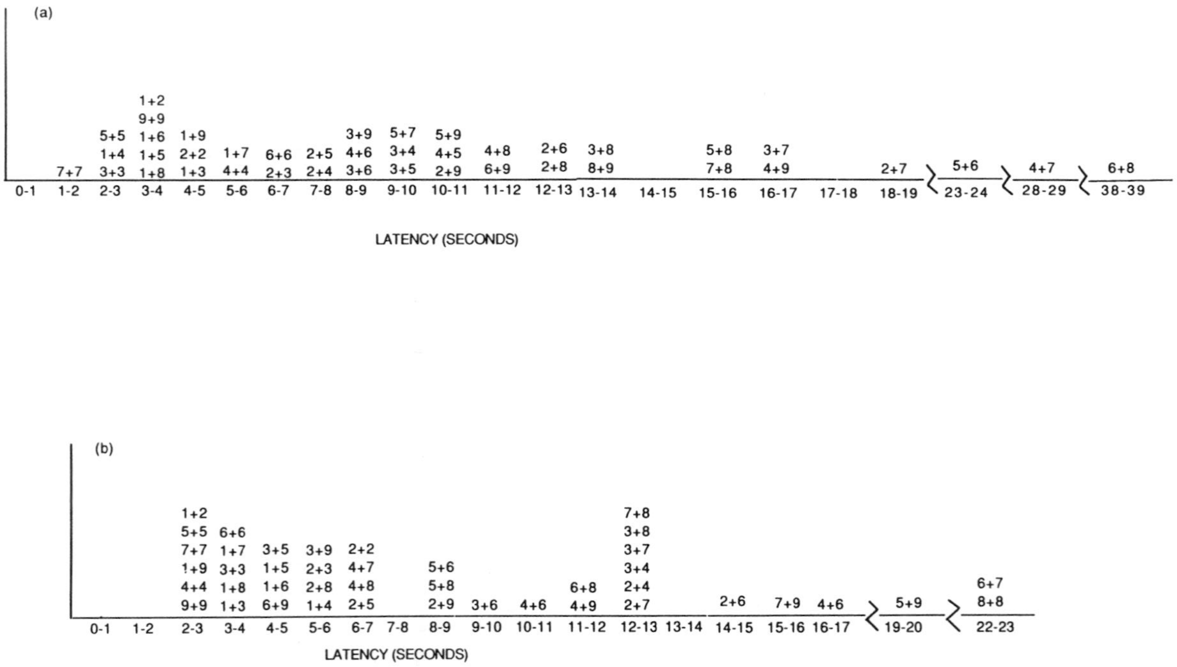

(a)

	1+2																				
	9+9																				
5+5	1+6	1+9			3+9	5+7	5+9														
1+4	1+5	2+2	1+7	6+6	2+5	4+6	4+5	2+6	3+8				5+8	3+7						
3+3	1+8	1+3	4+4	2+3	2+4	3+6	3+5	2+9	2+8	8+9			7+8	4+9	2+7	5+6	4+7	6+8		
7+7																				

0-1 1-2 2-3 3-4 4-5 5-6 6-7 7-8 8-9 9-10 10-11 11-12 12-13 13-14 14-15 15-16 16-17 17-18 18-19 23-24 28-29 38-39

LATENCY (SECONDS)

(b)

1+2
5+5 6+6
7+7 1+7
1+9 3+3   3+5 3+9 2+2   7+8
4+4 1+8   1+5 2+3 4+7   5+6   3+8
9+9 1+3   1+6 2+8 4+8   5+8   3+7   6+8   6+7
                  2+8 4+8 2+5   2+9 3+6 4+6 3+4 2+4 6+8 4+9 2+6 7+9 4+6 5+9 8+8
                                                             2+7   4+9

0-1 1-2 2-3 3-4 4-5 5-6 6-7 7-8 8-9 9-10 10-11 11-12 12-13 13-14 14-15 15-16 16-17 19-20 22-23

LATENCY (SECONDS)

FIG. 3.3. Pretest (a) and posttest (b) histograms for one group of "slow responding" learning disabled children. Problems are ordered by ascending latency within each one second interval class. Plots are based on per problem mean correct latency, aggregated over individual subjects. From Goldman, Pellegrino, and Mertz (1988).

SOME DIRECTIONS FOR FUTURE RESEARCH

Left unanswered by the research on basic mathematics skills are questions associated with the maintenance and transfer of the apparent gains induced by the intervening practice. Further work is needed to determine whether these increases in speed are maintained or can be further improved and what the outcomes of increased speed on basic facts might be for more complex mathematical problems such as multicolumn addition etc. We have argued elsewhere (Goldman & Pellegrino, 1987) that increases in speed of basic facts production are only important because they permit the allocation of attentional resources to other components of task performance such as keeping track of place value information and/or monitoring of one's place in a complex procedure. If learning disabled students lack the ability to correctly solve more complex mathematics problems, then as they become adolescents, proficiency differences may well become ones of developmental difference rather than delay. This would occur because the likelihood increases that complex problems will either not be solved at all or solved using fundamentally different strategies, ones that are within the attentional resources of the individual.

Our results for basic mathematics skills raise a number of further questions when set in the context of the corresponding cognitive science theories of the development of knowledge and skill. Computational models of the acquisition process emphasize the gradual growth and development of a knowledge base of associations for basic mathematics facts such that direct retrieval can always occur. Younger children can only retrieve a few basic facts given their level of practice or familiarity with such facts and must therefore compute answers using various simple or more sophisticated counting procedures. Most of the learning disabled children we studied appear to be developmentally delayed but we do not have an explanation for the delay. Most also seemed to profit from the intervening concentrated practice. What is required then is some explanation for the apparently slow initial rate of knowledge acquisition. We wonder whether exposure frequency can be the sole causal factor. There is no a priori reason to assume that learning disabled students have had fundamentally different experiential histories when compared to normally achieving peers, although that is certainly a possibility. If they have not had vastly different experiences, the question remains as to why, by grades two or three, they are well below grade level in mathematics achievement and substantially slower in basic facts performance. It would appear that these children do in fact manifest a "learning problem." An obvious critical area for intensive study is the detailed analysis of what constitutes a "learning problem."

The topics of learning and skill acquisition have received considerable recent attention within the cognitive science field (e.g., Ackerman, 1986, 1987; Anderson, 1981, 1982, 1987). Detailed theories and models of the processes and stages of knowledge acquisition are now available and they have been applied to specific domains of expertise. At the same time, however, we lack precise knowledge and understanding of individual variation in learning processes. For example, we do not know how much of individual differences in knowledge acquisition is attributable to simple quantitative differences in rate parameters and how much is due to qualitative differences in processing activities and structural capacities. In short, there remains a large agenda for future research on individual differences in learning. Such an agenda is obviously critical for the general field of learning disabilities.

Even though there is considerably more to do on the topic of individual differences in learning, we should not lose sight of the fact that current concepts within cognitive science that relate to skill acquisition, concepts such as automatization, proceduralization and restructuring, remain relevant for analyzing, understanding and potentially remeliorating the cognitive competence of children exhibiting specific academic deficits. Detailed analyses of knowledge and processing activities are clearly preferable to reliance on global intelligence and achievement test scores. The latter may have heretofore been operationally "useful" with respect to defining intelligence and learning disabilities but conceptually and instructionally useless.

ACKNOWLEDGMENTS

The research described in this chapter was supported in part by grant #G0083-002860 from the Office of Special Education and Rehabilitation Services, U. S. Department of Education, to Project TEECh, University of California, Santa Barbara.

REFERENCES

Ackerman, P. L. (1986). Individual differences in information processing: An investigation of intellectual abilities and task performance during practice. *Intelligence, 10,* 101–139.

Ackerman, P. L. (1987). Individual differences in skill learning: An integration of psychometric and information processing perspectives. *Psychological Bulletin, 102,* 3–27.

Anderson, J. R. (Ed.). (1981). *Cognitive skills and their acquisition.* Hillsdale, NJ: Lawrence Erlbaum Associates.

Anderson, J. R. (1982). Acquisition of cognitive skill. *Psychological Review, 89,* 369–406.

Anderson, J. R. (1983). *The architecture of cognition.* Cambridge, MA: Harvard University Press.

Anderson, J. R. (1987). Skill acquisition: Compilation of weak-method problem solutions. *Psychological Review, 94,* 192–210.

Ashcraft, M. H. (1987). Children's knowledge of simple arithmetic: A developmental model and simulation. In J. Bisanz, C. Brainerd, & R. Kail (Eds.), *Formal methods in developmental psychology* (pp. 302–338). New York: Springer-Verlag.

Boring, E. G. (1923.) Intelligence as the tests test it. *New Republic,* June, pp. 35–37.

Carpenter, T. P., Moser, J. M., & Romberg, T. A. (Eds.). (1982). *Addition and subtraction: A cognitive perspective.* Hillsdale, NJ: Lawrence Erlbaum Associates.

Embretson, S. E. (Ed.). (1985). *Test design: Developments in psychology and psychometrics*. New York: Academic Press.

Fredriksen, N., Lesgold, A., Glaser, R., & Shafto, M. (Eds.). (in press). *Diagnostic monitoring of skill and knowledge* Hillsdale, NJ: Lawrence Erlbaum Associates.

Gentner, D., & Stevens, A. L. (Eds.). (1983). *Mental models*. Hillsdale, NJ: Lawrence Erlbaum Associates.

Ginsburg, H. P. (Ed.). (1983). *The development of mathematical thinking*. New York: Academic Press.

Glaser, R. (1976). Components of a psychology of instruction: Toward a science of design. *Review of Educational Research, 46*, 1–24.

Glaser, R. (Ed.). (1978). *Advances in instructional psychology*. (Vol. 1). Hillsdale, NJ: Lawrence Erlbaum Associates.

Glaser, R. (1981). The future of testing. *American Psychologist, 36*, 923–936.

Glaser, R. (Ed.) (1982). *Advances in instructional psychology*. (Vol. 2). Hillsdale, NJ: Lawrence Erlbaum Associates.

Goldman, S. R., & Pellegrino, J. W. (1987). Information processing and educational microcomputer technology: Where do we go from here? *Journal of Learning Disabilities, 20*, 144–154.

Goldman, S. R., Pellegrino, J. W., & Mertz, D. L. (1988). Extended practice of basic addition facts: Strategy changes in learning-disabled students. *Cognition and Instruction, 5*, 223–265.

Kail, R., & Pellegrino, J.W. (1985). *Human intelligence: Perspectives and prospects*. New York: Freeman.

Kolligian, J., & Sternberg, R. J. (1987). Intelligence, information processing, and specific learning disabilities: A triarchic synthesis. *Journal of Learning Disabilities, 20*, 8–17.

Lesgold, A., & Perfetti, C. A. (Eds.). (1981). *Interactive proceses in reading*. Hillsdale, NJ: Lawrence Erlbaum Associates.

Lesh, R., & Landau, M. (Eds.). (1983). *Acquisition of mathematics concepts and processes*. New York: Academic Press.

Lidz, D. (Ed.). (1988). *Dynamic assessment: Foundations and fundamentals*. New York: Guilford Press.

Newell, A., & Simon, H. A. (1972). *Human problem solving*. Englewood Cliffs, NJ: Prentice-Hall.

Pellegrino, J. W. (1988). Mental models and mental tests. In H. Wainer & H. I. Braun (Eds.), *Test validity* (pp. 49–60). Hillsdale, NJ: Lawrence Erlbaum Associates.

Pellegrino, J. W., & Goldman, S. R. (1987). Information processing and elementary mathematics. *Journal of Learning Disabilities, 20*, 23–32.

Resnick, L. B. (Ed.). (1976). *The nature of intelligence*. Hillsdale, NJ: Lawrence Erlbaum Associates.

Samuels, S. J. (1987). Information processing abilities and reading. *Journal of Learning Disabilities, 20*, 18–22.

Schoenfeld, A. H. (1985). *Mathematical problem solving*. Orlando, FL: Academic Press.

Segal, J. W., Chipman, S. F., & Glaser, R. (Eds.). (1985). *Thinking and learning skills. Vol. 1 Relating instruction to research*. Hillsdale, NJ: Lawrence Erlbaum Associates.

Siegler, R. S. (1987). The perils of averaging data over strategies: An example from children's addition. *Journal of Experimental Psychology: General, 116*, 250–264.

Siegler, R. S., & Shrager, J. (1984). Strategy choices in addition and subtraction: How do children know what to do? In C. Sophian (Ed.), *Origins of cognitive skills* (pp. 229–293). Hillsdale, NJ: Lawrence Erlbaum Associates.

Snow, R. E., Federico, P. A., & Montague, W. E. (Eds.). (1980). *Aptitude, learning, and instruction. Vol. 1: Cognitive process analyses of aptitude*. Hillsdale, NJ: Lawrence Erlbaum Associates.

Spear, L. C., & Sternberg, R. J. (1986). An information-processing framework for understanding learning disabilities. In S. Ceci (Ed.), *Handbook of cognitive, social, and neuropsychological aspects of learning disabilities* (Vol. 2., pp. 2–30). Hillsdale, NJ: Lawrence Erlbaum Associates.

Sternberg, R. J. (Ed.). (1982). *Advances in the psychology of human intelligence* (Vol. 1). Hillsdale, NJ: Lawrence Erlbaum Associates.

Sternberg, R. J. (Ed.). (1984). *Advances in the psychology of human intelligence* (Vol. 2). Hillsdale, NJ: Lawrence Erlbaum Associates.

Sternberg, R. J. (1985). *Beyond IQ: A triarchic theory of human intelligence.* New York: Cambridge University Press.

Sternberg, R.J. (1986). *Advances in the psychology of human intelligence* (Vol. 3). Hillsdale, NJ: Lawrence Erlbaum Associates.

Sternberg, R. J., & Berg, C. A. (1986). Quantitative integration: Definitions of intelligence: A comparison of the 1921 and 1986 symposia. In R. J. Sternberg & D. K. Detterman (Eds.), *What is intelligence?* (pp. 155–162). Norwood, NJ: Ablex.

Sternberg, R. J., Conway, B. E., Ketron, J. L. & Bernstein, M. (1981). People's conceptions of intelligence. *Journal of Personality and Social Psychology, 41,* 37–55.

Sternberg, R. J., & Detterman, D. K. (Eds). (1986). *What is intelligence?* Norwood, NJ: Ablex.

Swanson, H. L. (1987a). Information processing theory and learning disabilities: An overview. *Journal of Learning Disabilities, 20,* 3–7.

Swanson, H. L. (1987b). Information processing theory and learning disabilities: A commentary and future perspective. *Journal of Learning Disabilities, 20,* 155–166.

4 A Sideway Glance at This Thing Called LD: A Context X Process X Person Framework

Stephen J. Ceci
Cornell University

Some astute observer of human nature is reputed to have once remarked that the only constant in life is change. Well, then, perhaps it should come as no surprise to find that my own thinking about the nature of learning disabilities has undergone change. There was a time when I conceptualized learning disabilities along the lines of definitions found in the sort of textbooks used in teacher training programs that stressed the specificity of the impairment, the adequate intelligence and motivation of the child, the breakdown of an underlying process that supported language-related performances, etc. The latter part of the 1970s were days of heady euphoria when we researchers shepherded over child study teams as they put their collective skills together to determine the eligibility of children to receive services for the learning disabled and to document the specificity of the impairment and the adequate level of so-called ''general intelligence.''

I no longer view textbook definitions as the best way to conceive of (or provide services for children with) learning disabilities. There are two interrelated reasons for this change in my thinking. One has to do with my own research on this population over the past decade and the other deals with my dismay with the phenomenology itself, unveiled through a fairly regular association with learning disabilities programs in the schools over the past 12 years.

Let me say something about this second reason first. We cannot, I think, ignore the reality that many—perhaps even most—of the children who are sitting in classes for LD, or who are being served in resource rooms by LD specialists, do not conform to the textbook definitions. Others have written at length about this situation (e.g., Shepard, Smith, & Vojir, 1983) but it warrants our renewed concern nevertheless. The category of learning disabilities, like it or not, is a conceptual hodgepodge; many knew that it was a hodgepodge from the very beginning (see Doris, 1986, for review of the historical events leading up to the current definition). From its outset, the term *LD* reflected political and economic realities to at least as great an extent as it reflected scientific realities. In our schools today, children who are having difficulties in one or more school subjects are labeled LD and there are a diversity of reasons for their difficulties—only a few of which are congruent with textbook definitions. A cottage industry of school psychologists, pediatric neurologists, occupational therapists, speech and language specialists, and others has sprung up to justify the many divergent cases that do not meet the definitional criteria. For those readers familiar with the "interiors" of the certification process, you already have seen cases (perhaps a lot of cases) in which a school psychologist working with a youngster will attempt to "fit" the youngster to the definitional criteria through a "creative" interpretation of test results.

In my earlier research I carefully defined what I meant by learning disabilities in terms of observable cognitive characteristics. I then proceeded to examine these underlying cognitive characteristics in a group of children who exhibited learning problems (e.g., Ceci, 1983, 1984; Ceci & Baker, 1986; Ceci, Lea, & Ringstrom, 1980). I usually, but not always, discovered some cognitive peculiarity about these youngsters. For instance, in several studies I discovered that LDs had semantic processing deficits that I characterized as *purposive* in nature (e.g., Ceci, 1983, 1984). When the task required the deployment of active semantic processes such as clustering, elaboration, or advanced encoding, the children labeled LD were found to suffer. In other studies I found that LDs' memory difficulties could be remediated by the presentation of encoding and retrieval cues (Ceci et al., 1980). Interestingly, there was often substantial *intra* individual variability in these studies. Some LDs might suffer on one task but not on another; or recall fewer words from one category than from another. This within-subject variability became an important reason for shifting my view of LD, but I discuss this later.

It is not that I now think my earlier insights into the nature of learning disablement were wrong—in fact, I do not, as they have been confirmed repeatedly by others (e.g., Swanson, 1986). But I think my researched missed an important point: The textbook definition of LD represents only a portion of those being served as LDs in our schools. And research that adheres to this definition may have little relevance for many of these youngsters. This has been one of the reasons that has prompted me to rethink my research strategy. But it has not been my main reason.

So much for my dismay with the mismatch I see between what textbooks claim LD to be and what schools see it as. Another reason for my shifting view about the nature of LD had to do with my own research findings. In 1980 when Lea, Ringstrom, and I published our paper in the *Journal of Experimental Psy-*

chology on coding characteristics of LD children, we suggested, only half in earnest, that our findings indicated that many of the coding problems exhibited by LDs could be accounted for on the basis of a deficit in semantic memory. Such a view was, of course, not original with us. Where we did differ from others, however, was in our suggestion that operations that accessed knowledge (e.g., encoding, rehearsal, inference) were duplicated in every domain of knowledge. For instance, *encoding* operations that are involved in the recognition and transformation of information arise repeatedly throughout the course of development and are tied to specific domains of knowledge. Thus, we might think of children as having an efficient encoding operation in one domain but a deficient encoding operation in another domain. The same goes for other cognitive operations such as inferential processing, rehearsal, and so on. The idea is simply that in the course of development some semantic domains are elaborated earlier than others and it is in these domains that cognitive operations should first occur with any efficiency. For example, a child cannot draw inferences if she is lacking the relevant background knowledge to do so. Keil (1984) has shown that asymmetries (often spanning several years) exist between the onset of some cognitive operation in one domain and its broader use throughout all domains.

The notion that the same cognitive operation had to be replicated in every domain struck many of us as problematic and we complained about our own suggestion: After all, it was terribly dyseconomic to posit that cognitive operations such as *encoding* and *rehearsal* had to be duplicated in every domain of knowledge. No one since Franz Joseph Gall, the father of phrenology, had proferred such a view. And we were inclined to look elsewhere ourselves. We mentioned that this view did not seem to be parsimonious—not pressing the obvious fact that "organized complexity" has an advantage over parsimony when the latter fails to account for some findings. And finally, if identical operations had to be replicated in each processing domain, then why were across-domain correlations so well established? For example, if duplicative encoding operations were cropping up all over the cognitive system, why is there not inconsistency in performance across tasks that require encoding operations— assuming some of these tasks would access domains in which encoding operations were fully developed and others would not? The answers, I believe, are to be found in a *person X process X context* view of learning disabilities.

In this chapter I lay out the broad assertions of this *person X process X context* view of cognitive processing and describe its implications for the field of learning disabilities. I argue that it shifts the emphasis from the rather global view of intellect we now endorse (at least implicitly) to a more modular view of the intellect. Recently, Fodor (1983) has made a related claim to the one that will be put forward here, though it is different in many important respects that are discussed elsewhere (Ceci, 1990) and his was not intended as a model for individual differences.

A PERSON X PROCESS X CONTEXT MODEL

Traditionally, it has been customary to think in terms of two factors when trying to explain differential cognitive outcomes, *person* and *process* ones. The thesis of this chapter is that a fuller understanding of the educational capacities of children who currently receive services for learning disabled is available only if we consider a third factor, namely, *context*. About the first factor *(person),* I need only say that here I am referring to the biological bases of cognitive behavior. This is the level of a lot of cognitive analysis, that is the individual's biologically given capacities. In addition to the *person,* it is customary to consider the processes themselves, e.g., encoding, memory, inference. The effectiveness of these processes or operations is a function of both their biological limits and the context in which they occur; they do not occur in a vacuum but rely upon the motivational and informational context. So, in a very real sense, the model being put forward here is one that elevates context to the same level of importance as the other two factors.

I believe that *context* is important in understanding learning disabilities because it entails not only the physical and social address where cognition unfolds, but also the knowledge structure that cognitive operators access. Depending on the knowledge structure, operators act more or less efficiently, as is seen below. So, a requirement of talking about operational efficiency is an understanding of the context in which the operations take place as well as the person's biologically imposed limits (e.g., the signal-to-noise ratio of information transmission in the central nervous system). It has become increasingly clear to those of us who work in the area of differential cognition that context plays a crucial role in task performance. Traditionally, the role of context has either been unrecognized or minimized—for a variety of reasons. To be sure, some psychologists have acknowledged the importance of context, especially those researchers in social, personality, and developmental psychology. But this message has never been fully appreciated by those of us who conduct individual differences research. All too often we administer batteries of standardized tests or well-fashioned laboratory tasks to all sorts of children, from all sorts of backgrounds, and slavishly try to expunge all aspects of context from playing a role in their performance, unless they are so pervasive and well understood that they can be statistically manipulated. Pointing out context effects on task performance to researchers from this tradition is akin to commenting on the emperor's sparse wardrobe! In our search for cognitive universals we have rarely sought evidence of subtle contextual influences that may, collectively, throw a spanner into the outcome by altering the factor structure or the sequence of processing steps.

Most of us were trained to view context-specific test variance as "noise," to be statistically controlled or, better yet, eliminated completely, rather than built into our models of the way people think. I suppose this way of thinking was natural for my generation. We were weaned on behaviorism and on general (some might even say "overarching") laws of learning. Even the most promising recent developments in multiple latent trait modeling are predicated on an assumption of noncontext specific variance. Susan Whitely (1983), one of the most astute thinkers in the area of cognitive testing, referred to theories that guide test construction in the following way: "A good theory should contain variables that are general across tasks. Thus, if across-task generalizability is not shown for individual differences measurements on the theoretical variables, the quality of the theory can be questioned" (p. 195). The very idea that cognition is altered in a fundamental manner by aspects of the context seems inimical to much of what modern differential psychology has strove for.

SINGULARITY VS. MODULARITY OF MIND

Consider for a moment textbook definitions of learning disabilities (e.g., PL 92-142) that stress the specificity of the impairment, the adequate intelligence and motivation of the child, the breakdown of an underlying process that is required for performance, etc. This is implicitly a *singular* view of the mind for it presupposes that there exists an entity called intelligence and that some children can be identified who have adequate quantities of this entity but who nevertheless exhibit weak spots in their cognitive profile. That is, there are children whose measured intelligence is higher than what one might think if they were to examine only their area of particular weakness (e.g., reading comprehension). Departures from an educational expectancy based on an overall IQ score is traditionally the way that LD children have been certified in order to receive special services. A child is thought to possess a single level of intelligence that permeates all of his or her abilities and that a deviation of any one ability from this level must be the result of a breakdown in some underlying process that supports it. After all, if this were not assumed, then why would children who exhibit problems in a specific area be thought to suffer from a learning disability? Why not simply assume that the mind is a modular computational device made up of many independent processing centers, each of which is in an important sense "encapsulated" (i.e., not influenced by the operation of other centers and not profitting from their output). And why not assume that each processing center falls somewhere along an "efficiency continuum," independent of the positioning of the others?

Consider two extreme cases in a child's cognitive profile: In case 1, the child is low functioning in all areas except one and in case 2, she is high functioning in all areas except one. The former case resembles some of the features of persons called *idiot savants,* though that term is technically a misnomer (i.e., these individuals are neither *idiots* in the psychometric sense of that term, nor are they *savants*). The latter case, in contrast, is a candidate for the label LD. When we are confronted with instances in which a child performs in a way that is thought to be inconsistently high compared with her performances in other areas, we are left with the suspicion that her expertise in the former was a manifestation of some hypertrophied skill that she has been honing for much of her life, not that she has some highly efficient, albeit highly encapsulated, computational device that subserves this performance. (For example, we wouldn't think that a child brought up in circus, the offspring of jugglers, had any special aptitude for juggling if she were a better juggler than 99% of children her age; she may simply be the most practiced!) In contrast, if a child is highly proficient at many things but is poor at only one thing, then we often attribute his poor performance to the presence of a specific disability.

A *singular* view of the mind rejects the above assumption in favor of one that posits a common intellectual resource pool that underpins and energizes *all* intelligent behavior. So, if a child with a high IQ does poorly in reading or math, the inference is drawn that a specific deficit (perhaps the result of a neural lesion to the relevant processing site) exists amidst this child's otherwise efficient brain. At the most general level of this view, significant unevenness in a child's cognitive profile is taken as a sign of a learning disability, provided that the earlier exclusionary criteria apply (e.g., no motivational explanation or sensory deficit to account for the unevenness). To be worse at one skill than others is regarded as a sign of a learning disability. Thus, high IQ children who excel in many skill areas but who are perhaps not quite as excellent in one or two areas as the others, can be regarded as learning disabled according to this singular view of the intellect.

According to a modular view, however, we might suppose that there exists not a single resource pool (or processing center) that energizes *all* cognitive endeavors, but rather many independent resources or processing centers. Although difficult to distinguish empirically from a singular view, there are two variants of the modular view that are relevant to this discussion. The first view of the modular cognitive processing system posits that there are "galaxies" of cognitive operations that are associated with each individual modular processing center. For example, the linguistic processing center may be connected (in some neurological as well as functional sense) to a galaxy of cognitive operations that are intimately bound to language processing, such as auditorization, segmentation, and memory. Similarly, the visual-perceptual processing center would be connected to a galaxy of cognitive operations that are tied to visual perception (e.g., visualization, analogical transformations, memory). According to this view of the modular system, the cognitive operations that are linked to each processing center may be shared. So, for instance, *memory* could be tapped both by the language and visual-perceptual centers, as needed. In such a view, it is unnecessary to postulate the existence of a singular resource pool that flows into all of cognition because across-task continuities as well as discontinuities can be accounted for without such a device.

The claim made by an alternative modular view is that each of the processing center requires its own cognitive operations. The only thing shared in the system is the knowledge base upon which each center operates. (Knowledge is not duplicated in each processing center even though the operations may be.) So, if encoding operations in a language processing center are highly efficient, this may say little about their efficiency in a perceptual processing center, a motoric processing center, and so on. According to this view, the saying ''a rose is a rose is a rose'' may be more true of flowers than of cognitive operations. In the latter case, an operation may be differentially effective across processing centers.

Now we need to add the following complication to the modular models: The efficacy of cognitive operations in both models is a function of two parameters: (1) their biologically based upper limit, and (2) the degree of elaboratedness of the knowledge bases they access. Concerning the first, the claim being made is that each cognitive operation is akin to a muscle; it has a definite biological limit on its potential size, though there may be an enormous range of reactions for any given muscle that results from environmental variations in general, and from differences in the amount and type of knowledge children possess in particular. So, for example, the ultimate capacity to store and retrieve information may be biologically constrained but the functional size of that capacity will depend on a host of developmental and experiential factors. In this sense, nature *proposes* and the child's ecology *disposes,* or, as my friend and colleague, Urie Bronfenbrenner has noted: the advantage of good biology are manifest only in a good ecology.

About the second claim, I simply mean that we do not deploy cognitive operations like encoding, memory, or inferencing in the abstract; rather we deploy them within an informational context. And the amount of background information that a child brings to the encoding, memory, or inferential task determines to a large extent how efficiently he will encode, remember, or infer. For example, those with an elaborate knowledge base in a particular domain will remember more things having to do with that domain than individuals who are without elaborate knowledge, assuming an equivalency in their biological limit to store and retrieve. This is precisely what has been found recently by researchers. Schneider, Korkel, and Weinert (in press) reported that among children with equivalent IQs, those who were highly knowledgable about soccer were able to remember and infer better about soccor stories than their less knowledgable peers. Michelene T. H. Chi and her colleagues have reported a similar finding for children who were highly knowledgable about chess or families of dinosaurs (e.g., Chi, Hutchinson, & Robin, 1989; Chi & Ceci, 1987). Such children remember more, reason better, and draw more appropriate inferences than matched controls who lack the same informational context. In all of these studies the amount of background knowledge children possess dictates their memory performance, even though they are equivalent in other respects, including the amount they can remember in other domains.

As you can see, a modular approach, even more so than a "singularity" view, makes it quite difficult to establish the basis for individual differences in processing because they could be the result of either biological differences (i.e., "person" variables) in the cognitive muscle, to continue that analogy, or to differences in children's knowledge-base (i.e., "context"). This can be seen in even the most "microlevel" tasks that are sometimes taken to index underlying cognitive processes in a relatively knowledge-pure manner. As is seen below, many researchers have noted the differential performance of children as a function of their ability profiles on simple reaction time tasks that require apparently little background knowledge and have concluded that the basis for these differences is biological. I think this work is misguided.

Eysenck (1986), Jensen (1982), Vernon, Nador, and Kantor (1985) and many others, although acknowledging the crucial role played by background knowledge in cognitive performance, go on to point out that individual differences on simple reaction time tasks are undoubtedly due to differences in the biological efficiency of the processes themselves because the role of knowledge in such tasks is negligible. The most commonly used task in this research is the Posner and Mitchell (1967) same–different paradigm: Subjects are asked to judge whether two letters are physically identical (A, A) or whether they have the same name (A, a) or different name (a, b). The difference between the time needed to make a physical identity match and that needed to make a name identity match is taken to be a measure of the time required to access and manipulate overlearned lexical codes that reside in long-term memory. (It takes longer to make name identity matches than physical identity matches and this extra time is how long it takes to retrieve a name code once its physical template has been accessed.) According to such a view, individual differences in intelligence are the result, in part, of underlying differences in this singular biological resource pool associated with high speed scanning and manipulation of the contents of one's long-term memory (itself thought to be the result of a high "signal-noise-ratio" in nervous system transmission). This biologically determined resource pool is presumably needed for *all* cognitive tasks, though we seldom think about it because it is deployed so unconsciously and effortlessly.

Yet, it is possible to show that knowledge (context) can exert powerful effects even on simple tasks such as the same-different one and to the extent this is true the assumption about the biological basis of individual differences falls down. If we go beyond the crude measures of knowledge that are often used in such studies (e.g., knowledge is assumed to be equivalent across ability groups if children of all IQs or ability profiles can name the stimuli), and attempt to employ finer-grained assessments of knowledge, we immediately see that it can have an important influence on processing efficiency. For instance, if we look at the age at which children acquire a letter, number, or word or if we examine all that they know about these items, such knowledge-base parameters predict a large part of the processing variance (Ceci, 1990; Lorsbach & Gray, 1986). For example, some children understand numbers as odd/even, or greater than/less than, while others also understand them in terms of their "cardinality," "roots," and other properties. The more dimensions a child uses to understand simple stimuli, the more efficiently he or she can encode, retrieve and infer about them.

A similar argument can be made for the role of knowledge in producing individual differences in other seemingly "basic" cognitive operations. For example, Tetewsky (1988) has demonstrated that knowledge plays an important role in how fast adults can decide whether two letters are mirror images of each other or can be rotated into angular congruence. (For example, the processes one goes through to mentally rotate two letters that have different vertical alignments is a function of how familiar those letters are, not simply whether everyone can name them.)

One final example of this same phenomenon concerns the role of knowledge in producing individual differences in analogical reasoning. Baker, Ceci, and Herrmann (1987) have shown that subtle differences in the amount and type of semantic knowledge children possess influences their analogical reasoning efficiency. For example, consider the following analogy:

TALL: SHORT::   (a) married : single, (b) hot : cold, (c) dead : alive

Although unable to articulate their reasons, many adolescents will choose *b* as the best answer because it is the only choice that captures the continuous nature of the TALL–SHORT contrast. That is, *hot:cold* is the only choice that, like the stem item, can be preceded by the adverb "very." (One cannot be "very alive" or "very married"—except in the metaphorical sense!) LDs as a group have less of this subtle semantic knowledge than their non-LD peers and this accounts for their poor performance on this task. But when they do possess equivalent knowledge, they reason just as well as their non-LD peers. This illustrates how one could arrive at very different conclusions, depending on the model's assumptions: The modularity view suggests that LDs' poor performance is not due to an absence of some biological (person) deficit that impairs their higher-level cognitions (in this case "analogical reasoning"), nor to a deficit in the analogical process itself. Rather, LDs may lack knowledge (context) and it is this deficit that constrains their analogical processing performance, not any deficit in either their reasoning skills or in the biological capacity to encode the terms, map them on to their meanings, and evaluate them. As already pointed out, however, these knowledge differences may themselves have been due to underlying deficits. The only way to disentangle the independent influences is through the systematic manipulation of person, process and context.

These sort of demonstrations suggest that it would be unwise to draw inferences about biologically based processing deficiencies in the absence of controls for ability-related differences in knowledge. Figure 4.1 shows a traditional "singularity" processing model. Each cognitive operation is depicted as carried

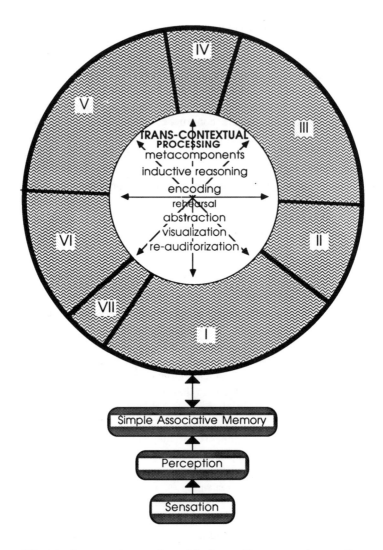

FIG. 4.1 A trans-contextual model of cognitive processing . . . Domains of knowledge are represented by Roman numerals and cognitive processes are not embedded in specific contexts but assumed to operate across all contexts of knowledge . . .

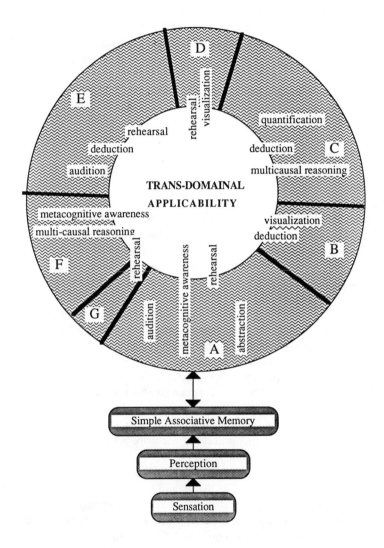

FIG. 4.2. Schematization of proposed model of cognitive complexity. In the model domains of knowledge are represented by letters and cognitive processes are tied to specific domains, to varying degrees. Note: Metacomponents are also initially domain-specific.

out within a central, singular, processing space. For example, *rehearsal* is depicted as an operation that occurs in a central work space and is deployed to *any* domain of knowledge, presumably with equal ease and efficiency. An expectation of this assumption is that there ought to be high across-task correlations, since the same operation and the same single energizing force is involved in all tasks. In terms of this sort of model (and I have simplified it greatly), a learning disability might be thought of as a breakdown in one or more of these cognitive operations that underlie more global cognition such as reading comprehension or math. In fact, this is how the original PL 94-142 conceived of it—as a breakdown in an underlying process, especially one that supports language-based performance. So, we can imagine the learning disabled child as someone who has adequate central processing space (i.e., intellectual potential) but whose performance on specific tasks is depressed because of a deficit in an underlying process like encoding, inference, rehearsal, and so on.

Figure 4.2 depicts each cognitive process as being tied to particular domains of knowledge (i.e., contexts), at least initially. Multiple resource pools are assumed but not shown in this model. Each cognitive process carries with it its own resources for its conductance. With development, some of these processes become trans-contextual (shown as movement into the central area of the ring, as in the case of *rehearsal,* which is beginning to emerge as a trans-contextual process). This happens when the individual notices similarities in processing in various domains. When this migration of process occurs, it suggests that it is now applicable to all domains or contexts and that the resource pools that energized it have been consolidated. But for many children, cognitive processes are tied to specific domains of knowledge and never achieve the status of being truly general (trans-contextual). Thus, process can be effective in one domain because of that domain's elaborate knowledge structure and yet be less effective in another domain because of its limited knowledge structure. This would indicate that the biological limit for this process is adequate but the knowledge base on which it must operate is the limiting factor.

Although these two figures are quite simplified, it is not possible to go into the various details of why this is so, as that would take me beyond the goal of this chapter to a considerable degree. The interested reader is referred to Ceci (1990) for a more detailed description of these two models. For our purposes, suffice to say that these models can be reconfigured to take into consideration various psychometric findings such as hierarchical models in which "families" of processing units are embedded at various levels (e.g., see Rabbitt, 1988 for one such model).

IMPLICATIONS OF A MODULAR VIEW OF LD

Most cognitive researchers today view performance on complex tasks like reading comprehension and math as multidetermined. They require an assortment of lower-level processes of the kind I have mentioned here (e.g., *encoding, memory, inference, rehearsal*). If each of these lower-level processes each have their own biological potential and depend critically on the organization of the knowledge base for their effectiveness, it follows that individual differences can result from either a biologically faulty operation or an impoverished knowledge domain (which itself could be the result of a biological deficiency or an experiential deficit). Importantly, this model not only allows for individual differences but actually requires them, as each operation is associated with its own source of variance. Thus, to take one example, there ought to be a range of biologically determined encoding efficiencies, from the most to the least, and these will be associated with a range of performances within a similarly structured knowledge base. Alternatively, an identical biologically based cognitive process will be associated with different performance outcomes if it is deployed on knowledge bases of varying degrees of elaborateness and structure. (Two children who have biologically equivalent processes may perform differently because of the elaborateness of their respective knowledge bases.) Thus, the same mechanism that is responsible for producing differences between individuals is responsible for producing within-subject variability. This is because individuals possess many domains that differ in their degree of elaborateness and therefore are more or less efficient as a result. And, individuals also possess a variety of cognitive processes that differ in their biologically determined efficiency. Carried forward, this means that we should expect that children will differ on global tasks such as reading comprehension and some of these differences will be due to biology and some will be due to knowledge base differences. But it can at times be difficult to disentangle these two sources of within-subject and between-subject variance, given the symbiotic nature of the person x process x context relationship.

IS LD UNIQUE?

The modular view just sketched implies that youngsters labeled "learning disabled" may not be unique in the sense of differing from higher or lower functioning peers who happen to have less variable performance profiles—at least not in the sense that they differ in the nature of their processes. A modular view is compatible with the idea that all children possess many different processing centers, each with its specific biological constraints and informational requirements that contribute to differential cognitive outcomes. Cast in these terms, the difference between mildly mentally retarded, LD, normal, and gifted children is one of the number and extent of deficits in these processes and not in any differences between these groups in their "overall level of intelligence," an assumption made by the singular view. Thus, an LD child may not differ from other youngsters in the number of processes they possess or in the mental steps they go through during the course of cognizing. Rather, more of their processes may be located at the low end of the efficiency continuum (because of biological disposition and/or lack of informational elaboratedness) than their higher-functioning peers.

Some empirical support for this view comes in the form of research that shows that LDs, EMRs, and normally developing children all go through the same information processing steps. In a microanalysis of their memory characteristics, Baker, Lorenz, and Ceci (1985) demonstrated that the three groups' encoding, storage, and retrieval processes were equivalent. No support was found for the view that one or more groups failed to exhibit a process that was used by the other groups. What was not the same among these three groups was the efficiency with which they used the identical process. The notion that LDs exhibit a qualitatively different mode of processing is unsupported in these data. Instead, they appear to differ quantitatively, deploying the very same underlying operations as their higher-functioning peers but with less efficiency.

REFERENCES

Baker, J. G., Ceci, S. J., & Herrmann, D. (1987). Semantic structure and processing: Implications for the learning disabled child. In H. L. Swanson (Ed.), *Advances in learning and behavioral disabilities: Memory and learning disabilities, 2,* (pp. 83–109). Greenwich, CT: JAI Press.

Baker, J. G., Lorenz, C., & Ceci, S. J. (1985, March). *Quantitative versus qualitative models of memory development.* Paper presented at the Eastern Psychological Association meeting, Boston.

Ceci, S. J. (1983). Automatic and purposive processing characteristics of normal and LD children. *Developmental Psychology, 19,* 427–439.

Ceci, S. J. (1984). A developmental study of learning disabilities and memory. *Journal of Experimental Child Psychology, 38,* 352–371.

Ceci, S. J. (1990). *On intelligence . . . more or less: A bio-ecological treatise on intellectual development.* Englewood Cliffs, NJ: Prentice-Hall, Century Series in Psychology.

Ceci, S. J., & Baker, J. G. (1986). How shall we conceptualize the language problems of learning disabled children? In S. J. Ceci (Ed.), *Handbook of cognitive, social, and neuropsychological aspects of learning disabilities* (Vol. 2, pp. 103–112). Hillsdale, NJ: Lawrence Erlbaum Associates.

Ceci, S. J., Lea, S. E. G., & Ringstrom, M. (1980). Coding characteristics of normal and learning disabled 10-year-olds: Modality-specific pathways to the cognitive system. *Journal of Experimental Psychology: HLM, 6,* 685–697.

Chi, M. T. H., & Ceci, S. J. (1987). Content knowledge: Its restructuring with memory development. In H. W. Reese & L. Lipsett (Eds.), *Advances in Child Development and Behavior, 20,* 91–146.

Chi, M. T. H., Hutchinson, J. E., & Robin, A. F. (1989). How inferences about novel domain-related concepts can be constrained by structured knowledge. *Merrill Palmer Quarterly, 35,* 27–63.

Doris, D. D. (1986). Learning disabilities. In S. J. Ceci (Ed.), *Handbook of cognitive, social, and neuropsychological aspects of learning disabilities* (Vol. 1, pp. 3–53). Hillsdale, NJ: Lawrence Erlbaum Associates.

Eysenck, H. J. (1986). Inspection time and intelligence: An historical introduction. *Personality and Individual Differences, 7,* 603–607.

Fodor, J. (1983). *Modularity of mind: An essay on faculty psychology.* Cambridge, MA: MIT Press.

Jensen, A. R. (1982). Reaction time and psychometric "g". In H. J. Eysenck (Ed.), *A model for intelligence*. NY: Springer-Verlag.

Keil, F. (1984). Mechanisms of cognitive development and the structure of knowledge. In R. J. Sternberg (Ed.), *Mechanisms of cognitive development* (pp. 81–100). New York: W. H. Freeman.

Lorsbach, T., & Gray, J. (1986). Item identification speed and memory span performance in learning disabled children. *Contemporary Educational Psychology, 46,* 68–78.

Posner, M. I., & Mitchell, R. (1967). Chronometric analysis of classification. *Psychological Review, 74,* 392–409.

Rabbit, P. M. (1988). Does it last? Is speed a basic factor determining individual differences in memory? In M. M. Gruneberg, P. Morris, & P. Sykes (Eds.), *Practical aspects of memory, Vol. 2.* 106–112. London: Wiley

Schneider, W., Korkel, J., & Weinert, F. (In Press). Expert knowledge and general abilities and text processing. In W. Schneider & F. Weinert (Eds.), *Interactions among aptitudes, strategies, and knowledge in cognitive performance*. New York: Springer-Verlag.

Shepard, L., Smith, M. L., & Vojir, C. P. (1983). Characteristics of pupils identified as learning disabled. *American Educational Research Journal, 20,* 309–331.

Swanson, H. L. (1986). Do semantic memory deficiencies underlie learning disabled readers' encoding processes? *Journal of Experimental Child Psychology, 41,* 461–488.

Tetewsky, S. J. (1988). *An analysis of familiarity effects in visual comparison tasks and their implications for studying human intelligence*. Unpublished doctoral dissertation. Yale University.

Vernon, P. A., Nador, S., & Kantor, L. (1985). Reaction times and speed measures of processing: Their relationship to timed and untimed measures of intelligence. *Intelligence, 9,* 357–374.

Whitely, S.E. (1983). Construct validity: Construct representation versus nomothetic span. *Psychological Bulletin, 93,* 179–197.

5 Implications of the Distinction[+] Between Academic and Practical Intelligence for Learning-Disabled Children

Richard K. Wagner
Janet A. Kistner
Florida State University

The aspect of new conceptions of intelligence that we have chosen to consider in the context of learning disabilities is the distinction between academic and practical intelligence. We begin by describing the characteristics of academic and practical problems, and the conceptions of academic and practical intelligence that we have adopted for present purposes. Next, we discuss relations between academic intelligence and learning disabilities by considering two specific questions: Are deficits in academic intelligence responsible for the impaired academic performance of children with learning disabilities, and conversely, is the impaired academic performance of children with learning disabilities likely to result in deficits in academic intelligence? Then, we ask the same two questions about relations between practical intelligence and learning disabilities.

ACADEMIC AND PRACTICAL INTELLIGENCE

Consider two school-related problems. The first is the arithmetic word problem, "If a zoo has 5 zebras and 3 run away, how many are left?" The second is the problem of how to improve the grade of F you received for the last grading period in reading.

The first problem is an academic one, representative of the kinds of problems that are found on IQ tests and in textbooks. The content of the second problem also concerns school achievement, but, because of characteristics that we discuss shortly, we consider this problem to be a practical one, representative of the kinds of problems found in the everyday world, including the everyday world of the school. These two problems differ in a number of characteristics that commonly differentiate academic and practical issues (Neisser, 1976; Wagner & Sternberg, 1985).

First, academic problems tend to be well-defined relative to practical problems. There can be little question that for the arithmetic word problem, you are to figure out how many zebras are left. But what really is the nature of the problem of getting an F in reading? Second, for academic problems, the relevant information that is needed for solving the problem is obvious. For practical problems, it usually is necessary to distill what is relevant from an abundance of irrelevant information. Third, there is a single solution to the arithmetic word problem (2), and one method of obtaining it (subtract 3 from 5). But consider the practical problem of improving your reading grade. There are a number of possible solutions (e.g., get help, get in a lower reading group), and a number of methods for obtaining each (e.g., for getting help, ask the teacher or ask your parent; for getting in a lower reading group, ask the teacher or ask your parent to ask the teacher). Fourth, feedback is direct, immediate, and reliable for your answer to the arithmetic word problem. Because of the immediacy and reliability of the feedback, it is often possible to employ a trial-and-error approach to learning. For the practical problem, feedback in the form of a grade given at the end of the next grading period is less immediate (although there may be indications of how well you are doing in grades on specific assignments), and sometimes is less systematically related to your performance. Finally, if you know how to solve the arithmetic word problem, chances are that you learned how as a result of formal instruction.

But learning how to solve many practical problems, including the problem of how to bring up your reading grade, happens in the absence of formal instruction. Until recently, almost all of what was known about intelligence concerned the set of intellectual competencies that are required to solve academic-type problems. We refer to this kind of intelligence as *academic intelligence*. It largely is this kind of intelligence that is measured by traditional IQ tests. The hallmark of the academically intelligent individual is facile acquisition of academic knowledge in formal schooling.

By *practical intelligence,* we refer to the set of intellectual competencies that are required to solve practical-type problems. It is important to note that whether a problem is primarily academic or practical depends on the characteristics of the problem, rather than whether the problem is encountered in school or in the everyday world. It also should be noted that most problems and tasks require some degree of both kinds of intelligence.

Whereas the hallmark of the academically intelligent individual is facile acquisition of formal knowledge, the hallmark of the practically intelligent individual is facile acquisition of *tacit knowledge* (Wagner, 1987). Tacit knowledge refers to practical know-how that usually is not openly expressed (*Oxford English Dictionary,* 1933) nor taught formally (see Polanyi, 1976, and Schon, 1983, for related conceptions of tacit knowledge, and Sternberg & Wagner, 1986, for a collection of other conceptions of practical intelligence).

One approach to measuring practical intelligence has been to follow the model of the IQ test that samples formal knowledge, but to sample *tacit* knowledge rather than formal knowledge. Support for the distinction between academic and practical intelligence is provided by the fact that performance on such measures has been related to performance in career pursuits such as academic psychology and business management, but appears to be only weakly related to performance on IQ tests (Wagner, 1987; Wagner & Sternberg, 1985). Additional support for a distinction between academic and practical intelligence has been provided by Ceci and Liker's (1986) studies of the practical intelligence of race-track bettors, and Mercer, Gomez-Palacio, and Padilla's (1986) cross-cultural studies of the practical intelligence of school children.

Having introduced the distinction between academic and practical intelligence, we are ready to review relations between each kind of intelligence and learning disabilities.

ACADEMIC INTELLIGENCE AND LEARNING DISABILITIES

In this section, we consider whether deficits in academic intelligence are responsible for the impaired academic performance of many children with learning disabilities, and conversely, whether the impaired academic performance of children with learning disabilities is likely to result in deficits in academic intelligence.

Are Deficits in Academic Intelligence Responsible for the Impaired Academic Performance of Children with Learning Disabilities?

This question is at the heart of the debate about whether the cognitive deficits of learning disabled children are specific or general.

In attempting to answer the question of whether children with learning disabilities have deficits in academic intelligence, it may be helpful to make a distinction between two kinds of deficits. What we refer to as *normative deficits* are deficits relative to an appropriately selected normative sample of children without learning disabilities. What we refer to as *environmentally relative deficits* are deficits relative to what the environment demands. A lack of correspondence between the two kinds of deficits is possible if the school environmental demands on academic intelligence are different for children with learning disabilities compared to their nondisabled peers, a possibility we entertain shortly.

Normative deficits in academic intelligence. Traditional definitions notwithstanding, there is overwhelming evidence that children with learning disabilities perform reliably worse than their nondisabled peers on a surprisingly wide range of cognitive tasks (see Stanovich, 1986a, for a recent review of this evidence). Of course, it is expected that children with learning disabilities would perform poorly on tasks that involve their particular deficit. We thus expect disabled readers, many of whom have difficulty in making use of phonological codes or sounds of the language when reading, to perform more poorly than their peers on tasks that require phonological coding. And they do, on tasks such as (a) matching sounds and symbols in a reading analogue tasks (Snowling, 1980), (b) using verbal labels to code stimuli for short-term recall (Cohen & Netley, 1981; Katz, Shankweiler, & Liberman, 1981; Torgesen, 1977; Torgesen & Houck, 1980), and (c) accessing the name codes of pictures of common objects, letters and numbers (Ellis, 1981; Spring & Capps, 1974).

What is unexpected is that disabled readers also perform poorly on tasks that are not directly related to their specific areas of deficit, including tasks that involve listening comprehension (Berger, 1978; Kotsonsis & Patterson, 1980; Smiley, Oakley, Worthen, Campione, & Brown, 1977), and processing the syntax of oral language (Newcomer & Magee, 1977; Vogel, 1974). The poor performance relative to nondisabled peers holds true for tasks that are commonly found on IQ tests, including tasks found on the nonverbal, performance part of the scales. The typical performance IQ for learning-disabled samples is approximately 90 (Stanovich, 1986a). Even when researchers attempt to match on IQ by selecting their learning-disabled and nondisabled samples so as to yield a nonsignificant difference in IQ between the groups, the IQ of the learning-disabled sample tends to run about 6 points less than that of the control-group sample (Torgesen & Dice, 1980; Vellutino, 1979; Wolford, 1981).

Should we reconceptualize learning disabilities as a pervasive, though perhaps mild, deficit in academic intelligence, as opposed to a specific deficit and normal intelligence? We give a brief answer to this question, and refer the interested reader to two recent articles by Stanovich, who, in the spirit of the football coach who could take his players and beat yours, and then turn around and take your players and beat his, has made the case for (Stanovich, 1986b) and against (Stanovich, 1986a) the assumption that the deficits of children with learning disabilities are specific rather than general.

We are not compelled by the evidence of pervasive cognitive deficits in children with learning disabilities to argue for reconceptualizing the basic nature of learning disabilities for at least four reasons;

1. As commonly observed, children who are referred and receive special education services are a biased sample of children with learning disabilities (Keogh, 1983; Wong, 1986). Two children, one with an IQ of 125 and another with an IQ of 85, whose achievement in reading in terms of standard and scores falls 25 points below their IQs, are not equally likely to be referred for, nor recipients of, special education services. For the most part, children with learning disabilities who receive special education services tend to be the children

with the most severe academic problems whose discrepancy between IQ and achievement meets eligibility requirements, rather than the children who show the largest discrepancy between IQ and achievement. Because IQ is correlated with achievement, employing the former selection strategy necessarily yields a school-identified population of children with learning disabilities with an average IQ lower than that of their peers. This bias extends to the many research samples that have been drawn from school-identified populations.

2. Some and perhaps much of the evidence for wide-ranging cognitive deficits with learning disabilities is suspect because of the regression to the mean artifact that is generated by the commonly employed IQ matching procedure (Crowder, 1984).

3. Group comparisons can sometimes be misleading. The rather pervasive group-average performance deficit of LD samples may not reflect the nature of the deficit performance of any individuals making up the sample. For example, if LD samples really represent an amalgamation of several distinct subtypes, each of which is characterized by marked deficits in different specific areas, averaging across the subtypes would suggest, erroneously, a modest but pervasive deficit.

4. A primary specific deficit that prevents school learning at a rate comparable to nondisabled peers will inevitably lead to secondary more generalized deficits on tasks, including IQ tests, that depend on school learning. We develop this point further when we consider whether the impaired academic performance of children with learning disabilities is likely to result in deficits in academic intelligence

Environmentally relative deficits in academic intelligence. We can do no more than speculate whether the school environmental demands on academic intelligence are greater for children with learning disabilities than for their peers because we know of no studies that have addressed this issue. However, it is likely that there are greater demands on academic intelligence for children with learning disabilities on tasks related to their area of deficit compared to the demands faced by their nondisabled peers.

Consider the case of reading disability. There is strong evidence that good and poor readers differ in the degree to which they rely on "top down" or conceptually driven versus "bottom-up" or data-driven processing (Perfetti, Goldman, & Hogaboam, 1979; Perfetti & Roth, 1981; Stanovich, 1986a). Conceptually driven processing refers to using cues such as the meanings of nearby words and syntax to guess the identity of words; data-driven processing refers to simply decoding the words. The evidence, which contradicts the previous view that the problem for disabled readers is an inability to use semantic and syntactic cues to predict the next word (Goodman, 1976; Smith, 1971), is that poor readers make *more* use of these contextual cues in word recognition than do good readers. It is not that poor readers are any better than good readers at using contextual cues, it is just that it is more efficient for good readers to rely on their faster data-driven processes. Because of their deficit decoding skills, poor readers are forced to rely on contextual cues, that is, their knowledge of word meanings and syntax, to make sense of the impoverished data that are provided by their inefficient and inaccurate data-driven processes.

Because disabled readers must rely more on conceptually driven processes than nondisabled readers, and because academic intelligence, in the form of knowledge of word meanings and syntax, is involved more in conceptually driven than in data-driven processing, decoding the words of a reading passage probably demands more academic intelligence of a disabled reader than of a nondisabled reader. If decoding as well as comprehension itself requires academic intelligence, disabled readers with low IQs may be doubly penalized in their ability to learn via reading: Their low IQs make them less successful at decoding as well as at comprehension, and poor decoding exacerbates the problem of poor comprehension because some of the words will not be decoded accurately.

Is the Impaired Academic Performance of Children with Learning Disabilities Likely to Result in Deficits in Academic Intelligence?

Perhaps the fact about children with learning disabilities we can be most sure of is that they are markedly impaired in academic performance. Might there be consequences for the development of academic intelligence associated with their impaired academic performance?

We think that it is nearly impossible for the development of academic intelligence to proceed unimpeded in the face of marked impairment in academic performance, especially if the area of impaired academic performance includes reading. Consider the case of reading and general vocabulary. Measures of vocabulary are the best predictors of total IQ. Following Merton (1968) and Walberg (Walberg & Tsai, 1983), Stanovich (1986b) has described how "Matthew effects" might explain why the cognitive deficits of older disabled readers seem to be so pervasive. The label Matthew effects comes from the Gospel according to Matthew (XXV:29), "For unto every one that hath shall be given, and he shall have abundance: but from him that hath not shall be taken away even that which he hath."

The basic idea applied to the present context is that good readers will profit from the educational experience more than will poor readers. The outcome will be an increasingly greater discrepancy between the level of performance of good and poor readers over time. This discrepancy should be found not only in reading, but also in more general cognitive abilities that depend in part on school learning for their development. Specifically, Stanovich (1986b) makes the following case. Much of the development of one's vocabulary does not occur as a result of direct instruction, but rather from a process of inferring the meanings of words from their context when they are encountered in written and oral language (Jenkins & Dixon, 1983; Nagy, Herman, & Anderson, 1985; Sternberg & Powell, 1983). Differences in the amount of reading thus can result in differences in vocabulary development.

There is reason to believe that disabled readers have much less experience at reading, in terms of words read and also perhaps in terms of time spent reading, if time spent in free reading is added to that spent in reading instruction. Allington (1984) counted the number of words read per week in 1st-grade reading groups and found a range of 16 words per week for the poorest reader to 1,933 for the best. Nagy and Anderson (1984) also estimated that the difference in words read in school by good and poor readers is two orders of magnitude.

Given the facts that (a) vocabulary development, perhaps the single best indicator of academic intelligence, is partially determined through reading experience, and (b) there are several orders of magnitude of difference in the amount of reading experience that disabled and nondisabled readers obtain, it is a wonder that the generalized cognitive deficits noted for older reading-disabled children are not more severe than they appear to be. If Stanovich's (1986b) analysis is correct, the issue of how to minimize the secondary effects of a primary problem of specific learning disability on academic intelligence is crucial to developing more effective educational interventions for children with learning disabilities.

PRACTICAL INTELLIGENCE AND LEARNING DISABILITIES

The idea that LD children have deficits of intelligence runs counter to most conceptions of learning disabilities. To suggest that LD children may be deficient in *practical intelligence* is even harder to accept since LD children are thought to be perfectly normal in situations that do not require formal instruction. Unlike hypothesized deficits of academic intelligence, for which there was a fairly strong empirical base, practical intelligence has not been a topic of research in the learning disabilities field. So why postulate that LD children may be deficient in this regard?

Well, for one thing, there is considerable question regarding the narrowness of domains in which LD children are deficient. Recent research indicates that LD children differ from their peers in areas outside the classroom as well. Most notably, LD children experience significant problems of social interactions (Bryan & Bryan, 1981; Gresham, 1981). We think it's reasonable to argue that getting along with others in social settings is a good example of the application of tacit knowledge, and that deficits in this area may reflect deficits of practical intelligence. While findings of deficits of social interactions/skills among LD children is consistent with the notion that these children are deficient in practical intelligence, there are also other explanations for these research findings, including bias in identifying children as learning disabled and the difficulties in matching children with and without learning disabilities. Rather than focus on the presence of deficits outside the academic domain to support our hypothesis that LD children are characterized by deficits of practical intelligence, we think a compelling case can be made by examining everyday behaviors in the classroom that are indicative of practical intelligence.

We focus here on two types of tacit knowledge that appear to be especially relevant to understanding the academic performance of LD children. The first consists of the achievement-related beliefs and informal theories that one acquires from one's school experience about such things as how success and failure are related to one's abilities and one's efforts. The second kind of tacit knowledge that is relevant to understanding the academic performance of children with learning disabilities is practical knowledge about how to do academic tasks that is characterized by (a) improvisation, and (b) having been acquired through informal learning. An example of this second kind of knowledge is the spontaneous application of strategies to cognitive tasks. Torgesen (1982) describes three levels of strategies that are applied to school tasks. The first level refers to very specific task strategies (e.g., sound-blending strategies) that are typically part of direct instruction by teachers. The second level includes strategies that are also important for successful school performance but tend not to be taught directly such as those required for memorizing information in preparation for recall. The third level of strategies, frequently associated with metacognition, includes problem-solving approaches that are important for both academic and nonacademic tasks, such as identifying when there is a problem, generating solutions to the problem, and selecting the most appropriate strategy for solving the problem at hand. This third level of strategy is also one that is not directly taught by teachers although there is evidence that applications of the second and third levels of strategies are facilitated by attending school (Sharp, Cole, & Lave, 1979; Wagner, 1978). Although not a result of direct instruction (i.e., teachers do not directly teach students in the use of these strategies), the demands to master cognitive tasks, and the indirect feedback regarding the utility of various strategies for obtaining successful outcomes, are thought to lead to the spontaneous application of strategies. In this sense, use of these second and third levels of strategies fits what we have described as a practical problem as opposed to an academic problem.

Our discussion of deficits in practical intelligence among children with learning disabilities will parallel the previously presented one regarding academic intelligence. We consider whether deficits in practical intelligence are responsible for the impaired academic performance of LD children, and conversely, whether the impaired academic performance of LD children results in deficits in practical intelligence.

Are Deficits in Practical Intelligence Responsible for the Impaired Academic Performance of Children with Learning Disabilities?

As in our discussion of academic intelligence, two types of deficits in practical intelligence are considered. Normative deficits in which LD children are deficient relative to an appropriately selected normative sample of children without learning disabilities; and environmentally relative deficits in which the school environmental demands placed on practical intelligence are greater for LD children, and exceed the limits of most LD children.

Normative Comparisons. Comparisons of LD and normally achieving children indicate differences in the first kind of tacit knowledge, specifically in achievement-related beliefs. LD children have more negative perceptions of their abilities and lower expectations for future success than do children without learning problems. When confronted with real or hypothetical failures, LD children are less likely than their peers to view insufficient effort as a cause and more likely to attribute their failures to insufficient ability or external sources (for review, see Kistner & Torgesen, 1987).

LD children's perceptions of their abilities and control over achievement outcomes are related to their persistence in difficult achievement situations, and have even been shown to predict their progress in school. For example, Kistner, Osborne, and LeVerrier (1988) found that LD children's causal attributions of hypothetical failures predicted how much academic progress they made over a two year interval. As predicted, attributions of failure to insufficient effort were positively associated with gains in achievement, whereas the tendency to blame academic failures on insufficient ability was negatively associated with academic progress. The tendency to attribute failures to external factors (as measured by the EAX) did not significantly predict academic progress.

There are also several studies in which the causal attributions of children with learning disabilities have been modified, resulting in more persistence and less debilitation in the face of failure (Dweck, 1975), suggesting that attributions held by children with learning disabilities are causally related to achievement behavior.

Clearly, the achievement-related beliefs of LD children are deficient in the normative sense (or perhaps we should say their beliefs are less adaptive) and these beliefs are related to their academic performance. It is not possible to say that their beliefs are the initial cause for their learning problems, but there are sufficient data to indicate a causal role of achievement-related beliefs to continued progress in academic achievement.

Turning to our second example of tacit knowledge, that of spontaneously applied strategies to cognitive tasks, a large body of research indicates that children with learning disabilities are deficient relative to nondisabled peers. These deficiencies have been most consistently demonstrated on short-term memory tasks for which a mnemonic strategy improves performance. For example, Torgesen (1977) found that LD children were less likely to sort cards according to category when preparing for a recall test, and that they recalled fewer pictures than did children without learning disabilities. Similar results have been reported for tasks requiring rehearsal and other forms of elaborative encoding (for review, see Pressley, Johnson, & Symons, 1987).

Not only have strategic deficits been found on laboratory tasks, but even on more academically relevant tasks such as reading comprehension and studying for tests (Bos & Filip, 1984; Bransford, Stein, & Vye, 1982; Wong & Jones, 1982). To the extent that academic performance is benefited by spontaneous application of these kinds of strategies, then it is expected that strategic deficits would contribute to LD children's academic problems.

Environmentally relative deficits in practical intelligence.   As we discussed in the corresponding section on academic intelligence, we can do no more than speculate on whether the school environmental demands on practical intelligence are greater for children with learning disabilities than for their peers. There are several reasons for suggesting that demands on practical intelligence are likely to be greater for children with learning disabilities than for those without learning disabilities. First of all, there are the anecdotal reports of LD children who derive unique and convincing ways of hiding their learning problems. Every year there is at least one story that reaches the popular press about a child who has graduated from high school, despite having never learned to read. To be able to present oneself as a reader and successfully complete a high school curriculum while unable to read would certainly demand considerable practical intelligence.

Second, the frequency with which LD children experience failure would also seem to greatly tax their abilities to maintain adaptive beliefs about themselves. Experimental studies clearly show that repeated failures lead to changes in one's achievement-related beliefs, particularly one's causal attributions for successes and failures. To maintain adaptive beliefs concerning one's abilities and the role of one's effort to achievement outcomes places greater demands on LD children than those without learning disabilities, because of their more frequent encounters with failure.

Finally, if one assumes LD children to have an underlying processing deficit, then it is likely that the strategies and techniques for acquiring specific academic knowledge will differ for LD children, requiring them to create new approaches to solving problems or to modify the strategies and techniques used by their peers. This demand on practical intelligence is much greater for LD children than for those without learning disabilities. Greater demands, coupled with evidence that many LD children may be deficient (relative to nondisabled children) in improvisation and development of strategies that are not directly taught, leads us to conclude that practical intelligence has important implications for academic progress of LD children.

Is the Impaired Academic Performance of Children with Learning Disabilities Likely to Result in Deficits in Practical Intelligence?

Just as we argued that academic intelligence is likely to be adversely affected by impaired academic performance, we also think development of practical intelligence is likely to be impeded. Practical intelligence is assumed to develop as a function of appropriate models, demands for performance on tasks that require self-regulated behavior, and feedback that follows successful mastery attempts. The experiences of LD children are not conducive to the development of practical intelligence.

First of all, a strong case can be made that repeated failures may result in maladaptive achievement-related beliefs that lead to avoidance of achievement situations and, consequently, fewer opportunities to acquire appropriate tasks strategies. Adding to this, parents and teachers may inadvertently encourage behaviors that are incompatible with practical intelligence through feedback they provide LD children, and communicate debilitating thoughts and attributions that increase the likelihood that LD children will not develop tacit knowledge related to success in the classroom. For example, being labeled LD and placed in special classes may lead children to believe that they are incapable of learning and that their efforts are not related to successful outcomes. Also, there is a tendency for parents and teachers of LD children to provide more help to them, perhaps reinforcing them for dependency rather than for active attempts to solve their own learning problems.

Some recent studies of teacher–student interactions also suggest that differential patterns of feedback may impede development of children's active and improvised attempts to solve their learning problems, and lead them to be overly reliant on external direction (Allington, 1980; Brown, Palincsar, & Purcell, 1986; McNaughton, 1981). For example, teachers tended to interrupt immediately after errors were made by low-ability students, typically by supplying the correct word for the child (Allington, 1980). In contrast, teachers usually delayed their feedback to high-ability students until they reached a natural pause in their reading (i.e., at the end of a phrase or sentence). This delay provided high-ability students the opportunity to self-correct, thus reducing the likelihood that teachers would have to provide corrections.

These findings suggest that because of their academic difficulties, children with learning disabilities are exposed to different types of interactions with adults, and that some of these interactions may impede development of tacit knowledge indicative of practical intelligence.

GENERAL DISCUSSION

Given the recency with which the distinction between academic and practical intelligence has been examined, our analysis of the implications of this distinction for understanding relations between intelligence and learning disabilities has admittedly been speculative. We think our framework serves a useful purpose by organizing a number of empirical findings about children with learning disabilities, but in the end, the proof of the pudding is in whether our speculations can be verified. In this final section, we will briefly summarize our main points and their implications for educating individuals with learning disabilities, and also consider how interested researchers might put some of these speculative ideas to empirical test.

Academic Intelligence and Learning Disabilities

In examining the potential role of deficits in academic intelligence in the deficient academic performance of children with learning disabilities, we have made a distinction between two kinds of deficits, normative and environmentally relative ones. There can be no doubt, from the many studies that show LD samples to perform lower than comparison samples of nondisabled children on a wide variety of measures, including performance IQ, that LD samples are characterized by mild but pervasive deficits in academic intelligence. The hard part is figuring out what it all means.

We have argued that the evidence of a mild but pervasive deficit in academic intelligence does not make a compelling case for reconceptualizing learning disabilities as a rather general though mild deficit in academic intelligence as opposed to one of more specific cognitive deficits but normal intelligence because of four limitations of the studies from which the evidence is drawn: (a) sampling bias, (b) regression artifacts associated with IQ-match designs, (c) the possibility of subtypes, and (d) the possibility that the deficit in academic intelligence is a consequence rather than a cause of learning disabilities.

We think that it now is possible for careful researchers to make considerable progress in resolving the issue of the specificity of learning disabilities by addressing the abovementioned limitations. Sampling bias can be minimized by applying one's inclusionary criteria (e.g., 20-point discrepancy between IQ and achievement) to the general school population rather than to the population of school-identified disabled learners. Regression artifacts associated with IQ-matched designs can be avoided by not matching groups on IQ but rather using statistical procedures to hold constant between-group variance that is due to group differences in IQ. Various cluster-analytic techniques can be used to identify subtypes, although this requires large samples. Finally, determining whether a deficit in academic intelligence is more a consequence than a cause of learning disabilities could be accomplished by study of the developmental pattern of deficits in academic intelligence. We say more about this last possibility shortly.

The possibility that environmentally relative deficits in academic intelligence might exist independent of the existence of normative deficits could be subject to empirical verification. We would expect such deficits to be more pronounced on tasks related to the area of deficit but which are not simply tests of the deficit skill itself. An example would be reading comprehension for disabled readers whose problem is confined to decoding individual words. If modal academic tasks such as reading comprehension demand more academic intelligence of children with learning disabilities than is demanded by their peers, there should be a stronger correlation between IQ and task performance for children with learning disabilities, provided that appropriate procedures and statistical adjustments are made to correct for differences in range of IQ and other potential confounds.

In examining the potential role of impaired academic performance on subsequent development of deficits in academic intelligence, we alluded to the possibility that because many children with learning disabilities receive a different educational experience (e.g., fewer words read over the academic year) and may be less able to profit from part of their educational experience to the same degree (e.g., retaining fewer words that are learned or retaining them for less duration), it is almost inevitable that a modest deficit in academic intelligence will occur. A longitudinal study that compared the change in IQ over time for a sample of learning disabled children and a sample of their nondisabled peers would provide a test of this notion: The slope of the line representing IQ over time should be significantly negative for the LD group relative to the control group.

Practical Intelligence and Learning Disabilities

If there is value to our application of the construct of practical intelligence in the present context, it is that it serves to organize research on children with learning disabilities from what currently are considered to be very diverse areas (e.g., achievement motivation; metacognition; social competence). This reorganization may lead to more cohesive theories of the nature and causes of learning disabilities, and should provide some direction for future research in the field.

In this chapter, we considered two possibilities: deficits in practical intelligence cause learning disabilities; and achievement deficits cause deficits in practical intelligence. We believe that both remain reasonable hypotheses.

The issues that we have just discussed concerning academic intelligence also apply to practical intelligence, but making substantial progress in testing possible relations between practical intelligence and learning disabilities requires more attention to ways of measuring practical intelligence in children (most of the existing measures are appropriate for adults). We think this effort is warranted. One place to start may be to examine convergence of measures that we (and others) consider to be products of practical intelligence. For example, the relations between spontaneous applications of strategies to cognitive tasks, achievement-related beliefs (e.g., attributions for one's successes and failures), and social competence have not been investigated. Demonstration that these measures covary would add strength to the notion of practical intelligence and provide some direction to development of tests to measure practical intelligence in children.

A good measure of practical intelligence for children would allow researchers to determine whether individual differences in practical intelligence account for the tremendous variability found in the academic success of learning disabled children that is not accounted for by the severity of their academic deficits. There are cases of children who are virtually nonreaders, yet whom are graduated from high school without having been discovered. There also are cases of children with apparently minimal cognitive deficits whose levels of academic achievement remain frozen year after year. Contrasting these two groups of achievers might provide insight into (a) practical knowledge that can help facilitate the achievement of children with learning disabilities, and (b) achievement-related beliefs about the nature of one's abilities that are adaptive in the face of the repeated failure that is commonly experienced by such children.

In addition to accounting for some of the tremendous variability in academic success of LD children, an unrecognized deficit in practical intelligence might account for the fact that, for the most part, the academic progress of many children with learning disabilities is less than might be expected on the basis of their nominal processing deficit and their measured academic intelligence. Such a deficit may also help to explain achievement problems of LD children in areas not typically associated with their identified processing deficit (i.e., problems with math as well as reading for children identified as having specific reading disabilities due to process deficits involving phonological codes). Finally, deficits in practical intelligence may be helpful to understanding those children whose academic progress continues to be below expectations after their specific processing deficits have been overcome.

A strong case was made that a deficit in practical intelligence is a likely consequence of the experiences associated with the deficient academic performance of children with learning disabilities. Repeated failures (characteristic of LD children) are associated with negative beliefs regarding one's abilities, and the perception that one's efforts are unrelated to achievement outcomes. These types of self-beliefs have been labeled as maladaptive because they are associated with lack of persistence in mastery efforts, thus increasing the likelihood of failure. Also, withdrawal of effort from difficult tasks and/or avoidance of challenging schoolwork reduces children's opportunities to acquire strategies to benefit their performance. It is likely that this interplay of beliefs and achievement behaviors produces the strategic deficits found to be characteristic of many LD children.

There clearly is a need for more specific information regarding the types of experiences likely to produce deficits in these kinds of practical intelligence. Certainly frequent failures contribute to these deficits. Yet despite the fact that all LD children have experienced frequent failures, not all are characterized by maladaptive beliefs and strategic deficits. Furthermore, frequency and severity of failure, as indexed by extent of achievement deficits, are not good predictors of which children exhibit these deficits.

Improving our knowledge of determinants of practical intelligence is likely to have several benefits. Prediction of academic progress of LD children may be facilitated. Also, knowledge of these determinants is likely to produce ideas of how to remediate, or possibly prevent, deficits of practical intelligence. One area of research that we think is particularly promising is the interactions between teachers and their LD students. By carefully examining the types of timing of feedback provided to LD children, Allington's (1980) work has been very informative. Further research employing a fine-grained analysis of teacher-student interactions is warranted. In addition to closer examination of teacher–student interactions, research on parent–child interactions is likely to shed light on determinants of practical intelligence. Early patterns of adult–child interactions are precursors to development of independent problem-solving strategies, as well as the beliefs we develop about our abilities.

The idea that preschool experiences (i.e., the types of adult–child interactions experienced prior to school) may cause deficits of practical intelligence is consistent with some hypotheses regarding a potential cause of learning disabilities. Kistner and Torgesen (1987) suggested that some children labeled as learning disabled may enter school unprepared to assume an active, adaptive role of learner due to family experiences. Perhaps these children have not been given adequate opportunities to engage in independent problem-solving actions, or dependence on adults to solve most difficulties has been strongly encouraged. These children would be at a disadvantage in the early school years and it is likely that their academic achievement would be negatively affected. Although most definitions of learning disabilities attempt to exclude from classification those children whose learning problems are primarily due to an impoverished background with insufficient opportunity for an adequate education, this is usually interpreted as children from poor families who do not support their children's achievement efforts. It does not consider more subtle types of parenting styles that cut across economic groups, that might adversely influence children's achievement in the early school years.

Continued research on the experiential determinants of tacit knowledge is critical both for understanding the academic problems of LD children, and for altering the future course of these children. While for decades there have been pessimistic data regarding modifiability of academic intelligence, nothing is known about the extent to which practical intelligence can be enhanced. It is our belief that experiences and types of adult–child interactions associated with individual differences in practical intelligence can be identified. This information might then be used to remediate, or possibly prevent, deficits among children with learning disabilities.

A final possible implication of our framework, particularly the distinction between normative and environmentally relative deficits in intelligence, may suggest another reason why it is so very hard for many children with learning disabilities to achieve in school. The implication is that children with learning disabilities may be doubly disadvantaged: Because of their learning disability, the environment demands more academic and practical intelligence (i.e., environmentally relative deficits) of children with learning disabilities than that required by their nondisabled peers for a similar level of success; however, the impaired academic performance that results from the learning disability also makes it likely that development of academic and practical intelligence will be impaired (i.e., normative deficits). In short, a learning disability *increases the demand* but *diminishes the supply* of both academic and practical intelligence. Finding out what can be done to break out of this potentially debilitating ''Catch 22'' is a problem for researchers of unsurpassed importance.

ACKNOWLEDGMENTS

Address correspondence to either author at the Department of Psychology, Florida State University, Tallahassee, Florida 32306-1051. Preparation of this chapter was supported by Contract MDA90385K0305 from the Army Research Institute.

REFERENCES

Allington, R. L. (1980). Teacher interruption behaviors during primary-grade oral reading. *Journal of Educational Psychology, 72*, 371–377.

Allington, R. L. (1984). Content coverage and contextual reading in reading groups. *Journal of Reading Behavior, 16*, 85–96.

Berger, N. (1978). Why can't Johnny read? Perhaps he's not a good listener. *Journal of Learning Disabilities, 11*, 633–638.

Bos, C. S., & Filip D. (1984). Comprehension monitoring in learning disabled and average students. *Journal of Learning Disabilities, 17*, 229–233.

Bransford, J. D., Stein, B. S., & Vye, N. J. (1982). Helping Students learn how to learn from written text. In M. Singer (Ed.), *Competent reader, disabled readers: Research and Application.* Hillsdale, NJ: Lawrence Erlbaum Associates.

Brown, A. L., Palincsar, A. S., & Purcell, L. (1986). Poor readers: Teach, don't label. In U. Neisser (Ed.), *The school achievement of minority children: New perspectives* (pp. 105–143). Hillsdale, NJ: Lawrence Erlbaum Associates.

Bryan, T., & Bryan, J. (1981). Some personal and social experiences of learning disabled children. In *Advances in special education* (Vol. 3. Greenwich, CT: JAI Press.

Ceci, S. J., & Liker, J. (1986). Academic and nonacademic intelligence: An experimental separation. In R. J. Sternberg & R. K. Wagner (Eds.), *Practical intelligence: Nature and origins of competence in the everyday world* (pp. 119–142). New York: Cambridge University Press.

Cohen, R., & Netley, C. (1981). Short-term memory deficits in reading disabled children, in the absence of opportunity for rehearsal strategies. *Intelligence, 5,* 69–76.

Crowder, R. G. (1984). Is it just reading? *Developmental Review, 4,* 48–61.

Dweck, C. S. (1975). The role of expectations and attributions in the alleviation of learned helplessness. *Journal of Personality & Social Psychology, 31,* 674–685.

Ellis, N. (1981). Visual and name coding in dyslexic children. *Psychological Research, 43,* 201–218.

Goodman, K. S. (1976). Reading: A psycholinguistic guessing game. In H. Singer & R. Ruddell (Eds.), *Theoretical models and process of reading* (pp. 497–508.) Newark, DE: International Reading Association.

Gresham, F. (1981). Social skills training with handicapped children: A review. *Review of Educational Research, 51,* 139–176.

Jenkins, J., & Dixon, R. (1983). Vocabulary learning. *Contemporary Educational Psychology, 8,* 237–260.

Katz, R., Shankweiler, D., & Liberman, I. (1981). Memory for item order and phonetic recoding in the beginning reader. *Journal of Experimental Child Psychology, 32,* 474–484.

Keogh, B. K. (1983). Classification, compliance and confusion. *Journal of Learning Disabilities, 16,* 25.

Kistner, J., Osborne, M., & LeVerrier, L. (1988). Causal attributions of learning disabled children: Developmental patterns and relation to academic progress. *Journal of Educational Psychology, 80,* 1, 82–89.

Kistner, J. A., & Torgesen, J. K. (1987). Motivational and cognitive aspects of learning disabilities. In B. Lahey & A. Kazdin (Eds.), *Advances in Clinical Child Psychology,* (Vol. 10, pp. 289–334). New York: Plenum Press.

Kotsonis, M., & Patterson, C. (1980). Comprehension-monitoring skills in learning-disabled children. *Developmental Psychology, 16,* 541–542.

McNaughton, S. (1981). The influence of immediate teacher correction on self-corrections and proficient oral reading. *Journal of Reading Behavior, 13,* 267–271.

Mercer, J. R., Gomez-Palacio, M., Padilla, E. (1986). The development of practical intelligence in cross-cultural perspective. In R. J. Sternberg, & R. K. Wagner, (Eds.). *Practical intelligence: Nature and origins of competence in the everyday world* (pp. 307–337). New York: Cambridge University Press.

Merton, R. (1968). The Matthew effect in science. *Science,* 56–63.

Nagy, W. E., & Anderson, R. C. (1984). How many words are there in printed school English? *Reading Research Quarterly, 20,* 233–253.

Nagy, W. E., Herman, P. A., & Anderson, R. C. (1985). Learning words from context. *Reading Research Quarterly, 20,* 233–253.

Neisser, U. (1976). General, academic, and artificial intelligence. In L. Resnick (Ed.), *The nature of intelligence* (pp. 135–144). Hillsdale, NJ: Lawrence Erlbaum Associates.

Newcomer, P., & Magee, P. (1977). The performance of learning (reading) disabled children on a test of spoken language. *The Reading Teacher, 30,* 896–900.

Oxford English Dictionary. (1933). Oxford: Clarendon Press.

Perfetti, C. A., Goldman, S., & Hogaboam, T. (1979). Reading skill and the identification of words in discourse context. *Memory & Cognition, 7,* 273–282.

Perfetti, C. A., & Roth, S. (1981). Some of the interactive processes in reading and their role in reading skill. In A. Leshold & C. Perfetti (Eds.), *Interactive processes in reading* (pp. 269–297). Hillsdale, NJ: Lawrence Erlbaum Associates.

Polyani, M. (1976). Tacit knowing. In M. Marz & F. Goodson (Eds.), *Theories in contemporary psychology* (pp. 330–344). New York: Macmillan.

Pressley, M., Johnson, C. J., & Symons, S. (1987). Elaborating to learn and learning to elaborate. *Journal of Learning Disabilities, 20,* 76–91.

Schon, D. A. (1983). *The reflective practitioner: How professionals think in action.* New York: Basic Books.

Sharp C., Cole, M., & Lave, C. (1979). Education and cognitive development: The evidence from experimental research. *Monographs of the Society for Research in Child Development, 44,* (1-2, Serial No. 178).

Smiley, S., Oakley, D., Worthen, D., Campione, J., & Brown, A. (1977). Recall of thematically relevant material by adolescent good and poor readers as a function of written versus oral presentation. *Journal of Educational Psychology, 69,* 381–387.

Smith, F. (1971). *Understanding reading.* New York: Holt, Rinehart & Winston.

Spring, C., & Capps, C. (1974). Encoding speed, rehearsal, and probed recall of dyslexic boys. *Journal of Educational Psychology, 66,* 780–786.

Stanovich, K. E. (1986a). Cognitive process and the reading problems of learning disabled children: Evaluating the assumption of specificity. In J. Torgesen & B. Wong (Eds.), *Psychological and educational perspectives on learning disabilities* (pp. 87–131). New York: Academic Press.

Stanovich, K. E. (1986b). Matthew effects in reading: Some consequences of individual differences in the acquisition of literacy. *Reading Research Quarterly, 21,* 360–407.

Sternberg, R., & Powell, J. (1983). Comprehending verbal comprehension. *American Psychologist, 38,* 878–893.

Sternberg, R. J., & Wagner, R. K. (1986). *Practical intelligence: Nature and origins of competence in the everyday world.* New York: Cambridge University Press.

Torgesen, J. K. (1977). Memorization processes in reading disabled children. *Journal of Educational Psychology, 69,* 571–578.

Torgesen, J. K. (1982). The learning disabled child as an inactive learner: Educational implications. *Topics in Learning & Learning Disabilities,* April, 45–52.

Torgesen, J., & Dice, C. (1980). Characteristics of research in learning disabilities. *Journal of Learning Disabilities, 13,* 531–535.

Torgesen, J., & Houck, D. (1980). Processing deficiencies of learning-disabled children who perform poorly on the digit span test. *Journal of Educational Psychology, 72,* 141–160.

Vellutino, F. (1979). *Dyslexia: Theory and research.* Cambridge, MA: MIT Press.

Vogel, S. (1974). Syntactic abilities in normal and dyslexic children. *Journal of Learning Disabilities, 7,* 103–109.

Wagner, D. A. (1978). Memories of Morrocco: The influence of age, schooling, and environment on memory. *Cognitive Psychology, 10,* 1–28.

Wagner, R. K. (1987). Tacit knowledge in everyday intelligent behavior. *Journal of Personality and Social Psychology, 52,* 1236–1247.

Wagner, R. K., & Sternberg, R. J. (1985). Practical intelligence in real-world pursuits: The role of tacit knowledge. *Journal of Personality and Social Psychology, 48,* 436–458.

Walberg, H. J., & Tsai, S. (1983). Matthew effects in education. *American Educational Research Journal, 20,* 359–373.

Wolford, G. (1981, April). *Reading deficits: Are they specific to reading?* Paper presented at The Meeting of the Society for Research in Child Development. Boston: Society for Research in Child Development.

Wong, B. Y. L. (1986). Problems and issues in the definition of learning disabilities. In J. K. Torgesen & B. Y. L. Wong (Eds.), *Psychological and educational perspectives on learning disabilities* (pp. 3–26). New York: Academic Press.

Wong, B. Y. L., & Jones, W. (1982). Increasing metacomprehension in learning disabled and normally achieving students through self-questioning training. *Learning Disabilities Quarterly, 5,* 228–240.

6

The Diagnostic and Educational Utility of Thinking Aloud During Problem Solving

Elizabeth J. Short
Cara L. Cuddy
Sarah E. Friebert
Chris W. Schatschneider
Case Western Reserve University

Learning disabled (LD) children are distinguished by one feature consistently: a significant incongruence between their academic performance as predicted by their mental ability on the one hand, and their actual performance in a learning situation on the other (Short, Feagans, McKinney, & Appelbaum, 1984). Performance in this context is measured either by achievement on objective tests or in the classroom; achievement in both cases is based on what LD children do on their own (independently). Thus, the crucial issue becomes to determine what interferes between their mental ability and their independent achievement. This IQ-achievement discrepancy has been explained according to various models. One such model is that of a neurological deficit (Rourke, 1985) which selectively interferes with the ability of the LD child to process information presented in visual or auditory modalities. Another explanation, known as the attention deficit hypothesis, assumes that attention deficit disordered (A.D.D.) children are not able to sustain their attention on academic tasks, and their poor academic progress is therefore the net result of an accumulation of missed academic experiences (Krupski, 1986). A third model explains the gap in terms of motivation and learned helplessness. Learning disabled children are characterized as passive learners who accept total responsibility for their failure while accepting little, if any, responsibility for their success (Torgesen, 1977). As a result of this maladaptive attributional profile, LD students simply give up in the learning situation. A fourth explanatory model, focusing on information processing theory, highlights the cognitive processes brought to the learning situation (Swanson, 1988) and argues that the disability experienced by the LD student results from specific difficulties with information processing components (i.e., encoding, storage, and retrieval).

Learning disabled children experience a multitude of skill deficits. As a group, the learning disabled are quite heterogeneous, with few children presenting the same clinical profile (McKinney, 1988). The great variability that exists in the LD population has made it difficult to pinpoint the skills critical to both academic and social success (McKinney, Short, & Feagans, 1985). One such skill—problem solving—appears to be critical to success in both domains (Bash & Camp, 1985; Swanson, 1988). In light of this research, the importance of problem-solving skills for academic and social success is the focus of this chapter.

First, we review briefly the nature of academic and social problem solving and the difficulties experienced by the LD child. Next, a rationale is presented for the need for dynamic assessment of problem-solving performance, with special emphasis on the feasibility of the think aloud technique as a diagnostic tool in academic and social situations. Finally, the educational utility of the think aloud technique for academic and social problem solving is discussed, with particular attention directed toward the LD child.

WHAT IS PROBLEM SOLVING?

One of the most important skills required in everyday life is the ability to solve problems efficiently (Cowan & Clary, 1978). A problem can be seen as a situation in which an individual has a goal but is unsure of how to reach it. Given an initial problem state and a desired goal state, successful problem solvers need to implement a plan to move from one to the other, minimizing the obstacles along the way (Duncker, 1945; Newell & Simon, 1972). Problem-solving goals and the skills used to achieve them cut across environmental, social, and academic domains. Everyday problems can be as basic as deciding what to buy at the grocery store, or as complicated as navigating around an unfamiliar city at rush hour. Problems of a social nature involve more direct interactions with one's peers. Examples of social problem solving include a child's strategy for making friends and for getting to know his or her teachers in school. When examining problem solving, problems from an academic setting are perhaps most often called to mind; some common areas include reading comprehension, mathematics, analogies, and series completion tasks.

Apart from the particular problem-solving domain, however, successful problem solvers engage in a 5-step process aimed at achieving their goals (Polya, 1948). The first step in this general problem-solving process is *identification of the problem,* since recognition of the existence of a problem is paramount to problem solution. Once the problem has been understood, the second step involves the *generation of possible solutions.* Several plans need to be considered for the solution, weighing the likelihood that alternative strategies will lead to success. After considerable decision making on the part of the problem solver, *selection and implementation of the optimal solution* occurs. Step four of the process, *monitoring the effectiveness of the solution,* immediately follows. Good problem solvers always look back to determine whether the strategies selected enabled them to achieve the problem goal. Depending on the outcome of the evaluation step, good problem solvers utilize step five, *feedback,* either to allow the generation of future plans and strategies or to initiate a new strategy to achieve a failed goal. Successful problem solvers are therefore flexible in their transactions with the problem-solving environment, profiting from subtle feedback cues by altering strategic performance.

INDIVIDUAL DIFFERENCES IN PROBLEM SOLVING

All five steps in the problem-solving process have proven to be problematic for LD learners (Meltzer, Solomon, & Fenton, 1987). Individual differences in problem-solving skills, and particularly differences in strategic awareness, have fascinated researchers and educators alike. Researchers have focused on the domain of problem solving for three main purposes: to explore in more detail students' ability to formulate or define problems; to observe their selection of appropriate strategies to solve these problems; and to monitor their progress toward achieving task solutions (Pressley, 1986; Pressley, Borkowski, & Schneider, 1987; Sternberg, 1977; Stone & Michals, 1986; Swanson, 1988). The findings suggest that LD students are less efficient than their nonlearning disabled (NLD) counterparts in problem-solving performance. That is, LD students are ineffective in planning, self-monitoring, and approaching the task in an organized fashion (Hallahan & Bryan, 1981; Torgesen, 1982). Learning disabled students are not only less efficient in problem solving but are also less flexible in their selection of strategies than their NLD peers. In addition, LD students experience great difficulty shifting their attention from one dimension of a problem to another (Short, Friebert, & Andrist, 1988). Finally, LD students appear to be unaware of the utility of a variety of strategies and fail to monitor the effectiveness of the strategy adopted (Brown & Palincsar, 1982; Flavell, 1979).

Given the vast array of problem-solving differences between LD and NLD students, it is not surprising that LD learners have been described as ''inactive learners'' and ''other regulated'' (Torgesen, 1982). Self-regulated learning involves active participation on the part of the learner in the planning and monitoring of the learning process (Corno, 1986). Students' awareness of their own cognitive activity and of the methods employed to regulate their own cognitive processes has been defined as metacognition (Brown, 1978). Although metacognitive research has clearly described the deficiencies of LD students in these areas (Wong, 1985), the need to move from descriptive studies to explanatory studies of group differences has long been recognized (Brown, Bransford, Ferrara, & Campione, 1983). Because of the desire to understand more fully the factors responsible for disparities in competence, researchers and educators have moved from static to dynamic techniques in examining differences in problem solving.

THE NEED FOR DYNAMIC ASSESSMENT OF PROBLEM SOLVING

Vygotsky (1978) clearly pointed out the need for the dynamic assessment of cognitive performance when he stated, "What children can do with the assistance of others might be in some sense more indicative of their mental development than what they can do alone" (p. 85). No statement could be more true for the learning disabled child. Recent research efforts designed to understand the nature of learning disabilities have thus concentrated on active evaluation of specific cognitive processes (Lidz, 1987).

Recognition of the importance of dynamic assessment of cognitive potential arose out of a dissatisfaction with standardized testing procedures. Current assessment procedures have been referred to as static because they focus exclusively on the end product (e.g., achievement test scores; Barr & Samuels, 1988). In addition, static assessments yield scores perceived to be irreversible, with little insight regarding factors that either impede or facilitate learning. Feuerstein (1980) expressed the importance of evaluating the learning process in action. Rather than emphasizing the student's manifested level of functioning, the focus of dynamic assessments should be on the student's potential for change, since it is this "potential for change" that provides insight into the malleability of underlying competence. The issue of malleability is particularly relevant to LD populations. Educators have been quite frustrated by standard measures of competence (e.g., IQ and achievement tests) that neither specify the deficient processes (e.g., encoding, planning, retrieval) nor suggest prescriptions for remediation. According to Das (1984), a good measure of cognitive ability must not only measure competence, but must also pinpoint the cognitive processes responsible for differences in competence and thereby shed insight into the remediation process.

Dynamic assessment presents the educator with a "good measure of cognitive ability" by giving an indication of overall competence and a measure of responsivity to instruction as well. Dynamic assessment adopts a "test-teach-test" approach. Rather than examining global test performance, the approach emphasizes the improvement over independent performance that the child can achieve, in conjunction with minimal adult guidance (Hall & Day, 1982). One such method that offers hope of enabling a more dynamic assessment of cognitive ability is the think aloud technique (Short, Evans, Dellick, & Cuddy, 1988). By asking subjects to think aloud about a problem to be solved, an adult can offer more contingent feedback and thereby improve the independent performance of the child.

THE DIAGNOSTIC UTILITY
OF THINK ALOUD TECHNIQUES

The think aloud technique has been used by cognitive psychologists (Duncker, 1945; Newell & Simon, 1972) to provide information on the processes and strategies employed by the learner during problem solving. In asking subjects to describe aloud what they are thinking about during problem solving, it is assumed that the think aloud protocol obtained will be a complete record of the problem-solving strategies employed by the learner (Ericsson & Simon, 1980). The think aloud technique is assumed not to alter task performance; therefore, it should prove to be a beneficial technique for assessing overall performance.

More recently, researchers have begun to explore the utility of the think aloud technique as a diagnostic tool. Rather than simply providing a static score (e.g., IQ, percentiles, grade equivalency), the think aloud technique yields a more dynamic assessment of academic performance because ability to profit from minimal instruction is also recorded. Preliminary evidence for the value of this approach as a diagnostic tool with normally achieving and learning disabled students has been obtained in the problem solving and reading domains. Specifically, studies have addressed the diagnostic utility of think aloud techniques for LD students in reading comprehension (Bereiter & Bird, 1985; Davey, 1983; Kavale, 1980; Olshavsky, 1976/77), mathematics problems (Havertape & Kass, 1978), analogical reasoning (Short, Cuddy, & Schatschneider, 1988), and picture arrangement tasks (Swanson, in press).

Although think aloud protocol analysis was originally applied in the area of problem solving (Ericsson & Simon, 1985), it was first introduced with LD students in the area of reading comprehension (Kavale, 1980; Olshavsky, 1976/77). In one of the first think aloud studies in reading comprehension, Olshavsky (1976/77) taught 10th grade skilled and disabled readers to utilize a modified version of the think aloud technique. This version required subjects to read a short clause or phrase of text and then think aloud about each segment. Olshavsky's purpose for employing the think aloud technique was to obtain useful information about the strategies employed by successful readers. Based on his analysis of students' think aloud protocols, ten commonly employed strategies were isolated. Three of the strategies pertain to words (e.g., use of context to define a word, synonym substitution, failure to understand), six of the strategies pertain to phrases (e.g., rereading, inference, addition, personal identification, hypothesis formation, and stated failure to understand), and one of the strategies pertains to the story (e.g., use of story information). Although both skilled and disabled readers used all of these strategies, skilled readers used them more frequently than disabled readers. Thus differences in reading performance can be attributed to differences in strategic performance.

Analogous findings were reported by Kavale (1980) for LD and NLD 6th graders' problem-solving performance during reading comprehension under the think aloud condition. After modeling the think aloud technique for his subjects,

97

Kavale asked them to think aloud as they read passages and answered questions. Based on the protocol analysis, differences were obtained in type of strategy and success of strategy employed. NLD students typically employed a lexical strategy (i.e., they extracted a word from the passage and developed a reasoning strategy around it) and a generalization strategy (i.e., comparison, classification, and definition). In contrast, LD students typically employed the most inefficient strategies (i.e., elimination or semantic fit) or no strategy at all (i.e., random response or no response). Not only were LD students unlikely to employ effective strategies, but the think aloud protocol also revealed that even when they were using the most efficient strategy, success was not the likely outcome. In light of the information obtained in this dynamic assessment, it seems clear that simply providing the LD learner with the appropriate strategy does not guarantee successful execution of the task.

The diagnostic utility of the think aloud technique with LD students has extended to mathematical problem solving as well. Havertape and Kass (1978) explored the differences between junior high and senior high school LD and NLD students' problem-solving skills on mathematical and reading tasks. By asking LD students to think aloud during problem solving, deficiencies in the data gathering process were illuminated. Thirty-three percent of the LD students gathered appropriate information to solve the problem, whereas 80% of the NLD students gathered relevant task information. In addition, 40% of the LD students indicated comprehension of the problem, while 80% of the NLD indicated comprehension. Also, 16% of the LD students used logical and efficient steps to solve the problems, while 57% of the NLD students approached the problem in a logical and efficient fashion. It should be noted that instead of approaching the problem in a logical fashion, 40% of the LD students were impulsive and random in their responses. Finally, even when LD students were using task appropriate strategies, they were not likely to complete the problem successfully. By employing the think aloud technique, Havertape and Kass (1978) discovered that the problem-solving inadequacies experienced by LD students were due in part to inefficient encoding strategies. Without the think aloud technique, the factors responsible for differences in performance (i.e., encoding, storage, and retrieval) could not be isolated. Finally, despite pronounced skill level differences, no developmental differences emerged.

Two more recent studies have extended the think aloud technique to the area of problem solving with LD students. In the first study, Short, Cuddy, and Schatschneider (1988) asked 5th grade NLD, LD, and educable mentally retarded (EMR) students to think aloud while solving a variety of verbal and nonverbal analogies. The analogies were of five types: simple matching, addition, subtraction, alterations, and progressions. Think aloud protocols were scored qualitatively for verbal ability (i.e., fluency and complexity), as well as self-regulation of learning (i.e., problem definition, strategic awareness, and amount of adult assistance via prompts). Despite no differences in verbal fluency, NLD students used more complex language throughout their think aloud protocol than did LD and EMR students, who did not differ from each other. In order to examine differences in self-regulation (i.e., problem definition, strategic awareness, and number of prompts), multivariate analyses were conducted with IQ and linguistic complexity as covariates. NLD students demonstrated superior skills in all aspects of self-regulation. While LD and EMR students did not differ in terms of problem definition, LD students demonstrated greater awareness of strategies than did their EMR counterparts. This superior awareness of strategies parallels the differences observed in overall performance; that is, NLD students solved more problems correctly than LD students, who in turn solved more problems correctly than EMR students. In addition, LD subjects required more prompting than either the NLD or the EMR students. This finding on the amount of adult assistance required by LD learners is consistent with the inactive learner hypothesis. Taken together, these findings suggest that LD students are quite aware of task appropriate strategies, but they experience great difficulty gathering relevant information to solve a problem. When provided with minimal adult assistance, LD students are capable of demonstrating considerable improvement in problem solving as compared to their independent performance.

In the second problem-solving study, Swanson (1988) asked LD and NLD 3rd graders to think aloud as they completed the picture arrangement subtest of the WISC-R. Verbal protocols were analyzed for linguistic complexity, global mental processing, heuristic processing, and strategic processing. LD and NLD were comparable in terms of overall problem-solving performance, global processing, and heuristic processing, but were quite different in terms of linguistic complexity and strategic processing. Additionally, strategic processing was a useful predictor for NLD students, whereas heuristic processing was a useful predictor for LD students.

All of the studies presented here suggest that the think aloud technique is quite effective as a diagnostic tool for assessing the processing difficulties of students, especially LD students. No studies to date have focused exclusively on the diagnostic potential of the think aloud technique in social domains, but it seems likely that it would be useful socially as well as academically. The think aloud technique provides a more dynamic measure of the existing skills of the LD student. It is quite possible that the think aloud technique will be useful for remediation as well, in that interventions can be systematically designed based on the information obtained from the think aloud protocol analysis. Preliminary studies investigating the remediation potential of the think aloud technique indicate that it has promise not only diagnostically, but educationally as well (Bereiter & Bird, 1985; Bash & Camp, 1985; Davey, 1983; Short, Evans, Dellick, & Cuddy, 1988).

Originally, cognitive psychologists assumed that the think aloud method would be a valuable diagnostic technique because it enabled an examination of the internal workings of the mind without altering task performance. As a result, educational benefits from the think aloud technique were assumed to be possible. Because of the mediational deficiencies experienced by some LD children, it was hypothesized that thinking aloud during problem solving would provide the mediational support necessary for optimizing the performance of the LD students. The think aloud technique was employed to maintain the proper frame of mind during learning and therefore was seen as a learner's "support strategy" (Dansereau, 1985). Thinking aloud during problem solving directed the learner's attention to the task and increased the concentration skills of the handicapped learners. Although the think aloud manipulation would presumably improve children's problem-solving performance (facilitative effects), the possibility nevertheless existed for neutral or debilitative effects. Neutral effects would result if children were already attending to the task in a comprehensive fashion and thereby had nothing to gain from thinking aloud, while debilitative effects would arise due to an overloading of the limited processing system (i.e., insufficient resources available for the task at hand).

REMEDIATION OF PROBLEM SOLVING DEFICIENCIES

The think aloud technique has been used as an instructional tool in three main areas. First, one study fashioned interventions after information obtained from think aloud protocols (Bereiter & Bird, 1985). Second, other studies have employed the think aloud technique as a means for modeling effective problem solving for poor learners (Davey, 1983; Duffy, Roehler, & Herrmann, 1988; Palincsar & Ransom, 1988). Finally, several studies have examined whether improved performance results from simply thinking aloud during problem solving (Short, Evans, Dellick, & Cuddy, 1988; Whimbey & Lochhead, 1986). All three aspects of educational intervention are discussed.

The Use of Think Aloud Techniques to Design Interventions

A classic study by Bereiter and Bird (1985) extended the use of the think aloud technique from that of a straightforward diagnostic tool to that of a method designed to inform interventions. Ten adult experts were asked to think aloud as they read a variety of passages ranging from expository writing to personal opinion. Based on a set of 60 transcripts, Bereiter and Bird (1985) isolated the strategies most commonly used by skilled readers to comprehend texts. Four main strategies were isolated through the think aloud technique: *backtracking* to the point of comprehension failure; *restatement,* or rephrasing of complicated text; *demanding relationships,* or designing text-related questions that signaled missing information; and *problem formulation,* or resolution of problematic text through inferential processes or a closer examination of the text.

After isolating the strategies from the expert think aloud protocols, Bereiter and Bird (1985) examined the utility of the think aloud technique as an instructional tool. Seventh grade average readers served as the subjects in this instructional phase of the study. Using the think aloud technique, teachers modeled the use of all four strategies and explicitly instructed students as to the advantages of each strategy. In addition, students were allowed the opportunity to practice their newly learned strategies while thinking aloud. Three of the strategies—backtracking, restatement, and problem formulation—were adequately mastered by students in this training study. Modeling of each strategy through the think aloud technique and direct explanation were both necessary in order to improve performance of the seventh graders. Thus, this study presents preliminary evidence for the feasibility of developing training techniques based on the data obtained from the think aloud protocols of skilled readers.

The Use of the Think Aloud Technique to Model Effective Strategies

The use of the think aloud technique to model effective teaching strategies has been demonstrated not only for academic problem solving, but for social problem solving as well. Most of the strategies modeled have been derived from an extensive review of the problem-solving literature and not from expert protocols. We first review the academic training programs and subsequently review the social training programs.

Although Davey (1983) developed her intervention strategies based on a comprehensive review of the reading literature rather than from direct observation of skilled readers, analogous training effects for normal and disabled readers were obtained. Davey (1983) taught readers four strategies: (1) making predictions; (2) imagery; (3) use of analogy to bridge the gap between new and known information; and (4) fix up or repair strategies. By utilizing think aloud techniques, the mysterious, invisible cognitive processes employed by the skilled reader can be made concrete and visible for the poor reader. Thus, through "mental modeling," teachers can demonstrate effective strategies for tackling unfamiliar information, thereby minimizing the mystery behind successful reading performance for disabled readers (Palincsar & Ransom, 1988; Duffy et al., 1988).

Other instructional methods that rely heavily on the think aloud technique for demonstration and monitoring of trained strategies are "paired problem solving" (Whimbey & Lochhead, 1986) and reciprocal teaching (Palincsar & Brown, 1984). Both techniques are designed to encourage the learner to adopt an active stance in the educational process and thus to develop a more positive attitude and strategic approach toward problem solving. These authors argue that to foster an active stance in learning, educators must change the role of both the teacher and the learner in educational settings.

Typically, the role of teachers is to cultivate the exchange of ideas and the growth of knowledge. Teachers play two major roles: (1) problem identification (i.e., teachers pose questions); and (2) solution monitoring (i.e., teachers provide feedback regarding accuracy). Students play a more minor role in the learning process (i.e., they supply a solution). The participation level of the student is minimized by the teacher's active role in problem identification and solution monitoring.

By definition, paired problem solving involves pairs of students jointly solving a set of problems, while the classroom teacher takes the role of the coach (Lochhead, 1985). One student serves as the reader/thinker, in that she or he reads the problem while thinking aloud. The partner of the pair serves as the listener/critic, in that he or she continually checks for accuracy while constantly demanding vocalizations. Upon solution of a problem, the students switch roles, so that each member of the pair has the opportunity to play both the role of the reader/thinker and that of the listener/critic. Though paired problem solving has not been formally evaluated by Whimbey and Lochhead (1986), a considerable amount of research does support its efficacy. This research does not refer to "paired problem solving" per se; rather it exists under such titles as peer teaching, cooperative learning, and peer mediation of learning (Lambiotte, Dansereau, O'Donnell, Young, Skaggs, Hall, & Rocklin, 1987; Lloyd, Crowley, Kohler, & Strain, 1988; Uttero, 1988). Yet all three approaches adopt a comparable format to that of paired problem solving.

In a recent study by Lambiotte et al. (1987), the effectiveness of cooperative teaching, cooperative learning, and cooperative microlearning was compared. Cooperative teaching involves flexible roles, with each child reading and preparing to teach one passage while his or her partner reads and prepares to teach the other passage. Because partners have not read the information being taught to them, students participating in cooperative teaching are not able to infer what their partner is communicating and are therefore dependent on their peer for enlightenment. Thus, the role of the student teacher in the cooperative teaching group is to organize information coherently, to choose effective memory aids, and to decide which details are critical in order that his or her partner understands the text. Cooperative teachers think aloud about the text, and learners signal lack of comprehension by red flag directives. In contrast, cooperative learners are each allowed to read both passages, and they each teach one of the passages. Less cooperation is necessary since both participants have read the passages and are completely informed as to their contents. Finally, the cooperative microlearning situation involves both participants reading half of and teaching half of each passage. These students are partially informed about the texts and can therefore make some inferences during the teaching of the passage. Cooperative teachers appeared to be more motivated, to have a greater sense of responsibility, to be more satisfied with their learning, and to be more active in the learning process than were the other groups. By employing the think aloud technique, cooperative teachers can highlight the thought processes that are critical for understanding the problem.

Reciprocal teaching (Palincsar & Brown, 1984) is another instructional technique that seems to rely heavily on the use of the think aloud technique. The procedure employes the method of Socratic teaching to disseminate information. Like the paired problem-solving approach, reciprocal teaching is based on the modeling of mental processes through the think aloud technique. The training program is designed to teach four strategies via the think aloud format: summarization, prediction, question generation, and clarification. Initially the teacher models the use of the strategies while thinking aloud. Strategic behavior is thus "other-regulated" (Vygotsky, 1978). Eventually students learn to assume both the role of the learner and that of the teacher during the teaching process. Students accept increasingly more responsibility for their learning and eventually become "self-regulated" (Corno, 1986). The major differences between reciprocal teaching and paired problem solving are that (1) reciprocal teaching techniques are more specifically focused on strategies, and (2) reciprocal teaching is designed to involve the teacher and students, not simply the student pairs. Reciprocal teaching techniques are quite effective in improving the comprehension performance of disabled readers, for both individualized and group settings (Palincsar & Brown, 1984; Palincsar & Ransom, 1988). Again, the think aloud technique enables teachers to model effective thinking skills successfully for their students and to monitor the effectiveness with which learners have mastered their newfound skills.

The major application of the think aloud training technique to social problems has been conducted with aggressive boys by Bonnie Camp and her colleagues (Camp & Bash, 1981; Camp, Blom, Hebert, & van Doorninck, 1977). In an attempt to teach effective social problem-solving skills, Bash and Camp (1985) have developed a program of 30 lessons covering such topics as making friends, predicting consequences, and recognizing different perspectives. Camp and her colleagues employ the think aloud technique to model effective strategies with young aggressive boys. Her studies have been very effective in reducing aggressivity and improving prosocial behaviors of kindergarten through third grade males. These studies suggest that thinking aloud during problem solving improves not only academic performance but social skills as well.

Does Thinking Aloud Facilitate Problem-Solving Performance?

Whether or not thinking aloud facilitates independent problem solving is somewhat uncertain to date. Most researchers who have employed the think aloud technique have failed to include an independent assessment of problem solving, leaving the question open to debate (Havertape & Kass, 1978; Kavale, 1980; Swanson, in press). However, despite little evidence directly addressing this question, substantial indirect evidence suggests that the think aloud manipulation would facilitate problem solving. Cognitive behavior therapists have long recognized the importance of overt verbalizations and self-instructions in guiding the performance of learners, particularly children (Kendall & Braswell, 1985; Meichenbaum, 1977). By encouraging students to externalize their thoughts and behaviors during problem solving, performance gains have been observed in a variety of content domains (Ryan, Short, & Weed, 1086; Vygotsky, 1978). Moreover, reliable changes in off-task behaviors such as aggressivity and impulsivity have also been observed (Bash & Camp, 1985). Finally, Stone and Wertsch (1984) argue that red flag directives (i.e., Why did you choose that one?) employed by the listener in the think aloud condition encouraged a more reflective style of problem solving. Thus, the assumption that the think aloud technique does not alter independent task performance may be a faulty one.

Recently Short, Evans, Dellick, & Cuddy (1988) attempted to address this question with NLD, LD, and EMR 5th graders. They hypothesized that the inability of LD children's IQ to predict their achievement may perhaps be a function of either a production or a mediational deficiency (Flavell, 1977; Reese, 1962). That is, LD students do not achieve on their own as would be expected based on their intelligence due to their failure to produce and/or use verbal mediators. In order to test this hypothesis, Short, Evans et al. (1988) asked 5th-grade NLD, LD, and EMR students to solve verbal and nonverbal analogies on their own (independent condition) or when they thought aloud (think aloud condition). No specific training in the use of the think aloud technique was provided; rather, the experimenter prompted the subjects consistently for overt verbalized thoughts. The assessment of independent problem solving revealed that NLD students were superior to LD and EMR students, who did not differ from each other. This finding was surprising given that LD students were vastly superior to their EMR peers in intelligence (X = 93 vs. X = 73). The think aloud manipulation improved the problem-solving performance of children in the NLD and LD groups as compared to their independent problem solving, despite minimal interaction with the experimenter. Of the problems used in the think aloud condition, NLD children solved 63% of the problems in the independent condition and 74% of the problems in the think aloud condition. Similarly, LD children solved 44% of the problems in the independent condition and 54% of the problems in the think aloud condition. Finally, EMR children solved 38% of the problems in the independent condition and 41% of the problems in the think aloud condition. It should be noted that the material covered during the think aloud condition consisted of moderate and hard problems, which accounts for the low percentage by all groups.

Despite the fact that all three groups demonstrated some improvement as a function of the think aloud manipulation, uniform improvement was not observed within each group. As expected, NLD children were more homogeneous as a group and therefore most children experienced the facilitative effects of the think aloud manipulation. In contrast, great variability in the facilitative effects of the think aloud manipulation was observed within both handicapped groups. Two thirds of the LD group and half of the EMR group experienced facilitative effects from the think aloud manipulation. From the correlational analyses, some insights can be offered as to why certain children profited from the manipulation. As was noted in previous studies with handicapped learners (Speece, McKinney & Appelbaum, 1985), classroom behavior is an important predictor of future academic difficulty. Correlational data from the Short, Evans et al. (1988) study suggested that students who profited from the think aloud manipulation appeared to be the most socially withdrawn and perhaps had previously adopted a passive approach to learning.

The merits of the think aloud approach have been clearly demonstrated in this study. NLD and LD students both profited from the manipulation, whereas EMR children did not seem to profit much from the think aloud technique. The method seems to engage the student in an active problem-solving stance. Future studies might systematically investigate the relative merits of the think aloud approach with handicapped, socially withdrawn, and aggressive children. Determination should then be made regarding which children profit from the think aloud techniques and which children do not.

EDUCATIONAL IMPLICATIONS

The preliminary evidence suggests that the think aloud technique is not only an effective diagnostic tool, but also a potentially useful remediation technique. The think aloud technique is beneficial for diagnosing the problem-solving difficulties of all learners, and is especially effective for the LD child. In addition, the think aloud technique proved to be quite a valuable tool for demonstrating the thought processes that typically occur in the successful learner. For many LD learners, success in school is but a mystery. Some students are lucky and they are successful, whereas others are less fortunate. The think aloud technique demystifies the learning process for those students (Short & Weissberg-Benchell, 1989). Additionally, it was assumed that the think aloud technique would facilitate problem-solving performance because the overt verbalizations would guide students' problem-solving behavior, especially for LD students (Ryan et al., 1986; Short & Weissberg-Benchell, 1989). The studies reported in this chapter shed greater insight into the difficulties experienced by the LD student than would typically be achieved with group difference studies. The think aloud technique offers considerable hope for isolating the difficulties experienced by the LD student and tailoring the instructional interventions to the student's needs.

Several caveats should be offered regarding the think aloud technique. The first concerns the wording of the instructions in the think aloud manipulation.

Ericsson and Simon (1980), who hold that the think aloud manipulation does not affect performance, have suggested that think aloud instructions should be bland, enabling the learner to give first priority to performing the task. This point must be strongly considered when developing a think aloud study. Complex instructions and excessive verbalizations could, in fact, overload the cognitive system and thereby adversely affect problem-solving performance, especially for handicapped students (Short, Evans et al., 1988). The second caveat concerns the difficulty associated with eliciting verbalizations from the children. Without some type of modeling of the think aloud technique, children have great trouble knowing what to say and do, which subsequently detracts from their task performance. Given the verbal difficulties experienced by LD students, the fact that the think aloud technique emphasizes verbal skills could be problematic. With sufficient modeling and opportunity to practice the think aloud technique, LD students appear to benefit greatly from the technique. Finally, the fact that in the Short, Friebert, and Andrist (1988) study, facilitative, neutral, and debilitative effects were obtained for the think aloud technique for the sample of LD and EMR students suggests that differential effects emerge for age and handicapping condition. In particular, young children may be more susceptible to mediational benefits than are older children or adults. Developmental and skill level differences should be researched in future studies.

In summary, several conclusions can be drawn from the studies reported in this chapter. First, important information about the cognitive processes responsible for differences in competence can be obtained through the use of the think aloud technique. The evidence reported here strongly supports the utility of the think aloud technique as a diagnostic tool. This procedure enables a more dynamic view of the problem-solving process. Second, the think aloud technique is useful for modeling effective problem-solving strategies, as well as the ability to cope with ineffective strategies. If the thought processes employed by the successful learner are explicitly verbalized, the mystique behind skilled performance is eliminated. Third, children's ability to solve problems is improved by demanding constant verbalization of the steps required in the problem-solving process. These overt verbalizations appear to guide the problem-solving performance of the learner. Finally, it appears to be an inaccurate assumption that thinking aloud does not alter the performance of a task for many children. The findings presented here suggest that verbalizations improve performance for normally achieving children, whereas for handicapped learners there may be facilitative, neutral or debilitative effects. For some children, overt verbalizations may help to encourage an active approach to problem solving and a complete analysis of the task. However, this issue should be further pursued in future research. Perhaps the improvement evidenced for many children is a function of the type of task employed or the verbal skills of the child. Researchers should therefore approach this manipulation with great care.

ACKNOWLEDGMENTS

Preparation of this manuscript was supported in part by a grant to the first author from the Little City Foundation: Center for Research and Innovation in Mental Retardation. Portions of this paper were presented at both the International Association for Research in Learning Disabilities and the Gatlinburg Conference on Mental Retardation/Developmental Disabilities. Requests for reprints should be directed to the first author at the Department of Psychology, Case Western Reserve University, Cleveland, Ohio 44106.

REFERENCES

Barr, P. M., & Samuels, M. T. (1988). Dynamic assessment of cognitive and affective factors contributing to learning difficulties in adults: A case study approach. *Professional Psychology: Research and Practice, 19*(1), 6–13.

Bereiter, C., & Bird, M. (1985). Use of thinking aloud in the identification and teaching of reading comprehension strategies. *Cognition and Instruction, 2,* 91–130.

Brown, A. L. (1978). Knowing when, where, and how to remember. In R. Glaser (Ed.), *Advances in instructional psychology* (Vol. 1, pp. 77–167). Hillsdale, NJ: Lawrence Erlbaum Associates.

Brown, A. L., Bransford, J. D., Ferrara, R. A., & Campione, J. C. (1983). Learning, remembering, and understanding. In P. H. Mussen (Ed.), *Handbook of child psychology: Cognitive development* (Vol. III, pp. 77–166). New York: Wiley.

Brown, A. L., & Palincsar, A. S. (1982). Inducing strategic learning from texts by means of informed, self-control training. *Topics in Learning and Learning Disabilities, 2,* 1–18.

Camp, B. W., & Bash, M. A. (1981). *Think aloud: Increasing social and cognitive skills—A problem solving program for children.* Champaign, IL: Research Press.

Camp, B. W., Blom, G. E., Hebert, F., & van Doorninck, W. J. (1977). Think aloud: A program for developing self-control in young aggressive boys. *Journal of Abnormal Child Psychology, 5,* 157–169.

Corno, L. (1986). The metacognitive control components of self-regulated learning. Annual meeting of the American Educational Research Association (1986, San Francisco, CA). In *Contemporary Educational Psychology, 11,* 333–346.

Cowan, R. E., & Clary, R. C. (1978). Identifying and teaching essential mathematical skills— items. *Mathematics Teacher, 71,* 130–134.

Dansereau, D. F. (1985). Learning strategy research. In S. F. Chipman, J. W. Segal, & R. Glaser (Eds.), *Thinking and learning skills (Vol. 1): Relating instruction to research* (pp. 209–240), Hillsdale, NJ: Lawrence Erlbaum Associates.

Das, J. P. (1984). Intelligence and information integration. In J. R. Kirby (Ed.), *Cognitive strategies and educational performance* (pp. 13–31). New York: Academic Press.

Davey, B. (1983). Think aloud: Modeling the cognitive processes of reading comprehension. *Journal of Reading, 27,* 44–47.

Duffy, G. G., Roehler, L. R., & Herrmann, B. A. (1988). Modeling mental processes helps poor readers become strategic readers. *The Reading Teacher, 41,* 762–767.

Duncker, K. (1945). On problem solving. *Psychological Monographs, 58*(6), Whole No. 270.

Ericsson, K. A., & Simon, H. A. (1980). Verbal reports as data. *Psychological Review, 87,* 215–251.

Ericsson, K. A., & Simon, H. A. (1985). Protocol analysis. In T. A. Van Dijk (Ed.), *Handbook of discourse analysis* (Vol. 2). London: Academic Press.

Flavell, J. H. (1977). *Cognitive development*. Englewood Cliffs, NJ: Prentice-Hall.

Flavell, J. H. (1979). Metacognition and cognitive monitoring. *American Psychologist, 34*, 906–911.

Feuerstein, R. (1980). *Instrumental enrichment: An intervention program for cognitive modifiability*. Baltimore, MD: University Park Press.

Hall, L. K., & Day, J. D. (1982, March). *A comparison of the zone of proximal development in learning disabled, educable mentally retarded, and normal children*. Paper presented at the Annual Meeting of the American Education Research Association, New York.

Hallahan, D. P., & Bryan, T. H. (1981). Learning disabilities. In J. M. Kaufman & D. P. Hallahan (Eds.), *Handbook of Special Education* (pp. 141–164). Englewood Cliffs, NJ: Prentice-Hall.

Havertape, J. F., & Kass, C. E. (1978). Examination of problem solving in learning disabled adolescents through verbalized self-instructions. *Learning Disability Quarterly, 1*, 94–100.

Kavale, K. A. (1980). The reasoning abilities of normal and learning disabled readers on measures of reading comprehension. *Learning Disability Quarterly, 3*(4), 34–45.

Kendall, P. C., & Braswell, L. (1985). *Cognitive-behavioral therapy for impulsive children*. New York: Guilford Press.

Krupski, A. (1986). Attention problems in youngsters with learning handicaps. In J. K. Torgesen & B. Y. L. Wong (Eds.), *Psychological and educational perspectives on learning disabilities* (pp. 161–192). New York: Academic Press.

Lambiotte, J. G., Dansereau, D. F., O'Donnell, A. M., Young, M. D., Skaggs, L. P., Hall, R. H., & Rocklin, T. R. (1987). Manipulating cooperative scripts for teaching and learning. *Journal of Educational Psychology, 79*, 424–430.

Lidz, C. S. (1987). *Dynamic assessment: An interactional approach to evaluating learning potential*. New York: Guilford Press.

Lloyd, J. W., Crowley, E. P., Kohler, F. W., & Strain, P. S. (1988). Redefining the applied research agenda: Cooperative learning prereferral, teacher consultation, and peer mediated interventions. *Journal of Learning Disabilities, 21*(1), 43–52.

Lochhead, J. (1985). Teaching analytic reasoning skills through pair problem solving. In J. W. Segal, S. F. Chipman, & R. Glaser (Eds.) *Thinking and learning skills (Vol. 1): Relating instruction to research* (pp. 109–132). Hillsdale, NJ: Lawrence Erlbaum Associates.

McKinney, J. D. (1988). Research on conceptually and empirically derived subtypes of specific learning disabilities. In M. C. Wang, M. C. Reynolds, & H. J. Walberg (Eds.), *The handbook of special education: Research and practice*, (Vol. 2, pp. 253–281). Oxford, England: Pergamon Press.

McKinney, J. D., Short, E. J., & Feagans, L. (1985). Academic consequences of perceptual-linguistics subtypes of learning disabled children. *Learning Disabilities Research, 1*, 6–17.

Meichenbaum, D. (1977). *Cognitive behavior modification: An integrative approach*. New York: Plenum Press.

Meltzer, L. J., Solomon, M. A., & Fenton, T. (1987, August). *Problem solving strategies in children with and without learning disabilities*. Paper presented at the 95th Annual Convention of the American Psychological Association, New York.

Newell, A., & Simon, H. (1972). *Human problem solving*. Englewood Cliffs, NJ: Prentice-Hall.

Olshavsky, J. E. (1976/77). Reading as problem solving: An investigation of strategies. *Reading Research Quarterly, 12*, 654–674.

Palincsar, A. S., & Brown, A. L. (1984). Reciprocal teaching of comprehension-fostering and comprehension-monitoring activities. *Cognition and Instruction, 1*, 117–175.

Palincsar, A. S., & Ransom, K. (1988). From the mystery spot to the thoughtful spot: The instruction of metacognitive strategies. *The Reading Teacher, 41*(8), 784–789.

Polya, G. (1948). *How to solve it: A new aspect of mathematical method*. Princeton, NJ: Princeton University Press.

Pressley, M. (1986). The relevance of the good strategy user model to the teaching of mathematics. *Educational Psychologist, 21,* 139–161.

Pressley, M., Borkowski, J. G., & Schneider, W. (1987). Cognitive strategies: Good strategy users coordinate metacognition and knowledge. In R. Vasta & G. Whitehurst (Eds.), *Annals of Child Development* (Vol. 4, pp. 89–129). Greenwich, CT: JAI Press.

Reese, H. W. (1962). Verbal mediation as a function of age level. *Psychological Bulletin, 59*(6), 502–509.

Rourke, B. P. (1985). *Neuropsychology of learning disabilities: Essentials of subtype analysis.* New York: Guilford Press.

Ryan, E. B., Short, E. J., & Weed, K. A. (1986). The role of cognitive strategy training in improving the academic performance of learning disabled children. *Journal of Learning Disabilities, 19,* 521–529.

Short, E. J., Cuddy, C. L., & Schatschneider, C. W. (1988). *Individual differences in strategies during problem solving.* Paper presented at the 21st Annual Gatlinburg Conference on Mental Retardation and Developmental Disabilities, Gatlinburg, TN.

Short, E. J., Evans, S., Dellick, D. M., & Cuddy, C. L. (1988). *Thinking aloud during problem solving: Facilitation effects.* Manuscript submitted for publication.

Short, E. J., Feagans, L., McKinney, J. D., & Applebaum, M. I. (1984). Longitudinal stability of LD subtypes based on age- and IQ-achievement discrepancies. *Learning Disability Quarterly, 9,* 214–225.

Short, E. J., Friebert, S. E., & Andrist, C. G. (1988). *Individual differences in attentional processes as a function of age and skill level.* Manuscript submitted for publication.

Short, E. J., & Weissberg-Benchell, J. (1989). The triple alliance for learning: Cognition, metacognition, & motivation. In C. McCormick, G. Miller, & M. Pressley (Eds.), *Cognitive Strategy Research: From basic research to educational applications* (pp. 33–63). New York: Springer-Verlag.

Speece, D. L., McKinney, J. D., & Appelbaum, M. I. (1985). Classification and validation of behavioral subtypes of learning disabled children. *Journal of Educational Psychology, 77,* 67–77.

Sternberg, R. J. (1977). *Intelligence, information processing, analogical reasoning: The componential analysis of human abilities.* Hillsdale, NJ: Lawrence Erlbaum Associates.

Stone, A., & Michals, D. (1986). Problem solving skills in learning disabled children. In S. J. Ceci (Ed.). *Handbook of cognitive, social, and neuropsychological aspects of LD* (Vol. 1, pp. 291–316). Hillsdale, NJ: Lawrence Erlbaum Associates.

Stone, C. A., & Wertsch, J. V. (1984). A social interactional analysis of learning disabilities. *Journal of Learning Disabilities, 17,* 194–199.

Swanson, H. L. (1988). Learning disabled children's problem solving: Identifying mental processes underlying intelligent performance. *Intelligence, 12*(3), 261–278.

Torgesen, J. K. (1977). The role of nonspecific factors in the task performance of learning disabled children: A theoretical assessment. *Journal of Learning Disabilities, 10,* 27–34.

Torgesen, J. K. (1982). The learning disabled child as an inactive learner: Educational implications. *Topics in Learning and Learning Disabilities, 2*(1), 45–51.

Uttero, D. A. (1988). Activating comprehension through cooperative learning. *The Reading Teacher, 41*(4), 390–395.

Vygotsky, L. S. (1978). *Mind in society: The development of higher psychological processes,* (M. Cole, V. John-Steiner, S. Scribner, & E. Souberman, Eds. and trans.). Cambridge, MA: Harvard University Press.

Whimbey, A., & Lochhead, J. (1986). *Problem solving and comprehension.* Hillsdale, NJ: Lawrence Erlbaum Associates.

Wong, B. Y. L. (1985). Metacognition and learning disabilities. In D. L. Forrest-Pressley, G. E. MacKinnon, & T. G. Waller (Eds.), *Metacognition, cognition, and human performance* (Vol. 2, pp. 137–180). New York: Academic Press.

7 IQ and Learning Disabilities: R.I.P.

Linda S. Siegel
The Ontario Institute for Studies in Education

Larry, age 8, received a score of 78 on an IQ test. He was placed in a class for mentally retarded children. He remained in classes for the mentally retarded until age 14. Today, at age 34 he is enrolled in a graduate program in a major Canadian university after completing a BA in psychology with an A average. Larry had great difficulty learning to read, spell, write, and do arithmetic calculations. When tested at age 34 his IQ score was in the high average range; however, he still had significant problems with reading and spelling. His score on the reading (word recognition) subtest on the Wide Range Achievement Test (WRAT) was at the 18th percentile and his score on the spelling subtest of the WRAT was at the 4th percentile. His score on the Woodcock Word Attack subtest, a measure of phonic skills, was at the 6th percentile. He had difficulties on short-term memory tasks and had occasional difficulty with verb tenses and word finding in spontaneous speech. He had good general knowledge and vocabulary and an average score on a reading comprehension test. Larry at age 34 displays a profile of a reading disabled individual; yet at age 8 he was called mentally retarded.

The case of Larry is a very dramatic example of the consequences of using an IQ test score as part of the definition of a reading disability. At age 8 Larry was *reading disabled* but, instead, was called *mentally retarded*. Larry was fortunate enough to have a very determined personality and very supportive parents who "believed in him."

This case is a real one. Fortunately, it has a happy ending, but for many children with genuine learning problems the ending is not college or graduate school but jail, alcohol abuse, and/or suicide. Larry's supportive environment did not prevent or cure his reading disability; his reading problem remained

throughout his schooling and into adulthood. However, his environment probably prevented Larry from developing the serious social problems that are often a
consequence of an undetected and untreated learning disability. Is Larry a rare
exception? No, today a child with poor reading skills and an IQ of 78 would be
labeled mentally retarded and not reading disabled. Unfortunately, children with
low IQ scores who show signs of severe reading problems are still called mentally retarded, even today. A great deal of weight is still given to the IQ score in
the definition of a reading disability.

The purpose of this chapter is to address the role of IQ test scores and other
variables in the definition of learning disabilities. These definitional issues have
plagued the field of learning disabilities. There are no reliable estimates of
prevalence rates of learning disabilities; clearcut definitions do not exist, and
generalizations about the characteristics of learning disabled individuals are hard
to produce. There is a great deal of controversy over who is learning disabled,
whether there are subtypes of learning disabilities and, if there are, what the
nature of these subtypes is.

The reason for this chaos is the lack of consistency in determining who is
learning disabled. There are several fundamental problems with existing definitions of learning disabilities: (1) the assumption that there must be a discrepancy
between intelligence and achievement for an individual to be defined as learning
disabled; (2) the inconsistent and illogical definitions of achievement; (3) the
illusion of specificity, that is, a learning disability must exist in only one specific
area.

An additional objective of this chapter is to consider several aspects of the
definition of learning disabilities and to examine the validity of the assumptions
underlying the typical definitions of learning disabilities.

Learning disabled individuals are defined as being of average or above average intelligence but having significant problems in reading, spelling, writing,
language, and/or arithmetic. *Normal intelligence is a critical part of this definition.* Intelligence must be average, or above average, and individuals with below
average intelligence are not typically considered learning disabled. Often, the
definition of a learning disability involves a discrepancy between intelligence as
measured by an IQ test and achievement as measured by a particular reading or
arithmetic test. For most definitions of learning disability, a child must be reading or solving arithmetic problems *below* his or her IQ level to be called learning
disabled.

BASIC ASSUMPTIONS

There are four basic assumptions inherent in this IQ-achievement discrepancy.
These assumptions are as follows: (1) IQ tests measure intelligence; (2) Intelligence and achievement are independent and the presence of a learning disability

will not affect IQ test scores; (3) IQ scores predict reading; children with low IQ scores should be poor readers and children with high IQ scores should be good readers; (4) Reading disabled individuals of different IQ levels have different cognitive processes and information processing skills. Specifically, individuals who have poor reading scores and low IQ scores are different from individuals who have poor reading scores and higher IQ scores. This chapter examines these assumptions and determines whether they are valid.

IQ Tests and What They Measure

The first assumption of the discrepancy definition is that IQ tests measure intelligence. The term intelligence implies problem solving and/or logical reasoning skills. The definition of intelligence, as it is operationalized in the IQ test, includes virtually no skills that are identifiable in terms of this definition.

In order to examine how ''intelligence'' is measured by the intelligence test, let us consider the usual measure of intelligence in the field of learning disabilities, the Wechsler Intelligence Scale for Children-Revised (WISC-R, Wechsler, 1974). This scale is composed of two parts, a Verbal and a Performance scale. A combined IQ is calculated on the basis of scores in the two scales.

Verbal Scale.   An examination of these subtests will help us understand what is being measured on the IQ test. One of the subtests is called Vocabulary. The child is given a word and asked to define it. More credit is given if the child uses a general term than specific exemplars or attributes. For example, more points are awarded for defining donkey as an animal than saying, ''goes slow, put heavy stuff on it'' or ''it has got a tail and four legs and a mouth.'' Some of the words to be administered to the older children are relatively uncommon ones, such as *obliterate, imminent,* and *dilatory.* Another of the WISC-R subtests, Similarities, also relies on specific word knowledge and ability to find the right word to express an idea. Reading disabled children have poor language skills (e.g., Siegel & Ryan, 1984, 1988; Vellutino, 1978, 1979), so they may have more difficulty finding the precise words necessary to produce this type of definition. Vocabulary growth is, at least in part, a function of reading. Reading disabled children read less than non-reading disabled children (e.g., Biemiller, 1977–78). Therefore, reading disabled children are likely to know fewer words and, consequently, have lower IQ scores.

Another subtest that relies on expressive language skills is called Comprehension, which measures the childs' factual knowledge, and understanding of social situations and acceptable behavior, such as, ''Why do we put stamps on letters?'' Again, specific knowledge and vocabulary are important determinants of the score. In the Information subtest, the child is asked for specific facts such as

"Who invented the electric light bulb?" These specific facts are probably acquired as a result of schooling and reading.

The Arithmetic subtest requires the child to do mental arithmetic and measures short-term memory skills, calculation ability, and knowledge of number facts and arithmetic operations. The Digit Span subtest requires the child to repeat numbers and is a test of short-term memory.

It is obvious that specific knowledge, vocabulary, expressive language, and memory skills are required in varying degrees by each subtest.

Performance Scale.   One might assume that the Performance IQ, or the less verbal subtests, of the WISC-R, might be freer of these difficulties. However, there are similar problems. The Performance subtests of the WISC-R require visual-spatial, fine-motor, attention, and concentration skills. Studies such as those of Rourke and Finlayson (1978) and Siegel and Feldman (1983), have shown that there are certain kinds of learning disabled children, specifically, those with an arithmetic disability, who have impaired fine motor skills and visual-spatial abilities. Therefore, in the case of these children, the performance IQ would not be an accurate measure of their "intelligence."

All of these Performance subtests are timed and in three of them, Picture Arrangement, Block Design, and Object Assembly, the more quickly the child completes the task within the time limit, the higher the score the child receives. Children who solve the problems more quickly receive higher IQ scores. Valerie Barsky and I have shown that learning disabled children, particularly at the older ages, are able to solve as many problems as nonlearning disabled children within the allowed time limit; however, they do so more slowly but *still within the time limit* (Barsky & Siegel, 1988). Therefore, learning disabled children are less likely to receive the bonus points for quicker performance and, consequently, obtain lower IQ scores.

IQ as a construct.   The subtests of both the Verbal and Performance Scales measure a diverse set of cognitive functions. Lezak (1988) has argued that the IQ score is insensitive to the complexities of behavior, and that the lumping of the diverse functions measured by the subtests into global IQ scores leaves us with a meaningless number. IQ is a *construct;* it does not measure any real function or structure. As Lezak has said, "Yet today, most psychologists, psychiatrists, educators, judges, the United States Social Security Administration, among others, think, write, talk, and make decisions as if an IQ score represented something real and essentially immutable with a locus somewhere in the cranium" (p. 356). The fact that IQ is not a real entity but only a construct is typically and conveniently forgotten in discussions of learning disabilities.

Obviously, there is a problem in using tests such as these to measure intelligence. Upon detailed examination, IQ tests such as the WISC-R do not appear to measure "potential" or basic reasoning skills and IQ scores depend on expressive language skills, memory, fine-motor abilities, and specific factual knowledge. *It seems inappropriate to use IQ tests as measures of intelligence.*

Are Measures of Intelligence Independent of Measures of Reading?

An implicit part of the discrepancy definition of a learning disability is the assumption that intelligence can be measured independently of academic achievement. Performance on an IQ test is assumed to be independent of the learning disability and it is assumed that the presence of a learning disability will not affect an IQ test score. Intelligence and achievement are treated as separate and independent variables in equations that are used to calculate whether there is a reading disability. There must be a discrepancy between measured IQ and measured achievement and reading failure must be "unexpected" in the basis of IQ.

An example of this type of reasoning is indicated in the concepts of Rutter (1978), Rutter and Yule (1975), and Yule (1973) who argue that there are two subtypes of reading disabled children, the *specific reading retarded* who are poor readers in relationship to their age and IQ and the *reading backward* who are poor readers in relationship to their age but whose reading scores are not lower than would be predicted by their IQ.

But can intelligence and achievement really be measured independently? Let us examine this assumption more closely. As we have already seen, standard IQ tests measure, among other abilities, expressive language skills, short-term memory abilities, speed of processing information, speed of responding, and knowledge of specific facts. There are many studies that indicate that each of these functions is deficient in many learning disabled individuals (e.g., Siegel, 1985; Siegel & Feldman, 1983, Siegel & Linder, 1984; Siegel & Ryan, 1984, 1988; Vellutino, 1978, 1979). Therefore, an IQ test that relies on some combination of these functions can not possibly be a true measure of intelligence in learning disabled individuals and IQ cannot be measured independently of achievement.

There is even evidence that a learning disability may be causally related to a lower IQ score. Stanovich (1986) has described what he has called "Matthew effects" in relationship to the development of reading problems and reading skills. Reading disabled children read fewer books; therefore they may fail to acquire new vocabulary and their IQ test scores may decline. From a longitudinal study of Bishop and Butterworth (1980), there is suggestive evidence that the reading disabled child's verbal IQ score may decrease over time. They showed that a large discrepancy between performance and verbal IQ scores at 4½ years did not predict subsequent reading problems, while such a discrepancy was more common in 8½-year-old reading disabled children. Share and Silva (1987) found that the language skills, particularly vocabulary and syntax, declined from ages 3 to 11 in children who were reading disabled but not in normal readers. Arnold,

Barneby, McManus, Smeltzer, Conrad, Winer, and Desgranges (1977) found that learning disabled children not exposed to an intensive remedial program showed significant decreases in IQ scores over a period of 18 months, whereas a group of learning disabled children who received intensive remediation showed significant improvements in IQ scores. A lower IQ score is a consequence of the learning disability and IQ scores underestimate the real intelligence of the learning disabled individual. There is evidence that children who have difficulty learning to read have less experience with print, and lower self-esteem and motivation, which lead to further problems in the development of these skills. There may be a decrease in the IQ test scores of the reading disabled, perhaps, as a consequence of reading failure.

Can Reading Performance be Predicted from IQ Scores?

The third assumption is that there is a strong correlation between reading and IQ, that is, a low IQ means the child should be a poor reader, and a higher IQ means the child should be a better reader. In order to be considered reading disabled, a child must be reading significantly *below his or her IQ level*. This concept leads to some paradoxical situations. If a child has a high IQ and an average or slightly above average reading level, he or she would be called reading disabled by a discrepancy definition. However, these children are not really reading disabled in that they do not have difficulty with reading and can read words and understand letter sound correspondences very well. Clearly, these children with high IQ scores and average reading scores may be quite good readers and do not require remediation in the same sense as severely reading disabled children who have very low scores on reading tests. For the purposes of studying the reading disabled, it seems illogical to consider both average readers with high IQ scores and poor readers with average scores to be reading disabled.

According to the discrepancy definition, it should *not* be possible for a child with a low IQ to be a good reader; however, a significant number of such cases exist. The existence of this type of children, that is children with low IQ scores and good reading skills, would seem to be a paradox. Their existence means children with low IQ scores can learn to read. *Therefore, children with low IQ scores who fail to read, are genuinely reading disabled, and do not fail to read because of low IQ scores.*

IQ and Cognitive Processes in the Learning Disabled

The fourth assumption is that the cognitive processes of learning disabled individuals with low IQ scores are different from those of learning disabled individuals with high IQ scores. By measuring IQ in the learning disabled child, we are assuming that IQ should be related to cognitive functioning.

There are two competing hypotheses in regard to the possible relationship between IQ and cognitive processes in the reading disabled. One hypothesis is that IQ is a significant factor in reading disability and that within the reading disabled population performance on a variety of tasks should be related to IQ. The other hypothesis is that reading disability is a unitary disorder and that reading disabled children at any IQ level should perform in a similar manner to each other but significantly different from non-reading disabled children. However, there is some suggestive evidence that certain cognitive processes may not be significantly different in learning disabled children with lower IQ scores and those with higher IQ scores. Hall, Wilson, Hymphries, Tinzmann, and Bowyer (1983) found that this was the case for short-term memory tasks and Taylor, Satz, and Friel (1979) found that this was the case for a variety of processes including reversal of letters or letter sequences within a word, neurological status, and mathematical ability. These studies provide some evidence but a critical test of these hypotheses requires the examination of reading and spelling skills as a function of IQ scores in the reading disabled.

IQ AND READING DISABILITY: SOME EVIDENCE

I have conducted a study to examine the performance of reading and non-reading disabled children at a wide range of IQ levels to determine whether these reading disabled children of different IQ levels actually differed on performance on a variety of reading, spelling, language, memory, and arithmetic tests (Siegel, 1988). The basic design involved the comparison of two factors, reading disability and IQ level, to determine which was the better predictor of performance on a variety of tests. The children were divided into 4 groups on the basis of IQ scores, IQ scores less than 80, 80–90, 91–109, and greater than 109. The performance of reading disabled and non-reading disabled children at these IQ levels was compared.

To be considered reading disabled, a child is required to have a score less than or equal to the 25th percentile on the Reading Test of the Wide Range Achievement Test (WRAT–Jastak & Jastak, 1978). Normally achieving children were defined as those having WRAT Reading scores greater than or equal to the 30th percentile. The WRAT Reading Test, which involves reading single isolated words (word recognition), as opposed to a reading comprehension test, was chosen for a variety of reasons. A definition of reading disability based on a word recognition deficit was chosen because of the belief that impaired decoding skill constitutes the bases of a reading problem. These reasons are outlined in detail in Siegel (1984a), Siegel (1986), Siegel and Heaven, (1986), and Siegel and Ryan (1989). Reading comprehension tests confound the measurement of a number of skills. Reading comprehension tests are timed and speed of reading is important in test performance. Andrew Biemiller and I have shown that giving children as much time as they want to complete a reading test (usually no more than 15 extra minutes) results in a significantly higher score than with the standard time limits of the test (Biemiller & Siegel, 1988). Many of the questions on reading comprehension tests involve prior knowledge; therefore, the answer is not necessarily derived from reading the passage in question. Most of the questions do not really require an inference but instead involve extracting information that is directly in the passage, that is, they are literal, rather than inferential, questions. Therefore, what is being measured by the test is speed of visual search rather than any conceptual process. Vocabulary and the knowledge of specific words can play an important part in answering the questions on a reading comprehension test. For all these reasons, there are a variety of confounding factors which means that scores derived from reading comprehension tests are not really measures of reading comprehension.

However, word recognition tests are not without their problems. Words can vary in a variety of dimensions, such as regularity, part of speech, frequency, etc., but word recognition is a less problematic measure than reading comprehension. As Siegel and Heaven (1986) have noted, nonword (pseudoword) reading would be an even purer and more accurate measure of reading ability but one that has not been used to study reading disabilities.

It is interesting to note that it was possible to find some normal readers who had IQ scores lower than 80. According to the logic of the assumptions described earlier, this type of individual should not exist. For example, in the 7- to 8-year-old age group, the mean WRAT reading percentile of the individuals with IQ scores less than 80 who are not reading disabled was 65.8 and for the 9- to 10-year-old group the mean was 53.0; so it is not a matter of their scores being close to the cut off. They were clearly *not* reading impaired in spite of low IQ scores. In addition, Share, McGee, and Silva (in press) have found 13-year-olds with low IQ scores who were reading at age appropriate levels.

Comparison of Reading Tasks

One of the most important questions is whether the reading disabled children at a variety of IQ levels differ in their actual reading skills. If IQ scores are important, we should predict that they would differ. If IQ scores are not, one would expect similar patterns of reading at a variety of IQ levels. Within the reading disabled group, there were no differences in the WRAT reading percentile scores as a function of IQ level. The non-reading disabled children with IQ scores greater than 109 did have higher word recognition scores. The latter is not surprising, as at the higher levels, the WRAT requires the reading of low frequency words such as *desuetude* and *egregious* and, thus, becomes more a test of vocabulary than reading skills. Most of the non-reading disabled children had good evidence of phonic skills, in terms of sounding out these unfamiliar words. Nevertheless, because they did not have experience with the specific word, they sometimes made an error, but this error was very close in pronunciation to the correct word. However, there was certainly no indication of significant differences among reading disabled children as a function of IQ; their word recognition skills were universally poor.

The reading of pseudowords, pronounceable combinations of letters which are not English words such as *bim, toaf,* and *shum,* is measured on the Woodcock Word Attack subtest of the Woodcock Reading Mastery test (Woodcock, 1973) and Reading of Symbols subtest of the GFW Sound Symbol Tests (Goldman, Fristoe, & Woodcock, 1974). As with word recognition, there were no differences in pseudoword reading skills among the reading disabled children at different IQ levels. Within the reading disabled group, there were no differences as a function of IQ level.

A variety of other measures of reading skills was used. The children were required to read a list of 36 regular and 36 exception words (Baron, 1979). The regular words included words such as *cut* and *gave,* and the exception words were words such as *put* and *have.* The exception words could not be read by applying the letter sound correspondence rules of English. There were no indication of differences among IQ levels within the reading disabled population on the tasks. The reading disabled children, at all IQ levels, had significantly lower scores than the non-reading disabled children.

The children were administered two reading tasks, adapted from Olson, Kliegl, Davidson, and Folz (1984), which were designed to test the knowledge of orthographic and phonological aspects of English. For the orthographic tasks the child was presented with a real word and a pseudoword, e.g., *rain* and *rane* and was asked to specify which of the two was a real word. Successful performance on this task depended on visual recognition of the correct spelling of a word. There were no differences as a function of IQ level within the reading disabled or the non-reading disabled children. However, there were very significant differences between the reading and the non-reading disabled children on this task. Reading disabled children at all IQ levels had trouble with orthography. For the phonological task, the child was asked to specify which of two visually presented pseudowords, e.g., *kake* and *dake,* sounded like a real word if pronounced. Again, the reading disabled children demonstrated very poor performance on this task and even at the oldest age levels performed at a level not significantly different from chance. However, there were no differences of function of IQ.

Spelling

The pattern was very similar on several spelling tasks, the WRAT spelling, which is a spelling to dictation task, the spelling of nonwords from the GFW Sound Symbol tests and the Recognition of a Visual Form of a Sound from the Gates and McKillop Tests (1962). On all of these tasks reading disabled children had similar performance at all the IQ levels and, in all cases, their performance was significantly below that of the non-reading disabled children.

Language, Short-Term Memory, Reading Comprehension, and Arithmetic

As van der Wissel and Zegers (1985) have noted, it is reasonable to expect differences on variables clearly related to IQ within the reading disabled population. In some cases, there were significant differences among the IQ levels for scores on memory, language, reading comprehension, and arithmetic tasks, although often these differences were small in magnitude and the differences between the reading disabled and the non-reading disabled were much greater.

Poor readers of any IQ level had similar scores on many cognitive tasks and, in all cases, demonstrated significantly poorer performance than the normally achieving children. This finding suggests that there is really no need to differentiate poor readers on the basis of IQ, if one is studying basic processes that are involved in reading.

There are other demonstrations of the irrelevance of IQ scores in the definition of a reading disability. Share, Jorm, McGee, Silva, Maclean, Matthews, and Williams (1987) compared the reading and spelling skills of normal IQ poor readers and low IQ poor readers and found that there were no significant differences between these two groups on 27 out of the 28 measures. In another study, Share, Jorm, Matthews, and Maclean (1988) found that, specifically, both disabled readers and children who were reading backward (with lower IQ scores) were less accurate and slower than normal readers in reading function words, but did not differ from each other. Therefore, IQ does not seem to be related to reading and spelling skills within the group of reading disabled children.

THE TEST NAME FALLACY
AND OTHER MEASUREMENT PROBLEMS

Definitions of intelligence are problematic. It is not clear that the IQ test score needs to play a role in the definition of a reading disability. But definitions of achievement are also often illogical. We need to be very cautious about assuming a test measures the skill indicated in the name of the test. Reading tests are a dramatic example of this problem. The problems with reading tests are described in detail earlier in this chapter and in Siegel and Heaven (1986). Basically the reading "comprehension" tests measure a variety of skills but understanding of what has been read is not prominent among them. Furthermore, if the definition of reading disability is confined to poor word recognition or word attack skills, a very clear picture of what a reading disability is emerges in terms of reading, language, spelling, and memory functions (Siegel & Ryan, 1987). If one uses a reading comprehension deficit definition, the group is much more heterogeneous on these functions. Siegel and Ryan (1987) have shown that poor readers defined on the basis of inadequate phonics skills (based on nonword reading tests) and/or word recognition skills (based on single word reading tests) had significantly below average language and short term memory skills. Children who had poor reading comprehension test scores but adequate word recognition skills did not have difficulties with language. Therefore, the type of reading test used to define the disability will determine the conclusions about the nature of the disability.

SPECIFICITY ISSUES

There is often the assumption that IQ scores should not be influenced by a reading disability. As Stanovich (1988) and others have noted, the concept of reading disability implies the concept of specificity, that is, that reading is the only function that is impaired while virtually everything else remains intact. There are a number of very serious problems with this assertion and the available empirical evidence contradicts it. For example, the idea that in order to be considered reading disabled, a child can not have problems in other subjects, but most particularly in arithmetic, is a common one. If one uses a computational arithmetic test such as the Arithmetic subtest of the WRAT, one will find that most individuals with reading problems also have difficulties with computational arithmetic. Computational arithmetic involves short-term memory, symbolic processing, and attention and concentration, all of which may be problematic for a reading disabled child. There is empirical evidence (e.g., Rourke & Finlayson, 1978; Siegel & Linder, 1984), that it is relatively difficult to find reading disabled children who do not also have problems with arithmetic.

Hall and Humphries (1982) assert that reading disabled children must be free of arithmetic problems; however, in their reading disabled samples they use the PIAT arithmetic test, a multiple choice test, to measure arithmetic problems. I have found that children who have low scores on the WRAT arithmetic do not necessarily have lower scores on the PIAT arithmetic. So children who would be considered to have arithmetic problems on the WRAT would not necessarily be considered to have arithmetic problems on the PIAT. At this point in time, it is impossible to tell which is the "right" arithmetic test, but the point is that different arithmetic tests produce different results and depending on the definition, there will be different conclusions about the specificity of the reading disability. In any case, it is rare to find a reading disabled individual whose only major cognitive deficit is reading.

OTHER DEFINITIONAL ISSUES

As Stanovich (1988) has noted, reading and reading disability are really part of a continuum. The cut-off between what we call reading disabled and what we call non-reading disabled is entirely arbitrary. For the purposes of learning more about this problem, it makes logical sense to deal with extreme cases, that is, to consider the lower end of the distribution as reading disabled and the higher end as not reading disabled. But it must be kept in mind that the division is an arbitrary one. One solution to this problem is to examine the effects as a function of different cut-off scores. That is, it would be helpful to examine what the results look like when we use different definitions. If we examine the data from this point of view and give recognition to the arbitrary nature of the definitions and the fact that we are really not dealing with discrete entities, then I believe the field will begin to make progress.

Often, investigators use learning disabled and non-learning disabled groups matched on IQ. But should IQ matching be used in reading, in the studies of reading disability? Some of the difficulties with this approach are discussed in Stanovich (1986). However, the problem is that matching is virtually impossible to achieve because as noted earlier in the chapter, IQ test performance is influenced by the cognitive deficits characteristic of the learning disabled child.

In defining a learning disability, standard scores or percentiles should be used rather than performance below grade level (e.g., Reynolds, 1981; Siegel, 1984b). Performance below age appropriate grade level should not be used because, as Reynolds (1981) has noted, "This method substantially overstates disabilities at upper grade levels while underestimating the severity of difficulties in the early grades" (p. 350).

If investigators would use clearer definitions perhaps findings would be more consistent and generalizable. The definitional problems in the field would be helped by abandoning the IQ score in the analysis of the learning disabled child. A similar proposal has been made by van der Wissel and Zegers (1985). The time and money spent administering and analyzing the IQ test and training people to use it, could be far better spent on administering specific tests of achievement that might give a better idea of the child's actual functioning. It is important to know what words the child is having difficulty reading, what letter sound correspondences present problems for the child, what types of spelling errors are made, what number facts are not known, what arithmetic operations are not understood, what types of errors are made, etc. Remediation based on a detailed knowledge of the child's academic skills makes more sense than some extrapolation of what reading (or arithmetic or spelling) should be, based on some imprecise IQ measure and an illogical discrepancy definition.

It has been argued that IQ tests do provide information about the child's cognitive skills and that learning disabled children have distinctive patterns of performance on the IQ test. However, Smith, Coleman, Dokecki, and Davis (1977) report that children with below normal intelligence scores exhibited patterns of performance on the WISC-R that were similar to those of children who were learning disabled by the traditional definition. It appears that patterns of performance on the WISC-R can not be used reliably to differentiate learning and non-learning disabled children.

The use of discrepancy definition penalizes children from different cultural or minority backgrounds because they may have low IQ scores and low reading scores, but are not called reading disabled because of their low IQ. Because of the specific knowledge and experience that is required for at least some of the questions, children from minority backgrounds, lower social class families, and/or different ethnic groups may be disadvantaged and may have lower IQ scores. Consequently, they may not be called reading disabled but instead labeled as slow learners and not be considered intelligent enough to benefit from remediation. The consequence is that they do not get the help that they need. The case of Larry, reported earlier, is a dramatic example how an IQ test score can be misused. I have shown that there are children with IQ scores below 90, even IQ scores below 80, who can learn to read, develop reasonable word recognition, reading comprehension, and word attack skills. A lower score on an IQ test does not necessarily mean that a child cannot learn to read.

Of course, we do not yet know much about the relationships between IQ tests scores and the ability to benefit from remediation. It is entirely possible that children with different IQ scores may benefit differentially from remediation. However, the studies that are available indicate that IQ is not significantly related to the ability to benefit from remediation (Arnold, Smeltzer, & Barneby, 1981). Lytton (1967) reports that learning disabled children with low IQ scores made significant gains from remediation. On the other hand, Yule (1973) reported that reading backward children made more gains in reading than the specifically reading disabled but it is important to note that the gains by both groups were very small and both groups still had significant reading problems at older ages. In a study of learning disabled Dutch children, van der Wissel and Zegers (1985) report that educational progress was not related to whether a child was a backward reader or specifically reading disabled. There does not seem to be strong evidence to use the IQ score to predict the effects of remediation. If the IQ test is used, one would have to demonstrate that achievement test scores could not do as well in predicting ability to benefit from remediation and that it made enough difference to warrant the expense of IQ testing.

We do not know about the differential error of patterns in reading and spelling tasks of children of different IQ levels. Should it be the case, then this information may be useful in remediation, and, therefore, there may be some reason to do IQ tests, although direct assessments of the error patterns may prove to be more profitable.

TOWARD A RESOLUTION
OF THE DEFINITIONAL ISSUES

I have written a great deal about how not to define a learning disability. I do believe there are some positive steps that we can take to resolve the definitional issues. Stanovich (1988) has provided us with an analyses of reading disability that may be helpful in the resolution of definitional problems.

Stanovich (1988) has advanced the hypothesis that characterizations of reading disabled as being deficient in rule learning, linguistic awareness, etc., are not really capturing the presence of a reading disability. He writes,

> The hypothesis that I wish to advance is that all characterizations of the reading disabled child like those just outlined are on the wrong track; that global processes like linguistic awareness, comprehension, strategic functioning, rule learning, active/inactive learning in generalization meta-cognitive functioning are the wrong places to look for the key to reading disability. . . . In short, phonological awareness is relatively dissociated from other higher-level cognitive skills. Thus, it is a good candidate for the mechanism that leads to a specific reading disability. (p. 8)

Stanovich suggests that the key to reading disability is a problem with phonological processing. Phonological processing is not necessarily regulated by any kind of central processing system, and that even efficient and meta-cognitive functioning can not remedy deficits in this area. It is independent of intelligence. If we accept this characterization of reading disability as a result of a deficit in phonological processing and that this process is independent of intelligence (however defined), then logically we should not need IQ in the definition of reading disability. Instead, we should study phonological processing in the reading disabled and base the definition of reading disability on a measure (or measures) of phonological processing.

I agree with Stanovich and think that the key to a reading problem lies in deficient phonological processing. However, there is a great paradox in the literature on reading disability. I think Stanovich's argument needs to be carried one step further when we examine the definition of reading disability. As I have noted in Siegel and Heaven (1986), the logical conclusion is that we should use poor performance on a pseudoword reading test to define reading disability. I believe a pseudoword reading test constitutes the most accurate test of a reading disability. Word recognition tests are the next best alternative, although words vary in frequency, regularity, and grammatical function, among other dimensions, and all of these may influence the individuals ability to read the words in ways that we do not yet fully understand. Reading comprehension tests suffer from a variety of problems that have been discussed previously.

Phonological processing is orthogonal to intelligence as measured by the IQ test. Evidence of this dissociation is seen in good readers with low IQ scores.

The most extreme case of good readers with low IQ scores are the hyperlexics who can decode and recognize words but have very low IQ scores, and significantly poor language, fine motor and memory skills (e.g., Siegel, 1984b). They are a type of "idiot savant" with very good reading skills but very poor functioning in other areas. The hyperlexic children are "word callers," that is, they read words without having knowing the meaning of them. They can read pseudowords very well. For example, the child described in my study, with an IQ score of 58, scored at the 86th percentile on a word recognition test, and at the 61 percentile on a pseudoword reading test. She could read many of the words on the Peabody Picture Vocabulary Test but could not point to the picture that was the correct definition of the word. She had very little understanding of spoken language. Yet her word recognition and decoding skills were clearly intact and even above average. The performance of this hyperlexic is a striking example of the dissociation between IQ and phonological skills.

SOLUTIONS

The resolution of the definitional issues in the field of learning disabilities is not hopeless. I propose the following solution. For the school-age child, we can define two types of academic learning disabilities, a reading disability and an arithmetic disability, and a third type of disability which is an Attentional Deficit Disorder (ADD). Attentional Deficit Disorder is also important but definition of ADD is quite controversial as is the extent to which it should be considered a learning disability. The measurement of the first two are more straightforward. I would suggest that we disregard the IQ and consider children who have severe problems with reading and/or arithmetic as learning disabled. Children who have problems decoding (reading pseudowords) and/or with word recognition should be called reading disabled. Children with difficulties in computational arithmetic should be called arithmetic disabled. Children, of course, have problems in spelling, writing, "reading comprehension" and/or language. In my experience, there are very few children whose only problems are spelling, writing, or language and who do not also have significant difficulties in reading and/or arithmetic. Of course none of these academic problems should be ignored. But for the sake of conceptual and empirical simplicity and scientific parsimony, reading and arithmetic problems should be the focus of our concentrated efforts.

There may be some objection to ignoring reading comprehension. In regard to reading comprehension, there are two issues. I have already described some very significant measurement issues in relation to this concept. Until better measures are developed in which the questions involve true inferences and not just finding literal material in the text, in which questions cannot be answered unless the passage is read, in which performance is not dependent on vocabulary or knowledge of the subject matter, and where a significant portion of the variance is not due to the fact that there is a time limit on the test, the measurement of reading comprehension as it now exists should be abandoned. Even when the perfect or near perfect test of reading comprehension is developed, there should be evidence presented that this processing deficit is specific to *reading* and would not occur with listening comprehension.

I believe we should abandon the use of the IQ test score in the definition of learning disability. If the field is not yet ready to abandon the IQ, I would propose another solution. A cut-off IQ score of 80 could be used. If a child achieves a score of 80 on an IQ test, it is clearly possible for that child to learn to read. Children with lower IQ scores should also receive remedial help and should not be ignored or assumed to be hopeless. However, for investigations, the admittedly arbitrary IQ of cut-off 80 should be considered, if investigators do not want to ignore IQ. In any case, the IQ-achievement deviation definition should be abandoned because of its illogical nature. Of course, we could also search for better measures of "intelligence." However, the multifaceted nature of mental processes and the possible influence of educational and cultural factors on test performance make it unlikely that a suitable intelligence test could be developed.

There are a variety of theoretical, empirical, and social reasons why the IQ test has outlived its usefulness in the field of learning disabilities. There are problems in assuming that the IQ test measures what is typically understood by intelligence and there is no reason to believe that a discrepancy between intelligence and achievement is necessary. Some children with lower IQ scores read at age appropriate levels, so a low IQ score is not a *cause* of poor reading. There are no differences among children of different IQ levels in basic cognitive processes. For all these reasons, there is no reason to use the IQ test to define a learning disability.

ACKNOWLEDGMENTS

The preparation of this chapter was made possible by a grant from the Natural Sciences and Engineering Research Council of Canada. Portions of this chapter have appeared in an article in the *Journal of Learning Disabilities*, 1989, 22, 469–478.

REFERENCES

Arnold, L. E., Barneby, N., McManus, J., Smeltzer, D. J., Conrad, A., Winer, G., & Desgranges, L. (1977). Prevention by specific perceptual remediation for vulnerable first-graders. *Archives of General Psychiatry, 34*, 1279–1294.

Arnold, L. E., Smeltzer, D. J., & Barneby, N. S. (1981). Specific perceptual remediation: Effects related to sex, IQ, and parents' occupational status; behavioral change pattern by scale factors; and mechanism of benefit hypothesis tested. *Psychological Reports, 49*, 198.

Baron, J. (1979). Orthographic and word-specific mechanisms in children's reading of words. *Child Development, 50,* 60–72.

Barsky, V. E., & Siegel, L. S. (1988). *The speed factor and WISC-R Performance IQ: Effects on subtypes of learning disabled children.* Unpublished manuscript.

Biemiller, A. (1977–78). Relationships between oral reading rates for letters, words, and simple text in the development of reading achievement. *Reading Research Quarterly, 13,* 223–253.

Biemiller A., & Siegel, L. S. (1988). *Developmental changes in relationships between reading comprehension, reading speed, reading accuracy, and working memory.* Unpublished manuscript.

Bishop, D. V. M., & Butterworth, G. E. (1980). Verbal-performance discrepancies: Relationship to birth risk and specific reading retardation. *Cortex, 16,* 375–389.

Gates, A. I., & McKillop, A. S. (1962). *Gates-McKillop Reading Diagnostic Tests.* New York: Teachers College Press.

Goldman, R., Fristoe, M., & Woodcock, R. W. (1974). *GFW Sound-Symbol Tests.* Circle Pines, MN: American Guidance Service.

Hall, J. W., & Humphries, M. S. (1982). Research on specific learning disabilities: Deficits and Remediation. *Topics in Learning and Learning Disabilities, 2,* 68–78.

Hall, J. W., Wilson, K. P., Humphries, M. S., Tinzmann, M. B., & Bowyer, P. M. (1983). Phonemic similarity effects in good vs. poor readers. *Memory and Cognition, II,* 520–527.

Jastak, J. R., & Jastak, S. R. (1978). *Wide Range Achievement Test.* Wilmington, DE: Jastak Associates.

Lezak, M. D. (1988). IQ: R.I.P. *Journal of Clinical and Experimental Neuropsychology, 10,* 351–361.

Lytton, H. (1967). Follow-up of an experiment in selection for remedial education. *British Journal of Educational Psychology, 37,* 1–9.

Olson, R., Kliegl, R., Davidson, B. J., & Folz, G. (1984). Individual and developmental differences in reading disability. In T. G. Waller (Ed.), *Reading research: Advances in theory and practice* (Vol. 4, pp. 1–64). New York: Academic Press.

Reynolds, C. R. (1981). The fallacy of "two years below grade level for age" as a diagnostic criterion for reading disorders. *Journal of School Psychology, 19,* 350–358.

Rourke, B. P., & Finlayson, M. A. J. (1978). Neuropsychological significance of variations in patterns of academic performance: Verbal and visual-spatial abilities. *Journal of Abnormal Child Psychology, 6,* 121–133.

Rutter, M. (1978). Prevalence and types of dyslexia. In A. L. Benton & D. Pearl (Eds.), *Dyslexia: An appraisal of current knowledge* (pp. 3–28). New York: Oxford University Press.

Rutter, M., & Yule, W. (1975). The concepts of specific reading retardation. *Journal of Child Psychology and Psychiatry, 16,* 181–197.

Share, D. L., Jorm, A., McGee, R., Silva, P. A., Maclean, R., Matthews, R., & Williams, S. (1987). *Dyslexia and other myths.* Unpublished manuscript. University of Otago Medical School. Dunedin, New Zealand.

Share, D. L., Jorm, A. F., Matthews, R., & Maclean, R. (1988). Lexical decision and naming times of young disabled readers with function and content words. *Australian Journal of Psychology, 40,* 11–18.

Share, D. L., McGee, R., & Silva, P. A. (in press). IQ and reading progress: A test of the capacity notion of IQ. *Journal of the American Academy of Child and Adolescent Psychiatry.*

Share, D. L., & Silva, P. A. (1987). Language deficits and specific reading retardation: Cause or effect? *British Journal of Disorders of Communication, 22,* 219–226.

Siegel, L. S. (1984a). On the adequacy of the Wide Range Achievement Test (WRAT): A reply to Snart, Dennis, and Brailsford. *Canadian Psychology, 25,* 73–74.

Siegel, L. S. (1984b). A longitudinal study of a hyperlexic child: Hyperlexia as a language disorder. *Neuropsychologia, 22,* 577–585.

Siegel, L. S. (1985). Psycholinguistic aspects of reading disabilities. In L. S. Siegel & F. J. Morrison (Eds.), *Cognitive development in atypical children* (pp. 45–66). New York: Springer-Verlag.

Siegel, L. S. (1986). Phonological deficits in children with a reading disability. *Canadian Journal of Special Education, 2,* 45–54.

Siegel, L. S. (1988). Evidence that IQ scores are irrelevant to definition and analysis of reading disability. *Canadian Journal of Psychology, 42,* 201–215.

Siegel, L. S., & Feldman, W. (1983). Non-dyslexic children with combined writing and arithmetic difficulties. *Clinical Pediatrics, 22,* 241–244.

Siegel, L. S., & Heaven, R. (1986). Defining and categorizing learning disabilities. In S. Ceci (Ed.), *Handbook of cognitive, social and neuropsychological aspects of learning disabilities* (Vol. 1, pp. 95–121). Hillsdale, NJ: Lawrence Erlbaum Associates.

Siegel, L. S., & Linder, B. A. (1984). Short-term memory processes in children with reading and arithmetic learning disabilities. *Developmental Psychology, 20,* 200–207.

Siegel, L. S., & Ryan, E. B. (1984). Reading disability as a language disorder. *Remedial and Special Education, 5,* 28–33.

Siegel, L. S., & Ryan, E. B. (1989). *Subtypes of developmental dyslexia: The influence of definitional variables. Reading and Writing: An Interdisciplinary Journal, 1.*

Siegel, L. S., & Ryan, E. B. (1988). Development of grammatical sensitivity, phonological and short-term memory skills in normally achieving and learning disabled children. *Developmental Psychology, 24,* 28–37.

Smith, M. D., Coleman, J. M., Dokecki, P. R., & Davis, E. E. (1977). Intellectual characteristics of school labelled learning disabled children. *Exceptional Children, 43,* 352–357.

Stanovich, K. E. (1986). Matthew effects in reading: Some consequences at individual differences in the acquisition of literacy. *Reading Research Quarterly, 21,* 360–407.

Stanovich, K. E. (1988). *The right and wrong places to look for the cognitive focus of reading disability.* Paper presented at the Orton Dyslexia Society, New York.

Taylor, H. G., Satz, P., & Friel, J. (1979). Developmental dyslexia in relation to other childhood reading disorders: Significance and clinical utility. *Reading Research Quarterly, 15,* 84–101.

van der Wissel, A., & Zegers, F. E. (1985). Reading retardation Revisted. *British Journal of Developmental Psychology, 3,* 3–9.

Vellutino, F. (1978). Toward an understanding of dyslexia: Psychological factors in specific reading disability. In A. L. Benton & D. Pearl (Eds.), *Dyslexia: An appraisal of current knowledge* (pp. 61–112). New York: Oxford University Press.

Vellutino, F. R. (1979). *Dyslexia: Theory and research.* Cambridge, MA: MIT Press.

Wechsler, D. (1974). *Manual for the Wechsler Intelligence Scale for Children—Revised.* New York: Psychological Corporation.

Woodcock, R. W. (1973). *Woodcock Reading Mastery Tests.* Circle Pines, MN: American Guidance Service.

Yule, W. (1973). Differential prognosis of reading backwardness and specific reading retardation. *British Journal of Educational Psychology, 43,* 244–248.

II SOCIAL COGNITION: MOTIVATIONAL AND SOCIAL ASPECTS

8 Social Factors in Learning Disabilities: An Overview

Tanis Bryan
University of Illinois at Chicago

James Bryan
Northwestern University and University of Illinois at Chicago

THE WEDDING OF SOCIAL FACTORS
AND LEARNING DISABILITIES

The following three chapters focus on varying aspects of social factors in learning disabilities. Vaughan, Hogan, and Kouzekanani's chapter addresses the predictive power of social status for subsequent diagnosis of learning disabilities. Pearl and Bryan relate learning disabled adolescents' social cognitive skills to the likelihood of crime victimization. Robert Thompson presents research on linkage of diagnostic states, including learning disabilities, to various forms of psychopathology. The divergence of topics and interests across these chapters is clear, but perhaps more striking is that the social and emotional life of the learning disabled youngster is now part and parcel of scholarly life in the field of learning disabilities. Indeed the wedding of interest in the social/emotional conditions of children to children with academic problems and alleged conditions of brain dysfunction now has been consummated. To some the wedding may seem surprising insofar as the concept of learning disabilities was generated from the medical, not the psychological community, and the original definitions of learning disabilities did not mention that such children might suffer the slings and arrows of social and personal misfortune. On the other hand, the wedding may have been a shot gun variety; a necessity driven by the demands of reality. That a divorce is unlikely is suggested by the fact that the two most recent definitions of learning disabilities include references to social problems as a possible distinguishing feature. The definition adopted by the Association for Children and Adults with Learning Disabilities (ACLD, 1985) includes the statement that: "Throughout life the condition can affect self-esteem, education, vocation, socialization, and/or daily living activities'' (Special Education Today, 1985, p. 1). Even more recently, in a mandated report to the Congress, the Interagency Committee on Learning Disabilities (1987) submitted a revised definition that included the statement: ''Learning disabilities is a generic term that refers to a heterogeneous group of disorders manifest by significant difficulties in the acquisition and use of listening, speaking, reading, writing, reasoning, or mathematical abilities, *or of social skills* (italics in original, p. 222).

Historically the courtship was spawned by a host of factors. Some sensitive clinicians reported that LD children might indeed experience emotional and social problems (Griffiths, 1970). Some astute researchers more systematically sampled teacher opinions, the results of which furthered the romance (Keogh, Tchir, & Windeguth-Behn, 1974). Finally, peers as well as parents and teachers became a relevant audience and studies were initiated addressed to the simple question of whether LD children's social status among their peers might differ from those of achieving children. Given the converging evidence that this group of underachieving children appeared to have difficulties that transcended the boundaries of intellectual activities, questions concerning the processes, the specific nature, and the consequences of these problems were pursued. So far, the emphasis has been on the social rather than the emotional. Thus, studies have been conducted addressing determinants of LD children's feelings about themselves, their social status, their thinking about social relationships, and their conduct vis-à-vis important others in their lives. A neglected area of research, which Thompson's work starts to correct, has been the emotional or psychological disturbances which might characterize children typically diagnosed as learning disabled. This neglect may not be surprising insofar as those people most directly involved in learning disabilities are educators, not psychologists, and research clinical psychologists have by and large eschewed involvement with such children. Moreover definitions of this problem contain an exclusionary clause regarding the linkage of emotional problems with learning disabilities. But neither the dynamics of children nor of diagnosticians may dictate conformity or even sensitivity to such clauses. In this regard, Thompson's work is quite important and even may be prophetic of future efforts.

Whatever the direction of future efforts, the following chapters by Vaughan, Hogan, and Kouzckanani, Pearl and Bryan, and Thompson reflect the field's continuing interest in the intra and interpersonal experiences of the learning disabled child.

SOCIAL STATUS OF CHILDREN AND YOUTH
WITH LEARNING DISABILITIES

That learning disabled children are held in lower regard than their classmates has been repeatedly demonstrated. Thus in the past 15 years about 20 studies have been conducted, with almost all of them reporting that children with learning disabilities either receive fewer votes on measures of popularity and/or more votes on measures of rejection than their higher achieving classmates. Vaughan et al. have further contributed to this body of literature by focusing on the social status of young children prior to their confrontation with academic difficulties or diagnosticians. They use a sociometric measure, teacher ratings of behavior, and children's self-perceptions of social status to assess which, if any, might be predictive of LD status 1 year later. The results are important as they show: (1) peer ratings 2 months into kindergarten are predictive of LD diagnosis, (2) peer rejection of classmates is prior to teacher awareness of either academic or social problems, and (3) those children who become labeled LD perceive their social status as higher than their more socially accepted classmates. If replicated, these results suggest that social problems may be entrenched much earlier than predicted. Now this area of research is being expanded beyond simple demonstrations that there are main effect differences between the learning disabled and their achieving classmates. Recent research in this area, most involving children other than the learning disabled, is now considering a variety of issues related to measurement, categorization, mediating characteristics, and social contexts.

For example, investigators have compared social status indexes when ratings versus nominations techniques are employed (Morrison, 1981). Although the initial studies categorized children's status as popular or rejected, recent efforts have expanded upon these categories to more specifically describe the child's social status suggesting typing a child's status as popular, amiable, rejected, and isolated. And there are good reasons to assume that such refinements may indeed sharpen our predictive powers (Parker & Asher, 1987). Classification systems have been further expanded to consider a child's social impact; the number of votes which the target receives on both popularity and rejection measures.

Another important direction being followed is that of the influence of situational influences, or more particularly the social context, on sociometric status. For example, Perlmutter, Crocker, Cordray, and Garstecki (1983) compared learning disabled students' sociometric status in regular classrooms and in resource rooms, controlling for familiarity. Sabornie and Kaufmann (1986) conducted their study in physical education classes, reporting outcomes that differed from earlier studies particularly as these relate to sex differences. They found more favorable ratings for learning disabled females than males in contrast to studies in the regular classroom (Bryan & Wheeler, 1972; Scranton & Ryckman, 1979) and on the playground (Gottlieb, Gottlieb, Berkell, & Levy, 1986). The results of these studies suggest that while learning disabled youngsters are at risk for problems in establishing positive peer relationships, there may be important factors of measurement, sex, and social context that influence research outcomes.

The results of these studies also suggest that a more complex model of determinants of social status are needed. Studies by Hops, Lewin, Stevens, and

Powers report research on primary school age children using multiple measures involving peer and teacher ratings and children's behavior on the playground and in the classroom. Although the study is not concerned with learning disabilities per se, Hops et al.'s model extends our understanding of the determinants of boys and girls sociometric status by convincingly demonstrating the potential role of the teacher in affecting such status.

Sociometric studies are expensive, and it is often difficult to enlist school district support, especially when rejection items are included in the assessment. Yet the results of the sociometric studies make it clear that social status is a significant issue in characterizing the learning disabled, that the findings of research suggest age, sex, cognitive and contextual differences must be further delineated if we are to understand learning disabled youngsters' social problems.

BEHAVIOR PROBLEMS IN LEARNING DISABLED CHILDREN

In addition to the sociometric approach to study learning disabled children's social status, other investigators turned to studies of their behavior. Several issues generated research on learning disabled students behavior. First, there was the question of whether the early clinical descriptions had social validity; e.g., were these children actually emotionally labile or perseverative? Second, there was concern for the impact of mainstreaming on children. Third, given the results of sociometric studies, there was interest in identifying those behaviors that might be producing social rejection from peers. If behaviors distinguishing the learning disabled from their achieving peers could be identified then social skills training interventions might be warranted.

What has been the result of these efforts? First, classroom observation studies that compared the learning disabled and their classmates have typically failed to find that the learning disabled were engaging in those behaviors cited in the early literature. That is, there was precious little evidence of perseveration, emotional lability, acting out or aggressiveness. Now it may be that individual children referred to hospital clinics for assessment may well engage in such behaviors, but children who are school labeled as learning disabled were not found to be engaging in the myriad of nasty behaviors attributed to them. Perhaps the most reliable finding that confirms the early ideas concerning the classroom activities of the learning disabled student is that they are more likely to be off task than their achieving classmates (Bryan & Wheeler, 1972; Richey & McKinney, 1978; McKinney, McClure, & Feagans, 1982), a finding confirmed by Vaughan et al.'s study of teachers' ratings of kindergardeners.

But the sociometric data also directed attention to the social interactions of the LD youngster, particularly and perhaps myopically, within the classroom context. By and large the results of these studies have failed to find radical differences in classroom interactions between learning disabled and achieving children. There appear to be no differences in the frequency of interactions (Bryan & Wheeler, 1972; McKinney, McClure, & Feagans, 1982; Schumaker, Sheldon-Wildgen, & Sherman, 1982), although qualitative analyses find differences in verbal communications (Bryan & Bryan, 1986). On the play ground, two studies reported that the learning disabled tended to have more difficulty than their peers in entering and remaining in activity groups (Gottlieb et al., 1986; Levy & Gottlieb, 1984) with a result of increased isolated play. The results of these studies provide some reason for concern, but in general it cannot be said that the results of classroom observation studies provide strong evidence as to the reasons underlying LD children's low repute.

While observational studies have generally yielded disappointing results, they have been consistent in suggesting that the LD child is not markedly deviant, in behavior or emotional expression, within the classroom setting. That they too might suffer, however, from severe emotional and psychological disturbances is suggested by the work of Thompson. As this investigator focused his attention on clinic referred patients, it is not surprising that emotional difficulties among LD children were found. It is however informative that distinct differences between LD children and children with other forms of disturbances were relatively few. Moreover, his concern with family structure introduces a relatively neglected field of study, an area that might yield a rich harvest. Whether the reported differences will prevail upon cross-validation attempts remains to be seen. What is of importance is the introduction of clinical psychology into the field of learning disabilities.

SOCIAL COGNITIVE DEFICITS

The tidal wave of the cognitive psychology movement during the past decade or so has picked up some new surfers, namely researchers interested in learning disabilities. This turning to cognition, especially those involving social processes or content, is understandable in light of the lack of knowledge yielded by observational studies as to the determinants of LD children's social status. Although the determinants of sociometric status are multidimensional, one factor likely to contribute to it are children's social cognitions. We suggest that some children with learning disabilities may be at risk for peer status difficulties because they lack, to some degree, the social cognitive skills of their achieving classmates, especially in situations in which the social cues are ambiguous or implicit (Pearl & Cosden, 1982), or when the learning disabled must take a dominant role in a social interaction (Bryan, Donahue, & Pearl, 1981).

The etiology of these difficulties is certainly far from clear. It may be that poorer social cognitive skills are the result of learning disabled students' social experiences. As yet, it is unclear that the LD child has either fewer friends or is more isolated than his achieving peers. But given the results of the sociometric studies, it is possible that such is the case. If so, then it is possible that children who have difficulty making friends may have fewer opportunities to learn about people. With less or different experiences, they may develop less knowledge about how people express their emotions and intentions which may in turn lead them to be less able to generate, recognize, or interpret overtures to or from others.

Conversely, it may be the case that social cognitive deficits are a part of the learning disability, and thus the cause of learning disabled children's social problems. The notion here is that learning disabled youngsters who experience problems in the social domain may lack awareness or ability to understand others' emotions, motives and intentions: feelings that are communicated through verbal and nonverbal channels. These deficits may cause learning disabled children to interact clumsily with peers, thereby provoking a negative response. The chapter by Vaughan et al. supports the notion that LD children may have social cognitive difficults that contribute to their social problems insofar as their self-perceptions of their social status were at variance with peer ratings. These young children appear to be unaware of their social standing in the classroom.

Whatever the etiology, there has been a host of studies that fall, somewhat clumsily, under this domain of inquiry. The research on social cognition has examined comprehension of social situations (Bryan, 1977; Maheady, Maitland, & Sainato, 1984; Weiss, 1984), role taking skills (Dickstein & Warren, 1980; Matthews,Whang, & Fawcett, 1980; Stone & LaGreca, 1984; Wong & Wong, 1980), referential communication (Donahue, Pearl & Bryan, 1980; Noel, 1980), and immediate first impressions (Bryan, & Sherman, 1980). The results of these studies suggest that many learning disabled children experience greater difficulty than achieving classmates in comprehending social situations when the cues are ambiguous or implicit, but not when the situations are routine, and well known. The role taking and referential communication studies find the learning disabled tend to give less adequate messages, and fail to ask for clarification when the situation demands. The immediate first impressions studies find that the learning disabled make worse first impressions, but that this difference is reduced when told in advance to make a good first impression.

The chapter by Pearl and Bryan provides an extension of studies on social cognition to crime victimization of learning disabled adolescents. Studies are reported that assessed learning disabled students understanding of deception and their role-playing of situations in which peers might cajole them into engaging in various criminal acts and substance abuse. As predicted the results find that learning disabled preadolescents are less skilled than their classmates in comprehending others' deception. The role playing results find the main difference related more to expectations (the learning disabled expect a more direct appeal from peers to engage in nefarious acts) and to a smaller repertoire of responses.

Whether this innocence will result in greater vulnerability in the LD adolescents everyday intercourse remains to be determined. The possibility that such is the case looms larger as a result of these studies.

Across these chapters, diverse in theory, method, and sample, it is clear that the inclusion of social factors in conceptions of learning disabilities is a fait accompli. The data base provides strong support for continued support for and interest in research on social factors in learning disabilities. It is expected that the next decade will see many gaps in our knowledge base filled in. Given evidence from so many directions that the learning disabled are likely to experience problems in the social domain, it is important that research continues to identify the nature of such problems, their etiology and the appropriate interventions.

REFERENCES

Bryan, J. H., & Sherman, R. (1980). Audiences' immediate impressions of non-verbal ingratiation attempts by boys labeled learning disabled. *Learning Disability Quarterly, 3,* 19–28.

Bryan, T. (1977). Learning disabled children's comprehension of nonverbal communication. *Journal of Learning Disabilities, 10,* 501–506.

Bryan, T., & Bryan, J. (1986). *Understanding learning disabilities.* Palo Alto: CA: Mayfield.

Bryan, T., Donahue, M., & Pearl, R. (1981). Learning disabled children's peer interactions during a small-group problem-solving task. *Learning Disability Quarterly, 4,* 13–22.

Bryan, T., & Wheeler, R. (1972). Perception of children with learning disabilities: the eye of the observer. *Journal of Learning Disabilities, 5,* 484–488.

Dickstein, E., & Warren, D. (1980). Role-taking deficits in learning disabled children. *Journal of Learning Disabilities, 13,* 378–382.

Donahue, M., Pearl, R., & Bryan, T. (1980). Learning disabled children's conversational competence: responses to inadequate messages. *Applied Psycholinguistics, 1,* 387–403.

Gottlieb, B. W., Gottlieb, J., Berkell, D., & Levy, L. (1986). Sociometric status and solitary play of LD boys and girls. *Journal of Learning Disabilities, 19,* 619–622.

Griffiths, A. N. (1970). Self-concept in remedial work with dyslexic children. *Academic Therapy, 6,* 125–133.

Hops, H., Lewin, L., Stevens, T., & Powers, B. (Manuscript). *The relative importance of the academic setting on social acceptance and rejection in elementary school children.* Eugene, University of Oregon.

Interagency Committee on Learning Disabilities (1987). *Learning disabilities: A report to the Congress,* Secretary of Health and Human Services: Washington, D.C., p. 222.

Keogh, B. K., Tchir, C., & Windeguth-Behn, A. (1974). Teachers' perceptions of educationally high-risk children. *Journal of Clinical Child Psychology, 8,* 213–216.

Levy, L., & Gottlieb, J. (1984). Learning disabled and non-LD children at play. *Remedial and Special Education, 5,* 43–50.

Maheady, L., Maitland, G., & Sainato, D. (1984). The interpretation of social interactions by mildly handicapped and nondisabled children. *Journal of Special Education, 18,* 151–159.

Matthews, R. M., Whang, P. L., & Fawcett, S. B. (1980). *Behavioral assessment of occupational skills of learning disabled adolescents.* Unpublished manuscript, University of Kansas.

McKinney, J. D., McClure, S., & Feagans, L. (1982). Classroom behavior of learning disabled children. *Learning Disability Quarterly, 5,* 45–52.

Morrison, G. M. (1981). Sociometric measurement: methodological considerations of its use with mildly learning handicapped and non-handicapped children. *Journal of Educational Psychology,* *73,* 193–201.

Noel, M. M. (1980). Referential communication abilities of learning disabled children. *Learning Disability Quarterly, 3,* 70–75.

Parker, J. G., & Asher, S. R. (1987). Peer relations and later personal adjustment: are low-accepted children at risk? *Psychological Bulletin, 102,* 357–389.

Pearl, R., & Cosden, M. (1982). Sizing up a situation: LD children's understanding of social interactions. *Learning Disability Quarterly, 3,* 3–9.

Perlmutter, B., Crocker, J., Cordray, D., & Garstecki, D. (1983). Sociometric status and related personality characteristics of mainstreamed learning disabled adolescents. *Learning Disability Quarterly, 6,* 20–30.

Richey, D. D., & McKinney, J. D. (1978). Classroom and behavioral styles of learning disabled children. *Journal of Learning Disabilities, 11,* 297–302.

Sabornie, E. J., & Kauffman, J. M. (1986). Social acceptance of learning disabled adolescents. *Learning Disability Quarterly, 9,* 55–60.

Schumaker, J., Sheldon-Wildgen, J., & Sherman, A. (1982). Social interaction of learning disabled junior high students in their regular classrooms: An observational analysis. *Journal of Learning Disabilities, 15,* 355–358.

Scranton, T. R., & Ryckman, D. A. (1979). Learning Disabled children in an integrative program: sociometric status. *Journal of Learning Disabilities, 2,* 402–407.

Special Education Today. (1985), I, p. 1.

Stone, W. L., & LaGreca, A. M. (1984). Comprehension of nonverbal communication: a reexamination of the social competencies of learning-disabled children. *Journal of Abnormal Child Psychology, 12,* 505–518.

Weiss, E. (1984). Learning disabled children's understanding of social interactions of peers. *Journal of Learning Disabilities, 17,* 612–615.

Wong, B. Y. L., & Wong, R. (1980). Role-taking in normal achieving and learning disabled children. *Learning Disability Quarterly, 3,* 11–18.

9 Learning Disabled Adolescents' Vulnerability to Victimization and Delinquency

Ruth Pearl
Tanis Bryan
University of Illinois at Chicago

In March of 1988, a suburban Chicago couple discovered upon their return from a Florida vacation that their $260,000 home had been ransacked. A subsequent investigation revealed what had happened. The couple's 20-year-old son, who remained at home while his parents vacationed, talked to a girl on a telephone party line and invited her to come over. The girl invited other youths to join them, and the ensuing party resulted in the theft of jewelry, appliances, and the family car as well as $25,000 in damage to the house. According to the newspaper report the parents indicated that their son has a learning disability.

Is it the case that individuals with learning disabilities are more susceptible to being enticed into undesirable activities? In a series of studies, we have examined whether learning disabled students have acquired attitudes, knowledge, and skills likely to facilitate their ability to protect themselves in potentially dangerous situations. We have been particularly concerned about learning disabled students' susceptibility to pressure from peers to engage in delinquent activity or substance abuse. Although there is certainly reason to be concerned about the influence of peer pressure on all teenagers, the results of research, primarily involving elementary school children, led us to suspect that learning disabled adolescents may be especially vulnerable to the influence of their peers.

One reason is that many learning disabled students appear to be less well liked than their classmates (e.g., Bryan, 1974; Bruininks, 1978; Perlmutter, Crocker, Cordray, & Garstecki, 1983). These students, therefore, may be particularly receptive to seemingly friendly overtures from peers. They also may be especially eager to fit in, and thus more willing than other students to conform regardless of the nature of their peers' activity. There is some evidence to support these notions. For example, adolescents with learning disabilities have been found to be more likely to adopt group values than their own (Alley, Warner, Schumaker, Deshler, & Clark, 1980). In addition, learning disabled students have been found in some situations to be deferential and unassertive with their peers (Bryan, Donahue, & Pearl, 1981; Bryan, Donahue, Pearl, & Sturm, 1981).

The social cognitive deficits that appear to be typical of many learning disabled students are a second factor that might make these students particularly vulnerable to peer influence. Learning disabled students appear to have little difficulty understanding routine, concrete social situations (Maheady & Maitland, 1982), but may have difficulty in roletaking the perspective of others and in comprehending the meaning of implicit or ambiguous social cues (e.g., Bryan, 1977; Dickstein & Warren, 1980; Pearl & Cosden, 1982; Wong & Wong, 1980). This research suggests that learning disabled students with such problems may not recognize instances in which they are deliberately being misled. In addition, to the extent that learning disabled students have had experiences different from those typical of their classmates, they may not have acquired the same type of social knowledge about situations in which they could get in trouble. The lack of this type of knowledge could put them at greater risk.

Finally, linguistic and pragmatic limitations (Donahue, 1986) may make some learning disabled students less able to effectively deal with difficult situations. Problems in language comprehension could lead them to misunderstand what is being proposed. Problems in language production could make it difficult for them to fend off invitations in socially appropriate ways. To just say no may work for Nancy Reagan but considerably more finesse and aplomb helps the rest of us avoid or escape socially undesirable situations. It is harder to say "no" than "yes," at least from a pragmatic perspective.

The suggestion that there is a relation between learning disabilities and problems such as delinquency is not new. However, this suggestion has been made primarily on the basis of findings of an overrepresentation of learning disabilities among delinquent youth (Murray, 1976; Podboy & Mallory, 1978; Sawicki & Schaeffer, 1979); few studies have examined this issue by comparing learning disabled and nondisabled adolescents before they actually become involved in the criminal justice system. In addition, we are proposing that the same factors that may make learning disabled students susceptible to delinquency may also make them susceptible to being victimized. The same desire to win peer approval may make one student agree to join in a robbery and another to allow new "friends" to hold a raucous party in his home.

This chapter summarizes studies conducted with high school and junior high school students to test the vulnerability hypothesis. It should be noted that it is not possible to test students' vulnerability directly. To do so would involve studies that are not ethical (e.g., place children in a social situation in which their responses to peer pressure would be directly tested by having a confederate try to sell them marijuana or persuade them to cut school) or practical (e.g., observe the students during their normal interactions to see if they conform to peer pressure). Therefore, the studies that are described in this chapter investigated this hypothesis indirectly by examining whether learning disabled students differed from classmates in characteristics likely to help keep them out of trouble.

CONFORMITY STUDIES

One way of determining whether learning disabled students are likely to be vulnerable to peer pressure to conform is to ask them. Two studies did just that. Bryan, Werner, and Pearl (1982) asked junior high school students what they would do in a variety of situations in which friends pressured them to join in activities in which they did not wish to participate. The students were administered a questionnaire adapted from the work of Bronfenbrenner (1970) and Berndt (1979) that consisted of 20 hypothetical conformity situations, half involving antisocial acts and half, prosocial acts. In the antisocial situations the acts included cheating on a test, stealing or "borrowing" something without the owner's permission, defacing school property, and taking illicit drugs. Prosocial acts included collecting money for charity, welcoming a new child in the neighborhood, and teaching other children.

For each situation, the students were asked to imagine that they either had different plans for that time or were reluctant to engage in the behavior advocated by their friends. Students were asked to indicate which of two mutually exclusive actions (i.e., to conform or not to conform) they predicted they would take if placed in that situation, and then to rate on a 3-point scale how certain they were that they would adhere to that alternative. Supplementary items on the questionnaire assessed perceived friend and parent supportiveness, self-reports of actual behavior, and their feelings subsequent to participating in activities in which they knew they should not participate.

Subjects were 50 students attending a suburban junior high school. Results indicated that although the groups did not differ in their expressed willingness to conform to the prosocial activities, the learning disabled students expressed a greater willingness to conform to the antisocial activities than the nondisabled students. No differences were found between groups in perceived friend or parent supportiveness or self-reports of behavior. However, the learning disabled students reported feeling less concern after engaging in an undesirable act than did the nondisabled students.

In addition, the relation between the students' concern and parent and friend supportiveness differed for the two groups. For the nondisabled students, the more parental support they perceived, the more concern they indicated experiencing. For the learning disabled students, however, perceived parental supportiveness was unrelated to the concern they reported feeling subsequent to undesirable behavior, while perceived friends' supportiveness had a direct relationship: The more supportive they perceived their friends to be, the less concern they experienced.

In the second study, Bryan, Pearl, and Fallon (in press) used the same questionnaire with 43 7th and 8th graders from a junior high school in a different suburb. Results of the study replicated the Bryan, Werner, and Pearl (1982) finding that students with learning disabilities expressed greater willingness to conform to peer pressure in antisocial situations. However, none of the supplementary items yielded group effects.

Results of these two studies indicate the importance of taking into account the social context in which learning disabled students function. Typically, efforts to assess social skills in students with learning disabilities focus only on the individual student. Similarly, research investigating the link between learning disabilities and juvenile delinquency (Broder, Dunivant, Smith, & Sutton, 1981; Murray, 1976) for the most part has not considered the social context in which students with learning disabilities might, or might not, engage in delinquent actions. The conformity studies suggest that an important influence on learning disabled students' behavior, apparently even more than with other students, are the peers whom they perceive to be friends.

SELF-REPORTED EXPERIENCES
WITH UNDESIRABLE ACTIVITIES

Another way to investigate whether students with learning disabilities are vulnerable is to directly ask them whether they have been victims of or participants in undesirable activity. For this purpose, we (Bryan, Pearl, & Herzog, in press) administered a questionnaire to 198 learning disabled and nondisabled adolescents in five city and suburban high schools. As a summary indicator of social context, ethnicity was included as a variable in this study. Participants were Black and Hispanic students who attended primarily urban high schools in areas with high rates of crime, high school drops outs, and gang activity, as well as White students who attended primarily middle class suburban high schools.

The questionnaire consisted of three major parts: general concerns; concerns about and experiences with crime, drugs, and alcohol; and sexual experiences and concerns. The format consisted of a question followed by a number of items to which the participant responded on scales, either 3- or 5-point Likert agreement scales or scales of frequency of occurrence or use.

Analyses indicated group differences in a number of areas, some of which were apparent only in the White teenagers. Learning disabled males reported having been victimized by crime more frequently than did nondisabled males. White learning disabled males indicated feeling more pressure from peers to join in illegal activity, and indeed, indicated a greater frequency of involvement in illegal activity than did the White nondisabled students. White learning disabled males also reported using more tobacco, drugs, and alcohol than did their White nondisabled classmates. Learning disabled males expressed a more positive attitude toward having babies and believed it more likely that they would father a baby within the next 2 years than did nondisabled males.

Among girls, the learning disabled students believed more than nondisabled students that they would get caught by the police if they committed a crime. White learning disabled females believed more than White nondisabled females that factors like failing courses or emotional or family problems could keep them from graduating. White learning disabled females also indicated more approval of smoking marijuana and drinking alcohol, and tended to report more tobacco, drug, and alcohol use than did the nondisabled students. Learning disabled females also reported engaging in sex more frequently than did the nondisabled females, and, like the learning disabled males, believed it more likely than do their nondisabled classmates that they will have a baby within the next 2 years.

Thus, learning disabled boys reported being the victims of crime more frequently than did nondisabled boys. In addition, both learning disabled boys and girls indicated a stronger expectancy of becoming parents within the near future. These findings, along with the learning disabled girls' belief that they would get caught by the police if they committed a crime, cut across all the learning disabled groups in the study. Other differences between learning disabled and nondisabled students, however, were found only among the White teenagers. Group differences were not as apparent among Black and Hispanic youths, perhaps because most of these students lived in areas plagued by crime and gang activity, which are likely to put all students at risk. These results again point to the need to consider the social context in which the students interact.

While these are intriguing data, it is important to note the limitations in research of this type. Because a small number of students returned parent permission forms we are unable to determine whether we have a representative sample. The subjects may be the risk takers, or the good citizens, or those whose teachers made special efforts to encourage their participation. Because we lack background information on the students who elected not to participate we cannot adjust for differences between those who participated and those who did not. We are unable, therefore, to describe the degree of self-selection bias. In addition, self-report data are notable for socially desirable responses. Because the questionnaire dealt with illegal and intimate behavior, it is likely that some students, despite assurances of confidentiality, chose to present themselves in the best possible light.

In spite of the limitations of this type of research, and the possibility that sampling and social desirability factors to some extent may have compromised the validity of the results, the findings are consistent with the hypothesis that learning disabled students may be especially vulnerable to being victims and participants in undesirable activity.

SCRIPTS ABOUT SITUATIONS INVOLVING PEER PRESSURE

In the next study, we began to probe reasons why learning disabled students might be particularly susceptible to peer pressure. In this study (Pearl, Bryan, & Herzog, in preparation), we examined whether learning disabled students differed from other students in their expectations, or scripts, about situations in which students were pressured by peers to engage in misconduct. Scripts are defined as a "coherent sequence of events expected by the individual, involving him as either a participant or observer" (Abelson, 1976). Research on scripts suggests that individuals' expectations about events influence the way they respond when faced with those events. We thought that because many learning disabled students have difficulty obtaining peer acceptance, they might not have experienced the range of social experiences typical of their classmates, and because of this social inexperience, they may not have developed the same scripts about what is likely to occur in different situations where an overture is made by a seemingly friendly peer. In this study, we examined learning disabled and nondisabled students' scripts for situations in which one teenager requested another to engage in an activity. We hypothesized that the learning disabled students might differ from their classmates in their expectation of how such a request would be stated, and what would ensue if the request were accepted or refused. We also examined why the students thought the story character would agree or refuse in order to assess their beliefs about what would be likely to motivate these decisions.

The students were the same as those included in the previous study. They were individually interviewed about nine situations in which one student asked another to participate in an activity. In three of these situations the activity involved behavior that, according to distinctions about rule violations made by Turiel (1983) and his colleagues, would be characterized as a moral transgression, for example, stealing a car or shoplifting; and in three of the situations the activity consisted of a rule violation that would be characterized by Turiel's distinctions as falling in the personal domain, for instance drinking beer or smoking marijuana. The remaining three situations involved prosocial activities; responses to these were not analyzed for purposes of this study. After hearing the basic scenario in each story, the students were questioned to determine their expectations for what would happen if the person acquiesced to the request and for what would happen if the person refused the request. The sex of the story characters was matched to that of the subject.

For example, one scenario was the following: "Jim is walking down the street with a guy he likes, Bob. They pass a car that has the keys still in it. Bob wants to take the car for a joy ride around the neighborhood and wants Jim to go with him."

144

The students were asked the following questions: "What do you think Bob would say to Jim to get him to go on a joy ride with him? Suppose Jim decides to go along with Bob. Why do you think he would decide that? What would he say to Bob? What do you think would happen next? And then? How do you think Jim, the guy who was asked, would feel? How would he feel about Bob? How do you think Bob would feel? How would he feel about Jim?"

The students were then asked the same questions in regard to what would happen if the person in the story refused the request. All interviews were tape-recorded and later transcribed. The transcripts were then coded according to codes developed to categorize the major themes related in the students' responses; reliability checks indicated that interrater reliability for each code was at least 85%. For each type of question, totals were derived indicating the number of times each of the major categories was used over the six stories involving misconduct. Multiple analyses of variance (manovas) then examined whether there were overall differences in category use.

The first question addressed the issue of how the students think a request would be posed. The manova indicated a significant group difference, and so analyses of variance (anovas) on individual categories were examined. These revealed that the learning disabled students were more likely than the nondisabled students to expect a simple, direct request, while the nondisabled students were more likely than the learning disabled students to think the request would be couched in terms indicating the payoff involved to the listener or in a way that minimized the negatives involved in the act. In other words, the learning disabled students expected the request to be succinct and to the point— "Let's take this car"—while the nondisabled students expected the speaker to use persuasive ploys, e.g., "Let's go for a ride; it'll be exciting" or "Let's borrow this car; we'll bring it right back."

The most common responses to the questions regarding why the listeners would agree to the requests indicated that the listener would agree because he or she would get something out of the activity, for instance, fun or material benefit, and because of social factors, for instance, friendship. The manova indicated a group difference in responses; however, none of the anovas on individual categories was significant. Hence, the difference appears to have resulted from the nondisabled students describing more reasons than the learning disabled students.

No differences were found in the consequences expected for going along with the request. Students responded most frequently with the predictions that the request would be complied with and nothing of consequence would happen, and that the story characters would be caught. (We have not analyzed at this point whether these responses were differentially made to the different types of stories.) However, despite the fact that the interview did not request the students to describe alternative possible consequences, more nondisabled students spontaneously suggested that the outcome was not certain, and that more than one course of events was possible.

Responses to the question about why someone would not go along with the request most frequently centered on the possibility of getting caught, the action being undesirable (for instance, you might get sick if you smoked), and the action being wrong or against the law. The manova indicated group differences, which resulted from the fact that nondisabled students mentioned the possibility of getting in trouble as a reason for the refusal more than did learning disabled students. Responses to the question of how the listener would refuse the request indicated that while the students mentioned a variety of ways the request would be refused, such as using an excuse or citing that the action was wrong or that they would be caught, the most frequently cited strategy was a simple refusal.

Students predicted about equally that nothing much would happen as a result of refusing the request, and that the listener would suffer social consequences such as a disruption of friendship or social disapproval. No group differences were found, but again, the nondisabled students were more likely than the learning disabled students to spontaneously suggest alternative scenarios, although this did not happen often. The questions regarding the affect of the characters revealed that the learning disabled students were more likely to believe that the individual refusing the request would feel bad.

To summarize, the learning disabled students' expectations differed in several respects from those of nondisabled students. One difference was in their response to the question of how a request would be stated. Learning disabled students were more likely than nondisabled students to report that they thought the request would be brief and to the point, and were less likely to suggest that the request would be couched in terms indicating a payoff to the listener or minimizing the negatives involved in the act. Learning disabled and nondisabled students also differed in their explanation for why the individual would refuse the request to participate in misconduct, with nondisabled students more likely to mention the possibility of getting caught. A third difference was in the anticipated affect of the individual who refused the request; the learning disabled students were more likely than other students to predict that the individual would feel bad. Finally, the learning disabled students showed less insight about situations in which the suggestion to engage in misconduct is made in that they suggested fewer reasons for why someone would accept these requests, and spontaneously suggested fewer alternative scenarios for what might ensue if the requests were accepted or refused.

The expectations of the learning disabled students seem likely to make these students more vulnerable than their nondisabled classmates to pressure from other teenagers to engage in misconduct. For instance, the finding that learning disabled students expect requests to be straightforward suggests that these students might be less wary than other students when requests are not so directly stated. The nondisabled students appear to know that peers trying to involve them in undesirable activities will attempt to cajole them; if the learning disabled students are not as aware that persuasive attempts are likely, it is possible that they may be more susceptible to the persuasive attempts that are made. In other words, if their peers say "it isn't so bad," the learning disabled students may be more likely to take them at their word.

At this point, one can only speculate about this possibility, because in this study the students had to actually produce the request, and we are speculating about their comprehension. That is, just because the request the learning disabled students reported they expected was more direct than that expected by the other students, it does not necessarily mean that they would not recognize and comprehend a less direct statement if they heard it. We are currently evaluating this possibility in a study examining learning disabled and nondisabled students' reactions to requests stated in different ways to see if learning disabled students are more easily swayed by persuasive appeals than are the nondisabled students. If this finding holds up, it suggests that it may not be enough to just teach learning disabled students how to deal with peer pressure to engage in undesirable activities; it may be necessary to teach them to recognize when such attempts are being made.

Other differences in learning disabled and nondisabled students' expectancies may also be important. The fact that the possibility of getting caught was a less salient reason for refusing to participate in misconduct may mean that learning disabled adolescents are less discerning than their nondisabled classmates of when misconduct is likely to be detected. In addition, the greater negative affect expected by the learning disabled students upon refusing a proposal to engage in misconduct may serve as a disincentive for refusing. One of the conformity studies described earlier (Bryan, Werner, & Pearl, 1982) found that learning disabled students reported experiencing less concern after committing an undesirable act than did nondisabled students. If learning disabled students experience less negative affect after engaging in misconduct, and anticipate more negative affect if a peer's request to engage in misconduct is refused, it may be that these experienced and anticipated emotional responses make learning disabled students more susceptible than nondisabled students to peer pressure to engage in such acts.

DETECTION OF DECEPTION

The next study further investigated the processes that might underlie learning disabled students' vulnerability. In this study (Pearl, Bryan, Fallon, & Herzog, in press), we looked at junior high school students' ability to recognize when someone is deliberately lying, a skill that could help students protect themselves from others attempting to take advantage of them.

Recognizing deception is generally not an easy thing to do. The first step in the detection of deception, recognizing that a statement is at variance with the facts, is itself likely to be a difficult task for individuals of limited social cognitive skill. Further, to recognize that the statement was not simply mistaken but, rather, an intentional lie, the speaker's deceptive intent must also be identified. There is some evidence to suggest that learning disabled students are more apt to assume a speaker's veracity than are other students. The results of a number of studies on children's referential communication skill, for example, suggest that learning disabled students assumed that speakers were as forthcoming as possible (Donahue, 1984; Donahue, Pearl, & Bryan, 1983). It was hypothesized in this study, therefore, that learning disabled students would be likely to assume a speaker was being truthful, and therefore would be less likely to detect deception than would their nondisabled classmates.

Forty-three 7th- and 8th-grade learning disabled and nondisabled students participated in this study. The task, which had been constructed to examine developmental differences (Demorest, Meyer, Phelps, Gardner, & Winner, 1984) consisted of 12 tape-recorded stories. These stories described an interaction between two characters, and were concluded with a statement made by one of the characters. Each story was written in four versions, with the final remark being either sincere, deceptive, sarcastic, or neutral. All statements were said with appropriate intonation and were described as being accompanied by appropriate nonverbal behavior. For example, one story began:

> Kate wanted to go swimming in the pond near her house. It was no fun to go alone. Kate asked Libby to go swimming with her. At the pond, Libby did not want to go in the water if it was cold. Kate jumped into the water right away.

The different versions of the story varied from this point. The sincere version continued, "The water was warm and felt great. Kate looked over and saw Libby standing at the edge of the pond. Kate said to Libby: 'This water in here is very warm.' "

The deceptive version continued, "The water was very cold and felt icy. Kate smiled and floated on her back in the water. Kate said to Libby: "This water in here is very warm.' "

The sarcastic version continued, "The water was very cold and felt icy. Kate screamed and swam quickly for the shore. Kate said to Libby: 'This water in here is very warm.' "

The neutral version continued, "The water was very cold and felt icy. Kate looked over and saw Libby standing at the edge of the pond. Kate said to Libby: 'This water in here is very warm.' " These neutral versions were clearly false, but were meant to be ambiguous with regard to whether they were deceptive or sarcastic.

A series of questions was asked after each story to determine the students' recall of the story, their understanding of the facts in the story, their assessment of the speaker's belief and intent, and the evidence used to determine the speaker's belief and intent. To make sure the students remembered the story, if the students were unable to answer the initial questions, which required them to summarize the story, the story was re-presented and the questions repeated. By examining the pattern of responses to the remaining questions, it was possible to determine whether the students thought the speaker's statement was sincere and correct, sincere but wrong, deceptive, or sarcastic.

Analyses were performed to examine whether the learning disabled and non-disabled students differed in identifying the sincere, sarcastic, and deceptive statements. Group differences were not predicted for the sincere statements, and were not predicted on this task for the sarcastic statements since earlier studies suggested that correctly identifying sarcastic statements in this task was difficult for all students of this age group. The results indicated that, as expected, there were no group differences in accuracy of interpreting the sincere and sarcastic statements, but there were group differences in accuracy of interpreting the deceptive statements, with the learning disabled students less accurate than the nondisabled students.

The next question was if they did not recognize that the statement was deceptive, how did they view the statement? Were they assuming that the statement was correct, or did they recognize that the statement was incorrect but simply assume that the speaker must have been mistaken rather than deliberately deceptive. Analyses indicated that the learning disabled students were not more likely to think the statements were true; however, they were more likely to think that although the speaker was wrong, he or she was sincere and not intentionally deceptive. An examination of students' assumptions about the neutral stories, those stories where the statement was untrue but where the speakers' intent was ambiguous, found again that the learning disabled students were less likely to believe that the speaker was being deceptive than were the nondisabled students.

As predicted, then, the learning disabled students were not as skilled as nondisabled students in detecting deceptive statements. This was not because they did not recognize that the statements were untrue; they were as likely as the nondisabled students to understand that the facts were different from those implied by the speaker's statement. But whereas the nondisabled students consistently recognized that the speaker would have known the facts of the story and therefore must have been purposefully deceptive, the learning disabled students were likely to assume that the speaker's statement was sincere.

Why did the learning disabled students more often fail to recognize the speaker's deceptive intent? One possibility is that the learning disabled children did not fully comprehend the stories. However, the questioning after the stories required the students to first relate the major facts of the story, which the learning disabled students were able to do.

Another explanation is that the students recognized the speaker's insincerity but felt reluctant to disparage another's motives because of perceptions that such assertive behavior would be inappropriate for them. However, in this study, the students were asked about fictional story characters and did not have to directly confront a conversational partner. Indeed, they never had to explicitly say that the speaker was lying, merely whether the speaker thought, to return to the example cited earlier, the water was "cold" or "warm." Although students' self-perceptions may certainly influence their behavior in real interactions, the design of the present study makes this an unlikely explanation for these data.

Another possibility is that the learning disabled students considered the possibility of deception but dismissed it because they believed it plausible that the speaker might not have known the facts, or might not have reacted to them in the assumed way. However, had the learning disabled students made such an analysis, it seems unlikely that they would have concluded that the speaker had a different perspective of the facts since in these stories the facts presented were explicit and extreme. For example, in the story in which the speaker said, "This water in here is very warm," the story had related that "the water was very cold and felt icy." In another story, the speaker said, "This is a beautiful house you live in" after the story had related that "the house was very ugly." It seems doubtful that even unskilled roletakers would come to the conclusion that the speakers really might have meant their statements in light of such clear and unambiguous facts.

A more likely possibility is that the students did not consistently attempt to determine the speaker's perspective or reconcile the speaker's statement with the facts because they were more likely to simply assume, as was suggested by the study on students' scripts, that the speaker would be frank and straightforward.

This study suggests, then, that in some situations, learning disabled students may be less able than other students to detect when they are being deliberately misled. This might manifest itself in a relatively innocuous way, for example, being gullible to the playful baiting of peers. A more serious possibility is that the relative difficulty learning disabled students had in detecting deception may leave them open to victimization by others who take advantage of their trust.

CONCLUSION

Across these studies, the differences that were found almost uniformly point to greater vulnerability among learning disabled students. The results suggest that one part of this vulnerability may be that these students are simply more willing than other students to submit to the wishes of peers. The students with learning disabilities reported a greater willingness to acquiesce to friends' requests to engage in antisocial activities, less concern after participating in such activities, and more anticipated negative affect for refusing requests to join in such activities.

However, the data from these studies also suggest that many learning disabled students seem to lack knowledge and skills that could serve as "antennae" in alerting them to the possibility that they might be victimized by ostensibly friendly peers. The learning disabled students expected direct, straightforward requests, rather than the persuasive appeals predicted by the nondisabled students. Compared to the nondisabled students, they had a lesser awareness of the possible consequences of undesirable actions, and appear to be less skillful in recognizing lies. Indeed, the direct reports of the learning disabled students suggest a greater vulnerability, particularly among boys. In comparison to the nondisabled boys, boys with learning disabilities reported more frequent victimization by crime. In addition, White learning disabled boys reported receiving more pressure from peers to engage in undesirable activities than did White nondisabled boys, and in fact admitted more frequent involvement in such activities.

Although these findings lend support to the hypothesis, there are reasons to interpret these findings cautiously, as we have previously mentioned. First, we do not know if we have a random sample of learning disabled and nondisabled adolescents in our studies. Especially in the studies involving high school students, we found it extraordinarily difficult to get the students to return their parent permission slips, and it is certainly possible that those who did differed from those who did not. Second, we don't know if the students who participated were candid in their responses. We did all we could to assure confidentiality, but we do not know for sure if the students were as frank as we hope they were. It is possible too that learning disabled students' greater social naivete—what we were attempting to investigate—manifested itself in the studies, though in a different way than we expected: perhaps they responded truthfully, while the more savvy nondisabled students distorted their responses to look more virtuous. In the studies on social scripts and the detection of deception we asked about fictitious students, and so it is not as likely that social desirability factors played much of a role. Nevertheless, it is important to be aware that these possible problems are inherent in research on sensitive topics of this type.

Despite these potential limitations, the fact that findings consistent with the vulnerability hypothesis were found in both junior high school and high school students, in city and suburban schools, and in the variety of areas investigated lends some degree of confidence that the results were not merely an artifact produced by a selection or response bias. Yet even assuming the verity of the results, many questions remain. More research is needed to evaluate our proposition that similar factors place students at risk for being victims of as well as participants in undesirable behavior. We also do not know whether it is the case, as we have assumed, that delinquent acts performed by learning disabled students are often done in the company of peers. To our knowledge, there are no data addressing this issue. Nor do we know how the differences we found actually manifest themselves in the students' ongoing interactions with peers.

Other issues have to do with identifying the processes placing individual learning disabled students at risk. Do the willingness to join in with peers and the social cognitive limitations we found coexist in the same students, or are these different forces (as well as other possible factors we have not examined) operating to different degrees in different students? If the latter is true, as it undoubtedly is, how can we determine how to help students who are vulnerable for different reasons? Do we need vulnerability profiles of individual students, or is it possible to develop interventions that will be effective with all learning disabled students? Do we even need special interventions for learning disabled students? Are potentially effective interventions for learning disabled students any different from those that would be effective for other at risk students? We have suggested that learning disabled students are at risk, but we are not convinced that they are *uniquely* at risk; nondisabled students who have experienced similar degrees of social rejection or isolation may be equally vulnerable. This too is a topic for further research.

Other questions relate to the learning disabled students who neither become victims nor victimizers. Clearly, most learning disabled students are not delinquents, and certainly a minority can legitimately be considered victims, although the incidence of victimization of the handicapped is largely unknown (Lang, 1987). Are these students less vulnerable because they are less concerned about peer acceptance or because they are more knowledgeable and skilled in avoiding trouble? Or are they as vulnerable but have avoided problems because they are in an environment in which they are exposed to less undesirable pressure from peers? Studies investigating the impact of IQ, type of academic deficit, social cognitive skill, sociometric status, and social environment would further help to clarify the factors that increase and reduce learning disabled students' risk.

There are, then, many issues needing investigation in order to definitively understand the degree to which learning disabled adolescents are vulnerable to negative peer influence, and the factors that actually turn the vulnerable learning disabled student into a victim or victimizer. Nevertheless, the findings from these studies do strengthen the hypothesis that learning disabled adolescents may be at risk, and suggest that this should be an area of continued concern.

ACKNOWLEDGMENTS

Preparation of this chapter was supported in part by a grant from the U.S. Department of Education.

REFERENCES

Alley, G. R., Warner, M. M., Schumaker, J. B., Deshler, D. D., & Clark, F. (1980). *An epidemiological study of learning disabled and low-achieving adolescents in secondary schools: Behavioral and emotional status from the perspective of parents and teachers.* Unpublished manuscript, University of Kansas.
Abelson, R. P. (1976). Script processing in attitude formation and decision making. In J. S.

Carroll, & J. W. Payne (Eds.), *Cognition and social behaviors* (pp. 33–45). Hillsdale, NJ: Lawrence Erlbaum Associates.

Berndt, T. (1979). Developmental changes in conformity to peers and parents. *Developmental Psychology, 15,* 608–616.

Broder, P. K., Dunivant, N., Smith, E. C., & Sutton, L. P. (1981). Further observations on the link between learning disabilities and juvenile delinquency. *Journal of Educational Psychology, 73,* 838–850.

Bronfenbrenner, U. (1970). Reaction to social pressure from adults versus peers among Soviet day school and boarding school pupils in the perspective of an American sample. *Journal of Personality and Social Psychology, 15,* 179–189.

Bruininks, V. L. (1978). Peer status and personality of learning disabled and nondisabled students. *Journal of Learning Disabilities, 11,* 29–34.

Bryan, T. H. (1974). Peer popularity of learning disabled children. *Journal of Learning Disabilities, 7,* 621–625.

Bryan, T. H. (1977). Children's comprehension of non-verbal communication. *Journal of Learning Disabilities, 10,* 501–506.

Bryan, T., Donahue, M., & Pearl, R. (1981). Learning disabled children's peer interactions during a small group problem-solving task. *Learning Disability Quarterly, 4,* 13–22.

Bryan, T., Donahue, M., Pearl, R., & Sturm, C. (1981). Learning disabled children's conversational skills: The "TV talk show". *Learning Disability Quarterly, 4,* 250–259.

Bryan, T., Pearl, R., & Fallon, P. (in press). Learning disabled students' conformity to peer pressure. *Journal of Learning Disabilities.*

Bryan, T., Pearl, R., & Herzog, A. (in press). Learning disabled adolescents' vulnerability to crime: Attitudes, anxieties, experiences. *Learning Disabilities Research.*

Bryan, T., Werner, M., & Pearl, R., (1982). Learning disabled students' conformity responses to prosocial and antisocial situations. *Learning Disability Quarterly, 5,* 344–352.

Demorest, A., Meyer, C., Phelps, E., Gardner, H., & Winner, E. (1984). Words speak louder than actions: Understanding deliberately false remarks. *Child Development, 55,* 1527–1534.

Dickstein, E. B., & Warren, D. R. (1980). Role taking deficits in learning disabled children. *Journal of Learning Disabilities, 13,* 378–382.

Donahue, M. (1984). Learning disabled children's conversational competence: an attempt to activate the inactive listener. *Applied Psycholinguistics, 5,* 21–35.

Donahue, M. L. (1986). Linguistic and communication development in learning-disabled children. In S. J. Ceci (Ed.), *Handbook of cognitive, social, and neuropsychological aspects of learning disabilities* (pp. 263–289). Hillsdale, NJ: Lawrence Erlbaum Associates.

Donahue, M., Pearl, R., & Bryan, T. (1983). Communicative competence in learning disabled children. In I. Bialer & K. D. Gadow (Eds.), *Advances in learning and behavioral disabilities Vol. II* (pp. 49–84). Greenwich, CT: JAI Press.

Lang, R. E. (1987). Crime prevention strategies for educable mentally retarded children and youth in unstructured and unsupervised conditions. Unpublished doctoral dissertation, University of Illinois at Chicago.

Maheady, L., & Maitland, G. (1982). Assessing social perception abilities in learning disabled students. *Learning Disability Quarterly, 5,* 363–370.

Murray, C. A. (1976). *The link between learning disabilities and juvenile delinquency:* Current theory and knowledge. Washington, DC: U.S. Government Printing Office.

Pearl, R., Bryan, T., Fallon, P., & Herzog, A. (in press). Learning disabled students' detection of deception. *Learning Disabilities Research.*

Pearl, R., Bryan, T., & Herzog, A. (in preparation). Resisting or acquiescing to peer pressure: Learning disabled and nondisabled adolescents' expectations of probable consequences.

Pearl, R., & Cosden, M. (1982). Sizing up a situation: LD children's understanding of social interactions. *Learning Disability Quarterly, 5,* 371–373.

Perlmutter, B., Crocker, J., Cordray, D., & Garstecki, D. (1983). Sociometric status and related personality characteristics of mainstream learning disabled adolescents. *Learning Disabled Quarterly, 6,* 20–30.

Podboy, J. W., & Mallory, W. A. (1978). The diagnosis of specific learning disabilities in a delinquent population. *Federal Probation, 42,* 26–33.

Sawicki, D., & Schaeffer, B. (1979). An affirmative approach to the LD/JD link. *Juvenile & Family Court Journal, 30,* 11–16.

Turiel, E. (1983). *The development of social knowledge,* Cambridge, England: Cambridge University Press.

Wong, B. Y., & Wong, R. (1980). Role-taking skills in normal achieving and learning disabled children. *Learning Disability Quarterly, 3,* 11–18.

10 Behavior Problems in Children with Learning Problems

Robert J. Thompson, Jr.
William Kronenberger
Duke University Medical Center

The study of children's behavior problems has been hampered by the absence of a classification system, based on empirically identified clinically and theoretically relevant dimensions of children's behavior, within which research findings could be integrated (Achenbach & Edelbrock, 1978; Thompson, 1986; Thompson, Kronenberger, & Curry, in press). With a satisfactory classification system, questions critical to the development of a behavioral-science knowledge base about children's behavior problems can be addressed. These critical questions include: What types and frequencies of behavior problems are demonstrated by normal children and by subgroups of children with developmental, medical, or learning problems; how do behavior problems in the various subgroups change over time; what is the association between behavior problems in early childhood and later adjustment; when and with what types of behavior problems is intervention necessary and effective? (Thompson, 1986). Moreover, a satisfactory behavior classification system would enable the study of children's behavior problems to proceed to theoretically driven research that seeks to evaluate the transaction of biological and psychosocial processes in the etiology, prevention, and remediation of behavior problems (Thompson, 1985a; 1986; Thompson et al., in press).

During the last decade, progress has been realized along two lines of research in developing empirical approaches to both the measurement and classification of children's behavior problems. One line of research has utilized peer nominations to identify children with specific types of behavior patterns, for example aggressive and withdrawn (Ledingham, 1981), and patterns of social relationships, for example rejected, neglected, popular, and controversial (Coie, Dodge, & Coppotelli, 1982). The social information processing deficits (Dodge, 1985) and the social behavior of children with specific types of behavior patterns (Milich & Landau, 1984) have subsequently been examined. A second line of research has utilized parent and teacher completed checklist ratings of children's behavior (Thompson, 1986) to identify children with behavioral disturbance. Despite the diversity of checklists, methods, and samples, considerable convergence has been found in the dimensions of children's behavior problems (Achenbach & Edelbrock, 1978; Dreger, 1981). Two broad-band syndromes are evident. One pattern is characterized by aggressive, acting-out, conduct disordered, and undercontrolled behaviors and is termed externalizing. Another pattern is characterized by inhibited, shy-anxious, personality disordered and overcontrolled behaviors and is termed internalizing.

Both of these lines of research have been extended to the delineation of behavior problems in children with learning problems and disabilities. Representative of the efforts to examine social relationships of learning disabled children is the work of Tanis Bryan and her colleagues. They have identified that learning disabled children have difficulties in their social relationships with peers and with teachers (see Bryan, 1978). Behavior checklists have also been utilized extensively to assess the frequency and types of behavior problems demonstrated by children with educational problems (see Thompson, 1986). In general, the findings indicate that the factor structure of behavior problems across various subgroups of children with educational problems is very similar to that found in the general population and other clinical subgroups. That is, both internalizing-personality problems and externalizing-conduct problems have been identified. Most studies report that subgroups of children with educational problems have higher levels of behavior problems than normal controls. In addition, research has addressed the question whether there are differences in behavior problems among the subgroups of children requiring special education, such as children with mental retardation, learning disabilities, or emotional problems. The findings have not been consistent regarding types of behavior problems as a function of subgroups of educational problems. However, findings have been consistent in demonstrating higher levels of behavior problems among children with emotional problems than among those with primary learning problems such as mental retardation or learning disabilities. In turn, children with primary learning problems have been found to demonstrate higher levels of behavior problems than normal controls but differences between the learning disabled and mentally retarded subgroups have been inconsistently reported (Thompson, 1986; Thompson, Lampron, Johnson, & Eckstein, in press).

DUKE RESEARCH SERIES

Because of a particular interest in how biological and psychosocial processes act together in development, we have embedded our study of children's behavior problems in the context of chronic developmental and medical problems. Chronic developmental or medical problems are viewed as potential stressors than can tax the adaptive resources of the child and family and with which there is an increased risk of psychosocial maladjustment (Thompson, 1985a). However, some children and their parents cope effectively with the stresses associated with their disorders. With this underlining conceptualization, the research program at Duke University Medical Center has several interrelated goals. One goal is to contribute to the efforts to derive standardized, objective, and reliable methods for empirically delineating theoretically and clinically relevant dimensions of children's behavior problems that would form the bases for a behavior classification system. A second goal is to delineate the types and frequencies of behavior problems in children with chronic developmental and medical problems. Goal three is to delineate the role of cognitive processes, social support in terms of family functioning, and coping processes in mediating the stresses associated with developmental and medical problems and psychosocial adjustment.

We have utilized the Missouri Children's Behavior Checklist (MCBC) (Sines, Pauker, Sines, & Owen, 1969) to assess children's behavior problems. The MCBC consists of 77 items that describe the behavior of children and that form 7 scales: Aggression, Inhibition, Activity Level, Sleep Disturbance, Somatization, Sociability, and Depression. Parents indicate (yes/no) for each item whether their child demonstrated that behavior during the previous 6 months. Through a series of studies beginning in 1973 the clinical utility of the MCBC has been demonstrated (Thompson, 1986). The MCBC has differentiated among children with developmental, psychiatric, and medical problems and nonreferred controls (Sines et al., 1969; Thompson & McAdoo, 1973; Thompson, Curry, & Yancy, 1979; Curry & Thompson, 1979, 1982, 1985; Thompson & Curry, 1983, 1985; Thompson, 1985b; Thompson et al., in press) and among preschoolers with, at risk for, and not at risk for developmental disabilities (Thompson, Curry, Sturner, Green, & Funk, 1982).

Recently, a new behavior classification system was devised using the MCBC (Thompson et al., in press). MCBC standard scores (Sines, 1986) were factor analyzed yielding three factors: Internalizing, Externalizing, and Sociable. These three factors form a multidimensional classification matrix. Hierarchical cluster analyses of these three factor scores yielded four behavior problem patterns: Internal Profile, External Profile, Mixed Internal and External Profile, and Undifferentiated Disturbance (not an empirically derived profile but a residual reflecting undifferentiated behavioral disturbance). Three behavior problem free patterns also emerged: Low Social Skills Profile, Problem Free Profile, and Sociable Profile. This new behavior classification system revealed different frequencies of behavior patterns among children with developmental, psychiatric, and medical problems and nonreferred controls (Thompson et al., in press). We currently are in the process of generating validity information regarding this new behavior classification system.

Developmental Evaluation Center

The contributions of our work to the emerging behavior science knowledge base regarding behavior problems in children with learning problems stems from the inclusion of these children within the population of children with developmental disabilities seen through the Developmental Evaluation Center (DEC) of Duke University Medical Center. The DEC was an outpatient clinic of the Department of Pediatrics supported by a contract from the Department of Human Resources of the state of North Carolina. Patients to 21 years-of-age with problems in more than one dimension of functioning, such as speech, neuromotor, or cognitive, that necessitated an interdisciplinary evaluation were eligible for services. The interdisciplinary team, consisting of representatives from the disciplines of pediatrics, psychology, speech pathology, special education, physical therapy, and social work, and the interdisciplinary process have been described in detail elsewhere (Thompson & O'Quinn, 1979). A problem-oriented approach to patient management and record keeping was utilized.

At intake, a developmental history and a preliminary assessment of the child's cognitive and academic functioning was obtained. This initial data base was supplemented with reports from the school and health care providers and was presented at an initial staff meeting at which it was the team's responsibility to identify problems and ascertain what additional evaluations were needed. Any functional deficit or complaint that required management or diagnostic workup, varying in degree of abstraction or specificity from symptom to specific diagnoses, was listed as a problem. Upon completion of all evaluations, the findings from the specific disciplinary evaluations were discussed at a second staff meeting at which the team arrived at a formulation, treatment plan, and recommendations.

After several years of functioning with this interdisciplinary model, a report was made (Thompson, 1982) of the multidimensional problems and findings in a sample of 301 patients seen at the DEC. The sample consisted of 69.4% males and 30.6% females, 64.1% Whites, 35.2% Blacks, and 0.7% of other races. Age ranged from 8 months to 17 years with 2% less than 2-years-of-age, 18.6% between 2- and 5-years-of-age, 47.5% between 5- and 9-years-of-age, 25.9% between 9- and 13-years-of-age, and 6% age 13 years or older. The Hollingshead Two Factor Index of Social Position (Hollingshead & Redlich, 1958) was obtainable on 277 of the 301 patients. There were 30.6% in classes I–III (high social economic status) and 69.4% in classes IV–V.

The most frequent presenting problems included poor school performance (57.8%), speech and language difficulties (51.8%), and behavioral management problems (25.9%).

Findings were recorded and reported in terms of dimensions of functioning such as cognitive, neuromotor, speech and language, and affective/behavioral. Notable among the findings was that mental retardation and borderline intellectual functioning occurred in 21.9% and 24.9% percent of the cases respectively.

Consequently, more than half of the children (53.2%) were functioning in the average or above average range of intelligence. An array of affective and behavioral problems in descriptive or functional terms as well as traditional mental health diagnoses were listed as findings in 82.1% of the cases. Educational recommendations were made in 85% of the cases and recommendations for counseling or therapy were made in 59.1% of the cases.

The remainder of this chapter focuses on three studies that have utilized the DEC to address questions regarding behavior problems in children with learning problems. The first study is a reanalysis, using the new MCBC behavioral classification system, of a previously reported study (Thompson et al., 1982) of children at risk for developmental and learning problems. The other two studies involve the subgroup of children referred to the DEC with the presenting problem of poor school performance. One of these studies involves a secondary analysis of the DEC data base described earlier. The other is a synopsis of a prospective study which is currently in press (Thompson et al., in press).

Preschool Children's Behavior Problems as a Function of Risk Status for Developmental and Learning Problems

The first study (Thompson et al., 1982) addressed two questions. First, do preschool children found to be at risk or not at risk for developmental and learning problems demonstrate different frequencies and/or types of behavior patterns? Second, do the frequency and/or types of behavior patterns demonstrated by at risk and nonrisk preschool children differ from that demonstrated by preschool children who had been referred to the DEC for evaluation of suspected developmental disabilities?

The subjects consisted of 105 children who were participants in a prekindergarten health screening program in a rural county in North Carolina. The children had completed the McCarthy Scales of Children's Abilities (McCarthy, 1972), and the MCBC had been completed by their parents at the time of the screening. This sample was divided into two groups based on their performance on the McCarthy Scales. Those obtaining a general cognitive index (GCI) more than one standard deviation below the mean (GCI < 84) were characterized as at risk. Those with a GCI ≥ 84 were characterized as nonrisk. There were 42 children at risk (28 males, 14 females; 18 Whites, 24 Blacks). There were 63 nonrisk children (33 males, 30 females; 44 Whites, 19 Blacks). The comparison sample of developmentally disabled preschool children were obtained from the previously described DEC data base. There were 20 children (14 males, 6 females; 11 Whites, 9 Blacks) who fell between the ages of 54 and 68 months, who comprised the developmentally disabled comparison group for the current study. The DEC sample did not differ significantly from the screening sample in regard to sex, race, or SES.

The means and standard deviations in terms of MCBC T scores for the 6 scales (the Depression scale had not been developed at the time of this study) and for the three factor scores (Sociability is both a scale score and a factor score) are presented in Table 10.1. An overall multivariate analysis of variance revealed significant group differences across the MCBC measures ($p < .0001$). Subsequently, univariate analysis of variance was conducted with each of the MCBC scale and factor scores. The probability levels associated with univariate F statistics are depicted in Table 10.1. Subsequently, comparisons of group means were conducted using the Duncan Multiple Range Test. The results indicate that significant differences among groups were obtained on the Aggression, Inhibition, and Activity Level scales and on the Internalizing and Externalizing factors. In each situation the highest level of behavioral problem was demonstrated by the children with developmental disabilities, followed by the at risk group and then the nonrisk group.

The percentage occurrence of MCBC behavior patterns is depicted in Table 10.2. It can be seen that 36% of the nonrisk group demonstrated a behavior problem pattern compared to 52% of the at risk group and 80% of the developmentally disabled group. The most frequent type of behavior problem in each group was Undifferentiated Disturbance which typically reflects mild elevation into the clinical range on one MCBC scale. Also notable was the relatively even distribution of Internal, External, and Mixed Internal and External behavior problem profiles in the nonrisk and at risk groups but the low frequency of the External profile in the DEC group. In addition to behavior problem patterns, 2% of the nonrisk group, 12% of the at risk group, and 5% of the developmentally disabled group demonstrated a Low Social Skills Profile. Thus, a problem pattern (Behavior Problem or Low Social Skills Profile) was demonstrated by 38% of the nonrisk group, 64% of the at risk group, and 85% of the DEC group. In contrast, 62% of the nonrisk group demonstrated either a Problem Free or a Sociable Profile compared to 36% of the at risk group and only 15% of the developmentally disabled group. The frequencies of those with or without a problem pattern varied significantly ($\chi^2 = 15.96$, df $= 2$, $p < .0001$) across the three groups.

These findings indicate that preschool children who were demonstrating the potential for developmental and learning difficulties were also demonstrating the potential for behavior problems. Since these children had not yet been exposed to school demands and expectations, the behavior problems could not have been in reaction to poor school functioning. Also of interest was the distribution of types of problem patterns within these preschool groups. Although undifferentiated disturbance was the most frequent pattern in the nonrisk group and there was a relatively even distribution across types of problem patterns within the at risk groups, there was a relatively low frequency of the External Profile in the developmentally disabled group. The low frequency of externalizing behavior problems and the relative preponderance of internalizing behavior problems has been a characteristic finding in our work with school aged children with chronic

TABLE 10.1
Means ($\overline{X}$) and Standard Deviations (SD) of MCBC Scale and Factor
Scores for Preschool Sample

| | | Subgroup | | | |
		Non Risk	At Risk	DEC	F
MCBC Scale/Factor		N = 63	N = 42	N = 20	
Aggression	$\overline{X}$	47.44[b]	49.62[b]	56.30[a]	6.03**
	SD	8.25	10.76	12.74	
Inhibition	$\overline{X}$	50.11[b]	54.02[b]	62.70[a]	16.13***
	SD	7.46	9.80	9.72	
Activity Level	$\overline{X}$	52.70[c]	57.74[b]	62.70[a]	6.86**
	SD	10.21	12.16	11.90	
Sleep Disturbance	$\overline{X}$	52.00	53.79	53.60	.38
	SD	10.83	12.23	9.39	
Somatization	$\overline{X}$	48.10	49.36	50.05	.49
	SD	6.83	11.05	9.14	
Sociability	$\overline{X}$	55.03	51.19	51.90	2.61
	SD	8.31	9.17	10.17	
Internalizing	$\overline{X}$	98.21[b]	103.38[b]	112.75[a]	9.70**
	SD	10.12	16.38	13.26	
Externalizing	$\overline{X}$	152.14[b]	161.14[a,b]	172.60[a]	5.21**
	SD	26.29	27.64	25.02	

Note. Subscales scores are T-scores. Factor scores are sums of subscales
T-scores. Means with different superscripts differ significantly. DEC =
Developmentally Disabled.

**$p < .01$.
***$p < .001$.

TABLE 10.2
Percentage of Occurrence of MCBC Behavior Profiles in Preschool Sample

| | Subgroup | | |
	Non Risk	At Risk	DEC
MCBC Behavior Profiles	N = 63	N = 42	N = 20
Behavior Problems	[36]	[52]	[80]
Internal Profile	5	12	20
External Profile	5	12	5
Mixed Internal and External Profile	6	10	25
Undifferentiated Disturbance	21	19	30
Low Social Skills Profile	2	12	5
Problem Free Profile	30	26	5
Sociable Profile	32	10	10

Note. Numbers may add to more than 100 due to rounding error.
DEC = Developmentally Disabled. Data in brackets [ ] indicate
the total percentage of Behavior Problem Profiles.

developmental and medical problems (Thompson et al., in press). The next step requires theoretically driven research to explicate the biopsychosocial processes involved in these findings.

Behavior Problems in Children Presenting With Poor School Performance

Poor school performance is one of the most frequent presenting problems prompting referral of children for psychoeducational assessment. Poor school performance occurred in 57.8% of the 301 children in our DEC data base, and was the most frequent presenting problem (Thompson, 1982). Diagnostically, the task is to delineate the biopsychosocial contributions to the child's poor school performance. However, reliance upon categorical models that view poor school performance as either a learning disability or as an emotional or behavioral problem has obscured the interaction of cognitive, motivational, and emotional/behavioral dimensions of functioning (Thompson, 1986). Recently, research questions have begun to address the association of poor school performance in general, and learning disabilities in particular, with emotional and behavioral problems (Thompson et al., in press).

We addressed two research questions in two separate studies. First, what are the frequencies and types of behavior problems demonstrated by children with poor school performance? Second, do subgroups of children with poor school performance differ in the frequency and/or types of behavior problems demonstrated?

One study consisted of drawing from the previously described DEC data base a subsample of school age children who presented with poor school performance. The MCBC data were reanalyzed using the new MCBC Behavior Classification system. Another study consisted of a 2-year prospective investigation of children presenting with poor school performance (Thompson et al., in press).

DEC Data Base Study

In the study utilizing the DEC data base, a subsample was drawn from the 301 children of all those with a presenting problem of poor school performance who were between the ages of 6½ and 15½ years. The subsample consisted of 126 children: 69% males, 31% females, 71% White, 29% Black.

Based on intellectual and achievement test scores four subgroups were formed initially. The mentally retarded subgroup (MR) consisted of 8 children with intelligence scores (Full Scale IQ score on the WISC-R or Stanford-Binet IQ score) $\leq$ 69 ($\bar{X}$ IQ = 60.5; range = 55–67). The borderline mentally retarded subgroup (BMR) consisted of 44 children with IQ scores $\geq$ 70 and $\leq$ 84 ($\bar{X}$ IQ = 77.2; range = 70–84). The learning disabled subgroup (LD) consisted of 47 children with IQ > 84 ($\bar{X}$ IQ = 92.1; range = 85–112) and achievement test scores less than the 20th percentile in one or more areas (as assessed by the Woodcock–Johnson Psycho-Educational Battery test of Achievement or the PIAT). A Residual subgroup of 27 children remained in which poor school performance occurred in the absence of cognitive deficits or learning disability ($\bar{X}$ IQ = 102.6; range = 85–139). Because of the small number of children in the mentally retarded subgroup, this subgroup was combined with the borderline mentally retarded subgroup for subsequent analyses (MR–BMR). Thus, these subgroups were operationally defined psychometrically and do not represent clinical diagnoses.

The three subgroups differed significantly on mean age with the LD subgroup (117.8 mos) being about 1 year older than the Residual (106.1 mos) and MR–BMR (103.2 mos) subgroups.

Subgroup differences on the MCBC scale and factor scores were analyzed by an overall multivariate analysis of variance ($p < .01$). Subsequently, univariate analyses of variance were conducted with each of the MCBC measures serving as the dependent variable. Table 10.3 depicts the means for the subgroups on the MCBC scale and factor scores and the results of the univariate analyses of variance. It can be seen that only on the Inhibition scale and on the Internalizing factor did significant differences among subgroups emerge. In both situations the mentally retarded and borderline mentally retarded subgroup (MR–BMR) scored significantly higher than the LD group but not significantly higher than the residual group and the residual and LD subgroups did not differ significantly.

Table 10.4 depicts the percentage occurrence of MCBC behavior patterns for the total sample of children with poor school performance and for the three subgroups. It can be seen that 78% of the total sample demonstrated a Behavior Problem Profile and 4% demonstrated a Low Social Skills Profile. A Problem Free Profile or Sociable Profile were demonstrated by 18% of the sample. The highest frequency of behavior problems occurred in the MR–BMR subgroup (85%), followed by the residual subgroup (81%), and the LD subgroup (68%). There is a relatively even distribution of type of behavior problem pattern with the exception of a relatively low frequency of the External Profile. Collapsing the data into problem pattern (Behavior Problem or Low Social Skills Profile) and no problem pattern (Problem Free or Sociable Profile) categories indicated that 82% of the total sample had a problem pattern with no significant difference in this distribution across the MR–BMR (88%), LD (74%), and Residual (82%) subgroups ($\chi^2 = 3.24$, df = 2, NS).

Thus, the findings of this study reveal that children having presented to the DEC with poor school performance had a relatively high frequency of problem profiles (82%) with 78% being classified as a behavior problem and 5% as having low social skills. While the frequency of problem behaviors in the total sample was high, there were no significant differences in frequencies of problem patterns across the three subgroups of children with poor school performance. The only significant difference among subgroups occurred with the Inhibition

TABLE 10.3

Means (X̄) and Standard Deviations (SD) of MCBC Scale and Factor Scores for DEC Poor School Performance Sample

		Subgroup			
MCBC Scale/Factor	Total Group N = 126	MR-BMR N = 52	LD N = 47	Residual N = 27	F
Aggression X̄	52.1	50.2	53.4	53.2	1.11
SD	11.7	10.6	12.1	12.7	
Inhibition X̄	58.1	61.2[a]	55.0[b]	57.5[a,b]	3.78*
SD	11.5	11.3	10.8	11.9	
Activity Level X̄	61.1	63.0	60.8	57.9	2.23
SD	10.3	9.5	11.5	9.8	
Sleep Disturbance X̄	54.9	53.7	54.6	57.9	1.12
SD	11.9	12.7	11.3	11.4	
Somatiza- tion X̄	55.3	57.7	54.0	53.2	1.69
SD	12.2	13.6	11.5	9.9	
Sociabil- ity X̄	50.7	50.5	50.2	51.9	.27
SD	9.9	10.5	9.9	8.8	
Internaliz- ing X̄	113.4	118.8[a]	109.0[b]	110.7[a,b]	3.60*
SD	19.6	20.1	19.4	17.3	
Externaliz- ing X̄	168.1	167.0	168.8	169.0	.09
SD	25.2	26.0	26.5	22.3	

Note. Subscale scores are T-scores. Factor scores are sums of subscale T-scores. Means with different superscripts differ significantly. MR-MBR = Mentally Retarded or Borderline Mentally Retarded; LD = Learning Disabled.

*p < .05.

TABLE 10.4
Percentage Occurrence of MCBC Behavior Profiles in DEC Poor School
Performance Sample

| MCBC Scale/Factor | Total Group | Subgroup | | |
		MR-BMR	LD	Residual
	N = 126	N = 52	N = 47	N = 27
Behavior Problems	[78]	[85]	[68]	[82]
Internal Profile	23	25	19	26
External Profile	10	6	13	15
Mixed Internal and External Profile	20	25	19	11
Undifferentiated Disturbance	25	29	17	30
Low Social Skills Profile	4	4	6	0
Problem Free Profile	11	6	17	11
Sociable Profile	7	6	9	7

Note. MR-BMR = Mentally Retarded or Borderline Mentally Retarded; LD =
Learning Disabled. Numbers may add to more than 100 due to rounding. Data
in brackets [ ] indicate the total percentage of Behavior Problem Profiles.

scale and the Internalizing factor. In both situations, the MR-BMR subgroup was significantly higher on these dimensions than the LD subgroup. The association of cognitive deficits with internalizing behavior problems is increasingly being noted in the literature (see Thompson et al., in press).

Prospective Study With Multiple Measures of Behavioral Disturbance

With the advances in the development of empirical measures of children's behavior problems, it has been recognized that checklists may be limited in reflecting affective problems, such as depression (Breslau, 1985; Thompson & Curry, 1985). Structured clinical interviews may be more effective for assessing this dimension of functioning (Breslau, 1985). Furthermore, findings from the studies that have addressed the agreement among alternative measurement strategies (Kazdin & Heidish, 1984; Steinhausen & Gobel, 1987) indicate the necessity for including multiple measures for the adequate assessment of children's behavioral disturbance.

In addition to multiple measures of behavioral disturbance, the study of children's behavior problems needs to proceed to theoretically driven research that addressed the transactions of biopsychosocial processes in the etiology, prevention, and remediation of behavior problems (Thompson, 1986; Thompson et al., in press). Our research program has moved to addressing the role of mediating processes associated with vulnerability and resiliency in the face of adversity or stress associated with chronic developmental and medical problems (Thompson,

1985a). More specifically, evidence suggests that perceived competency, in terms of self efficacy (Bandura, 1977) and self-esteem (Rutter, 1987a, 1987b), and social support, in terms of family functioning (Daniels, Moos, Billings, & Miller, 1987), are protective processes that reduce the impact of risk or stress situations (Thompson et al., in press).

With these considerations in mind, a prospective study was conducted for 2 years through the DEC (Thompson et al., in press). In addition to addressing the two previously articulated questions regarding the frequency and types of behavior problems demonstrated by children with poor school performance and among subgroups of children with poor school performance, a third question was addressed: Do family functioning and the child's perceived competency serve as mediational processes in the relationship between the stress of poor school performance and behavior problems?

During the study, in addition to the regular interdisciplinary evaluations, a research protocol was established for all school aged children with a presenting problem of poor school performance. Each child completed the Wechsler Intelligence Scale for Children–Revised (Wechsler, 1981), the Test of Achievement of the Woodcock–Johnson Psycho-Educational Battery (Woodcock, 1977), and the Perceived Competency Scale for Children (Harter, 1982). The parent, typically mother, completed the Family Environment Scale (Moos & Moos, 1981), the MCBC, and the Child Behavior Checklist (CBCL) (Achenbach & Edelbrock, 1983).

There were 79 children studied under this protocol, 70% males, 30% females, 61% White, 35% Black and 3% for whom race was not recorded. Age ranged from 6 years, 11 mos to 15 years, 1 mos with a mean of 10 years, 2 mos. Forty-seven percent of the children fell within SES levels (Hollingshead & Redlich, 1958) I–III and 53% within levels IV–V.

This sample of children with poor school performance was subsequently divided into subgroups. First, a learning disabled (LD) subgroup was derived. In doing so, it was necessary to confront the lack of conceptual and measurement consensus that has characterized the field of learning disabilities (e.g., see Keogh, Major, Omori, Gandara, & Reid, 1980; Schere, Richardson, & Bialer, 1980). We adopted Keogh's (Keogh et al., 1980) recommendation that "investigators provide enough information on common sampling variables to allow other researchers to determine equivalence" (p. 30). Our operational definition of learning disability was based on the conceptualization of average or above average intellectual functioning with a substantial deficit in academic functioning. In addition to poor school performance, two other criteria were established in the research protocol. First, the child had average intelligence as defined by WISC-R Verbal, Performance, or Full Scale IQ $\geq$ 85. Second, there was a substantial deficit in academic achievement as defined by either the Reading, Math, Written Language, or Knowledge cluster score on the Woodcock-Johnson Psycho-Educational Battery $\leq$ 20th percentile for age. There were 34 children (43%) who met this operational definition of learning disabled (LD).

Subsequently, the 45 children who were not classified as learning disabled were divided into subgroups on the basis of intellectual functioning. The Mental Retardation subgroup (MR) included those with a Full Scale IQ < 70 (n = 14; 18%). Thus, the MR subgroup was operationalized psychometrically and does not reflect a clinical diagnosis which must also be based on consideration of adaptive behavior. The Borderline mental retardation subgroup (BMR) included those with a Full Scale IQ of ≥ 70 ≤ 84 (n = 14; 18%). A Residual subgroup was comprised of those who were not LD, MR, or BMR (n = 17; 22%).

A key aspect of this prospective study was the use of three measures of children's behavior problems: two mother completed checklists, MCBC and CBCL; and DSM-III Axis I diagnoses, which were a product of the inter-disciplinary staffing of each patient. With the CBCL, Internalizing, Externalizing, and Total Behavior Problem scores were obtained. A Total Behavior Problem cutoff score equivalent to the 90th percentile was used to identify children with behavior problems in the clinical range. The MCBC and CBCL were combined into one checklist for ease in administration.

In terms of behavior problems as assessed by the MCBC, Table 10.5 depicts the means and standard deviations of MCBC scale and factor scores. Analyses of variance revealed that the four subgroups differed significantly only on the Somatization scale and on the Internalizing factor. In both situations, the MR subgroup had a significantly higher mean score than the other subgroups which

TABLE 10.5
Means ($\overline{X}$) and Standard Deviations (SD) of MCBC Scale and Factor Scores for Prospective Poor School Performance Sample

| MCBC Scale/Factor | | Total Group | Subgroup | | | | F |
			MR	BMR	LD	Residual	
		N = 79	N = 14	N = 14	N = 34	N = 17	
Aggression	$\overline{X}$	54.53	58.07	54.00	51.88	57.35	1.16
	SD	12.64	13.10	14.08	10.74	14.36	
Inhibition	$\overline{X}$	67.28	73.00	67.07	67.35	62.59	2.34
		11.17	12.69	11.84	10.25	9.77	
Activity Level	$\overline{X}$	66.76	69.07	62.93	66.29	68.94	1.02
	SD	10.98	12.93	12.51	10.99	7.26	
Sleep Disturbance	$\overline{X}$	57.85	60.14	57.64	57.15	57.53	0.13
	SD	15.32	14.43	15.68	16.89	13.44	
Somatization	$\overline{X}$	57.91	67.78[a]	56.07[b]	54.41[b]	58.29[b]	4.15**
	SD	12.85	12.53	10.62	13.55	9.59	
Sociability	$\overline{X}$	53.77	51.71	49.36	55.50	55.65	1.38
	SD	11.00	13.39	10.70	10.77	0.03	
Internalizing	$\overline{X}$	125.19	140.79[a]	123.14[b]	21.76[b]	120.88[b]	4.09**
	SD	19.52	17.61	19.36	19.25	16.63	
Externalizing	$\overline{X}$	179.14	187.29	174.57	175.32	183.82	0.74
	SD	30.44	33.05	36.01	27.83	29.10	

Note. Subscales scores are T-scores. Factor scores are sums of subscale scores. $\overline{MR}$ = Mentally Retarded; BMR = Borderline Mentally Retarded; LD = Learning Disabled. Means with different superscripts differ significantly.

**$p < .01$.

did not differ significantly among themselves. Table 10.6 depicts the percentage occurrence of MCBC behavior patterns for the total group and subgroups. Of the total group, 91% demonstrated a behavior problem with the Mixed Internal and External Profile (43%) and the Internal Profile (27%) the most frequently demonstrated profiles. There was a low percentage of the Problem Free Profile (5%) and of the Sociable Profile (2%). There was no significant difference in the distribution of those with (Behavior Problem or Low Social Skills Profiles) and without (Problem Free or Sociable Profiles) MCBC problem patterns across the four subgroups ($\chi^2 = 2.19$, df = 3, $p < .53$).

In terms of behavior problems as assessed by the CBCL, Table 10.7 depicts the means and standard deviations and the analyses of variance results. The four subgroups differed significantly only on the Internalizing score. The Borderline, Residual, and LD subgroups did not differ significantly among themselves, but the MR subgroup was significantly higher than the Residual and LD subgroups. On the basis of CBCL Total Behavior Problem Score, 39% of the total group were classified as having a behavior problem. Classification as a behavior problem differed significantly across the four subgroups ($\chi^2 = 17.79$, df = 3, $p < .001$) with the MR subgroup having an 86% occurrence, the Residual subgroup 35%, the Borderline subgroup 29%, and the LD subgroup 26%.

In terms of behavior problems by DSM–III axis I diagnoses, 71% of the total group had a diagnosis. An affective disorder was the most frequent and occurred in 40% of the total group. There was no significant difference in distribution of those with and without DSM-III diagnoses across the four subgroups ($\chi^2 = 0.56$, df = 3, $p < .91$).

Across the three measures, only three children (4%) were identified as not having a behavior problem. There were 60 children (76%) identified as having a behavior problem by two or three of the measures, and 24 children (30%) were identified by all three measures as having a behavior problem. It is notable that 100% of the MR subgroup were identified as having a behavior problem by two of the three measures.

The high frequency of behavior disturbance in these children presenting with poor school performance, and the corresponding low frequency of children without a problem pattern, hampered the effort to investigate the relationship of mediating processes and behavior problems. Those with a problem pattern on the MCBC, in comparison to those without a problem pattern, had significantly lower (t test) mean scores on the Self Worth dimension of the Perceived Competency Scale ($p < .004$) and on the Supportiveness factor ($p < .02$) of the Family Environment Scale and a significantly higher mean score on the Controlling factor ($p < .03$). The Supportiveness factor reflects degree of mutual commitment and support for expression of feelings and for active participation in social and recreational activities. The Controlling factor reflects an emphasis upon control, ethical and religious values, achievement orientation and a lack of independence. In terms of the DSM-III Axis I diagnoses, there were no signifi-

TABLE 10.6

Percentage of Occurrence of MCBC Behavior Profiles in Prospective Poor School Performance Sample

MCBC Behavior Profile	Total Group	Subgroups			
		MR	BMR	LD	Residual
	N = 79	N = 14	N = 14	N = 34	N = 17
Behavior Problems	[91]	[100]	[93]	[88]	[94]
Internal Profile	27	36	50	15	24
External Profile	5	0	7	3	12
Mixed Internal and External Profile	43	64	14	47	41
Undifferentiated Disturbance	16	0	14	24	18
Low Social Skills Profile	1	0	0	3	0
Problem Free Profile	5	0	7	9	0
Sociable Profile	2	0	7	0	6

Note. MR = Mentally Retarded; BMR = Borderline Mentally Retarded; LD = Learning Disabled. Data in brackets [ ] indicate the total percentage of Behavior Problem Profiles.

TABLE 10.7
Means ($\overline{X}$) and Standard Deviations (SD) of CBCL Scores for Prospective Poor School Performance Sample

CBCL T-Score		Total Group	Subgroups				F
			MR	BMR	LD	Residual	
Internalizing	$\overline{X}$	63.61	70.07[a]	64.93[a,b]	60.85[b]	62.71[b]	3.99**
	SD	9.06	9.18	7.25	9.31	7.42	
Externalizing	$\overline{X}$	64.04	68.07	62.29	63.00	64.24	1.50
	SD	8.36	7.13	6.26	9.41	8.13	
Total Behavior	$\overline{X}$	60.28	63.57	60.21	58.44	61.29	1.88
	SD	7.21	5.87	5.56	6.99	9.06	

Note. MR = Mentally retarded; BMR = Borderline Mentally Retarded; LD = Learning Disabled. Means with different superscrips differ significantly.
**$p<.01$.

cant differences between those with and without a diagnosis on any of the mediating variables. In terms of the CBCL only one significant difference occurred with those with a behavior problem having a higher mean on the Cognitive dimensions (perceived school competency) of the Perceived Competency Scale than those without a behavior problem ($p < .03$).

The correlation coefficients between the hypothesized mediating variables and the CBCL and MCBC measures were small and for the most part statistically insignificant, with several exceptions. The Social dimension of the Perceived Competency Scale was significantly ($p < .05$) negatively correlated with the CBCL Internalizing score ($-.24$) and the Self Worth dimension was significantly ($p < .05$) negatively correlated with the Externalizing dimensions of both the MCBC ($-.24$) and CBCL ($-.27$). In terms of the Family Environment Scale, the Family Relationship Index (a composite measure of the degree that the family is characterized by cohesion, expressiveness, and conflict) was significantly ($p < .05$) negatively correlated with the Internalizing dimensions of the MCBC ($-.28$) and CBCL ($-.26$) and the Controlling factor was significantly positively correlated with the Internalizing dimensions of the MCBC ($.26, p < .05$) and CBCL ($.35, p < .003$). The Supportiveness factor was also significantly ($p < .05$) negatively correlated with the CBCL Internalizing score ($-.26$).

The findings in this 2-year prospective study indicate that children with poor school performance had a very high frequency of behavioral disturbance, but for the most part, the frequency and types of behavioral disturbance did not differ significantly across the four subgroups. The few significant differences that did occur were attributable to the MR subgroup, in terms of frequency of behavioral disturbance and a specifically higher frequency of Internalizing problems. These findings are consistent with the accumulating evidence of the high rate of behavior problems in children with central nervous system impairment (e.g., Connell & McConnel, 1981; Rutter, 1981) and of the specific association of internalizing behavior problems with developmental and physical disabilities involving the central nervous system (Breslau, 1985; Thompson, 1985b). The high frequency of behavioral disturbance is particularly impressive. Of the total group, 91% had an MCBC behavior problem pattern and 1% had a low social skills profile yielding 92% with a behavioral disturbance. DSM-III Axis I diagnoses were found with 71% of the children and 39% had a CBCL behavior problem score in the clinical range. These findings are similar to those of the previous study in showing a high frequency of MCBC behavioral disturbance, few significant differences across subgroups, and a particular association of cognitive impairment with internalizing problems.

While preliminary, the pattern of findings regarding the role of the hypothesized mediating processes are of interest. Those with an MCBC problem pattern in contrast to those without were lower in perception of their self worth and their family functioning was characterized as less supportive and more controlling. These findings encourage further exploration of the role of these mediational processes in psychosocial adjustment.

CONCLUSION

The findings from this series of three studies indicate that:

1. nonreferred preschool children found to be at risk for developmental and learning problems are also at risk for behavioral disturbance;

2. children referred to a developmental disabilities clinic with a presenting problem of poor school performance have a very high frequency occurrence of behavior problem patterns, particularly internalizing, mixed internalizing and externalizing, and affective disorder;

3. there are few significant differences in frequency and types of behavior problems across learning disabled, mentally retarded-borderline, and nonlearning disabled nor cognitively impaired subgroups of children with poor school performance;

4. children's perceived competency and social support in terms of family functioning are dimensions that may have a role mediating between the stresses associated with chronic developmental and learning problems and psychosocial adjustment.

The findings regarding behavioral disturbance in children with poor school performance supports the movement away from categorical models that view poor school performance as either a learning or a behavioral problem (Thompson et al., in press). Interactional models rather than main effect models are now necessary. The need for early intervention to prevent poor school performance, in terms of cognitive enhancement programs, has been clearly recognized for some time. However, research studies now need to focus upon delineating the biopsychosocial processes that mediate learning and behavior problems so that early intervention efforts can also be guided to foster behavioral adjustment in the face of the stress of learning problems. That is, intervention programs also need to be interactive and to focus on fostering both cognitive and behavioral development.

REFERENCES

Achenbach, T. M., & Edelbrock, C. S. (1978). The classification of child psychopathology: a review and analysis of empirical effects. *Psychological Bulletin, 85,* 1275–1301.

Achenbach, T. M., & Edelbrock, C. S. (1983). *Manual for the Child Behavior Checklist and Revised Child Behavior Profile.* Burlington: University of Vermont.

Bandura, A. (1977). Self-efficacy: Toward a unifying theory of behavioral change. *Psychological Review, 84,* 191–215.

Breslau, N. (1985). Psychiatric disorder in children with physical disabilities. *Journal of the American Academy of Child Psychiatry, 24,* 87–94.

Bryan, T. H. (1978). Social relationships and verbal interactions of learning disabled children. *Journal of Learning Disabilities, 11,* 107–115.

Coie, J. D., Dodge, K. A., & Coppotelli, H. (1982). Dimensions and types of social status: A cross-age perspective. *Developmental Psychology, 18,* 557–570.

Connell, H. M., & McConnel, T. S. (1981). Psychiatric sequelae in children treated operatively for hydrocephalus in infancy. *Developmental Medicine and Child Neurology, 23,* 505–517.

Curry, J. F., & Thompson, R. J., Jr. (1979). The utility of behavior checklist ratings in differentiating developmentally disabled from psychiatrically referred children. *Journal of Pediatric Psychology, 4,* 345–352.

Curry, J. F., & Thompson, R. J., Jr. (1982). Patterns of behavioral disturbance in developmentally disabled children: A replicated cluster analysis. *Journal of Pediatric Psychology, 7,* 61–73.

Curry, J. F., & Thompson, R. J., Jr. (1985). Patterns of behavioral disturbance in developmentally disabled and psychiatrically referred children: a cluster analytic approach. *Journal of Pediatric Psychology, 10,* 151–161.

Daniels, D., Moos, R. H., Billings, A. G.,, & Miller, J. J., III (1987). Psychosocial risk and resistance factors among children with chronic illness, health, siblings, and healthy controls. *Journal of Abnormal Child Psychology, 15,* 295–308.

Dodge, K. A. (1985). Attributional bias in aggressive children. In P. Kendall (Ed.), *Advances in cognitive-behavioral research and therapy* (Vol. 4). New York: Academic Press.

Dreger, R. M. (1981). First, second, and third-order factors from the children's behavioral classification project instrument and an attempt at rapprochement. *Journal of Abnormal Psychology, 90,* 242–260.

Harter, S. (1982). The Perceived Competency Scale for Children. *Child Development, 53,* 87–97.

Hollingshead, A. B., & Redlich, F. C. (1958). *Social class and mental illness.* New York: Wiley.

Kazdin, A. E., & Heidish, I. E. (1984). Convergence of clinically derived diagnoses and parent checklists among inpatient children. *Journal of Abnormal Child Psychology, 12,* 421–436.

Keogh, B. K., Major, S. M., Omori, H., Gandara, R., & Reid, H. P. (1980). Proposed markers in learning disabilities research. *Journal of Abnormal Child Psychology, 8,* 21–31.

Ledingham, J. E. (1981). Developmental patterns of aggressive and withdrawn behavior in childhood: A possible method for identifying preschizophrenics. *Journal of Abnormal Child Psychology, 9,* 1–22.

McCarthy, D. (1972). *A manual for the McCarthy Scales of Children's Abilities.* New York: Psychological Corporation.

Milich, R., & Landau, S. (1984). A comparison of the social status and social behavior of aggressive and aggressive/withdrawn boys. *Journal of Abnormal Child Psychology, 12,* 277–288.

Moos, R. H., & Moos, B. S. (1981). *Family Environment Scale Manual.* Palo Alto: Consulting Psychologists Press.

Rutter, M. (1981). Psychological sequelae of brain damage in children. *The American Journal of Psychiatry, 138,* 1533–1544.

Rutter, M. (1987a). Psychosocial resilience and protective mechanisms. *American Journal of Orthopsychiatry, 57,* 316–331.

Rutter, M. (1987b). The role of cognition in child development and disorders. *British Journal of Medical Psychology, 60,* 1–16.

Schere, R. A., Richardson, E., & Bialer, I. (1980). Toward operationalizing a psychoeducational definition of learning disabilities. *Journal of Abnormal Child Psychology, 8,* 5–20.

Sines, J. O. (1986). Normative data for the Revised Missouri Children's Behavior Checklist—Parent Form (MCBC-P). *Journal of Abnormal Child Psychology, 14,* 89–94.

Sines, J. O., Pauker, J. D., Sines, L. K., & Owen, D. R. (1969). Identification of clinically relevant dimensions of children's behavior. *Journal of Consulting and Clinical Psychology, 33,* 728–734.

Steinhausen, H., & Gobel, D. (1987). Convergence of parent checklists and child psychiatric diagnoses. *Journal of Abnormal Child Psychology, 15,* 147–151.

Thompson, R. J. Jr. (1982). Multidimensional problems and findings in developmentally disabled children. *Journal of Developmental and Behavioral Pediatrics, 3,* 153–158.

Thompson, R. J., Jr. (1985a). Coping with the stress of chronic childhood illness. In A. N. O'Quinn (Ed.), *Management of chronic disorders in childhood.* Boston: G. K. Hall.

Thompson, R. J., Jr. (1985b). Delineation of children's behavior problems: a basis for assessment and intervention. *Journal of Developmental and Behavioral Pediatrics, 6,* 37–50.

Thompson, R. J., Jr. (1986). *Behavior problems in children with developmental and learning disabilities.* International Academy for Research in Learning Disabilities, Number 3. Ann Arbor: The University of Michigan Press.

Thompson, R. J., Jr., & Curry, J. F. (1983). A construct validity study of the Missouri Children's Behavior Checklist with developmentally disabled children. *Journal of Clinical Psychology, 39,* 691–695.

Thompson, R. J., Jr., & Curry, J. F. (1985). Missouri Children's Behavior Checklist profiles with developmentally disabled children: construct validity. *Journal of Clinical Psychology, 41,* 556–564.

Thompson, R. J., Jr., Curry, J. F., Sturner, R. A., Green, J. A., & Funk, S. G. (1982). Missouri Children's Behavior Checklist ratings of preschool children as a function of risk status for developmental and learning problems. *Journal of Pediatric Psychology, 7,* 307–316.

Thompson, R. J., Jr., Curry, J. F., & Yancy, W. S. (1979). The utility of parent's behavior checklist ratings with developmentally disabled children. *Journal of Pediatric Psychology, 4,* 19–28.

Thompson, R. J., Jr., Kronenberger, W., & Curry, J. F. (in press). Behavior classification system for children with developmental, psychiatric, and chronic medical problems. *Journal of Pediatric Psychology.*

Thompson, R. J., Jr., Lampron, L. B., Johnson, D. F., & Eckstein, T. L. (in press). Behavior problems in children with the presenting problem of poor school performance. *Journal of Pediatric Psychology.*

Thompson, R. J., Jr., & McAdoo, W. G. (1973). A comparison of mothers' and fathers' behavior checklist ratings of outpatient boys and girls. *Journal of Community Psychology, 1,* 387–389.

Thompson, R. J., Jr., & O'Quinn, A. N. (1979). *Developmental disabilities: etiologies, manifestations, diagnoses, and treatments.* New York: Oxford University Press.

Wechsler, D. (1981). *Manual for the Wechsler Adult Intelligence Scale-Revised.* New York: Psychological Corporation.

Woodcock, R. W. (1977). *Manual for the Woodcock Psychoeducational Battery.* Boston's Teaching Resources Corporation.

11 Social Competence and Learning Disabilities: A Prospective Study

Sharon Vaughn
Anne Hogan
University of Miami

> *"Oh, Diana,"* said Anne at last, clasping her hands and speaking almost in a whisper, *"do you think- oh, do you think you can like me a little-enough to be my bosom friend?"*
> —L. M. Montgomery, *Anne of Green Gables*

OVERVIEW OF SOCIAL COMPETENCE

Having a "bosom friend" is an important part of growth and development, as Anne of Green Gables reminds us. So much so, that the social competence of children has been the topic of increased attention in the behavioral sciences in the last 10 years. This mounting interest in the social behavior and relationships of children has also been reflected in research with learning disabled populations (Vaughn, 1985; Wiener, 1987).

Despite its importance, social competence has remained an elusive construct. In our current work, we have begun to consider social competence as a construct analogous to intelligence in several ways. First, we think of social competence as a higher-order construct made up of many components that can combine for effective behavior. Although we often measure only a subset of these components, it is nevertheless important to think of them as a *part* rather than the whole of our molar notion of social competence.

Using the analogy has also lead us to consider the study of social competence from both the individual difference perspective as well as a developmental one. The current concern with sociometric assessment is an example of the contribution of an individual difference orientation, while the study of children's developing social cognition regarding social relationships and behavior is an example from the developmental or age-normed orientation. Each contribute critical information for our ultimate understanding of social competence, in the same way that psychometric, developmental, and processing approaches assist in our understanding of the development of intelligence.

In our current thinking, social competence is considered to include the following four components:

1. Positive Relations with Others. This component includes general peer status, friendship patterns, family relations, and at later ages, intimate relations. In the study presented in this chapter, we have focused on peer relations.

2. Accurate/Age-Appropriate Social Cognition. This component includes interpersonal problem solving, self-evaluations as well as attributions and judgments about others' feelings, motivation, and behavior. In the study presented in this chapter, the focus is on accurate/age-appropriate social acceptance and academic competence.

3. Absence of Maladaptive Behaviors. This component includes the absence of serious behavior problems and noxious social behavior. In a more positive vein, it also includes the development of self-control. In this study we focus on problem behavior and disruptive conduct, poor attention, and anxiety.

4. Effective Social Behaviors. This component includes the range of specific social skills often targeted for behavioral observation or intervention.

These four components form the core for the higher-order construct, social competence. As with our intelligence analogy, each component has multiple skills associated. No single component in isolation can adequately define the overall competence construct. In fact, individual's competence can be made of unique patterns of strength and weakness across the components. In addition, although the components have some independence, we would expect modest patterns of interrelatedness as well.

In this chapter we briefly review the literature as it pertains to the four components of social competence outlined earlier, specifically as they relate to learning disabled students. Additionally, we report the initial findings from a prospective study examining the social competence of learning disabled students prior to identification. In an attempt to further explain factors related to social competence with learning disabled students, we have begun a longitudinal, prospective study investigating factors related to social competence with learning disabled students.

Social Competence in LD Students: Peer Relations

Repeated studies have found that children with learning disabilities are perceived by peers, teachers, parents, and even strangers as less desirable social partners than their nondisabled classmates. Since Bryan's initial research documenting the low peer acceptance of learning disabled children (Bryan, 1974), the peer relations of learning disabled students have been repeatedly studied (see Pearl, Donahue, & Bryan, 1986; Wiener, 1987 for reviews). Although there are certainly subgroups of LD students who are popular or average in popularity, more LD students are identified as rejected and fewer are identified as popular than their non-LD peers (see Pearl, Donahue, & Bryan, 1986; Wiener, 1987 for reviews). In addition to the overall finding of social competence difficulties, female LD children appear to be at greater risk for rejection and low peer acceptance than are male LD children (Bruck, 1986; Bryan, 1974; LaGreca, Stone, & Halpern 1988; Scranton & Ryckman, 1979). Given the heterogeneity of learning disabled students the persistent finding that LD students as a group are less popular than their nonLD peers requires further explanation.

Why are the peer relations of LD students the focus of such extensive research? The peer relations of children are of concern because they have been associated with later difficulties such as serious adjustment problems later in life, dropping out of school, and criminality (see Parker & Asher, 1987 for a review). The extensive number of studies investigating peer acceptance and its relationship to adjustment (e.g., Cantrell & Prinz, 1985; Hartup, 1983) has made peer acceptance an important research topic with children who are learning disabled. Peer relations are considered the best single early indicator of later social competence.

Self-Acceptance

A review of the literature on the self-perceptions of LD children has yielded inconsistent findings; some have suggested they have lower self-concepts (Battle, 1979; Black, 1974), other studies suggested comparable self-concepts to their nonhandicapped peers (Beck, Roblee, & Hanson, 1981; Silverman & Zigmond, 1983). In an attempt to interpret these conflicting results, Morrison (1985) demonstrated that two factors significantly influence the results of assessing self-perceptions with learning disabled students: type of classroom placement (self contained, resource, or regular classroom), and topic of self-evaluation (academic, social, behavioral, or anxiety). Depending upon the combination of these two factors, LD students self-perceptions are higher, lower, or the same as peers. When achievement is controlled, for example, there were no significant differences on self-perceptions between LD self-contained students, LD resource students, and NLD on the Piers-Harris Children's self-concept scale (Yauman, 1980).

LD students' self-perceptions have appeared to be surprisingly accurate. In general, their self-perceptions of academic ability were significantly lower than their NLD peers (Battle, 1979; Chapman & Boersman, 1980), whereas LD children overall feelings of self-worth are comparable to their peers (Bryan, 1986; Cooley & Ayres, 1988). LD students, unlike their NLD peers, distinguished between their self-perceptions of intellectual ability and academic ability (Renik, 1987). They perceived themselves as being relatively intelligent, yet having difficulty in some academic areas, most often reading and spelling. Bender (1987) determined that there were significant differences between LD and NLD 3rd through 6th graders on only two of the six subtests of the Piers-Harris self-concept scale (Piers, 1984): behavior and intellectual status. There were no differences on the subtests physical appearance, anxiety, popularity, and happiness.

Developmental data has suggested there is a relationship between increased age and the debilitating effects of failure on children's self-perceptions (Nicholls, 1978, 1979). Responses to failure situations appeared to be more devastating as children get older, with younger children (grade 2) more likely to show persistence after failure than older children (grade 6). The implications for LD students would be that their self-perceptions become increasingly more negative as they get older. Initial data, however, has suggested that this may not be the case. A longitudinal study by Kistner and Osborne (1987) indicated that LD students may differ from low achieving students in that they do not become more negative about themselves as they grow older. LD students appeared to be accepting of themselves despite their academic failures. A less optimistic interpretation of the data is that LD children did not value academic performance, thus their low academic ability had little influence on their overall self-worth. While this may produce a positive outcome for self-worth, it may result in LD students having less motivation for and interest in academic tasks. In summary, the self-perceptions of LD children have been remarkably accurate, with low self-perceptions in academic areas and comparable self-perceptions to their peers in areas not related to academic performance.

Behavior Problems

An examination of the behavior problems of 295 LD pupils on the Behavior Problem Checklist (Quay & Peterson, 1975) indicated that while there were no significant differences between LD and NLD on conduct disorders, LD students demonstrated greater maladjustment on the personality problem scale (Cullinan, Epstein, and Lloyd, 1981). In terms of their personality problems, both male and female LD students were identified by teachers as exhibiting more aberrant behavior such as self-consciousness, inferiority, shyness, social withdrawal, lack of self-confidence, hypersensitivity, reticence, anxiety, tension, and aloofness. Other investigators have found LD males (Stone & LaGreca, 1984) and LD females (Epstein, Cullinan, & Nieminen, 1984) to have more anxious-withdrawn behavior than NLD children.

On a different measure of behavior problems, the Child Behavior Checklist (Achenbach & Edelbrock, 1983), parents of LD children reported significantly lower levels of social competence, participation in activities, and social interaction (McConaughy & Ritter, 1986) than did parents of NLD children. In this same study, LD students were reported to have both higher scores on externalizing and internalizing behavior problems.

In addition to their behavior adjustment, the classroom behavioral patterns of LD students have been examined. In a 3-year longitudinal study, LD elementary children were consistently more "off task" and distractible in the classroom than their NLD peers (McKinney & Feagans, 1984). In contrast with these findings, when secondary LD students were compared with emotionally disturbed students and a nonhandicapped sample on such school related behaviors as prepared for class, on-task, compliance with requests, and asks appropriate questions, LD students did not perform significantly differently from their nonhandicapped peers (Zigmond, Kerr, & Schaeffer, 1988). Inasmuch as Zigmond et al. described all of the secondary students as relatively passive in their behavioral style, it could be that the passive learning style (Torgesen, 1982) of LD students is more compatible with the behavioral norms of secondary students.

Social Skills

Because LD children are more frequently rejected and receive lower ratings of peer acceptance than their NLD peers, the assumption has been made that they lack the appropriate social skills to interact with others. This assumption, in fact, was what initiated much of the social skills training with LD youngsters (e.g., LaGreca & Mesibov, 1979). Given the model of social competence we presented earlier, low peer acceptance does not necessarily correspond with low social skills. As we know, improving social skills does not guarantee increased acceptance or social competence (Bierman, 1986; Bierman & Furman, 1984). Nevertheless, research has focused more on identifying what types of social skills problems characterize LD students, and what subgroups of LD students are most at risk for social skills problems.

Considerable research has focused on the communicative behaviors of LD students that may interfere with their social interactions. Results have indicated that students with learning disabilities do not make appropriate modifications in their language to accommodate the listener (Knight-Arest, 1984; Soenksen, Flagg, & Schmits, 1981), perform more poorly on tests of referential communication (Noel, 1980), display a more egocentric communication style (Soenksen et al., 1981), and use social ingratiation strategies that are viewed by adults as less socially competent (Bryan, Sonnefeld, & Greenberg, 1981). It is likely that because their social communication is less responsive to their partner they are less desirable social partners. Because verbal interaction has been considered more important for female friendship making and maintenance than for males, the communicative difficulties of LD students may partially explain why female LD children have been at greater risk for peer rejection than males.

The prosocial behaviors of LD children, however, have not differed from their NLD peers (LaGreca, 1981; Levy & Gotlieb, 1984). LD children have interacted with peers as frequently as other children, and displayed comparable rates of sharing and helping behaviors (Bryan, Wheeler, Felcan, & Henek, 1976). Together, the findings on prosocial behavior have suggested a ''greater than usual'' willingness for LD children to help or go along with others (Bryan, Werner, & Pearl, 1982; Vaughn & LaGreca, 1988).

With regard to teacher perceptions of social skills, LD 3rd through 5th graders were perceived by teachers as displaying significantly lower social skills than their classmates (Cartledge, Stupay, & Kaczala, 1986). While as a group LD children have demonstrated less social competence than NLD, LD children are a heterogeneous group with a subgroup of LD performing equivalent to their NLD peers (Carlson, 1987). Some insight into which LD students might be at greater risk for social skills deficits was provided by a study examining the peer relationship problems of three subgroups of LD males (Landau, Milich, & McFarland, 1987). LD males were divided into three groups based on their verbal and performance scores from the WISC-R: verbal scores greater than performance, performance scores greater than verbal, and those who had equal verbal and performance scores. Results suggested that not all male LD children are at equal risk for peer problems, and those whose verbal scores were lower than their performance scores were particularly at risk.

Although we must be cautious in defining social skills deficits in the entire LD population, LD children do appear to be more at risk for social skills deficiencies than their NLD peers. Certainly a subgroup of LD students could benefit from direct social skills instruction (Vaughn, 1985), particularly in light of the fact that they do not outgrow their social difficulties (Leigh, 1987). We would expect these improved social skills could contribute to, although not insure, overall greater social competence.

This review of the literature of factors related to social competence, has shown that across all four areas—peer acceptance, social skills, self perception, and behavioral adjustment, LD children are at greater risk than their NLD peers. Several hypotheses for the low social competence of LD students have been posed. These hypotheses can be grouped into two broad categories: one focusing on the difficulty as being related to the learning disability, and one focusing on other related factors such as low achievement, low teacher perceptions, and reduced exposure to classmates (Vaughn & Hogan, 1988).

Within the first category, the rationale is that the same processing and cognitive difficulties that interfere with academic learning also interfere with social learning. Thus, the language deficiencies of many LD students may interfere with their ability to understand many of the subtle social messages as well as cause difficulty in their ability to adequately express themselves in social settings (Bryan, Donahue, Pearl, & Strum, 1981; Speckman & Roth, 1984). Additionally, the social cognition difficulties of LD students may interfere with their ability to successfully interpret social situations and use interpersonal problem-solving skills (Bryan, Werner, & Pearl, 1982; Maheady & Maitland, 1982; Oliva & LaGreca, 1988). Because LD children are described as inactive learners (Torgesen, 1982), who often do not use metacognitive skills to monitor, interpret, and adjust to academic learning, it is likely they behave as inactive learners in social situations as well. For example, during a small group problem-solving task, LD students were more submissive and less persuasive than NLD group members (Bryan, Donahue, & Pearl, 1981). LD students have shown fewer adaptations in their communication to accommodate the listener (Bryan & Pflaum, 1978; Soenksen et al., 1981) and requested more information when oral communication is ambiguous (Donahue, Pearl, & Bryan, 1980).

Within the second category, the low acceptance of LD students is considered a result of related factors such as low academic achievement, poor perceptions of LD students by teachers, and less exposure to classmates. As the relationship between low achievement and low peer acceptance has been well established (Dodge, Coie, & Brakke, 1982; Gottman, Gonso, & Rasmussen, 1975; Green, Forehand, Beck, & Vosk, 1980), and LD children are a subgroup of low achievers, it could be the low peer acceptance of LD students is more a function of low achievement than learning disabilities (Bursuck, 1983). Additionally, teacher perceptions of LD students are generally low (Garrett & Crump, 1980; Siperstein & Goding, 1985), which may influence the perceptions of classmates, particularly in the early grades. Since a positive relationship between friendship preferences and assignment to reading group has been documented (Hallinan & Sorensen, 1985), it could be many LD students miss an important interaction time which negatively influences their peer acceptance.

Unraveling all the factors that influence the social acceptance of LD children is challenging, and requires systematic, programmatic research. It appears, however, that a first step is to determine the extent to which social competence in LD students is a function of the child's interpersonal behavior or such factors as low achievement, teacher perceptions, and the influence of removal from the regular classroom. In an attempt to better understand the social competence of LD children, we are conducting a prospective study aimed at assessing factors related to social competence in learning disabled students and their classmates.

A PROSPECTIVE STUDY OF BEHAVIORAL ADJUSTMENT AND ACCEPTANCE OF LD STUDENTS PRIOR TO IDENTIFICATION

This study attempted to address the question: How do learning disabled students prior to identification (LDPA), low achieving (LA), average achieving (AA), and high achieving (HA) students compare on peer, teacher, and self-assessments of social status, adjustment, and social skills in the fall and spring of their kindergarten year? In order to address this question, an initial cohort of 239 kindergarten students (males = 120) are being followed for several years. There were 10 students (9 males, 1 female) from this group identified as learning disabled and they were matched with LA, AA, and HA peers from the same cohort. In an attempt to investigate their social competence patterns early in their formal school career, their scores on measures of social competence during the fall and spring of their kindergarten year were analyzed.

During the fall and spring of kindergarten year, all students were administered four measures corresponding to the four factors of social competence discussed earlier in this chapter. These four factors include:

Peer Relations.   Both peer ratings of social acceptance and positive friendship nominations were individually collected from each student. Thus, peers' perceptions of likability were obtained from the rating scale, and the identification of rejected and accepted students was obtained from the positive nominations and the lowest ratings on the rating scale (Asher & Dodge, 1986).

Self-Acceptance.   To assess self-acceptance the Pictorial Scale of Perceived Competence and Social Acceptance for Young Children (Harter & Pike, 1984) was individually administered. Two of the scales, peer acceptance and maternal acceptance were combined to yield a total social acceptance factor score.

Behavior Problems.   The Revised Behavior Problem Checklist (RBPC) (Quay & Peterson, 1987) is an 88-item teacher completed rating scale of children's behavior problems. The RBPC yielded the following 6 subscales: Conduct Disorder (CD), Attention Problem (AP), Anxiety-Withdrawn (AW), Socialized Aggression (SA), Psychotic Behavior (PB), and Motor Excess (ME).

Social Skills.   Based on the Social Skills Rating Scale for Teachers (SSRS-T) (Gresham & Elliott, 1986), an adapted version of the scale was constructed. Because a substantial modification of the instrument was used, the following section provides a description of the revision procedures for the SSRS-T.

Items were selected that focused solely on social skills with peers. Because this measure was selected specifically to assess social skills only, items with content describing behavior problems, and academic/school skills were deleted. This reduced the item pool from 60 to 26. Using the data on these 26 items from 338 kindergarten subjects, factor analyses were conducted to determine the most appropriate subscale format. The kindergarten sample was split in half with each sample consisting of approximately half boys, and ethnic distribution of one-third each for White, Black, and Hispanic.

Principal axis factoring was used, eigenvalues were set at 1.0, and a varimax rotation was performed. Nearly identical loading patterns were obtained for the two subsamples. The first factor accounted for 44% and 39% in the two subsamples respectively; the second factor accounted for 9% and 11%. Table 11.1 contains factor loadings and item content for the two subscales. Factor 1, Cooper-

TABLE 11.1
Social Skill Rating Factor Loadings

	Factor 1		Factor 2		Content Factor 1: C/R
Sample:	1	2	1	2	Cooperative/Responding
	.66	.48	(.25)	(.29)	accepts ideas
	.50	.48	(.40)	(.26)	gets along/other ethnic
	.63	.68	(.18)	(.13)	follows rules
	.76	.72	(.35)	(.22)	responds/teasing
	.76	.79	(.23)	(.09)	responds/aggression
	.59	.60	(.43)	(.28)	gets along/peers
	.70	.77	(.16)	(.07)	waits turn
	.79	.76	(.21)	(.14)	shares
	.81	.72	(.24)	(.20)	cooperates
	.62	.57	(.22)	(.08)	compromises
	.75	.77	(.07)	(.02)	controls temper
	.61	.62	(.30)	(.32)	polite refusal
	.67	.64	(.24)	(.32)	responds/false accusation
	.74	.64	(.29)	(.27)	responds/peer pressure
					Factor 2: O/I Outgoing/Initiating
	(.23)	(.17)	.75	.72	sense of humor
	(.35)	(.24)	.65	.64	acknowledges compliments
	(.24)	(.09)	.71	.75	invites
	(-.12)	(-.04)	.74	.75	initiates conversation
	(.22)	(.37)	.64	.49	participates
	(.27)	(.32)	.68	.70	joins
	(.23)	(.23)	.61	.59	introduces
	(.28)	(.17)	.57	.70	volunteers
	(.30)	(.10)	.62	.69	nonverbally expressive
	(.34)	(.41)	.74	.69	makes friends
					Items Excluded
	.57	.55	.43	.45	empathy
	.40	.46	.47	.41	expresses feelings when wronged

*Samples: Each subsample had approximately half boys, and was evenly distributed for White, Hispanic, and Black children.

**"Gives Compliments" is an item added to the OII factor but not included in this analysis.

ating/Responding (C/R), contains 14 items, and Factor 2, Outgoing/Initiating (O/I), contains 10 items. Across all items, the means ranged from .91 to 1.72 (0/2 total range), and item standard deviations ranged from .46 to .73. C/R and O/I scale scores were calculated for both fall and spring on all 338 children. Interscale correlations both concurrently and longitudinally ranged from .55 to .66.

Results

Descriptive statistics for each group on the major social variables appear in Table 11.2. To assess significant differences among the groups two multivariate repeated measures analyses of variance (MANOVA) were performed with one each for fall and spring data across the three measures; total social skills on the SSRS-T

TABLE 11.2
Means and Standard Deviations on Social Skills,
Self-Perceptions of Social Acceptance, and Peers'
Ratings of Acceptance

Group	Fall		Spring	
Social Skills (SOCIAL)				
	M	SD	M	SD
LDPI	1.36	.45	1.29	.30
LA	1.09	.45	1.37	.47
AA	1.74	.16	1.82	.28
HA	1.70	.35	1.59	.35
Self-Perception of Social Acceptance (SELF)				
	M	SD	M	SD
LDPI	43.30	2.83	41.40	5.93
LA	38.70	4.55	40.10	7.72
AA	36.90	5.63	37.70	8.35
HA	34.50	5.83	34.90	6.99
Peers' Perceptions of Acceptance (PEER)				
	M	SD	M	SD
LDPI	2.06	.34	2.08	.23
LA	2.40	.39	2.23	.46
AA	2.67	.27	2.42	.31
HA	2.68	.29	2.60	.31

(SOCIAL), self-perception of social acceptance (SELF), and peers' rating of acceptance (PEER). Because of the rather small sample size, we wanted to limit the number of dependent variables so we collapsed subscales for the SOCIAL and SELF measures.

Results indicated there were significant differences among the groups for both fall and spring data. In the fall, the LDPI children were significantly higher on SELF and lower on PEER than AA and HA children. For SOCIAL, the only significant difference was the LA students were rated lower than the AA students. For spring data, there were significant group differences on two variables, SOCIAL and PEER. LDPI and LA children were lower on SOCIAL than AA children. The LDPI group were also lower on PEER than HA.

Social Status Ratings. The mean number of positive nominations for students in each group follows: LDPI = 0.8; LA = 1.6; AA = 4.1; and HA = 4.4; resulting in LDPI scores being significantly lower than both AA and HA.

Using the Asher and Dodge (1986) procedure for classifying children by using positive nominations plus the lowest rating on the rating scale for negative nominations, 9 of the 40 subjects in the study were identified as rejected. Of these 9, 6 were in the LDPI group and 3 were in the LA group; no AA or HA children were identified as rejected. There were also 9 of the 40 subjects identified as popular. Of these 9, none were in the LDPI or LA groups, 3 were in the AA group, and 6 were in the HA group.

Teacher Ratings of Behavior Problems.   On the 6 subtests of the RBPC, there were significant group differences on two of the subtests, attention problems and psychotic behavior. On both subtests, LDPI children showed significantly elevated problem scores relative to both AA and HA children. It is important to note however, that on only the attention problem subtest were the mean T scores of the LDPI students (59.5 fall, 59.4 spring) significantly elevated based on the norms for their age (mean norm 50.0; SD 10). For all groups on all other scales the means were within the average range, from 46 to 52.

Interpretation and Implications

The study reported here attempted to provide a prospective perspective on the social competence of learning disabled students. We argued that social competence is much like cognitive competence or intelligence. Both are difficult to define and are often examined in terms of the factors perceived as contributing to them. This study examined the social competence of learning disabled students from the perspectives of teachers, peers, and self as they related to factors of social competence: social skills, behavioral adjustment, peer relations and social cognition.

The results of this study indicated that, as early as 2 months after their first formal school experience and maintained 6 months later, kindergarten children later identified as learning disabled (LDPI) received lower peer acceptance ratings than their average achieving (AA) and high achieving (HA) classmates. Of even greater concern was the high percentage of LDPI students identified as rejected (60%), and the low percentage of LDPI students identified as popular (0%). This contrasted sharping with the AA and HA samples who when combined have no rejected students and nearly 50% identified as popular. Because rejection status is relatively stable (Li, 1985), and is related to later adjustment difficulties (Parker & Asher, 1987), the high number of rejected LDPI students was of serious concern.

An important consideration when interpreting the low peer relations of LDPI students is the extent to which low peer ratings merely reflect lack of exposure on the part of classmates to the LD student. Thus, low peer ratings may have indicated that peers have interacted relatively little with the target students. If this were the case, it would be expected that significantly more LDPI students would be identified as socially neglected. For example, in Morrison's (1981) study of the social status of mainstreamed mildly handicapped students, she determined that mildly handicapped youngsters were more likely to be socially neglected when compared with their nonhandicapped classmates (Morrison, 1981). In the study reported here, there were few group differences in the number of students identified as neglected, with the LA group having the largest number (4), LDPI (3), and both AA and HA with two. Thus, the LDPI students in this group did not appear to be significantly more socially neglected than their peers.

In this chapter, the social competence of learning disabled students was discussed in light of several hypotheses that might explain their low social status. One hypothesis attempted to explain their low social acceptance in light of their cognitive and processing difficulties which may interfere with their social cognition and social behavior. The second hypothesis focused on such related factors as low achievement, low perceptions by teachers, and less exposure to classmates. As the peer rejection of the LDPI students occurred so early in their formal school career and the students were not yet referred for special services, the results of this study can be interpreted to provide support for hypotheses that suggest the difficulty is not merely a function of a history of low achievement, low teacher acceptance, and lack of involvement in the regular classroom.

An interesting pattern occurred relative to students' self-perceptions (see Table 11.3). Despite significantly low peer acceptance scores, LDPI children perceive themselves as having high social acceptance. In contrast, HA children who had high social acceptance from peers perceived themselves as having lower self-acceptance by peers than any other group. Though the primary interest of this study was in social acceptance, the pattern for achievement and self-perceptions of academic competence show a similar pattern. As can be seen in Table 11.3, HA students, whose achievement scores were above the 97th percentile, did not have corresponding extreme high scores on their self-perceptions of academic performance. While the academic self-perception scores of HA students were not low, they were only within the average range contrasting sharply with their extremely high achievement scores.

There are several possible explanations for lack of congruence between self-perception and performance (as determined by achievement tests and peers ratings) for both HA and LDPI populations. HA students may have already learned

TABLE 11.3
Self and Comparison Evaluation for Social and Academic Domains

Fall	Social				Academic			
	Peer		Self		Achievement		Self	
	M	SD	M	SD	M	SD	M	SD
LDPI	2.06	.34	22.0	2.05	35.5	35.3	21.9	1.45
LA	2.40	.39	18.9	3.31	11.5	7.24	21.0	2.94
AA	2.67	.27	18.0	4.20	77.0	4.08	21.2	2.20
HA	2.68	.29	17.1	4.12	97.6	.84	22.2	1.32
Spring	Social				Academic			
	Peer		Self		Achievement		Self	
	M	SD	M	SD	M	SD	M	SD
LDPI	2.08	.23	21.1	2.92	35.5	35.3	21.7	2.40
LA	2.23	.46	21.7	3.08	11.5	7.24	20.8	3.27
AA	2.42	.31	19.4	5.10	77.0	4.08	22.4	1.35
HA	2.60	.31	16.5	3.60	97.6	.84	22.0	2.05

the importance of modesty. While their self-perceptions are within the average range based on a normed sample, they are low when compared with other groups in this sample and certainly low when compared with their actual performance. While an alternative explanation might be that HA students are highly self-critical, the simplicity of the academic questions on the self-perception scale (know the letters in your name, say the alphabet) suggest they were not being self-critical but modest.

An appropriate question appears to be whether the LDPI children's self-perception scores of social acceptance are elevated or the AA and HA children are demonstrating low scores of self-perception. Harter and Pike's (1984) means for kindergarten children were very similar to the AA and HA means from this study. Thus, our LDPI group elevation of nearly a standard deviation is of special interest. As we discussed initially in this chapter, social cognition is considered an important aspect of social competence. It appears as though the social cognition of children in the LDPI group reflects a social obliviousness which may be related to further peer interaction problems. The self-perceptions of the LDPI students over time will be of interest as the self-perceptions of low achievers tend to become more negative as they get older (Black, 1974; Kifer, 1975).

Teacher reports on the behavior problems of students in this study indicated that LDPI students, when compared with AA and HA students, were significantly elevated on two subtests of the RBPC, psychotic behavior and attention problems. It is important to note that while the psychotic behavior scores of the LDPI group were significantly higher than both AA and HA groups, the LDPI's scores were well within the average normative range and can not be considered aberrant. The attention problem scores of the LDPI group, however, were both significantly higher than AA and HA groups, and their mean scores are one standard deviation above the normative mean. Not surprising, students who are later identified as LD have significantly high levels of attention problems as early as the beginning of their kindergarten year.

Summary

What do all of these findings mean and how do they relate to the social competence of LD children? These findings suggest that children who are later identified as learning disabled show patterns demonstrating risk for social competence problems as early as 6 weeks into their first formal schooling, kindergarten. Thus, hypotheses suggesting that the social competence difficulties of LD students can be explained *solely* by teachers' perceptions, withdrawal from the regular classroom, and being labeled LD are inaccurate.

Based on the model of social competence presented in this chapter, LDPI children display problems to some degree in all four factors of social competence. Relative to their relations with other children, they were more frequently rejected, less accepted, and received overall lower ratings of likability. These low ratings were maintained throughout their kindergarten year. Relative to their social cognition, LDPI children demonstrated inaccurate self-perceptions that were out of line with the data they were receiving. Both their self-perceptions of academic success and peer acceptance were distorted. It may be that LDPI students are less developmentally able to make these judgments and their perceptions will be more in line with performance as they get older. The third factor, absence of maladaptive behaviors, was problematic as these students had significantly high attention problems, although they were not rated by their teachers as having conduct disorders or other behavior problems. The final factor, social behaviors, was assessed by asking teachers to rate their social skills. While their social skills were less acceptable by teachers over time, they were not significantly lower than the other groups. In contrast with the performance of LDPI children on the factors of social competence, both AA and HA students had no scores on any of the factors which were problematic. The LA students scores were significantly different from AA and HA only on the fall ratings by teachers of social skills. Their overall scores on all four factors were low, but not significantly so as were LDPI students.

In order to more fully understand the social competence of LD students we intend to follow the students through their 4th-grade year. We hope to be able to determine the patterns of social competence of LD students over time, and provide more information on the patterns of social competence of LD children.

ACKNOWLEDGMENTS

This paper was supported in part by the Dade County Public Schools through the University of Miami, Florida Diagnostic Learning and Resources System. Special thanks to directors Keith Scott and Eleanor L. Levine and to school principals Donald Lape, William Renuart, and Maybelline Truesdell.

REFERENCES

Achenbach, T. M., & Edelbrock, C. S. (1983). *Manual for the child Behavior Checklist and Revised Child Behavior Profile*, Burlington, Vt: Department of Psychiatry, University of Vermont.

Asher, S., & Dodge, K. (1986). Identifying children who are rejected by their peers. *Developmental Psychology, 22*, 444–449.

Battle, J. (1979). Self-esteem of students in regular and special classes. *Psychological Reports, 44*, 212–214.

Beck, M. A., Roblee, K., & Hanson, J. (1981). Special education/regular education: A comparison of self-concept. *Education, 102*, 277–279.

Bender, W. N. (1987). Behavioral indicators of temperament and personality in the inactive learner. *Journal of Learning Disabilities, 20*(5), 301–305.

Bierman, K. L. (1986). Process of change during social skills training with preadolescents and its relation to treatment outcome. *Child Development, 57,* 230–240.

Bierman, K. L., & Furman, W. (1984). The effects of social skills training and peer involvement on the social adjustment of preadolescents. *Child Development, 55,* 151–162.

Black, F. W. (1974). Self-concept as related to achievement and age in learning disabled children. *Child Development, 45,* 1137–1140.

Bruck, M. (1986). Social and emotional adjustment of learning disabled children: A review of the issues. In S. J. Ceci, (Ed.), *Handbook of cognitive, social, and neuropsychological aspects of learning disabilities.* Hillsdale, NJ: Lawrence Erlbaum Associates.

Bryan, J. H., Sonnefeld, L. J., & Greenberg, F. Z. (1981). Childrens' and parents' views of ingratiation tactics. *Learning Disability Quarterly, 4,* 170–179.

Bryan, T. H. (1974). Peer popularity of learning disabled children. *Journal of Learning Disabilities, 7,* 621–625.

Bryan, T. H. (1986). Self-concept and attributions of the learning disabled. *Learning Disabilities Focus, 1,* 2, 82–89.

Bryan, T., Donahue, M., & Pearl, R. (1981). Learning disabled children's peer interactions during a small-group problem-solving task. *Learning Disability Quarterly, 4*(1), 13–22.

Bryan, T. H., Donahue, M., Pearl, R., & Strum, C. (1981). Learning disabled children's conversational skills—the T.V. talk show. *Learning Disability Quarterly, 4,* 250–259.

Bryan, T., & Pflaum, S. (1978). Social interactions of learning disabled children: A linguistic, social, and cognitive analysis. *Learning Disability Quarterly, 5,* 344–352.

Bryan, T., Werner, M., & Pearl, R. (1982). Learning disabled students' conformity responses to prosocial and antisocial situations. *Learning Disability Quarterly, 1,* 70–79.

Bryan, T. H., Wheeler, R., Felcan, J., & Henek, T. (1976). "Come on, dummy": An observational study of children's communication. *Journal of Learning Disabilities, 9,* 661–669.

Bursuck, W. D. (1983). Sociometric status, behavior ratings, and social knowledge of learning disabled and low achieving students. *Learning Disability Quarterly, 6,* 329–338.

Cantrell, V. L., & Prinz, R. J. (1985). Multiple perspectives of rejected, neglected, and accepted children: Relation between sociometric status and behavioral characteristics. *Journal of Consulting and Clinical Psychology, 53*(6), 884–889.

Carlson, C. I. (1987). Social interaction goals and strategies of children with learning disabilities. *Journal of Learning Disabilities, 20*(5), 306–311.

Cartledge, G., Stupay, D., & Kaczala, C. (1986). Social skills and social perception of LD and nonhandicapped elementary-school students. *Learning Disability Quarterly, 9*(3), 226–234.

Chapman, J. W., & Boersman, F. J. (1980). *Affective correlates of learning disabilities.* Lisse: Swets & Zeitlinger.

Cooley, E. J., & Ayres, R. R. (1988). Self-concept and success-failure attributions of nonhandicapped students and students with learning disabilities. *Journal of Learning Disabilities, 21*(3), 174–178.

Cullinan, D., Epstein, M. H., & Lloyd, J. (1981). School behavior problems of learning disabled and normal girls and boys. *Learning Disability Quarterly, 4*(2), 163–169.

Dodge, K. A., Coie, J. D., & Brakke, N. P. (1982). Behavior patterns of socially rejected and neglected preadolescents: The role of social approach and aggression. *Journal of Abnormal Child Psychology, 10,* 389–410.

Donahue, M., Pearl, R., & Bryan, T. (1980). Learning disabled children's conversational competence: Responses to inadequate messages. *Applied Psycholinguistics, 1,* 387–403.

Epstein, M. H., Cullinan, D., & Nieminen, G. (1984). Social behavior problems of learning disabled and normal girls. *Journal of Learning Disabilities, 17,* 609–611.

Garrett, M. K., & Crump, W. D. (1980). Peer acceptance, teacher preference, and self-appraisal of social status among learning disabled students. *Learning Disability Quarterly, 3,* 42–48.

Gottman, J., Gonso, J., & Rasmussen, B. (1975). Friendships in children. *Child Development, 46,* 709–718.

Green, K., Forehand, R., Beck, S., & Vosk, B. (1980). An assessment of the relationship among measures of children's academic achievement. *Child Development, 51,* 146–156.

Gresham, F. M., & Elliott, S. (1986). *Social skills rating scale for teachers.* Baton Rouge: Louisiana State University.

Hallinan, M. T., & Sorensen, A. B. (1985). Ability grouping and student friendships. *American Educational Research Journal, 22*(4), 485–499.

Harter, S., & Pike, R. (1984). The pictorial scale of perceived competence and social acceptance of young children. *Child Development, 55,* 1969–1982.

Hartup, W. W. (1983). Peer relations. In P. H. Mussen (Ed.), *Handbook of child psychology, Vol. 4* (pp. 374–402). New York: Wiley.

Kifer, E. (1975). Relationships between academic achievement and personal characteristics: A quasi-longitudinal study. *American Educational Research Journal, 12*(2), 191–210.

Kistner, J., & Osborne, M. (1987). A longitudinal study of LD children's self-evaluations. *Learning Disability Quarterly, 10*(4), 258–266.

Knight-Arest, I. (1984). Communicative effectiveness of learning disabled and normally achieving 10–13 year old boys. *Learning Disability Quarterly, 7,* 237–245.

LaGreca, A. M. (1981). Social behavior and social perception in learning-disabled children: A review with implications for social skills training. *Journal of Pediatric Psychology, 6,* 395–416.

LaGreca, A. M., & Mesibov, G. (1979). Social skills intervention with learning disabled children: Selecting skills and implementing training. *Journal of Clinical Child Psychology, 8,* 234–241.

LaGreca, A. M., Stone, W., & Halpern, D. A. (1988, February). *LD status and achievement: Confounding variables in the study of children's social and behavioral functioning?* Presented at the International Academy for Research in Learning Disabilities, Los Angeles.

Landau, S., Milich, R., & McFarland, M. (1987). Social status differences among subgroups of LD boys. *Learning Disability Quarterly, 10,* 277–282.

Leigh, J. (1987). Adaptive behavior of children with learning disabilities. *Journal of Learning Disabilities, 20,*(9), 557–562.

Levy, L., & Gotlieb, J. (1984). Learning disabled and non-LD children at play. *Remedial and Special Education, 5,* 43–50.

Li, A. K. F. (1985). Early rejected status and later social adjustment: A 3-year follow-up. *Journal of Abnormal Child Psychology, 13*(4), 567–577.

Maheady, L., & Maitland, G. E. (1982). Assessing social perception abilities in learning disabled students. *Learning Disability Quarterly, 5,* 363–370.

McConaughy, S. H., & Ritter, D. R. (1986). Social competence and behavioral problems of learning disabled boys aged 6–11. *Journal of Learning Disabilities, 19*(1), 39–45.

McKinney, J. D., & Feagans, L. (1984). Academic and behavioral characteristics of learning disabled children and average achievers: Longitudinal studies. *Learning Disability Quarterly, 7,* 251–265.

Morrison, G. M. (1981). Sociometric measurement: Methodological consideration of its use with mildly learning handicapped and nonhandicapped children. *Journal of Educational Psychology, 71*(2), 191–201.

Morrison, G. M. (1985). Difference in teacher perceptions and student self-perceptions for learning disabled and nonhandicapped learners in regular and special education settings. *Learning Disabilities Research, 1*(1), 32–41.

Nicholls, J. G. (1978). The development of the concepts of effort and ability, perception of academic attainment, and the understanding that difficult tasks require more ability. *Child Development, 49,*800–814.

Nicholls, J. G. (1979). Development of perception of own attainment and causal attributions for success and failure in reading. *Journal of Educational Psychology, 71,* 94–99.

Noel, M. (1980). Referential communication abilities of learning disabled children. *Learning Disability Quarterly, 3,* 70–75.

Oliva, A. H., & LaGreca, A. M. (1988). Children with learning disabilities: Social goals and strategies. *Journal of Learning Disabilities, 21*(5), 301–306.

Parker, J. G., & Asher, S. R. (1987). Peer relations and later personal adjustment: Are low-accepted children at risk. *Psychological Bulletin, 102*(3), 357–389.

Pearl, R., Donahue, M., & Bryan, T. (1986). Social relations of learning-disabled children. In J. K. Torgesen, & B. Y. L. Wong (Eds.), *Psychological and educational perspectives on learning disabilities,* Orlando, FL: Academic Press.

Piers, E. V. (1984). *Piers-Harris children's self-concept scale* (rev. ed.). Los Angeles: Western Psychological Services.

Quay, H. C., & Peterson, D. R. (1975). *Manual for the behavior problem checklist.* Coral Gables, FL: University of Miami.

Quay, H. C., & Peterson, D. R. (1987). *Manual for the revised behavior problem checklist.* Coral Gables, FL: University of Miami.

Renik, M. J. (1987). *Measuring the relationship between academic self-perceptions and global self-worth: The self-perception profile for learning disabled students.* Presented at the Society for Research in Child Development, Baltimore, MD.

Scranton, T., & Ryckman, D. (1979). Sociometric status of learning disabled children in an integrative program. *Journal of Learning Disabilities, 12,* 402–407.

Silverman, R., & Zigmond, N. (1983). Self-concept in learning disabled adolescents. *Journal of Learning Disabilities, 16,* 478–482.

Siperstein, G. N., & Goding, M. J. (1985). Teachers' behavior toward LD and non-LD children: A strategy for change. *Journal of Learning Disabilities, 18*(3), 139–144.

Soenksen, P. A., Flagg, C. L., & Schmits, D. W. (1981). Social communication in learning disabled students: A pragmatic analysis. *Journal of Learning Disabilities, 14,* 283–286.

Speckman, N. J., & Roth, F. P. (1984). Intervention strategies for learning disabled children with oral communication disorders. *Learning Disability Quarterly, 7,* 7–18.

Stone, W. C., & LaGreca, A. M. (1984). Comprehension of nonverbal communication: A reexamination of the social competencies of learning disabled children. *Journal of Abnormal Child Psychology, 12,* 505–518.

Torgesen, J. (1982). The learning disabled child as an inactive learner: Educational implications. *Topics in Learning and Learning Disabilities, 2*(1), 45–52.

Vaughn, S. (1985). Why teach social skills to learning disabled students? *Journal of Learning Disabilities, 18*(10), 588–591.

Vaughn, S., & Hogan, A. (1988, February). *Peer acceptance, self-perceptions, and social skills of LD students prior to identification.* Presented at the International Academy for Research in Learning Disabilities, Los Angeles.

Vaughn, S., & LaGreca, A. M. (1988). Social sills of LD students: Characteristics, behaviors, and guidelines for intervention. In K. Kavale (Ed.), *Handbook in learning disabilities,* San Diego: College Hill.

Wiener, J. (1987). Peer status of learning disabled children and adolescents: A review of the literature. *Learning Disabilities Research, 2*(2), 62–79.

Yauman, B. E. (1980). Special education placement and the self-concepts of elementary-school age children. *Learning Disability Quarterly, 3,* 30–35.

Zigmond, N., Kerr, M. M., & Schaeffer, A. (1988). Behavioral patterns of learning disabled and non-learning disabled adolescents in high school academic classes. *Remedial and Special Education, 9*(2), 6–11.

SUBTYPING RESEARCH

12 Subtyping in Learning Disabilities: Introduction to the Issues

Steven R. Forness
UCLA Neuropsychiatric Hospital

Most categories of educational handicap have attempted, with varying degrees of success, to arrive at systems of classification in order to reduce children's difficulties to more understandable or manageable types of problems. Such classifications are presumed necessary to develop convenient, if not more effective, instructional systems. Classification in the area of mental retardation, for example, is done by level of severity, e.g. educable, trainable, or severe mental retardation. In regard to behavioral disorders, broad distinctions have traditionally been made, for example, between internalizers and externalizers and with substantial justification, although there are points of overlap even in such apparently disparate subtypes (Forness, 1988). In learning disabilities, severity of disability is rarely used as a classification, even in research studies (Adelman & Taylor, 1986). The LD field, somewhat like the field of behavioral disorders, seems currently to be spending its classification efforts instead on determining subtypes according to patterns of disorder, particularly different areas of underlying cognitive or psychologic dysfunction.

Classification in this fashion has a long history in the LD field. Witness, for example, writings more than 2 decades ago, at or shortly after the first appearance of the term "learning disabilities," in which classification by underlying etiologic or related considerations is mentioned as a critical need (Bateman, 1965; Johnson & Myklebust, 1965; Kirk, 1962; Money, 1962). A decade thereafter (Cruickshank, 1972) and more than 2 decades thereafter (Adelman & Taylor, 1985; Keogh, 1986), classification and subtyping issues continue to be seen as fundamental.

Subtyping research, as it is currently practiced, strives to divide heterogeneous samples of LD youngsters into homogeneous subgroups based on their

195

patterns of performance across a variety of tests or other measurements thought to be critical to development of learning disabilities. In such studies, a variety of methods have been used to classify such samples. Early subtyping studies were often characterized by a clinical inferential approach (Boder, 1973; Denckla, 1973) or by factor analytic techniques (Doehring & Hoshko, 1977; Fiske & Rourke, 1979; Petrauskas & Rourke, 1979). More recent studies (e.g., Feagans & Appelbaum, 1986; Lyon, 1985; Lyon, Stewart, & Freedman, 1982; Lyon & Watson, 1981; McKinney, Short, & Feagans, 1985; McKinney & Speece, 1986; Satz & Morris, 1981, 1983; Speece, 1987; Speece, McKinney, & Appelbaum, 1985) have applied the statistical technique of cluster analysis in which individuals with similar patterns on such cognitive or psychologic processing measures are grouped together iteratively until a substantial portion of the sample is accounted for in presumably nonoverlapping groups. Such techniques have not been without their problems, however (Morris, Blashfield, & Satz, 1981); and subsequent chapters by Speece and by Kavale focus on these and other critical problems at some length.

To summarize adequately such complex methodological problems or to characterize LD subtypes to date is impossible in a brief introduction such as this; but a convenient heuristic is available in Table 12.1. This depicts an attempt by Weller and Strawser (1987) to summarize what they consider to be the "consensus" subtypes that have been arrived at thus far by researchers in the area. In fairness to these authors, it should be noted that their comprehensive review has been reduced to this tabular summary only for the purposes of a quick introduc-

TABLE 12.1
Consensus Summary of LD Subtypes *

Subtype	Cognitive of Social Patterns	Percent of LD
1. Non-LD Pattern	*Discrepancy from grade but not IQ *Possible frustration, absences	25-38%
2. Production Deficits	*Inefficient cognitive strategies *Possible inattention or hyperactivity	22-30%
3. Verbal Organization Disorders	*Poor understanding or language use *Possible aggression or acting out	14-17%
4. Nonverbal Organization Disorders	*Visual-spatial-motor deficits *Possible social misperception or withdrawal	11-15%
5. Global Disorders	*Multiple deficits in processing *Possible problems in all coping skills	8-10%

*Adapted from data in Weller and Strawser (1987).

tion to certain issues and may not do justice to their work. This table presents not only the 5 consensus subtypes that have been found to date; but the second column also depicts for each subtype both the cognitive deficits or processing patterns associated with each and, just below it, the social problems typically encountered by youngsters in that subtype, as found in some of the studies reviewed. The third column gives the approximate percentages of the typical LD sample accounted for by the particular subtype. Note that cognitive deficits seem often to relate to the type of social problem encountered. It should be noted that, although 5 consensus subtypes are presented here, the actual number found across various studies has ranged from 2 to 7, with anywhere from 1 to 32 different psychological or neurological measures being used to determine subtype patterns (Kavale & Forness, 1987a).

It is clear that such subtypes can be viewed as encompassing some of the long-standing, major issues in the LD field. Subtype 1, for example, in which no particular pattern of underlying deficit could be found, might be said to reflect the view that learning disabilities cannot be reliably distinguished from under-achievement given our current psychoeducational measures (Ysseldyke, Algozzine, Richey, & Graden, 1982). Subtype 2 tends to suggest the importance of cognitive strategies to address inefficient memory or attentional processes (Swanson, 1987a; Torgesen, 1977). Subtype 3 stresses the importance of underlying linguistic difficulties in the development of learning disabilities (Velluntino, 1979). Subtype 4 calls to mind original views of learning disabilities in which visual perceptual deficits were not only the primary symptomatology but also the focus of remediation. The last subtype suggests, perhaps along with all the others, the ultimate complexity of learning disabilities in which no one view prevails.

There are at least three problems with the LD subtyping movement, however. The first is that psychologic processing tests or related procedures typically used to determine underlying disorders are notoriously unreliable (Berk, 1984; Forness & Kavale, 1987a; Kavale & Forness, 1984). The second is that available studies frequently tend to have serious methodological and statistical limitations or often fail to account for significant amounts of variance within their LD samples, i.e., nearly 30% on average over 15 studies (Kavale & Forness, 1987a) as suggested earlier by subtype 1. Thus, such subtypes as have been recognized are on relatively unstable footing. The third difficulty is perhaps the most problematic. Most subtyping studies have not addressed the fact that such subtypes should not only extend our understanding of learning disabilities but must also possess predictive power, i.e., must be externally validated in terms of differential response to intervention. At present, only a few exceptions exist (Lyon, 1985; McKinney, Short, & Feagans, 1985), and these are admittedly tentative examinations of subtype response to specific instructional approaches.

Thus, despite more than a decade of research, LD subtypes have yet to result in well substantiated classroom applications. However such subtypes are determined, their worth would ultimately seem to depend, as indicated earlier, on response of children so identified to differential instruction. This unfortunately means at least some variation of aptitude-by-treatment interaction, the more than 2-decade history of research on which has largely upheld the null hypothesis, i.e., that grouping LD or other handicapped children by underlying learning style or demonstrated preference does not result in differential instructional effects. In a recent meta-analysis of 39 existing studies in this area, not only were effect sizes quite small at best; but even those modest results tended to disappear when less carefully designed studies were eliminated (Kavale & Forness, 1987b).

It may be that current educational research approaches are not equal to the challenge of establishing such relationships at least until temperament, attribution, instructional history, motivation, teacher competence, psychologic environment, self-concept, and other such variables affecting LD achievement can be factored into subtype interactions (Forness & Kavale, 1987b). It is possible, however, that more "holistic" or qualitative methods of inquiry offer some promise. Studying subtypes of children, derived from cluster analytic techniques, through holistic or ethnographic methods of documenting their differential responses to ongoing classroom instruction might be an interim solution (Forness, 1988). Other aspects of this validity question are addressed in the thoughtful chapter by McKinney.

In conclusion, it seems quite clear that subtyping research involves major methodological and substantive questions in the field of learning disabilities. Evidence is beginning to appear that subtyping research can, however, be helpful in reducing the variance and complexity of findings in other areas of learning disability inquiry (Swanson, 1987b). The number of learning disabled children in this country has nonetheless grown almost 135% in less than a decade, while companion special education categories such as speech impairments, mental retardation, and behavioral disorders are either markedly underrepresented or in actual decline (U.S. Department of Education, 1987). Whether other special education categories have been reduced commensurate with growth in the LD category is not clear; but it is interesting that *vestiges* of these other categories appear in Table 12.1, e.g., subtypes 1 and 5 as mildly mentally retarded, subtype 2 as behaviorally disordered, subtype 3 as speech or language handicapped, and so forth. The pursuit of LD subtypes, whether such investigators acknowledge it or not, may become at least partly motivated by the drive to bring order somehow to this burgeoning category of learning disabilities, a drive which current trends indicate may not diminish.

REFERENCES

Adelman, H. S., & Taylor, L. (1985). The future of the LD field: A survey of fundamental concerns. *Journal of Learning Disabilities, 18,* 423–427.

Adelman, H. S., & Taylor, L. (1986). The problems of definition and differentiation and the need for a classification schema. *Journal of Learning Disabilities, 19,* 514–520.

Bateman, B. (1965). An educator's view of a diagnostic approach to learning disorders. In J. Hellmuth (Ed.), *Learning disorders* (Vol. 1, pp 219–239). Seattle: Special Child.

Berk, R. (1984). *Screening and diagnosis of children with learning disabilities.* Springfield, IL: Charles C. Thomas.

Boder, E. (1973). Developmental dyslexia: A diagnostic approach based on three atypical reading-spelling patterns. *Developmental Medicine and Child Neurology, 15,* 663–687.

Cruickshank, W. M. (1972). Some issues facing the field of learning disability. *Journal of Learning Disabilities, 5,* 380–388.

Denckla, M. D. (1973). Research needs in learning disabilities: A neurologist's point of view. *Journal of Learning Disabilities, 6,* 441–450.

Doehring, D. G., & Hoshko, I. M. (1977). Classification of reading problems by the Q-technique of factor analysis. *Cortex, 13,* 281–294.

Feagans, L., & Appelbaum, M. (1986). Language subtypes and their validation in learning disabled children. *Journal of Educational Psychology, 78,* 358–364.

Fisk, J. L., & Rourke, B. P. (1979). Identification of subtypes of learning disabilities at three age levels: A neuropsychological, multivariate approach. *Journal of Clinical Neuropsychology, 1,* 289–310.

Forness, S. R. (1988). School characteristics of children and adolescents with depression. *Monographs in Behavioral Disorders, 10,* 177–203.

Forness, S. R. (1988). Reductionism, paradigm shifts and learning disabilities. *Journal of Learning Disabilities, 21,* 421–424.

Forness, S., & Kavale, K. (1987a). De-psychologizing special education. *Monographs in Behavioral Disorders, 9,* 2–14.

Forness, S., & Kavale, K. (1987b). Holistic inquiry and the scientific challenge in special education: A reply to Iano. *Remedial and Special Education, 8,* 47–51.

Johnson, D. J., & Myklebust, H. R. (1965). Dyslexia in childhood. In J. Hellmuth (Ed.), *Learning disorders* (Vol. 1, pp 259–292). Seattle: Special Child.

Kavale, K., & Forness, S. (1984). A meta-analysis assessing the validity of Wechsler Scale profiles and recategorization: Patterns or parodies? *Learning Disability Quarterly, 7,* 136–156.

Kavale, K., & Forness, S. (1987a). The far side of heterogeniety: A critical analysis of empirical subtyping research in learning disabilities. *Journal of Learning Disabilities, 20,* 374–382.

Kavale, K., & Forness, S. (1987b). Substance over style: Assessing the efficacy of modality testing and teaching. *Exceptional Children, 54,* 228–234.

Keogh, B. K. (1986). Future of the LD field: Research and practice. *Journal of Learning Disabilities, 19,* 455–460.

Kirk, S. A. (1962). *Educating exceptional children.* Boston, MA: Houghton Mifflin.

Lyon, G. R. (1985). Identification and remediation of learning disability subtypes: Preliminary findings. *Learning Disabilities Focus, 1,* 21–35.

Lyon, G. R., Stewart, N., & Freedman, D. (1982). Neuropsychological characteristics of empirically derived subgroups of learning disabled readers. *Journal of Clinical Neuropsychology, 4,* 343–365.

Lyon, G. R., & Watson, B. (1981). Empirically derived subgroups of learning disabled readers: Diagnostic characteristics. *Journal of Learning Disabilities, 14,* 256–261.

McKinney, J. D., Short, E. J., & Feagans, L. (1985). Academic consequences of perceptual-linguistic subtypes of learning disabled children. *Learning Disabilities Research, 1,* 6–17.

McKinney, J. D., & Speece, D. L. (1986). Academic consequences and longitudinal stability of behavioral subtypes of learning disabled children. *Journal of Educational Psychology, 78,* 365–372.

Money, J. (1962). Dyslexia: A postconference review. In John Money (Ed.), *Reading disability* (pp. 9–34), Baltimore: The Johns Hopkins University Press.

Morris, R., Blashfield, R. K., & Satz, P. (1981). Neuropsychology and cluster analysis: Potentials and problems. *Journal of Clinical Neuropsychology, 3,* 77–79.

Petraukas, R., & Rourke, B. P. (1979). Identification of subgroups of retarded readers: A neuropsychological, multivariate approach. *Journal of Clinical Neuropsychology, 1,* 17–37.

Satz, P., & Morris, R. (1981). Learning disability subtypes: A review. In F. J. Pirozzolo & M. C. Wittrock (Eds.), *Neuropsychological and cognitive processes in reading* (pp. 109–141). New York: Academic Press.

Satz, P., & Morris, R. (1983). Classification of learning disabled children. In R. E. Tarter (Ed.), *The child at psychiatric risk* (pp. 128–149). New York: Oxford University Press.

Speece, D. L. (1987). Information processing subtypes of learning-disabled readers. *Learning Disabilities Research, 2,* 91–102.

Speece, D. L., McKinney, J. D., & Appelbaum, M. (1985). Classification and validation of behavioral subtypes of learning disabled children. *Journal of Educational Psychology, 77,* 67–77.

Swanson, H. L. (1987a). Information processing theory and learning disabilities: An overview. *Journal of Learning Disabilities, 20,* 3–7.

Swanson, H. L. (1987b, October). *Subtyping the memory problems of learning disabled readers.* Paper presented at Council for Learning Disabilities, San Diego.

Torgesen, J. K. (1977). The role of nonspecific factors in the task performance of learning disabled children: A theoretical assessment. *Journal of Learning Disabilities, 10,* 33–40.

U.S. Department of Education (1987). *Ninth annual report to Congress on implementation of Public Law 94-142: The Education for All Handicapped Children act.* Washington, D.C.: U.S. Government Printing Office.

Weller, C., & Strawser, S. (1987). Adaptive behavior of subtypes of learning disabled individuals. *Journal of Special Education, 21,* 101–115.

Vellutino, F. R. (1979). *Dyslexia: Theory and research.* Cambridge, MA: MIT Press.

Ysseldyke, J. E., Algozzine, B., Richey, L., & Graden, J. (1982). Declaring students eligible for learning disability services: Why bother with the data? *Learning Disability Quarterly, 5,* 37–43.

13 Methodological Issues in Cluster Analysis: How Clusters Become Real

Deborah L. Speece
University of Maryland at College Park

Recently several articles and chapters have been written summarizing the problems and potential of classification efforts generally and cluster analysis specifically in adding to our understanding of learning disabilities (e.g., Kavale & Forness, 1987; McKinney, 1988; Torgesen, 1982). The focus of these works has been on the role of classification in science, surveys of various approaches to classification, and synthesis of findings across subtyping studies. Although most authors refer to the many decisions that face an investigator who chooses to use empirical methods, the decision points and consequences of the decisions have yet to be evaluated in relation to the study of learning disabilities.

The purpose of this review is not to insist on the superiority of empirical methods but rather to provide a discussion of the more vexing issues associated with applying cluster analysis techniques. Although social scientists typically are more interested in relationships that are derived after clusters are identified, lack of sufficient attention to the detail that leads to the formation of clusters will add more confusion than clarity to any field seeking methods of coping with intragroup variability. The goal of this review is to emphasize the flexibility of the method and to provide a framework from which rational decisions can be made.

Cluster analysis represents a family of empirical techniques designed to divide a heterogeneous sample of entities, usually subjects, into more homogeneous subgroups. In contrast to the emphasis of more familiar statistical methods, cluster analysis methods revere within group variability and seek to impose order on a group of individuals by classifying them into discrete subtypes.

The discussion of the technical aspects of cluster analysis methods will be restricted to hierarchical, agglomerative techniques in which every subject begins as a single entity followed by successive mergers of subjects or clusters until all subjects are contained in a single cluster. The reasons for this emphasis are that hierarchical techniques have received the most attention in the statistical literature and these techniques are most often selected by researchers in the social sciences. This focus does not imply the superiority of hierarchical over non-hierarchical methods (e.g., k means) as there is evidence that the latter perform equally as well under some conditions (Scheibler & Schneider, 1985) or may be useful in conjunction with hierarchical methods (Milligan, 1980; Morris, Blashfield, & Satz, 1986). The choice of hierarchical methods does represent a decision point and, consequently, presents some problems. The most obvious is determining what point in the hierarchy represents the best solution, that is, the correct number of clusters. If the sample size is 100, there are 99 possible solutions. A second issue is that subjects are not reassigned in later stages of clustering (as the number of clusters approaches 1) even though a subject may be more similar to members of a different cluster. Suggestions for addressing these issues are presented in a later section.

FRAMEWORK

The outline for this chapter loosely follows Skinner's (1981) three stage framework for the design of a study incorporating cluster analysis techniques: theory formulation, internal validity, and external validity. Theory formulation includes subject and variable selection and, in some cases, hypotheses. Although Skinner (1981) places choice of a similarity measure in the realm of internal validity, the decision on *how* entities are to be judged as similar is integral to one's theoretical orientation toward the problem at hand rather than a decision made independently. Thus, the choice of a similarity measure as well as an algorithm will be discussed within theory formulation.

Internal validity represents a set of procedures to assess the replicability of a cluster structure. Adams (1985) correctly notes that the use of the term validity in this case is really a misnomer as the procedures assess the *reliability* of a solution. As is true in measurement, reliability is a separate issue and should not be confused with evidence for validity. Success in replicating a solution does not insure validity.

External validity, or simply validity of a cluster solution, represents a set of procedures to determine if variables that are external to the data set used for clustering can differentiate among the clusters in some meaningful way. If variables are selected carefully, this step grounds the results of the reliability procedures to a reference point that is not confounded by earlier decisions in the clustering process.

The literature reviewed is drawn primarily from the statistical literature in education and psychology published since 1981. This benchmark was based on Milligan's (1981) thorough review of Monte Carlo investigations that summarized studies of reliability techniques prior to that date. In addition, papers in which hierarchical cluster analysis techniques were used by behavioral researchers are reviewed selectively to illustrate the methodological issues.

THEORY FORMULATION

The role of theory in learning disabilities has received thorough and careful treatment in the volume edited by Vaughn and Bos (1987) and by Torgesen (1986), as has the problem of sample definition (e.g., Keogh, 1987; McKinney, 1987; Senf, 1986). These issues are of general concern to research in learning disabilities and are not specific to classification efforts. However, when one's purpose is to describe a group of individuals by dividing them into discrete subtypes and then to assess the meaning of the subtypes via relationships with external criteria, the need for a theoretical rationale to set the foundation for the study becomes apparent. Success in obtaining subtypes is not related to logic or theory; one will always get subtypes regardless of whether there exists a system for interpretation. While this point is made so often in the literature it is becoming trite, the state of the art is such that it bears repeating.

For the most part, empirical subtype research in learning disabilities has not been theory driven per se, but in several cases the conceptual frameworks guiding the investigations were based on extensive evidence gleaned from research in single domains that used group difference designs. This is viewed as a step in the right direction but a comprehensive classification system of learning disabilities will need to incorporate measures across multiple domains (Kavale & Forness, 1987; McKinney, 1988). However, identification of a comprehensive system is not the only legitimate use of cluster analysis in learning disabilities and application of clustering techniques within domains may eventually lead to the identification of variables for a multiple domain study.

Problems regarding sample definition in learning disabilities are legion but will not be resolved here. Cluster analysis investigations have relied primarily on clinic or school defined samples with the notable exception of the Satz and Morris analysis of the Florida Longitudinal Study (Satz & Morris, 1981). In that study an unselected group of children was used in a cluster analysis to identify learning disabled subtypes, thus avoiding several problems related to selection bias. If one does not have the resources to study a sufficiently large group to obtain interesting subtypes for further classification, some care must be exercised in defining the population of interest, preferably on theoretical grounds. Torgesen (1987) proposed a continuum of useful suggestions regarding sample definition. For example we could drop the designator "learning disabilities" and define samples by the criterion or criteria of interest or apply stricter criteria for selection to a pool of school identified subjects. The latter approach was used to define a group of LD readers that was comparable to other research samples in the literature on reading and information processing (Speece, 1987). This method resulted in the clustering of only 55% of the available subjects. Although one could question the value of subtyping a subgroup, the goal was to understand heterogeneity of information processing skills in poor readers as opposed to learning disabilities generally.

A basic issue is how many subjects are required for cluster analysis. In contrast to more familiar statistical techniques, there are no rules for subject to variable ratios (the exception may be Q-factor analysis; see Fleiss & Zubin, 1969) or even variable to cluster ratios. This point is not widely understood. In general, the more subjects the better especially in regard to various reliability techniques. The critical issue is the degree of certainty one can have that the number of clusters identified in the sample reflect the number in the population. Obviously with small samples that are not selected randomly, one cannot have much confidence in this proposition. For this reason, it is best not to dismiss clusters with few members as "outliers" as more subjects may increase the n per cluster. For later analysis, however, the small clusters may need to be excluded on statistical grounds.

Selection of variables for both the clustering and as a method of validation is critical in the design of the study. As obvious as this statement is, one often finds investigators using measures that have little or no psychometric adequacy and no clearly delineated connection with theoretical propositions. The latter point is especially true of relationships between clustering variables and the external data set. When significant relationships are discovered, the investigator is often in the awkward position of employing ex post facto reasoning to explain the observed differences. Although this feat has been accomplished quite successfully, it clearly is not the strongest position. An exception to this criticism is the study of language subtypes by Feagans and Appelbaum (1986) in which a priori hypotheses were developed to predict the relationship between the subtypes and academic achievement. That the predicted relationships were obtained concurrently and longitudinally is a tribute to the power of theory.

Assuming that a reasonable nomological net can be cast about the problem of interest, this information can be used to select a similarity measure to define *how* subjects are to be judged as similar and an algorithm to define *why* these mergers are made. The more difficult of the two is similarity. In general, the choice is between correlation and distance measures and the problem can be cast into deciding the importance of elevation, scatter, and shape in defining the clusters (Cronbach & Gleser, 1953; Skinner, 1978). Given a single subject with scores across a multivariate data set, elevation refers to the mean level of performance across the variables, scatter is the standard deviation across the measures, and shape is the residual information after the mean and standard deviation have been removed from the subject's profile. Shape represents the "ups and downs" across the profile. A distance measure uses all three pieces of information in the form of raw scores (usually standardized) while correlation uses only shape.

The controversy in the statistical literature between correlation and distance measures appears to have subsided as recent Monte Carlo studies have compared the accuracy of both measures in conjunction with a variety of algorithms. This implies that both are tenable choices. It should be noted, however, that early papers by Cronbach and Gleser (1953) and Fleiss and Zubin (1969) question the logic of a correlation approach from the perspectives of interpretation and the advisability of deleting information (i.e., elevation and scatter) from the data set. Discussions of the issue emphasize that investigators provide a rationale for the choice based on knowledge of the consequences of the decision.

What, then, are the consequences in the context of research in learning disabilities? A correlation approach will judge as similar two subjects whose profile shapes are the same regardless of elevation and scatter. Thus a subjects's profile that resembles, for example, an "M" shape with points one standard deviation above the mean will evidence a high correlation with an "M" profile one standard deviation below the mean. Under what circumstances is this state of affairs reasonable? There appear to be at least two. Adams (1985) suggests that when the sample consists of learning disabled children known to have a similar level of performance, then one can reasonably ignore elevation and emphasize shape (see Speece, 1987).

A second possibility, that has not been addressed previously, relies on one's conception of learning disabilities in relation to "normal" performance. If there is evidence that LD children exhibit similar patterns of strengths and weaknesses as do non-LD children, albeit at different levels, then identification of pattern "types" that encompass the developmental spectrum may be the more appropriate choice. Using this rationale, one would expect LD and non-LD children to be members of the same clusters in some instances. The alternative to this position is that LD children exhibit a different developmental pattern, that is, represent a different population, and should not share cluster membership with non-LD children. The investigator can obtain either result via choice of correlation in the first instance and distance in the second. Unfortunately, most subtype studies to date have clustered only LD children and used performance of normals primarily as baseline data. The exceptions are the analyses of the Florida Longitudinal data (Satz & Morris, 1981; Morris, Blashfield, & Satz, 1986). Using distance as the measure of similarity to subtype normal and "reading disabled" children, Morris et al. (1986) obtained the result predicted earlier: Two clusters were identified and appeared to consist of normal and "poor" readers.

The existing subtype studies with learning disabled/reading disabled children have generally failed to present a strong rationale with respect to the connection between the various theoretical assumptions of the research and choice of a similarity index. Rather, preferences appear to be based within paradigms with neuropsychologists favoring distance (e.g., Lyon, Stewart, & Freedman, 1982; Morris et al., 1986) and educational psychologists preferring correlation (e.g., Edelbrock & Achenbach, 1980; Feagans & Appelbaum, 1986; Speece, McKinney, & Appelbaum, 1985). Although no single research group has the "high ground" regarding developmental constructs and learning disabilities, a compelling case can be made in favor of the developmental continuum perspective based on the results of studies that used either cluster analysis or a group difference methodology. To elaborate, a common finding in subtype studies, regardless of orientation, is that a "normal" profile of LD children is identified. An analysis of group difference results indicates overlap between LD and non-LD groups, significance notwithstanding (Weener, 1981). Taken together, one might expect some clusters of LD children to exhibit very different patterns of performance while others exhibit profiles similar to nonidentified children. A correlation approach would allow examination of this possibility while distance would likely mask it.

Some researchers who employ distance provide the rationale that they are interested in elevation or "severity." The problem with this logic is that distance indices use elevation, scatter, and shape, thus the formation of the clusters may be based on any combination of the three criteria, not simply mean level (Skinner, 1978). This confounding precludes statements regarding severity.

Skinner (1978) has provided one method of resolving the similarity dilemma. He proposed that initial clustering be based on correlation, that is, shape, with the resulting clusters reclassified by adding scatter and then elevation. This procedure allows examination of the influence of shape, scatter, and elevation to cluster formation. It also demands a large sample. Nonetheless, as we become more rigorous with respect to making theoretical assumptions explicit in the design stage, this formulation may become a viable approach in specific contexts (e.g., Speece & Cooper, in press).

Choice of an algorithm in applied situations depends primarily on choice of a similarity index. Both Milligan (1981) and Lorr (1983) provided excellent reviews of Monte Carlo studies that assess the ability of a variety of algorithms to recover known structures. Of interest here is the performance of the algorithm in conjunction with the similarity index. As summarized by Lorr (1983), Ward's minimum variance algorithm (Ward, 1963) performs best in combination with Euclidean distance; the average linkage algorithm performs best in combination with correlation. The degree of recovery is similar for these two combinations. These conclusions were confirmed in a recent Monte Carlo study by Scheibler and Schneider (1985) with the additional finding that the Lance Williams algorithm performed as well as Ward's when Euclidean distance was used as the similarity measure.

The difficulty with these recommendations is that they are based on performance on simulated data sets in which the structure is known, and clusters are compact and well separated. This knowledge, of course, does not exist with actual data. To address this problem, Morey, Blashfield, and Skinner (1983) used a real data set to evaluate the effectiveness of different combinations of algorithms and similarity indices. In addition to a comparison of methods, the authors used an extensive and detailed design to establish the validity of the subtypes. Of importance here is that they obtained the same results in the replication phase regarding Ward's and average linkage algorithms as did the Monte Carlo studies. Morey et al. (1983) found that Ward's algorithm with Euclidean distance provided the best discriminatory power across methods. They caution us, however, in noting that the Ward's method was particularly sensitive to the elevation dimension in their application (alcoholics) and that use of the technique may not be recommended with other problems. In any event, choice of these algorithms implies that the underlying clusters are compact as opposed to elongated and do not overlap. Although this is how we may choose to conceptualize empirical clusters, there is usually no a priori evidence to support this position.

RELIABILITY

Following selection of a similarity index and algorithm, three questions regarding reliability of the solution need to be addressed: (a) Are there any clusters? (b) How many? and (c) Can they be replicated? Kavale and Forness (1987) have correctly pointed out that investigators involved in cluster analysis do not seriously consider the possibility that no clusters exist. Generally, one skips this question, and proceeds to examine the second and third. In regard to the first question, Milligan and Cooper (1985) recently compared the effectiveness of 30 statistical stopping rules in recovering the correct number of clusters. Three of the six best performing rules have been incorporated in the most recent version of SAS (1985). These rules are referred to in the SAS manual as the pseudo F statistic, the pseudo t^2 statistic and the Cubic Clustering Criterion. They correspond, respectively, to the first, second, and sixth best rules evaluated by Milligan and Cooper (1985).

Although the positive evaluation of these rules and their incorporation in a popular software package is good news, some cautions are in order. First, the evaluation was based on a simulated data set with well-defined cluster structure (Milligan & Cooper, 1985). Second, the evaluation was based on clustering with Euclidean distance so performance with correlation as a similarity measure is unknown. Third, the tests are conservative; whereas significant tests provide confidence that clusters exist, nonsignificant tests do not rule out the presence of clusters (Duda & Hart, 1973; Hawkins, Muller, & ten Krooden, 1982; Sarle, 1983).

As an example of the last point, Sarle (1983) reported that the performance of the Cubic Clustering Criterion is not good when the number of clusters approximates the number of variables plus one (p. 11). In subtyping studies in learning disabilities this situation is a frequent occurrence. Given the current state of affairs, the recommendation is to use the tests cautiously but as Duda and Hart (1973), whose work provided the basis for the pseudo t^2 statistic, suggested, it may be best to assume that a "suspicious test is better than none" (p. 244).

Due to the recency of the evaluation and availability of the stopping rules, they have not been used extensively in the LD subtyping research. Instead, a number of heuristic techniques have been implemented to assess the number of clusters problem and replicability. There are many variations on basically two themes: comparison with different algorithms and use of some type of split sample or independent sample technique.

The logic of comparing solutions across different algorithms is that a cluster structure should not be algorithm-dependent (Anderberg, 1973; Johnson & Wichern, 1982; Lorr, 1983). Based on the results of methodological studies, when correlation is the similarity measure, a comparison of average linkage and Ward's method appears appropriate in that they perform similarly in regard to recovery rate (Milligan, 1981; Morey et al., 1983; Scheibler & Schneider, 1985). The equivalence of these algorithms with distance is not clear; based on Scheibler and Schneider's (1985) results, Ward's may be best compared with the Lance Williams algorithm using the above criterion.

The strongest case for replicability can be made when two different samples are both cluster analysed and the results compared. Morey et al. (1983) clustered samples A and B, assigned members of B to clusters identified in A, and compared the membership agreement between assigned clusters and empirical clusters. A version of this technique was incorporated in a study by Morris et al. (1986). In studies where sample size did not permit an even split, some proportion of the sample was randomly selected and independently clustered with membership agreement compared to results for the full sample (McKinney, Short, & Feagans, 1985; Speece, 1987; Speece, McKinney, & Appelbaum, 1985).

An issue related to the number of clusters problem is the determination of correct cluster membership, a problem with hierarchical techniques noted in the introduction. Since subjects are not reassigned as clusters or subjects are merged, it is necessary to assess the extent to which subjects maintain cluster identity within a specific solution. A discriminant function analysis technique referred to as "forecasting" is useful in this regard (see Speece, 1985). A discriminant function is derived for each cluster and subjects are "forecasted" into each cluster based on the fit of the data to the classification criterion resulting in a posterior probability of membership in each cluster. Reassignment is necessary when membership probability is higher for a cluster other than the original assignment. This general approach, outlined by Feild and Shoenfeldt (1975), also has been used to provide useful descriptive information with respect to cluster membership of normally achieving children (Speece et al., 1985) and longitudinal membership stability (McKinney & Speece, 1986). It must be emphasized, however, that tests of significance (e.g., MANOVA, discriminant function analysis) based on cluster differences across the classification variables are not valid and do not provide any evidence of cluster validation (Aldenderfer & Blashfield, 1984; Milligan & Cooper, 1987). When one considers that the purpose of cluster analysis is to minimize within cluster variability and maximize between cluster differences it becomes apparent that the testing of these differences is superfluous and should be avoided.

The last approach to assessing reliability to be discussed is the generation and clustering of a simulated data set and comparison of the results of these random clusters with those in the real data set. If the F ratios resulting from univariate ANOVA's on the "real" clusters are larger than those produced by the random clusters, some evidence is obtained regarding the presence of non-random cluster structure. Aldenderfer and Blashfield (1984) provided an overview of the method with examples. Watson, Goldgar, and Ryschon (1983) and Morris et al. (1986) have implemented the technique in their studies. If only a single random sample is generated for comparison purposes the technique is heuristic as a significance threshold for differences between F ratios cannot be determined. However, significance thresholds can be determined for simulated distributions if enough samples are generated. In the latter case the simulation method is regarded as a statistical, not heuristic, approach to cluster structure.[1]

Based on the foregoing, one firm conclusion can be drawn: There is no single set of procedures that has evolved as the superior approach to cluster analysis. One possible limitation of previous substantive work in cluster analysis is that researchers have been overly concerned about deriving "the correct" number of clusters in the replication stage of the design. It may be more useful to our goals and certainly more realistic to entertain several possible solutions at this stage and evaluate them against the external criteria. Since classification efforts in learning disabilities are primarily exploratory at this point, evaluating several solutions recognizes the subjective nature of the technique and the reality that it is virtually impossible to identify the single correct partition of a real data set. This recommendation is not put forth as support for unlimited tests of significance. Rather, it acknowledges that the guidance functions available are imperfect and that interesting subtypes may be missed if an early commitment to a single solution is made. It is incumbent upon the investigator to present fully all analyses with respect to reliability and validity efforts. If a reasonable framework linking clustering variables with external variables has been developed, then the evaluation of more than one solution should not be regarded as a weakness in the

VALIDITY

The importance of assessing external validity was detailed under theory formulation. Further discussion of validation methods can be found in Milligan and

---

[1] I thank Glenn Milligan for calling this difference to my attention and also for his insightful critique of this chapter.

Cooper (1987) and Skinner (1981) with applied examples in several papers including Feagans and Appelbaum (1986), Lyon, Stewart, and Freedman (1982), and McKinney and Speece (1986). A limitation of work in learning disabilities is that most studies employ ex post facto reasoning with regard to explaining observed differences among clusters. Another limitation is that validation is not perceived as a series of studies (Skinner, 1981) but rather as a one shot proposition. Reid Lyon's (1985) work in establishing the clinical utility of his subtypes is an important exception. Perhaps as more effort is put toward designing prospective studies with thorough understanding of the strengths and weaknesses of the methodology, investigators will devote more energy to the content of the study and become less enmeshed in the technique.

In conclusion, I offer a few observations from my perspective which is the *near* side heterogeneity. First, there is a notable difference in the degree of caution offered by methodologists in discussing the possible weaknesses of their studies as compared with researchers in the social sciences. Specifically, researchers in learning disabilities tend to reify their clusters based on scanty evidence. Much is to be learned by studying the content of the Discussion sections of Monte Carlo studies. Second, an investigator can justify any decision made in the context of cluster analysis if one reads narrowly in the statistical literature. As an example, Romesburg (1984) recently published a text entitled "Cluster analysis for researchers." This is an intriguing title for those who wish to use the method as a tool in their research. However, a review of this text by Milligan (1985) points out that the book contains misleading statements and uneven treatment of the limitations of algorithms. Specifically, Romesburg implies that only Euclidean distance can be used with Ward's algorithm and that hypothesis testing is not a legitimate activity in cluster analysis situations (Milligan, 1985). The lesson here is to read broadly. Third, and on a more positive note, the subtyping research in the field of learning disabilities appears to be gaining sophistication. The frequency of the methodological statement consisting of only "we used cluster analysis techniques and identified four clusters" is declining with movement toward at least mentioning the similarity measure, algorithm and computer program. Still missing, however, is a well conceived rationale guiding selection of variables and methods that is tied to some conceptual framework. We would do well to heed Cormack's concern "of the growing tendency to regard numerical taxonomy as a satisfactory alternative to clear thinking" (cited in Skinner, 1977, p. 142).

How, then, do clusters become real? To answer this, I searched for the perfect philosophical statement from a reknowned scientist (following Kavale & Forness, 1985, 1987). Regrettably, my reading of the great philosophers is limited these days to Dr. Seuss and his colleagues in my children's library. However, with a bit of editing, and apologies to Margery Williams (1981), I found the answer:

> "What is a Real cluster?" asked the Rabbit one day. "Does it mean having things that buzz inside you and a stick out handle?"

"Real clusters aren't how you are made," said the Skin Horse. "It's a thing that happens to you. When an investigator studies you for a long, long time, not just to play with, but REALLY studies you, then clusters become Real."
"Does it hurt?" asked the Rabbit.
"Sometimes," said the Skin Horse for he was always truthful.
"Does it happen all at once, like an F test," he asked, "or bit by bit?"
"It doesn't happen all at once," said the Skin Horse. "Clusters become. It takes a long time. That's why it doesn't often happen to investigators who break easily, or have sharp edges, or who have to be carefully kept. Generally, by the time your clusters are Real, most of your hair has fallen out, and your eyes drop out, and you get loose in the joints and very shabby. But these things don't matter at all, because once your clusters are Real you can't be ugly, except to editors and reviewers who don't understand."

ACKNOWLEDGMENTS

Preparation of this paper was partially supported by a grant from the U.S. Department of Education, Office of Special Education and Rehabilitative Services (Grant No. G008530155). Several colleagues have influenced my thinking on the issues presented in this paper, perhaps unknowingly. In this regard, I wish to acknowledge Mark Appelbaum, David Cooper, James D. McKinney, Elizabeth Short, and Lee Swanson. Although I would also like to share the blame for inaccuracies, any errors are my own.

REFERENCES

Adams, K. M. (1985). Theoretical, methodological, and statistical issues. In B. P. Rourke (Ed.), *Neuropsychology of learning disabilities* (pp. 17–39). New York: Guilford Press.

Aldenderfer, M. S., & Blashfield, R. K. (1984). *Cluster analysis.* Sage University Paper Series on Quantitative Applications in the Social Sciences, 07-044. Beverly Hills and London: Sage Publications.

Anderberg, M. R. (1973). *Cluster analysis for applications.* New York: Academic Press.

Cronbach, L. J., & Gleser, G. C. (1953). Assessing similarity between profiles. *Psychological Bulletin, 50,* 456–473.

Duda, R. O., & Hart, P. E. (1973). *Pattern classification and scene analysis.* New York: Wiley.

Edelbrock, C., & Achenbach, T. M. (1980). A typology of child behavior profile patterns: Distribution and correlates of disturbed children aged 5–16. *Journal of Abnormal Child Psychology, 8,* 441–470.

Feagans, L., & Appelbaum, M. I. (1986). Validation of language subtypes in learning disabled children. *Journal of Educational Psychology, 78,* 358–364.

Feild, H. S., & Schoenfeldt, L. F. (1975). Ward and Hook revisited: A two-part procedure for overcoming a deficiency in the grouping of persons. *Educational and Psychological Measurement, 35,* 171–173.

Fleiss, J. L., & Zubin, J. (1969). On the methods and theory of clustering. *Multivariate Behavioral Research, 4,* 235–250.

Hawkins, D. M., Muller, M. W., & ten Krooden, J. A. (1982). Cluster analysis. In D. M. Hawkins

(Ed.), *Topics in applied multivariate analysis* (pp. 303–356). Cambridge, England: Cambridge University Press.

Johnson, R. A., & Wichern, D. W. (1982). *Applied multivariate techniques.* Englewood Cliffs, NJ: Prentice-Hall.

Kavale, K. A., & Forness, S. R. (1985). *The science of learning disabilities.* San Diego: College Hill Press.

Kavale, K. A., & Forness, S. R. (1987). The far side of heterogeneity: A critical analysis of empirical subtyping research in learning disabilities. *Journal of Learning Disabilities, 20,* 374–382.

Keogh, B. K. (1987). A shared attribute model of learning disabilities. In S. Vaughn & C. S. Bos (Eds.), *Research in learning disabilities* (pp. 3–18). Boston: College-Hill Press.

Lorr, M. (1983). *Cluster analysis for social scientists.* San Francisco: Jossey-Bass.

Lyon, G. R. (1985). Educational validation studies of learning disability subtypes. In B. P. Rourke (Ed.), *Neuropsychology of learning disabilities* (pp. 228–253). New York: Guilford Press.

Lyon, G. R., Stewart, N., & Freedman, D. (1982). Neuropsychological characteristics of empirically derived subgroups of learning disabled readers. *Journal of Clinical Neuropsychology, 4,* 343–365.

McKinney, J. D. (1987). Research on the identification of learning disabled children: Perspectives on changes in educational policy. In S. Vaughn & C. S. Bos (Eds.), *Research in learning disabilities* (pp. 215–237). Boston: College Hill Press.

McKinney, J. D. (1988). Research on conceptually and empirically derived subtypes of specific learning disabilities. In M. C. Wang, H. J. Walberg, & M. C. Reynolds (Eds.), *The handbook of special education: Research and practice Vol. II* (pp. 253–281). Oxford, England: Pergamon Press.

McKinney, J. D., Short, E. J., & Feagans, L. (1985). Academic consequences of perceptual-linguistic subtypes of learning disabled children. *Learning Disabilities Research, 1,* 6–17.

McKinney, J. D., & Speece, D. L. (1986). Academic consequences and longitudinal stability of behavioral subtypes of learning disabled children. *Journal of Educational Psychology, 78,* 365–372.

Milligan, G. W. (1980). An examination of the effect of six types of error perturbation on fifteen clustering algorithms. *Psychometrika, 45,* 325–342.

Milligan, G. W. (1981). A review of Monte Carlo tests of cluster analysis. *Multivariate Behavioral Research, 16,* 379–407.

Milligan, G. W. (1985). [Book review of *Cluster analysis for researchers*]. *Journal of Classification, 2,* 133–137.

Milligan, G. W., & Cooper, M. C. (1985). An examination of procedures for determining the number of clusters in a data set. *Psychometrika, 50,* 159–179.

Milligan, G. W., & Cooper, M. C. (1987). Methodology review: Clustering methods. *Applied Psychological Measurement, 11,* 329–354.

Morey, L. C., Blashfield, R. K., & Skinner, H. A. (1983). A comparison of cluster analysis techniques within a sequential validation framework. *Multivariate Behavioral Research, 18,* 309–329.

Morris, R., Blashfield, R. K., & Satz, P. (1986). Developmental classification of learning disabled children. *Journal of Clinical and Experimental Neuropsychology, 8,* 371–392.

Romesburg, H. C. (1984). *Cluster analysis for researchers.* Belmont, CA: Lifetime Learning Publications.

Sarle, W. S. (1983). Cubic clustering criterion (SAS Technical Report A-108). Cary, NC: SAS Institute Inc.

SAS Institute Inc. (1985). *SAS User's guide: Statistics, Version 5 Edition.* Cary, NC: Author.

Satz, P., & Morris, R. (1981). Learning disability subtypes: A review. In F. J. Pirozzolo & M. C. Wittrock (Eds.), *Neuropsychological and cognitive processes in reading* (pp. 109–141). New York: Academic Press.

Scheibler, D., & Schneider, W. (1985). Monte Carlo tests of the accuracy of cluster analysis algorithms: A comparison of hierarchical and nonhierarchical methods. *Multivariate Behavioral Research, 20,* 283–304.

Senf, G. M. (1986). LD research in sociological and scientific perspective. In J. K. Torgesen & B. Y. L. Wong (Eds.), *Psychological and educational perspectives on learning disabilities* (pp. 27–53).Orlando: Academic Press.

Skinner, H. A. (1977). The eyes that fix you: A model for classification research. *Canadian Psychological Review, 18,* 142–151.

Skinner, H. A. (1978). Differentiating the contribution of elevation, scatter, and shape in profile similarity. *Educational and Psychological Measurement, 38,* 297–308.

Skinner, H. A. (1981). Toward the integration of classification theory and methods. *Journal of Abnormal Psychology, 20,* 68–87.

Speece, D. L. (1985). Information processing and reading in subtypes of learning disabled children. *Dissertation Abstracts International, 45,* 2459A. (University Microfilms No. 84-25, 518)

Speece, D. L. (1987). Information processing subtypes of learning-disabled readers. *Learning Disabilities Research, 2,* 91–102.

Speece, D. L., McKinney, J. D., & Appelbaum, M. I. (1985). Classification and validation of behavioral subtypes of learning-disabled children. *Journal of Educational Psychology, 77,* 67–77.

Torgesen, J. K. (1982). The use of rationally defined subgroups in research on learning disabilities. In J. P. Das, R. F. Mulcahy, & A. E. Wall (Eds.), *Theory and research in learning disabilities* (pp. 111–131). New York: Plenum Press.

Torgesen, J. K. (1986). Learning disabilities theory: Its current state and future prospects. *Journal of Learning Disabilities, 19,* 399–407.

Torgesen, J. K. (1987). Thinking about the future by distinguishing between issues that have resolutions and those that do not. In S. Vaughn & C. S. Bos (Eds.), *Research in learning disabilities: Issues and future directions* (pp. 55–64). Boston: College Hill Press.

Vaughn, S., & Bos, C. S. (Eds.). (1987). *Research in learning disabilities.* Boston: College-Hill Press.

Ward, J. H. (1963). Hierarchical grouping to optimize an objective function. *Journal of the American Statistical Association, 58,* 236–244.

Watson, B. V., Goldgar, D. W., & Ryschon, K. L. (1983). Subtypes of reading disability. *Journal of Clinical Neuropsychology, 5,* 377–399.

Weener, P. (1981). On comparing learning disabled and regular classroom children. *Journal of Learning Disabilities, 14,* 227–232.

Williams, M. (1981). *The velveteen rabbit.* Philadelphia: The Running Press.

14 A Critical Appraisal of Empirical Subtyping Research in Learning Disabilities

Kenneth A. Kavale
The University of Iowa

There has been a steady increase in and attention paid to empirical subtyping research in the field of learning disabilities (LD). The identification of subgroups has enhanced classification efforts in the field and are viewed as positive steps towards enhanced understanding of the LD phenomenon (Adelman & Taylor, 1985). While a significant contribution, empirical subtyping must still be viewed cautiously. It is not the solution to the many problems confronting the LD field and must be evaluated in relation to classification in other fields (e.g., botany, zoology) where taxonomic issues are primary concerns. Therefore, the purpose of this chapter is to analyze critically the present work in empirical subtyping.

THE NATURE OF LEARNING DISABILITIES AND SUBTYPE RESEARCH

The variability which marks the LD field is the reason why classification needs to be a central concern. This is the problem of heterogeneity, which implies a significant diversity within the LD population. In order to harness that diversity, the LD field is engaged in classification efforts that seek to order and to organize the variability which makes LD students so different from one another. Research in LD has been directed at finding differences between LD and normal comparison groups. The differences, however, have remained as discrete and isolated descriptions that have not coalesced into a unified conceptualization of LD. The consequences are found in vague boundary conditions that has led to a steady increase in the LD population which has become increasingly heterogeneous.

Classification thus becomes the means through which heterogeneity can be managed rationally. The life sciences (i.e., botany, zoology) whose variability is equal to if not greater than that found in LD, have addressed the problem through theoretically driven taxonomic efforts. Why can't the LD field do the same? A partial answer is the fact that most of us in LD have been nurtured on the idea that LD is a homogeneous disorder and our efforts are best directed at finding single-paradigm explanations. Keogh (1987) has argued cogently that LD is, in fact, many things and what is needed is a shared attribute notion. In a meta-analysis of 1400 studies, Kavale and Nye (1985–86) compared LD and normal groups across four domains and 38 variables but found no single area where LD and normal groups could be differentiated clearly. It was concluded that LD is not associated with a single area but is a complex and multivariate problem. Although inelegant, this conclusion must be reflected in conceptualizing LD and a major contribution of subtype research is to move the LD field towards recognition of the variegated nature of LD. Heterogeneity, rather than being villified, should be recognized as something to be studied in its own right for explicating the complexity inherent in LD.

By the mid-1970s, there appeared attempts to divide empirically the general population of LD students into more homogeneous subgroups (see Lyon, 1983; McKinney, 1984, 1988; Rourke, 1985; Satz & Morris, 1981, 1983 for reviews). Classification has always been an interest for special education in general (see Reynolds, 1984) and the fields of mental retardation (see Grossman, 1983; Zigler, Balla, & Hodapp, 1984) and behavior disorders (see Achenbach & Edelbrock, 1978) in particular. But classification in LD differs from these other areas in form and function. Classification in mental retardation is concerned primarily with degree in the form of severity levels while classification in behavior disorders is concerned primarily with a single dimension in the form of social/emotional indicators. In contrast, classification in LD is multivariate and is not aimed exclusively at dividing the population along a single dimension. Rather, classification in LD is aimed at identifying subgroups along a variety of dimensions which may then be used to describe the basic nature of LD. The scope of LD classification thus transcends simple categorization and is also concerned with enhancing the theoretical understanding of LD (Lyon & Risucci, 1988).

THE GOAL OF SUBTYPE RESEARCH IN LEARNING DISABILITIES

The goal of subtype research is to classify the general LD population into homogeneous subgroups for both practical and scientific purposes. Subtype research focuses on several purposes but questions arise about those purposes (see Sokal, 1974). For example, what is the object of classification (Warburton, 1967)? Is it individuals (i.e., those possessing LD) or behaviors (i.e., the attributes possessed by those individuals)? The distinction is not always clear since it is possible to identify LD subtypes that emphasize different features (e.g., linguistic, achievement, behavioral, neuropsychological) in individuals who possess multiple deficits. Should it be the single feature (i.e., deficit) or should it be the individual that is the primary object of classification? By not distinguishing which is the primary object, there is the risk of confusing the natural order of nature with that imposed upon it in subtype research. This is what biologists call essentialist versus population thinking (Hull, 1974). Population thinking stresses uniqueness with the individual being most important, not the type. There is no "typical" individual. Essentialist thinking focuses on essences that are defined by typical values. Average values are sought and variability is considered nothing but error. The problem is that the averages are not reflective of anything of real importance. Present subtype research may be presently dominated by essentialist thinking. But differences among LD individuals are real and are not captured by average values used as the grist for subtyping. Therefore, subtype research should strive for more population focused thinking.

Without an emphasis on the individual, a primary purpose of classification may be lost that is, to convey information about that individual (Fleishman, 1982). If, however, the emphasis is on attributes, there exists the risk of confusing the meaning of classification with diagnosis. These are different; classification refers to the process whereby categories are constructed while diagnosis refers to the assignment of individuals to an existing set of categories (Achenbach & Edelbrock, 1983). This is a conceptual confusion which needs to be recognized in subtype research.

It is probably the case that a focus on attributes leads to an emphasis on diagnosis. The educational utility of such efforts might be limited since an integral part of the process (i.e., intervention) is not addressed. Classification methods can, however, be applied in efforts aimed at both diagnosis *and* remediation. For LD, the problem is not only the validity of a diagnosis but also some insight in the question: What is the best educational treatment? Recent research by Lyon (1985a, 1985b) and McKinney, Short, and Feagens (1985) provide good examples of how classification systems can be used for educational purposes particularly by examining subtype x treatment interactions. Although these efforts represent a sound beginning to an important problem, it is necessary for studies to avoid both the conceptual and methodological pitfalls found in previous aptitude x treatment interaction research (see Kavale & Forness, 1987).

THE PRODUCTS OF SUBTYPE RESEARCH

Subtype research aims at dividing heterogeneous LD samples into homogeneous subgroups based on performance patterns obtained through multivariate classification techniques (e.g., cluster analysis, Q-factor analysis). The resulting patterns are the subtypes and a representative sample of subtype research is summarized in Table 14.1.

Table 14.1 reveals some commonality in subtype research. Although a variety of different tests are used, the measures fall under several general headings suggesting that similar areas of functioning are assessed. The average number of subgroups identified was 3.5 with the range being 2 to 7 which suggests limited variability in the number of subgroups emerging.

But the commonalities found in Table 14.1 also raise some questions. For example, what is the relationship between the measures used and subgroups identified? Are linguistic subgroups obtained because linguistic measures are used? Table 14.1 supports the view of a strong association between the measures

TABLE 14.1
Empirical Subtype Research in Learning Disabilities

Study	Measures (Number)	Technique	No. of LD Subtypes
Del Dotto and Rourke (1984)	Neuropsychological (21)	Q-Factor Analysis Cluster Analysis	3
Doehring and Hoshko (1977)	Neuropsychological (22) Reading (9)	Q-Factor Analysis	6
Doehring, Hoshko, and Bryans (1979)	Neuropsychological (22) Reading (9)	Q-Factor Analysis	3
Feagans and Appelbaum (1986)	Linguistic (6)	Cluster Analysis	5
Fisk and Rourke (1979)	Neuropsychological (32) Psychoeducational (2)	Q-Factor	3
Joschko and Rourke (1985)	Neuropsychological (Reitan Battery)	Cluster Analysis	4
Lyon et al. (1981)	Neuropsychological (2) Psychoeducational (6)	Cluster Analysis	5
Lyon et al. (1982)	Neuropsychological (2) Psychoeducational (7)	Cluster Analysis	4
Lyon and Watson (1981)	Neuropsychological (2) Psychoeducational (6)	Cluster Analysis	5
McKinney et al. (1985)	Perceptual (3) Linguistic (3)	Cluster Analysis	3
Petraukas and Rourke (1979)	Neuropsychological (32) Psychoeducational (2)	Q-Factor Analysis	3
Satz and Morris (1981)	Linguistic (2) Perceptual-Motor (2)	Cluster Analysis	5
Speece et al. (1985)	Behavioral (1)	Cluster Analysis	7
Watson et al. (1983)	Neuropsychological (8) Linguistic (4) Readings (6)	Cluster Analysis	2
Wolfus et al. (1980)	Linguistic (15)	Discriminant Analysis	2

used and the resulting subgroups. In fact, the correlation between assessments (i.e., names of tests) and outcomes (i.e., subtype name) was almost perfect ($r = .983$). It thus appears that the measures utilized to obtain data exerted a strong influence on outcomes and suggests that subtypes are actually defined in terms of the functions being assessed. In one sense, this is antithetical to scientific progress (Laudan, 1977). Scientific progress assumes the development of new concepts and their refinement. The high correlation between measures and subtypes suggests that present efforts really introduce no new concepts but only those that have already been established. These are not refined but rather only reiterated.

What then can be said about the subgroups identified? How different or how alike are subgroups defined by the same general class of assessments? Too much overlap among subgroups is a problem since classification may be analogous but they cannot be wholly analogous or they would, in fact, be identical. Classification is an act of distinction and demarcation but when there is overlap among resulting categories the outcome is what Hesse (1966) termed "negative analogies" (or disanalogies) which tend to be a source of confusion. Classifying involves the adjudication of boundaries, and it is the imposition of boundaries which provide the structure for the classification (Blackwelder, 1967). Classifications are thus arbitrary structural arrangements comprised of objects and boundaries in a binary system: this object belongs or this object does not belong. But overlap in a classification system obscures the boundaries and does not allow for the required binary reduction. The boundaries must be articulated clearly but presently in subtype research they are not. The problem here may be one where a complex system like LD is actually more than the sum of its parts. This is not in some metaphysical sense but rather in the pragmatic sense that given the properties of the parts and the nature of their relationships it is not a trivial matter to infer the properties of the whole (Medawar, 1984).

Another problem emerged from examining the studies listed in Table 14.1. On average, 30% (range 13% to 51%) of the subjects clustered into a subgroup showing no major deficits ("principally normal"). What conclusion can be drawn about these approximately 3 out of 10 subjects? Were they misidentified as LD initially? This is a possibility but it has also been suggested that measures used were possibly not robust enough to identify all facets of the general area under investigation (e.g., linguistic functioning, reading achievement) or that performance differences in the area under study were not the result of skill deficiencies in that area per se but rather the result of other factors interfering with performance (i.e., instruction, social/emotional) (Lyon, 1985b). This is a problem that needs to be addressed in empirical subtype research if the results are to be generalized to the entire LD population.

A final observation about Table 14.1. A majority of the studies identified what might be termed general subtypes which really only represent a first cut at the data. The outcome is best termed a macrotaxonomy where the process is one of grouping objects into classes (Mayr, 1982). Most of the studies have, in fact, identified classes that would be the biological equivalent of a genus, the lowest collective category. But a genus is a collective category that consists of an aggregate of lower order members termed species who, in turn, share joint properties. Thus, we have linguistic subtypes, perceptual subtypes, and the like. What is required now is microtaxonomy which refers to classification at the level of species (Mayr, 1982). A behavioral subtype may be considered a genus which now requires refinement into species. The LD field has provided microtaxonomies for behavioral subtypes (Speece, McKinney, & Appelbaum, 1985) and information processing subtypes (Speece, 1987). A broad class (genus) was analyzed into the lowest level of genuine discontinuity above the level of the individual (Blackwelder, 1967). Just like the red oak and the pin oak are different species so too are, for example, attention deficit and withdrawn behavior within the realm of behavioral subtypes. This type of refinement in classification results in scientific progress. This is not to say that microtaxonomy is better in any sense but rather that it is different. Both activities are necessary for a complete taxonomic effort.

THE DEVELOPMENT OF NUMERICAL TAXONOMY

During the last century, classical methods of taxonomy were formally developed to provide classification systems for life forms. These could be ultimate or proximate (Hull, 1974). Ultimate systems were based on assumptions about evolution and development. The underlying theme is *why* in the sense of attempting to order nature. Proximate systems were far more functional and attempted to determine *how* a system can be constructed. The how is found in measurement and quantification that are operationalized into a system. Although both ultimate and proximate perspectives are important, the development of numerical taxonomy (see Sokal & Sneath, 1963) favored a proximate perspective because of the possibility of analyzing numerical data from nature (e.g., Clifford & Stephenson, 1975; Dunn & Everitt, 1982; Jardine & Sibson, 1971). The rigor here is appealing but may provide a false sense of closure because insights into the why of a system are minimized (Johnson, 1970).

For example, a strictly proximate basis of taxonomy may confound temporal aspects involved in LD. Numerical taxonomies identify LD subtypes based upon data collected at a particular point in time. Such a cross-sectional approach cannot account for the developmental aspects of LD (see Kirk & Chalfant, 1984) which would require an ultimate perspective for complete understanding since developmental concerns are not presumed in the application of numerical (i.e., proximate) methods. Thus, proximate classification in LD is probably useful, regardless of how functional it may be, only if it is based on some rational ultimate perspective that incorporates what is known about the development of LD. Numerical methods are most useful then when they are applied not on the basis of some favored measures but rather on well-conceived conceptual models (see Lyon & Risucci, 1988).

NUMERICAL TAXONOMY AND CLUSTER ANALYSIS

With respect to actual methodology, there are an assortment of techniques that fall under the heading of numerical taxonomy. The most popular technique is cluster analysis (e.g., Anderberg, 1973; Everitt, 1980; Tryon & Bailey, 1970) and Speece (this volume) has provided us with valuable insights into the procedure.

But even before the selection of a clustering method, there is a most basic question: Does the structure of the data warrant any clustering effort? It is necessary to first test clustering tendency in the data to determine the extent to which there are homogeneous yet distinct groupings embodied in the data (see Dubes & Jain, 1979 for a review of methods). The point is that multivariate data sets do not automatically qualify for cluster analysis. The failure to detect clustering tendency may suggest that the variables chosen were not appropriate, the measures used were unreliable, or perhaps there exists only one cluster. If not tested, the results may be spurious since many clustering methods produce groupings from any data set—"garbage in, clusters out" as a take-off on the popular criticism of factor analysis.

As Speece (this volume) suggested, cluster analysis, does not represent a unitary technique but is represented by different methodological procedures that differ with respect to both form and function. The primary conclusion is that different clustering methods often generate very different classification schemes for the same data (e.g., Blashfield & Aldenderfer, 1978; Everitt, 1979; Fleiss & Zubin, 1969). The question becomes: Which solution is correct? It is at this point that the empirical nature of the process must be replaced by subjective decisions which, in turn, should be based on a rational strategy incorporating a well-defined purpose and a sound theoretical base. It is necessary to guard against naive empiricism (Morris, Blashfield, & Satz, 1981). Clustering algorithms are merely heuristic devices and there appropriateness is subject to debate (Simpson, 1964; Mayr, 1965). As Mayr (1982) suggested, "The question is to what extent numerical methods are useful and indeed superior to the human computer is not yet settled" (p. 245).

THE LOGIC OF CLUSTER ANALYSIS

In a theoretical sense, there is an ideal logical strategy to follow in applying cluster analysis techniques (Skinner, 1977):

1. Precise characterization of the data and the kind of representation wanted are set up;

2. Criteria of adequacy for such representations are established;

3. Then there is a quest for an efficient algorithm.

But, for the most part, this sequence is not followed and, in fact, it is more common for the inverse sequence to be followed. There seems to be a confusion between algorithms and the methods they implement. This leads back to the discussion of purpose for, in a field like LD, there exists, in general, no *unique* optimal solution and no algorithm which is guaranteed to find an optimal solution. A methodology (e.g., cluster analysis) cannot be believed in simply because it works well. The application of cluster analysis techniques is not an unreflective exercise wherein the "best" cluster solution is generalizable only to some *ex post facto* reconciliation with theory. Instead cluster analysis should be used with the goal being the representation of data to yield useful psychological/conceptual realities (e.g., about treatment) rather than simply a process to yield an answer to a problem (i.e., what subtypes can be found in these data).

Regardless of the actual methodology used to create a classification, the desired outcome is a taxonomy which represents a systematic distinguishing, ordering, and naming of elements within a domain (Cormack, 1971). It is also important to note that a taxonomy also represents an epistemic structure providing a description for the relationships between elements (Beckner, 1959). It is here that the relationship between theory and method becomes more important. Present subtype research, just like most LD research, appears method driven (Lyon, 1987). Data are collected, a method applied, subtypes found and then a theory is derived. But such *ex post facto* theory lacks the structure to provide the necessary insight into the LD phenomenon. It is too tied to method and data to stand alone and consequently does not lead to enhanced understanding. A system such as this does not result in scientific progress.

A better scheme would be for subtype research to be driven by theory (see Lyon & Risucci, 1988). Based on theoretical analysis, a rational conceptual structure could be created where the data collected and method applied result in subtypes that possess the important dimensions of meaningfulness (Hull, 1974). They would possess a reality that is tied to theory and could be verified. The procedure becomes one of testing theory rather than creating subtypes and is a continuous process. Subtypes may have immediate value for identification and diagnosis but ultimately their real worth is in the theoretical domain, specifically an understanding of LD. If that understanding does not emerge, then the theory is reexamined and modified to guide more research, not simply the application of alternate methodology. The focus is on theory with subtypes being the elements that are predicted and explained (Skinner, 1981).

VALIDATION OF TAXONOMIES

In general, taxonomies have fundamentals in common (1) they attempt to divide what appear to be almost continuous systems (e.g., all children with learning problems) into discrete entities, and (2) they compress complex multidimensional relationships into two-dimensional models (Hull, 1974). But the resulting taxonomy must be validated; numerical methods will always find a classification solution. Therefore, we need the taxonomies to be validated both internally and externally.

Internal validation evaluates a clustering solution in its own right: How adequate is the solution? It is primarily a statistical procedure whereby the obtained results are used as a standard against which other methods are employed to see if similar results are obtained. It is basically an evaluation of reliability, homogeneity, and coverage (Skinner, 1981). The primary purpose of internal validation is to determine whether the taxonomy appears to be more "natural" or "artificial" in the sense of being forced on the data.

External validation is ultimately more important because it deals with the whole notion of validity (i.e., in its classic sense: Does it measure what it purports to measure?) (Fletcher, 1985). It also refers to the relevance of a classification where relevance may be conceived of as incorporating two criteria: information content and predictive power. These concerns about external validity ultimately surround the question of stability. This is the importance of McKinney's research on subtypes (see McKinney et al., 1985; McKinney & Speece, 1986) since it deals with the important question of stability. This work also demonstrates that the question of external validity is not solely a statistical process. Rather, it is a problem that requires logic and reason for an optimal solution so as not to place too great a burden on numerical taxonomy and multivariate techniques. Statistical methods alone do not suffice for dealing with the subtle tasks and nuances of subtype research and, if the sole criterion, the external evaluations may be artificially recast into *ex post facto* justifications for any obtained classification scheme.

A FRAMEWORK FOR SUBTYPING RESEARCH

Classification is a fundamental activity of the mind; it provides order and a coherent look at things (Broadfield, 1946). The process goes back to Aristotle whose quest for natural classification was based on the search for *essence*—those qualities which an object must have in order to be entitled to its name (Peck, 1965). This basic approach was followed by Linneaus whose goal was to find the nature and extent of the connection between logical forms and natural forms (see Larson, 1971). This is accomplished through forming categories on the basis of common attributes. But the procedure is made difficult by the need to distinguish between attributes that are central to describing an object and hence contribute to its essence and those attributes which are merely incidental.

The goal is to take the central attributes and present them in a consolidated manner that provides insight into the characteristic variation of a specified population (Mukherjee, 1983). The process of classification aims at establishing mutually distinct but analogous classes and depends on a systematic arrangement of the properties of the trait common to the objects being classified (Hull, 1974).

The intracacies inherent in the classification process suggest that a fundamental and necessary prerequisite is a full and complete description of the phenomenon of interest (i.e., LD). There is considerable activity that precedes the actual classification activity and these can only be understood if it is completely clear what is being discussed. Classification in botany and zoology, for example, is based on such descriptions (see Willis, 1973, for botany and Schenk & McMasters, 1956, for zoology). It is through such fundamental description and ultimately naming as embodied in the codes of nomenclature (e.g., *International Code of Botanical Nomenclature* and *International Commission on Zoological Nomenclature*) that it is possible to recognize and to incorporate objects into the mental processes necessary for classification (Korner, 1970). The nomenclature is an integral part of classification method and provides consistency and uniformity wherein a "correct" application of any name can be discovered no matter how much concepts related to classification may change. A name in classification, however, does not really denote a thing but rather a concept (see Korner, 1970). Because this makes it a cognitive process, the description must be based on reason and experience.

Classification does not occur in a vacuum; the context of classification is now recognized to be as important as the quantifiable aspects of classification (Ellen & Reason, 1979). The context of classification in LD really lies beyond the particular sample chosen for examination and includes properties beyond those under consideration. For example, the sociological context of LD is often overlooked (Senf, 1987) and most LD subtyping efforts are not cast in a wider sociological context. One reason is the difficulty in quantifying such variables since they represent qualitative dimensions that are not easily (or meaningfully) scaled for analysis. Yet, exclusive attention to variables that can be measured hides, in fact, the concurrent role of context variables in producing the variation that needs to be classified. Classification thus must aim at the efficient coordination of measurable variables (quantitative) *and* contextual variables (qualitative) in order to provide classifications with wide relevance.

The LD field appears to be heading in the right direction with regard to description of both quantitative and qualitative variables through Torgesen's (1982) work on "rationally defined subgroups" and Keogh's work on "marker variables" (Keogh, Major-Kinglsley, Omori-Gordon, & Reid, 1982). These efforts show how a coordinated description of LD can be provided and draw attention to the fact that such comprehensive description is fundamental to understanding LD. Too often, it appears that LD is described solely through test scores which is really the end product ("the quantification"). The description required for understanding LD needs to be far more comprehensive than simply a "measurable variable" which will move the field from its present status of limited description provided through selected test instruments. It is probably the case that description needs to be much more formalized and that the LD field should move towards the development of an *International Code of Learning Disabilities* that can serve as the basis for all subtype research.

A code of this sort would provide the foundation for what is termed systematics in biology (Simpson, 1964). Systematics studies diversity and lays the foundation for taxonomy which is the theory and practice of classification. Thus, systematics can be viewed as a form of inventory taking in the sense of discovering and describing the elements that make up a particular phenomenon. This would not be an easy task for LD and may be asking too much but the dividends would be considerable for improved structure for the subtyping effort. The primary advantage here would be the elimination of any potential bias. A fundamental dilemma in present subtyping research is found in the fact that any population is essentially preselected (Morrison, MacMillan, & Kavale, 1985). But by fully describing an LD population, a sample can be selected that is not biased as it is based on a description wherein all subjects chosen would possess a common set of characteristics.

With description as complete as possible, the LD field can then move towards developing classification schemes. The difference, however, will be that now there would be a solid and rational foundation from which to pursue classification efforts. Before the application of empirical methods, subtype identification was based on clinical-inferential approaches that grouped LD students according to *a priori* decision rules (presumably based on theoretical considerations) and visual inspection techniques of large data sets (see Lyon, 1983; Malatesha & Dougan, 1982; Satz & Morris, 1981 for reviews). These resemble early taxonomic efforts like those carried out by Aristotle which were based on downward classification by logical division (Peck, 1965). The goal here is to provide a convenient identification scheme. The problem becomes one of information load. Downward classification works well for a limited domain but as that domain grows, there is too much information and any logical division breaks down. These "armchair" classifications (e.g., Boder's [1973] three types of developmental dyslexia: dysphonetic, dysiedetic, and mixed) should not be considered "false" but only limited (Rosenthal, Boder, & Callaway, 1982). Their coverage is restricted to only a portion of the population and thus does not possess wide applicability.

When the phenomenon to be classified is complex and multivariate like LD, downward classification must be replaced by upward classification by compositional analysis (Mayr, 1982). In this method, one starts at the bottom, sorts into groups, and combines these groups into a hierarchical arrangement. The advantage is a retreat from reliance on a single character which was replaced by the simultaneous use of many characteristics. It is evident, however, that compositional analysis demands an understanding of what one is classifying. It is only through something like an *International Code of Learning Disabilities* that this goal of understanding might be achieved and upward classification can proceed on a logical and rational basis.

Upward classification is typically associated with empirical techniques. But there is a danger here associated with the fact that good empirical solutions may lead to a false sense of closure. Although such classifications may provide integration, economy, and structural conformity, it may not possess reality since it is only an hypostasized system of categories. A classification per se can be neither right nor wrong; it is not a model but only a way of summarizing information in an intelligible form (Hull, 1974). Its value is assessed by consideration of the classification's usefulness to others in the field. Because LD is also a practical field, a strict modeling of botanical or zoological classification (e.g., Jeffrey, 1982, for botany and Simpson, 1961, for zoology) may not be appropriate. This may be particularly true given the poor state of LD theory (see Kavale, 1987) which suggests that attempts to find distinct subtypes may be a case of trying to fit complex phenomena into unnaturally simple, invalid, or nonexistent theoretical frameworks—a Procrustean bed problem. The role of theory in LD classification may be conceived of as a bipartite endeavor: basic processes can be explained in terms of classical scientific theory (i.e., cause and effect) while, at the individual level necessary for classification, explanation requires the addition of ecological and demographic data—the qualitative description encompassing sociological variables. The LD field thus needs to go beyond strict theoretical classification efforts because, regardless of the outcome's "truth," it may not be useful for the pragmatic demands of LD (i.e., intervention).

CONCLUSION

Heterogeneity has been a vexing problem for the LD field and has limited the generalization and replicability of research findings. Recent efforts, however, have been aimed at reducing this heterogeneity through the empirical identification of homogeneous subtypes (Fisk & Rourke, 1983). The purpose of this paper has been to examine critically these classification efforts. Although problems were noted, it can be concluded that subtyping research represents an important and valuable means of attacking the problems posed by heterogeneity.

The present classification efforts in LD, while a positive addition, may, however, be somewhat ahead of their time. To provide perspective, the LD field should retreat somewhat and devote greater effort to a more formalized description of LD. A detailed description of LD that provides a complete rendering of the phenomenon along many dimensions can then be the basis for empirical subtyping. In this way, a full range of purposes (e.g., theory development, clinical diagnosis, educational intervention) can be achieved and the classifications will possess relevance across a wide range of activities. In line with this suggestion, it would behoove the LD field to strive for more commonality and consensus in measurement and methodology. Subtyping research appears presently to be a series of independent efforts all more or less striving to achieve the same goal. Although the individual research programs are valuable, the outcomes could be even more powerful if the major individuals involved in subtype research would pool their efforts into producing a *single* classification scheme for the LD field. A single scheme would parallel those found in the life sciences (e.g., botany, zoology) and would bring needed order and objectivity to the LD field. This might move LD classification to a level beyond Lewis Carroll's description of classification where

> It next will be right
> To describe each particular batch;
> Distinguishing those that have
>   feathers, and bite
> From those that have whiskers,
>   and scratch.
> *(The Hunting of the Snark)*

REFERENCES

Achenbach, T. M., & Edelbrock, C. S. (1978). The classification of children psychopathology: A review and analysis of empirical efforts. *Psychological Bulletin, 85,* 1275–1301.

Achenbach, T. M., & Edelbrock, C. S. (1983). Taxonomic issues in child psychopathology. In T. H. Ollendick & M. Hersen (Eds.), *Handbook of child psychopathology* (pp. 65–93). New York: Plenum.

Adelman, H. S., & Taylor, L. (1985). The future of the LD field: A survey of fundamental concerns. *Journal of Learning Disabilities, 18,* 423–427.

Anderberg, M. R. (1973). *Cluster analysis for application.* New York: Academic Press.

Beckner, M. (1959). *The biological way of thought.* New York: Columbia University Press.

Blackwelder, R. E. (1967). *Taxonomy: A text and reference book.* New York: Wiley.

Blashfield, R. K., & Aldenderfer, M. S. (1978). The literature on cluster analysis. *Multivariate Behavioral Research, 13,* 271–295.

Boder, E. (1973). Developmental dyslexia: A diagnostic approach based on three atypical reading-spelling patterns. *Developmental Medicine and Child Neurology, 15,* 663–687.

Broadfield, A. (1946). *The philosophy of classification.* London: Grafton.

Clifford, H. T., & Stephenson, W. (1975). *An introduction to numerical classification.* New York: Academic Press.

Cormack, R. M. (1971). A review of classification. *Journal of the Royal Statistical Society* (Series A), *134,* 321–367.

Del Dotto, J. E., & Rourke, B. P. (1985). Subtypes of left-handed learning disabled children. In B. P. Rourke (Ed.), *Neuropsychology of learning disabilities: Essentials of subtype analysis* (pp. 89–130). New York: Guilford Press.

Doehring, D. G., & Hoshko, I. M. (1977). Classification of reading problems by the Q-technique of factor analysis. *Cortex, 13,* 281–294.

Doehring, D. G., Hoshko, I. M., & Bryans, B. N. (1979). Statistical classification of children with reading problems. *Journal of Clinical Neuropsychology, 1,* 5–16.

Dubes, R., & Jain, A. K. (1979). Validity studies in clustering methodologies. *Pattern Recognition, 11,* 235–254.

Dunn, G., & Everitt, B. (1982). *An introduction to mathematical taxonomy.* New York: Cambridge University Press.

Ellen, R. F., & Reason, D. (Eds.). (1979). *Classifications in their social context.* New York: Academic Press.

Everitt, B. S. (1979). Unresolved problems in cluster analysis. *Biometrics, 35,* 169–181.

Everitt, B. S. (1980). *Cluster analysis* (2nd ed). New York: Halsted.

Feagans, L., & Appelbaum, M. (1986). Language subtypes and their validation in learning disabled children. *Journal of Educational Psychology, 78*(5), 358–364.

Fisk, J. L., & Rourke, B. P. (1979). Identification of subtypes of learning disabilities at three age levels: A neuropsychological, multivariate approach. *Journal of Clinical Neuropsychology, 1,* 189–310.

Fisk, J. L., & Rourke, B. P. (1983). Neuropsychological subtyping of learning disabled children: History, methods, implications. *Journal of Learning Disabilities, 16,* 529–531.

Fleishman, E. A. (1982). Systems for describing human tasks. *American Psychologist, 37*(7), 821–837.

Fleiss, J. L., & Zubin, J. (1969). On the methods and theory of clustering. *Multivariate Behavioral Research, 4,* 225–250.

Fletcher, J. M. (1985). External validation of learning disability subtypes. In B. P. Rourke (Ed.), *Neuropsychology of learning disabilities: Essentials of subtype analysis* (pp. 187–211). New York: Guilford Press.

Grossman, H. J. (Ed.). (1983). *Classification in mental retardation.* Washington, DC: American Association on Mental Deficiency.

Hesse, M. B. (1966). *Models and analogies in science.* Indiana: University of Notre Dame Press.

Hull, D. L. (1974). *Philosophy of biological science.* Englewood Cliffs, NJ: Prentice-Hall.

Jardine, N., & Sibson, R. (1971). *Mathematical taxonomy.* New York: Wiley.

Jeffrey, C. (1982). *An introduction to plant taxonomy* (2nd ed). New York: Cambridge University Press.

Johnson, L. A. S. (1970). Rainbow's end: The quest for an optimal taxonomy. *Systematic Zoology, 20,* 203–229.

Joschko, M., & Rourke, B. P. (1985). Neuropsychological subtypes of learning-disabled children who exhibit the ACID pattern on the WISC. In B. P. Rourke (Ed.), *Neuropsychology of learning disabilities: Essentials of subtype analysis (pp. 65–88).* New York: Guilford Press.

Kavale, K. A. (1987). Theoretical quandaries in learning disabilities. In S. Vaughn & C. Bos (Eds.), *Research in learning disabilities: Issues and future directions* (pp. 19–29). Boston: Little, Brown/College Hill.

Kavale, K. A., & Forness, S. R. (1987). A matter of substance over style: A quantitative synthesis assessing the efficacy of modality testing and teaching. *Exceptional Children, 53,* 228–239.

Kavale, K. A., & Nye, C. (1985–86). Parameters of learning disabilities in achievement, linguistic, neuropsychological and social/behavioral domains. *Journal of Special Education, 19,* 443–458.

Keogh, B. K. (1987). A shared attribute model of learning disabilities. In S. Vaughn & C. Bos (Eds.), *Research in learning disabilities: Issues and future directions* (pp. 2–12). Boston: Little, Brown/College-Hill.

Keogh, B. K., Major-Kingsley, S., Omori-Gordon, H., & Reid, H. P. (1982). *A system of marker variables for the field of learning disabilities.* New York: Syracuse University Press.

Kirk, S. A., & Chalfant, J. C. (1984). *Academic and developmental learning disabilities.* Denver: Love Publishing Company.

Korner, S. (1970). *Categorical frameworks.* Oxford: Basil Blackwell.

Larson, J. L. (1971). *Reason and experience: The representation of natural order in the work of Carl Von Linne.* Berkeley, CA: University of California Press.

Laudan, L. (1977). *Progress and its problems.* Berkeley, CA: University of California Press.

Lyon, G. R. (1983). Learning disabled readers: Identification of subgroups. In H. R. Myklebust (Ed.), *Progress in learning disabilities* (Vol. 5, pp. 103–133). New York: Grune & Stratton.

Lyon, G. R. (1985a). Educational validation of learning disability subtypes. In B. P. Rourke (Ed.), *Neuropsychology of learning disabilities: Essentials of subtype analysis* (pp. 228–253). New York: Guilford Press.

Lyon, G. R. (1985b). Identification and remediation of learning disability subtypes: Preliminary findings. *Learning Disabilities Focus, 1*(1), 21–35.

Lyon, G. R. (1987). Learning disabilities research: False starts and broken promises. In S. Vaughn & C. Bos (Eds.), *Research in learning disabilities: Issues and future directions* (pp. 69–80). Boston: Little, Brown/College Hill.

Lyon, G. R., Rietta, S., Watson, B., Porch, B., & Rhodes, J. (1981). Selected linguistic and perceptual abilities of empirically derived subgroups of learning disabled readers. *Journal of School Psychology, 19,* 152–166.

Lyon, G. R., & Risucci, D. (1988). Classification of learning disabilities. In K. Kavale, (Ed.), *Learning disabilities: State of the art and practice* (pp. 44–70). Boston: Little, Brown/College Hill.

Lyon, G. R., Stewart, N., & Freedman, D. (1982). Neuropsychological characteristics of empirically derived subgroups of learning disabled readers. *Journal of Clinical Neuropsychology, 4,* 343–365.

Lyon, G. R., & Watson, B. (1981). Empirically derived subgroups of learning disabled readers: Diagnostic characteristics. *Journal of Learning Disabilities, 14,* 256–261.

Malatesha, R. N., & Dougan, D. R. (1982). Clinical subtypes of developmental dyslexia: Resolution of an irresolute problem. In R. N. Malatesha & P. G. Aaron (Eds.), *Reading disorders: Varieties and treatments* (pp. 69–92). New York: Academic Press.

Mayr, E. (1965). Numerical phenetics and taxonomic theory. *Systematic Zoology, 14,* 73–97.

Mayr, E. (1982). *The growth of biological thought: Diversity, evolution, and inheritance.* Cambridge, MA: Harvard University Press.

McKinney, J. D. (1984). The search of subtypes of specific learning disability. *Journal of Learning Disabilities, 17,* 43–50.

McKinney, J. D. (1988). Research on conceptually and empirically derived subtypes of specific learning disabilities. In M. C. Wang, M. C. Reynolds, & H. J. Walberg (Eds.), *The handbook of special education: Research and practice* (Vol. II, pp. 253–281). Oxford: Pergamon Press.

McKinney, J. D., Short, E. J., & Feagans, L. (1985). Academic consequences of perceptual-linguistic subtypes of learning disabled children. *Learning Disabilities Research, 1*(1), 6–17.

McKinney, J. D., & Speece, D. L. (1986). Academic consequences and longitudinal stability of behavioral subtypes of learning disabled children. *Journal of Educational Psychology, 78*(5), 365–372.

Medawar, P. B. (1984). *The limits of science.* New York: Harper & Row.

Morris, R., Blashfield, R. K., & Satz, P. (1981). Neuropsychology and cluster analysis: Potentials and problems. *Journal of Clinical Neuropsychology, 3,* 77–79.

Morrison, G. M., MacMillan, D. L., & Kavale, K. A. (1985). System identification of learning disabled children: Implications for research. *Learning Disability Quarterly, 8,* 2–10.

Mukherjee, R. (1983). *Classification in social research.* Albany, NY: State University of New York Press.

Peck, A. L. (1965). *Introduction to Aristotle's Historia Animalum.* Cambridge, MA: Harvard University Press.

Petraukas, R., & Rourke, B. P. (1979). Identification of subgroups of retarded readers: A neuropsy-chological, multivariate approach. *Journal of Clinical Neuropsychology, 1,* 17–37.

Reynolds, M. C. (1984). Classification of students with handicaps. In E. W. Gordon (Ed.), *Review of Research in Education, 11,* 63–92.

Rosenthal, J. H., Boder, E., & Callaway, E. (1982). Typology of developmental dyslexia: Evidence for its construct validity. In R. N. Malatesha, & P. G. Aaron (Eds.), *Reading disorders: Varieties and treatments* (pp. 93–120). New York: Academic Press.

Rourke, B. P. (Ed.). (1985). *Neuropsychology of learning disabilities: Essentials of subtype analysis.* New York: Guilford Press.

Satz, P., & Morris, R. (1981). Learning disability subtypes: A review. In F. J. Pirozzolo, & M. C. Wittrock (Eds.), *Neuropsychological and cognitive processes in reading* (pp. 109–141). New York: Academic Press.

Satz, P., & Morris, R. (1983). Classification of learning disabled children. In R. E. Tarter (Ed.), *The child at psychiatric risk* (pp. 128–149). New York: Oxford University Press.

Schenk, E. T., & McMasters, J. H. (Eds.). (1956). *Procedure in taxonomy* (3rd ed.). Stanford, CA: Stanford University Press.

Senf, G. M. (1987). Learning disabilities as sociologic sponge: Wiping up life's spills. In S. Vaughn & C. Bos (Eds.), *Research in learning disabilities: Issues and future directions* (pp. 3–12). Boston: Little, Brown/College Hill.

Simpson, G. G. (1961). *Principles of animal taxonomy.* New York: Columbia University Press.

Simpson, G. G. (1964). Numerical taxonomy and biological classification. *Science, 144,* 312–313.

Skinner, H. A. (1977). The eyes that fix you: A model for classification research. *Canadian Psychological Review, 18,* 142–151.

Skinner, H. A. (1981). Toward the integration of classification theory and methods. *Journal of Abnormal Psychology, 90*(1), 68–87.

Sokal, R. R. (1974). Classification: Purposes, principles, progress, prospects. *Science, 185*(4157), 1115–1123.

Sokal, R. R., & Sneath, P. H. (1963). *Principles of numerical taxonomy.* San Francisco: W. H. Freeman.

Speece, D. L. (1987). Information processing subtypes of learning disabled readers. *Learning Disabilities Research, 2,* 91–102.

Speece, D. L., McKinney, J. D., & Appelbaum, M. (1985) Classification and validation of behavioral subtypes of learning disabled children. *Journal of Educational Psychology, 77,* 67–77.

Torgesen, J. K. (1982). The use of rationally defined subgroups in research on learning disabilities. In J. P. Das, R. F. Mulcahy, & A. F. Wall (Eds.), *Theory and research in learning disabilities* (pp. 111–131). New York: Plenum.

Tryon, R. C., & Bailey, D. E. (1970). *Cluster analysis.* New York: McGraw-Hill.

Warburton, F. E. (1967). The purposes of classification. *Systematic Zoology, 26,* 241–245.

Watson, B. V., Goldgar, D. E., & Ryschon, K. L. (1983). Subtypes of reading disability. *Journal of Clinical Neuropsychology, 5,* 377–399.

Willis, J. C. (1973). *A dictionary of flowering plants and ferns* (8th ed., revised by H. K. A. Shaw). New York: Cambridge University Press.

Wolfus, B., Moscovitch, M., & Kinsbourne, M. (1980). Subgroups of developmental language impairment. *Brain and Language, 10,* 152–171.

Zigler, E., Balla, D., & Hodapp, R. (1984). On the definition and classification of mental retardation. *American Journal of Mental Deficiency, 89,* 215–230.

IV COGNITION AND ACADEMIC PERFORMANCE

15

Cognition and Academic Performance: An Introduction

Robert J. Hall
Texas A&M University

Michael M. Gerber
University of California, Santa Barbara

From the perspective of contemporary cognitive theory, achievement is best characterized in relation to cognitive competence, hence, it represents more than just score points on a standardized test. Achievement, in our view, includes some understanding of the declarative/procedural mix of ideas and actions that define skilled performance at a given point in time (Anderson, 1982, 1983). Performance underlying achievement is a constructive product, reflecting how and whether an individual responds to constraints imposed by the environment, the problem, or the question asker (Bolles, 1988). Learners able to bridge these constraints may well be judged to have achieved because they are on grade level or have answered enough questions correctly to be given credit for mastery of an objective. Evaluating only at the level of correct response, however, can be misleading as variance in the production of correct responses (i.e., latencies) may indicate mastery of a technique but uncertainty about content.

Framed in terms of cognitive competence, judgments about achievement should reflect not only the correctness of performance but also how performance comes to be initiated, sustained, and completed by the learner. Correct performance, then, may signal teachers that students have acquired a skill or action-sequence (i.e., procedures underlying the ability to carry out sequences of operations on symbols), but without careful analysis of products produced by their students, teachers may be unaware of the levels of proficiency or competence that characterize students' skill development. Equating skilled performance with correct performance may lead teachers to inappropriately assume a level of prerequisite skill that does not exist for some students. In turn, lack of prerequisite procedural knowledge creates an obstacle to learning new procedures; that is, conditions necessary for an action to occur are not present. Simply stated, we

233

believe that to understand achievement, one must go beyond statements about numbers of correct or incorrect responses. Acquisition of cognitive skill in any academic or social domain is a complex process, thus, attempts to teach children, who by definition, exact effort from the system (i.e., children with learning problems), demand expertise across a number of overlapping knowledge domains.

Teachers, we believe, are faced with teaching problems that may require, at minimum, not only attention to detail in student performance, but vast domain-specific knowledge repositories for interpreting performance in each subject area to be taught. Moreover, effective instruction requires knowledge about how individual differences tend to be supported or disrupted by particular educational environments, and appreciation for how contextual effects such as the presence or absence of certain environmental constraints, prompts, cues, or reinforcement can alter the quality of performance (Swanson, 1987).

Psychological characteristics of children are expressed through the filter of a context. Teachers and teaching are a part of that context such that academic and social interactions over time shape or modify the valence that teachers attach to children and that children attach to teachers. Negative valences may further contribute to breakdowns in communication between teachers and students, affecting the quality of products produced by students and/or the willingness of students to fully engage in problem-solving activities.

We recognize that calls for increased expertise and references to complexity generally reflect dissatisfaction with the status quo, and uncertainty about what to do next. But, our intent here, as well as the intent of the other chapters on achievement and academic performance appearing in this volume, reflects an interest in being constructive as well as critical. It is our feeling that the availability and portability of technology has led to a renewed interest in trying to model and understand how thinking and problem solving occur or fail to occur. It is also our view that the measurement and interpretation of achievement data can provide a "window on cognition," and, hence, can serve to inform the instructional process for children with learning problems. For this to occur, however, there is a cost, measured principally in the time needed (1) to plan instruction, (2) to systematically evaluate student performance, and (3) to modify instruction once evaluation has been interpreted. Following is a brief overview of what we consider to be pluses and minuses in the measurement and use of achievement data in educational settings. Included in this analysis is a look at standardized testing as it relates to teacher effectiveness and a short section identifying contributions to school learning emanating from cognitive psychology. We end this short chapter with an analysis of the work of an 8-year-old boy to illustrate how competence within an academic domain is better understood by mapping performance, in context, to domain-specific indicators of processing rather than by attempting to squeeze, from aggregated achievement scores, interpretations about process.

HOW VERSUS HOW MUCH

Quantitatively, standardized testing provides benchmarks or markers, allowing us to document child progress. Thus, educational practice in different parts of the country, different schools within a district, or even different classrooms within a school can be compared against some age or grade appropriate standard. The importance of a marker system for descriptive purposes has been discussed by Keogh (1986). In essence, a marker system, in which standardized test data would be but one of many markers, makes it easier for teachers and researchers to interpret and to contribute to the data-based literature. For the teacher, a well-marked sampling system means that relevant local norms can be more easily established. Factors empirically demonstrated to influence child performance and consonant with characteristics present in the classroom, curriculum, or individual can be taken into account when evaluating child or classroom progress. Consequently, teachers and administrators are less likely to overreact to unusually high or low scores because evidence, not intuition, creates the context for score interpretation. Standardized test scores viewed from this perspective provide data relative to the amount or quantity of information acquired by a particular child or group of children. We would argue, moreover, that this is a good use for standardized tests in that the interpretive emphasis is on quantity or "how much," a notion entirely consistent with how test items are generated and selected (Willson, 1987).

On the qualitative side, standardized achievement tests are often used to determine significant academic strengths or weaknesses, to establish whether performance in one or more academic areas warrants recommendation for remedial services, and to help teachers individualize instruction via analysis of student errors. Scores used for these purposes, we would argue, require a level of performance analysis that is generally not consistent with how test items were generated or chosen nor detailed enough to be informative about the acquisition of cognitive skills. As Bejar (1984) points out in the introduction to a paper on educational diagnostic assessment, "Standardized test results frequently have little or no impact on instruction because the test results offer little help in designing instruction that is optimal for an individual student" (p. 175).

Standardized Testing and Teacher Effectiveness

In reviewing what constitutes effective teaching, Mastropieri and Scruggs (1987) cite numerous studies to support the general notion that special educators can increase student achievement in special education by "(a) actively engaging students on task during instruction, (b) presenting information in clear, concise ways, (c) asking students questions relevant to the instructional objectives, (d) keeping students actively involved in relevant instructional activities, and (e) monitoring students' performance" (p. 3). What is remarkable here is not the content or phrasing of these tenets of teacher effectiveness, rather it is the absence of any reference to information typically provided by school psychologists for classroom teachers. If the primary role for school psychologists is to serve as gatekeepers, deciding who is or is not eligible for psychological services, then discussion of teacher effectiveness as related to psychoeducational assessment is not relevant. Two points argue against this general position, however. First, with the push to make School Psychology a doctoral level discipline, emphasis on the school psychologist as scientist/practitioner has re-emerged (Fuchs & Fuchs, 1986; Pryzwansky, 1987). This model serves to expands the contributions of school psychologists to include information about the status of a given child's academic development. A school psychologist functioning under this mandate might also be asked to help regular classroom teachers formulate and evaluate alternative instructional strategies for children referred for testing. In this role, the school psychologist decreases the probability that the regular classroom teacher's "suspicion of disability" does not result from haphazard, idiosyncratic, or chaotic referral methods whereby different teachers refer different types of students because certain individual difference characteristics are bothersome to them (Ysseldyke, Thurlow, Graden, Wesson, Deno, & Algozzine, 1983). Second, as Gerber and Semmel (1984) point out, school psychologists as gatekeepers may not serve a very useful or necessary function. Although teacher ratings are subjective and technically less valid than standardized measures, teachers are accurate in identifying those who need academic and behavioral programs beyond the scope of the regular classroom (Algozzine, Christenson, & Ysseldyke, 1982). Given this perspective, for school psychologists to remain viable in the school marketplace, the primary purpose of testing should be to determine (1) where a given child is relative to the attainment of some fluent cognitive skill, (2) how individual difference variables impact on skill development in a given academic area, and (3) what educational goals and objectives are critical to promote steady academic progress at a given point in time. If the central goal for testing is treatment/remediation then determining those variables that impact on teacher effectiveness (e.g., equating time allocated with time engaged) and how those variables can be positively affected (e.g., addressing precise behavioral objectives at the correct level of difficulty) become important for the school psychologist who wants to make substantive contributions to the instructional needs of children (Deno, 1986; Howell, 1986; Lentz & Shapiro, 1986; Sewell, 1987; Shinn, Tindal, & Stein, 1988). In that regard, there is a call to re-evaluate educational testing and assessment in light of advances in the cognitive psychology of human learning (Bejar, 1984; Glaser, 1981; Linn, 1986; Messick, 1984; Willson, 1987).

Teachers also have a stake in understanding the cognitive correlates of achievement-related, student performance. Consider, what may be the necessary **and** sufficient requirements for teaching children who have difficulty learning.

First, teachers must be able to generate models of efficient and inefficient problem solving for all tasks to be taught. This allows for the creation of specific correction subroutines and general instructional plans that can accommodate incomplete skill development. These task models require detailed understanding of the processes to be taught and typically go far beyond the content of preservice level classes designed to train future teachers. Second, knowledge about individual differences must be broad based and well organized enough to allow teachers to develop generic models of student development in order to understand the dynamic or changing character of competent performance. That is, what is competent behavior for an 8-year-old may be viewed as only marginal behavior for an 11-year-old. Moreover, what may be competent behavior for one 8-year-old given a certain start point may not reflect competence for another 8-year-old with a different start point. Thus, teachers must be able to generate a model of generic responding tempered by age, a model of the process to be instructed and developed, and a model of the specific child being evaluated (Gerber & Hall, in press; Kauffman, Gerber, & Semmel, 1988). These models are then compared, in abstraction, such that the teacher can decide whether (1) the model of the specific child is a good one, and (2) the knowledge domain has been modeled appropriately. Discrepancies can exist for either or both models, thus, leading to situations where children overemphasize the learning of techniques rather than content.

Contributions from Cognitive Psychology

Bejar (1984), Curtis and Glaser (1983), Glaser, (1981), Kolligian and Sternberg (1987), Snow and Peterson (1985), and Swanson (1987, 1988) are some of the researchers who have summarized work from the areas of cognitive psychology, information processing, and artificial intelligence that have implications for testing and test development. The basic premise that underlies this work is that student errors are often systematic (Brown & Burton, 1978; Tatsuoka & Tatsuoka, 1983). Variance associated with those errors provides a rich source of diagnostic information that is specific to an academic domain and highlights the general development of a given student's ability to be strategic in situations that are difficult but solvable. The work of Brown and Burton (1978), Goldman and Pelligrino (1987), and Nesher (1986) in the area of mathematics; Curtis and Glaser (1983), Beck and Carpenter (1986), Spache (1976), and Spear and Sternberg (1985) in the area of reading; Carey (1986) and Shana (1983) in the area of science; Gerber and Hall (1987) in the area of spelling; Webb, Herman, and Cabello (1983) in the area of language arts; and Bartholomue (1980) in the area of writing are all examples of developments in cognitive psychology that may impact construction of achievement tests beyond summary scoring.

A STORY BY JONATHAN

Following are two versions of a composition written by an 8-year-old boy. The classroom teacher prompted this work by asking children to write a story in which a hat or the use of a hat played a major role.

The Boy Who Traveled in Time

Once upon a time, there was a boy his name was Ralph. He was very very shy. Ralph earned some allowance with chores that he did earlier in the week. Ralph's total added up to $15.39 so he looked but he couldn't find anything he wanted. So finally he got tired of looking. When he was about to leave he saw an anteke shop so he went in. He found lots of things he liked over there espessialy a hat that he found. So he asked the clerk "how much does this cost" he asked. The clerk said "$15.00 he said i'll buy it. Later on he played with it for a little while he wondered what the bateries were for. So he put some bateries in it, and pushed a red button. The twirly thing on top started twirling Ralph said "wow"! with amazmnt in his eyes he put the hat on wait till my friends see this he said. So the next day Ralph showed his friends his new hat. Everybody laughed at it. So the next day he went in to the woods, and threw his hat down again and again and then he heard a beeping sound. And he dissapeared. The sun was moving very very fast faster than the speed of sound. Finally the sun stopped moving very fast. He wonderd where he was. After he wonderd off a little bit the place looked familiar it looked like 1940 when he was born. Soon he knew he was right it was when he was born. So he pushed the red button and lived happily ever after. The End

How is Jonathan's Performance to be Evaluated?

From a quantitative perspective, focus is on technical aspects of the writing process. For example, we might be interested in total number of words used, number of words spelled correctly, number of multisyllabic words, number of punctuation errors, number of descriptive words, number of incomplete sentences, percentage of subject/verb agreement, and so on. From the qualitative side, we might be interested in the texture of the story itself. Are the events portrayed in an orderly fashion? Does the story make sense? Is the story complete? How many characters appear in the story and is there any character development? Is the language used in the story roughly equivalent to the level of the child's language development? Is there cohesiveness in the story; that is, are linguistic elements present in text that tie propositions together and contribute to the overall continuity of the narrative? What kinds of errors does the child make? Is there a pattern to the child's errors?

The most straightforward questions to be answered, are those labeled quantitative. Answers to both types of questions, however, can be interpreted to suggest errors in judgment, errors in application or interpretation of rules, or insufficient knowledge about a subject matter area. It should also be evident that qualitative questions are more intricate than quantitative questions, leading to more involved investigations of processing. Seeking information about the richness and cohesiveness of narratives, rather than about the ability of children to generate error free texts, represents an attempt to understand how children's propositional networks are linked and how broadly and tightly their knowledge bases are organized. Observations might also include how children respond to time constraints and whether there has been any spontaneous effort to monitor intermediate or final products. Since much of the early language arts instruction focuses on learning and applying rule-based information, overall evaluations of performance should include both quantitative and qualitative analyses. Qualitative analysis of performance, however, means major time investments for regular and special classroom teachers if they are to develop the expertise in academic areas that will result in better, more informed instructional decisions.

But, simply developing a theoretical framework for interpreting academic performance based on an information-processing model may still not result in instructional decisions or student performance that is completely satisfactory. Other variables and background information also impact on whether or not instruction, often in the form of strategy training, is productive for the child (Borkowski, Weyhing, & Turner, 1986; Gelzheiser, Shepherd, & Wozniak, 1986; Palincsar, 1986).

Turnure (1986) has outlined a pentrahedronal model for analyzing problems of child development and education. At the base of this model are four components of the instructional process, characteristics of the learner, learning activities, criterial tasks, and nature of the materials. At the apex of the pentrahedron is the instructional agent. Turnure argues that, due largely to the impact of informational complexity and complicated tasks,

> It is abundantly clear that the crucial features of any educational experience revolve around what actually happens when teachers and students interact during instruction. To successfully coordinate curricular goals, instructional procedures, and pupil comprehension, teachers must become communicative experts. (p. 109)

Two basic tenets underlie Turnure's work: (1) information is best exchanged via familiar communication patterns, and (2) new information must make contact with familiar information for meaningful learning to occur (Craik & Tulving, 1975; Miller, 1981). To interpret performance, then, teachers must develop some understanding for the circumstances and child characteristics that may shape children's responses (Gavelek & Palincsar, 1988). In that regard, *What information about Jonathan might qualify or frame his performance?*

Jonathan is a high achiever. His standard scores on group and individual standardized measures of achievement consistently have been at or above the 95th percentile in reading, math, and spelling related activities. His grades consistently have been above the 90% mark in all subject areas, for all grading periods, during his first 2 years in school. At the time he was asked to write this essay, he was in the process of reading an abridged version of H. G. Wells', *The Time Machine*. Finally, he typed his composition directly into the computer using a simple but, unfamiliar to him, word processing program.

Analysis of Jonathan's performance, taking child factors into account, might lead us to the general conclusion that his performance in this area is flawed but competent considering his age. On the quantitative side, we might note that all sentences (22 in total) begin with a capital letter and end with a period. Apparently, he has proceduralized this information as his application of these rules was automatic or nearly automatic. A total of 276 words were produced in approximately 1 hour, a seemingly reasonable output, even for a bright 8-year-old. Six different words were misspelled, although only one, "anteke," involved something other than difficulty with a doubled consonant or a past tense marker. We might also note that there was an attempt to use demarcated dialogue and commas to set off pauses. Interestingly, the commas all precede the word "and."

Qualitatively, we are impressed by the overall structure of his story. A hat became a time machine and, thus, he mixed information from an organized knowledge base with a groundrule stated by the teacher. Importantly, Jonathan's story draws some parallels and insight from H. G. Wells' work, but it is not a veiled clone of that story line. Close scrutiny of the cohesiveness of his work, similar to the analysis offered by Ripich and Griffith (1988), would reveal that Jonathan had done a commendable job of initiating, sustaining, and elaborating a story line. While a more detailed analysis is not possible here, parameters for analyzing text structures are available in the literature (Halliday & Hasan, 1976; Kintsch, 1977; Page & Stewart, 1985; Stein & Glenn, 1979). Taken together, quantitative and qualitative information, we might suggest that instruction for Jonathan continue to focus on technical skill development in the writing process. We might also suggest that he be encouraged to read, as he seems to be able to draw appropriate links and to make substantive elaborations from old to new ideas. These simple suggestions seem warranted from the data, but appear to minimize the role of qualitative assessment, at least for Jonathan, or do they?

Asking children to work on skills that they feel they have some control or mastery over can be difficult and frustrating for both teacher and student. As Paris and Oka (1986) point out, "skill and will are forged together in learning and should be joint targets of instruction for handicapped students" (p. 104). Moreover, they suggest that self-regulated learning is a legimate educational objective for handicapped students, and that "self-regulated learning means that individuals manage their cognitive abilities and motivational effort so that learning is effective, economical, and satisfying" (p. 103). While Jonathan is not handicapped, Paris and Oka's comments seem pertinent to his learning as well. Our judgment at this point, then, is that not enough data has been collected; too many questions about his ability to perform remain unanswered. For example, would there be any systematic improvement in the quality of Jonathan's composition if he was asked to edit, independently, his own work? Similarly, what type of improvement would be realized from a request to edit with prompting from a teacher? Given changes in the quality of the final product, would we need to make adjustments in our instructional recommendations?

Following is the final edited version of Jonathan's story produced with the help of a teacher. Jonathan was asked to review his story on a sentence by sentence basis, and the teacher prompted him with questions about spelling, grammar, syntax, readability, and clarity of thought. He was also encouraged to ask questions about anything that he did not understand or thought was confusing.

The Boy Who Traveled in Time

Once upon a time, there was a boy named Ralph. He was very very shy. Ralph earned some allowance from chores that he did earlier in the week. Ralph's total added up to $15.39. He looked but he couldn't find any hats that he wanted to buy. Finally, he got tired of looking. When he was about to leave, he saw an antique shop and he went in. He found lots of things he liked over at the antique shop, especially a hat he had found. He asked the clerk "How much does this cost"? The clerk said "$15.00." Ralph said "I'll buy it." Later on he played with it for a little while. He wondered what the battery holder was for. He put some batteries in it, and pushed a red button. The copter on top started spinning. Ralph said "wow"! with amazment in his eyes. He put the hat on, "Wait till my friends see this!" he said. The next day Ralph showed his friends his new hat. Everybody laughed at it. The next day he went into the woods, and threw his hat down again and again and then he heard a beeping sound. Ralph didn't know that the hat was a time machine and when it started to beep, Ralph and the hat disappeared. The sun was moving very very fast, faster than the speed of sound. Finally the sun stopped moving. He wondered where he was. After he wandered off a little bit, the place looked familiar. It looked like 1940 when he was born. Soon he knew he was right it was when he was born. So he pushed the red button and went back into his own time and lived happily ever after. The End

In this version of the story, 19 words and 5 sentences have been added. In addition, logic, readability, and cohesiveness in the story have all shown considerable improvement. Use of the word "so" has, in many instances been replaced by more sophisticated and subtle linguistic devices. Questions about spellings that he was unsure about (i.e., anteke, dissapear, bateries, espessialy, wondered, and wandered) have led him to resolve his uncertainty either by looking the word up in the dictionary or by producing a correct spelling variant on his own (i.e., catching his mistakes). Prompted by questions from Jonathan, the teacher reviewed rules about the use of quotation marks and commas. This resulted in the swift, and generally error-free, application of those rules throughout the rest of his text (e.g., notice how punctuation changed from outside to inside quotation marks following a query in sentence 9). Questions by the teacher about clarity resulted in elaborations and changes in sentence structure to aid understanding of the story. Importantly, these changes, although prompted by teacher queries, were generated by Jonathan.

Two points, relative to the measurement of achievement, are apparent from analysis of Jonathan's edited story. First, the dynamic character of the educational and assessment process, touched upon by Paris and Oka (1986) and Turnure (1986) must be considered if we are to develop a complete picture of children's skill development. Alterations in context can lead to substantially different conclusions about what children know and how broadly what they know can be applied. Second, from a qualitative perspective, Jonathan's work can be analyzed in greater depth than it has been here. The result would be a much clearer picture of how he processes information, how quickly new information can be acted upon, how quickly old information can be accessed and applied, where he is uncertain about his performance, and whether overlays of technique, in the form of strategies or tactics, might help him to monitor, more carefully, his own performance. The benefit to teachers from systematic analysis of children's performance is (1) an investment in the development of their own expertise, (2) a more complete understanding of the children that they teach, and (3) more control over the disparity between skill and will that often creates problems in the classroom (see Hall, Gerber, & Stricker, 1989, and Gerber & Hall, in press for a more detailed discussion).

In summary, what is interesting about this brief analysis of Jonathan's work is that he represents the category of children whose learning we judge to be intact, yet to appreciate his achievement, what he knows well and what he knows something about, we must be willing to delve into the complexity of his performance. For children who have learning problems, descriptions of how and why they do what they do in response to requests to perform, represents an even more complex problem for teachers. Children with learning problems are often reluctant to perform and when they do, their responses are typically austere. This makes the data collection process much more difficult, requiring the teacher to be ever more vigilant. In Jonathan's case, individual difference variables such as task orientation, adaptability, or reactivity did not impede or constrain his ability to perform. Often this is not the case, however, and teachers are faced with instructing children in complex skill development while trying to accommodate individual differences in areas such as temperament or language. As Turnure (1986) suggests, "Special education is an exceedingly complex social and conceptual system, probably more so than regular education" (p. 109).

We began this chapter by arguing that questions or statements about what constitutes achievement require more demanding explanations than simply aggragating correct or incorrect scores on some measure of performance. It is our belief, however, that through the development of fine-tuned, automated analytic procedures and the acculumation of a richly detailed and organized knowledge base, the skilled, expert educational professional can quickly assess what a student is doing on an academic task and what must be done by the student to bring about performance that is "successful, economical, and satisfying" (Paris & Oka, 1986, p. 103). To become an expert is by no means easy and notable expertise may take some ten years to acquire, regardless of the domain (Simon, 1978). Nonetheless, simply being aware of how an information-processing approach can enhance the measurement and interpretation of achievement data and attempting to implement that approach, can improve the quality of services provided to students, even while the long and arduous task of expert skill is being pursued.

REFERENCES

Algozzine, B., Christenson, S., & Ysseldyke, J. E. (1982). Probabilities associated with the referral to placement process. *Teacher Education and Special Education, 5,* 19–23.

Anderson, J. R. (1982). Acquisition of cognitive skill. *Psychological Review, 89,* 369–406.

Anderson, J. R. (1983). *The architecture of cognition.* Cambridge, MA: Harvard University Press.

Bartholomue, D. (1980). The study of error. *College composition and communication, 31,* 253–269.

Beck, I. L., & Carpenter, P. A. (1986). Cognitive approaches to understanding reading: Implications for instructional practice. *American Psychologist, 41,* 1098–1105.

Bejar, I. I. (1984). Educational diagnostic assessment. *Journal of Educational Measurement, 21,* 175–189.

Bolles, E. B. (1988). *Remembering and forgetting: An inquiry into the nature of memory.* New York: Walker and Company.

Borkowski, J. G., Weyhing, R. S., & Turner, L. A. (1986). Attributional retraining and the teaching of strategies. *Exceptional Children, 53,* 130–137.

Brown, J. S., & Burton, R. R. (1978). Diagnostic models for procedural bugs in basic mathematical skills. *Cognitive Science, 2,* 155–192.

Carey, S. (1986). Cognitive science and science education. *American Psychologist, 41,* 1123–1130.

Craik, F. I. M., & Tulving, E. (1975). Depth of processing and the retention of words in episodic memory. *Journal of Experimental Psychology: General, 104,* 268–294.

Curtis, M. E., & Glaser, R. (1983). Reading theory and the assessment of reading achievement. *Journal of Educational Measurement, 20,* 133–147.

Deno, S. L. (1986). Formative evaluation of individual student programs: A new role for school psychologists. *School Psychology Review, 15,* 358–374.

Fuchs, L. S., & Fuchs, D. (1986). Linking assessment to instructional interventions: An overview. *School Psychology Review, 15,* 318–323.

Gavelek, J. R., & Palincsar, A. S. (1988). Contextualism as an alternative worldview of learning disabilities: A response to Swanson's "Toward a Metatheory of Learning Disabilities." *Journal of Learning Disabilities, 21,* 278–281.

Gelzheiser, L. M., Shepherd, M. J., & Wozniak, R. H. (1986). The development of instruction to induce skill transfer. *Exceptional Children, 53,* 125–129.

Gerber, M. M., & Hall, R. J. (1987). Information processing approaches to studying spelling deficiencies. *Journal of Learning Disabilities, 20,* 34–42.

Gerber, M. M., & Hall, R. J. (in press). Cognitive instruction and spelling. *Learning Disability Quarterly.*

Gerber, M. M., & Semmel, M. I. (1984). Teacher as imperfect test: Reconceptualizing the referral process. *Educational Psychologist, 19,* 137–148.

Glaser, R. (1981). The future of testing: A research agenda for cognitive psychology and psychometrics. *American Psychologist, 36,* 923–936.

Goldman, S. R., & Pelligrino, J. W. (1987). Information processing and educational microcomputer technology: Where do we go from here? *Journal of Learning Disabilities, 20,* 144–154.

Hall, R. J., Gerber, M. M., & Stricker, A. G. (1989). Cognitive training: Implications for spelling instruction. In J. N. Hughes & R. J. Hall (Eds.), *Cognitive behavioral psychology in the schools: A comprehensive handbook* (pp. 347–388). New York: Guilford Press.

Halliday, M., & Hasan, R. (1976). *Cohesion in English.* London: Logeman.

Howell, K. W. (1986). Direct assessment of academic performance. *School Psychology Review, 15,* 324–335.

Kauffman, J. M., Gerber, M. M., & Semmel, M. I. (1988). Arguable assumptions underlying the regular education initiative. *Journal of Learning Disabilities, 21,* 6–11.

Keogh, B. K. (1986). A marker system for describing learning-disability samples. In S. J. Ceci (Ed.), *Handbook of cognitive, social, and neurological aspects of learning disabilities* (Vol. 1, pp. 81–94). Hillsdale, NJ: Lawrence Erlbaum Associates.

Kintsch, W. (1977). On comprehending stories. In E. Just & H. Carpenter (Eds.), *Cognitive process in comprehension* (pp. 33–62). Hillsdale, NJ: Lawrence Erlbaum Associates.

Kolligian, J., & Sternberg, R. J. (1987). Intelligence, information processing, and specific learning disabilities: A triarchic synthesis. *Journal of Learning Disabilities, 20,* 8–17.

Lentz, Jr., F. E., & Shapiro, E. S. (1986). Functional assessment of the academic environment. *School Psychology Review, 15,* 346–357.

Linn, R. L. (1986). Educational testing and assessment: Research needs and policy issues. *American Psychologist, 41,* 1153–1160.

Mastropieri, M. A., & Scruggs, T. E. (1987). *Effective instruction for special education.* Boston: Little, Brown.

Messick, S. (1984). The psychology of educational measurement. *Journal of Educational Measurement, 21,* 215–237.

Miller, G. A. (1981). *Language and speech.* San Francisco: W. H. Freeman.

Nesher, P. (1986). Learning mathematics. *American Psychologist, 41,* 1114–1122.

Page, J., & Stewart, S. (1985). Story grammar skills in school-age children. *Topics in Language Disorders, 5,* 16–30.

Palincsar, A. S. (1986). Metacognitive strategy instruction. *Exceptional Children, 53,* 118–124.

Paris, S. G., & Oka, E. R. (1986). Self-regulated learning among exception children. *Exceptional Children, 53,* 103–108.

Pryzwansky, W. B. (1987, June). The School Psychologist as scientist and practitioner. *The School Psychologist,* 1–2.

Ripich, D. N., & Griffith, P. L. (1988). Narrative abilities of children with learning disabilities and nondisabled children: Story structure, cohesion, and propositions. *Journal of Learning Disabilities, 21,* 165–173.

Sewell, T. (1987, June). Perspectives. *The School Psychologist,* 1–5.

Shana, S. (1983). *Diagnosing student errors: An example from science.* Los Angeles, CA: UCLA Center for the Study of Evaluation.

Shinn, M. R., Tindal, G. A., & Stein, S. (1988). Curriculum-based measurement and the identification of mildly handicapped students: A research review. *Professional School Psychology, 3,* 69–85.

Simon, H. A. (1978). Information-processing theory of human problem-solving. In W. K. Estes (Ed.), *Handbook of learning and cognitive processes.* Hillsdale, NJ: Lawrence Erlbaum Associates.

Snow, R. E., & Peterson, P. L. (1985). Cognitive analyses of tests: Implications for redesign. In S. Embertson (Ed.), *Test design: Contributions from psychology, education, and psychometrics* (pp. 149–166). New York: Academic Press.

Spache, C. D. (1976). *Diagnosing and correcting reading disabilities.* Boston: Allyn & Bacon.

Spear, L. C., & Sternberg, R. J. (1985). Cognitive assessment with disabled readers. *Special Services in the Schools, 2,* 71–84.

Stein, N., & Glenn, C. (1979). An analysis of story comprehension in elementary school children. In R. Freedle (Ed.), *New directions in discourse processing,* Vol. 2 (pp. 53–102). Norwood, NJ: Ablex.

Swanson, H. L. (1987). Information-processing theory and learning disabilities: An overview. *Journal of Learning Disabilities, 20,* 3–7.

Swanson, H. L. (1988). Toward a metatheory of learning disabilities. *Journal of Learning Disabilities, 21,* 196–209.

Tatsuoka, K. K., & Tatsuoka, M. M. (1983). Spotting erroneous rules of operation by the individual consistency index. *Journal of Educational Measurement, 20,* 221–230.

Turnure, J. E. (1986). Instruction and cognitive development: Coordinating communication and cues. *Exceptional Children, 53,* 109–117.

Webb, N., Herman, J., & Cabello, B. (1983). *Optimizing the diagnostic power of tests: An illustration from language arts.* Los Angeles, CA: UCLA Center for the Study of Evaluation.

Willson, V. L. (1987, August). *Cognitive psychology and test development: Out with the old.* Invited address, Division 5, annual meeting of the American Psychological Association, New York.

Ysseldyke, J. E., Thurlow, M. L., Graden, J. L., Wesson, C., Deno, S. L., & Algozzine, B. (1983). Generalizations from five years of research on assessment and decision making. *Exceptional Education Quarterly, 4,* 75–93.

16

Toward an Interactive Model: Teaching Text-Based Concepts To Learning Disabled Students

Candace S. Bos
Patricia L. Anders
University of Arizona

Learning disabled (LD) students face challenging reading demands as they enter secondary school settings. While many of these students continue to face difficulties with basic reading skills such as fluent decoding, they now need to use a cadre of comprehension and metacomprehension strategies for learning information from text. In addition to increased reading demands, secondary students are expected to deepen and broaden their content knowledge through reading. Unfortunately, many LD students may lack the background in various domains of content knowledge because their instructional focus has been on basic decoding skills and low level reading comprehension. Because LD students spend much of their in-school time learning how to read, they are deprived of opportunities to read for learning concepts and information (Snider & Tarver, 1987). Furthermore, school observational research suggests that students attending resource rooms in elementary schools miss out on content instruction (McGill-Franzen & Allington, 1987; Richardson, Casanova, Placier, & Guilfoyle, 1989). The compounding of limited reading skills and strategies plus limited content area background knowledge poses a tremendous threat for the learning disabled adolescent.

Another threat lies in the organization and conventions of the secondary school. Not surprisingly, the secondary setting has some predictable demands for these students. First, textbooks are content loaded. In response to declining achievement test scores during the past 20 years and the ever-increasing amounts of information to be learned, textbooks have become more content dense than ever before (Chall & Conard, 1984). Second, teachers focus on the content knowledge to be learned and expect that the skills needed for effective learning from texts are already known. Content area teachers typically do not perceive process or procedural instruction to be their responsibility (Estes & Vaughan, 1985). Third, tasks that require the use and application of higher level thinking skills such as evaluation, synthesis, and abstraction are more prevalent. These types of thinking processes are an important goal of the secondary school and are what is needed for a literate and informed citizenry capable of making decisions. This is the situation faced by LD students and consequently, researchers focusing on intervention research at the secondary level.

During the last decade, this situation has received increasing attention. A considerable amount of intervention research has focused on teaching comprehension and comprehension monitoring skills to learning disabled adolescents (e.g., Clark, Deshler, Schumaker, Alley, & Warner, 1984; Graves, 1986; Jenkins, Heliotis, Stein, & Hayes, 1987; Palincsar & Brown, 1984; Wong, Wong, Perry, & Sawatsky, 1986). Results from these and other works in cognitive training and learning strategies intervention have been promising in that improved performance on comprehension tests has occurred.

Although strides have been made in learning strategy instruction (Wong & Wong, 1988), there is a growing concern among educators and intervention researchers that providing students with learning strategies is not sufficient for learning in the content areas or for accomplishing other real world literacy tasks (Bos & Anders, 1988; Bulgren, Schumaker, & Deshler, 1988). Consequently, a complimentary set of research has developed that focuses on teaching strategies appropriate for implementation during the teaching and learning of content area subjects (e.g., Bos, Anders, Filip, & Jaffe, 1989; Bulgren et al., 1988; Darch & Carnine, 1986). While the learning strategies research is based on cognitive training and cognitive behavior modification, much of the teaching strategies research is grounded in theoretical constructs such as schema theory (Rumelhart, 1980), the closely related knowledge hypothesis (Anderson & Freebody, 1981), the psycholinguistic model of the reading process (Goodman, 1984) and concept learning and development theory (Klausmeier, 1984). The purpose of this chapter is to elaborate on this theoretical rationale for interactive instructional strategies, review research investigating these strategies, particularly that of the authors, and to draw together evidence toward an interactive instructional model for teaching text-based concepts to learning disabled students.

TOWARD AN INTERACTIVE MODEL

The interactive model for teaching content area concepts represented in text relies upon assumptions found in three different but complimentary lines of inquiry and theory. This section explicates the assumptions within each of the theories that are relevant to the interactive model of teaching concepts.

Schema Theory and the Knowledge Hypothesis

Schema theory explains how knowledge is structured in memory and how these structures affect incoming information. Schemata are data structures for representing generic concepts stored in memory (Anderson, 1984; Rumelhart, 1980). Schemata provide an organizational framework or scaffolding on which new information can be integrated. "Schemata are employed in the process of interpreting sensory data (both linguistic and nonlinguistic), in retrieving information from memory, in organizing actions, in determining goals and subgoals, in allocated resources, and generally, in guiding the flow of processing in the system" (Rumelhart, 1980, pp. 33–34).

Schema theory has been used by reading comprehension researchers to explain the importance of prior knowledge for learning new information (Anderson, Reynolds, Schallert, & Goetz, 1977; Anderson, Spiro, & Anderson, 1978). Assumptions from schema theory have also been used to explain the powerful and consistent correlation between vocabulary knowledge and reading comprehension. Anderson and Freebody (1981) referred to this as the knowledge hypothesis: Understanding a concept or knowing a vocabulary word implies that one knows not only the definitional meaning but also its relationships to other concepts and its semantic characteristics. Instructional principles can be derived from schema theory and the knowledge hypothesis in developing an instructional model for teaching text-based concepts:

1. The richness of a reader's related schemata and the degree to which a reader activates these schemata should affect both concept learning and text comprehension.

2. The degree to which the instructional intervention provides opportunities for developing relationships between and among concepts should affect conceptual learning and reading comprehension.

3. The degree to which the instructional intervention allows analysis of the semantic features of a concept should affect conceptual learning and reading comprehension.

Psycholinguistic Model of Reading

According to the psycholinguistic model of reading (Goodman, 1984), readers utilize three information systems when comprehending texts: the grapho-phonic system, the syntactic system, and the semantic system. The reader uses certain cognitive strategies to engage these systems. Key among the cognitive strategies are sampling or selecting, predicting, confirming, and justifying. Goodman argues that these processes are engaged at every level of discourse, from letters to entire texts, as readers construct meaning. Although the psycholinguistic model is compatible with schema theory, it is different in that Goodman's model explains comprehension while schema theory explains knowledge acquisition and memory.

Thus, certain additional instructional principles can be derived from the psycholinguistic model for teaching text-based concepts:

1. The degree to which the instructional intervention allows for opportunities to access all systems of language affects the quality of comprehension.

2. The degree to which the instructional intervention explicates the cognitive strategies of selecting, predicting, confirming, and justifying affects the quality of comprehension and conceptual learning.

Concept Learning and Development Theory

Research and theories about concepts and conceptual attainment is rich, drawing on the psychology of both Piaget and Bruner and the fields of cognitive psychology and information processing theory. Klausmeier and his colleagues (Klausmeier & Sipple, 1980) have developed a model to describe the attainment of concepts within school curriculum areas that corresponds well with the schema theorists and Goodman's model of the reading process. This concept learning and development theory hypothesizes four levels of attaining a concept: concrete, identity, classification, and formal. Concepts are attained in long term memory when a learner engages the concept at all four levels (Klausmeier, Ghatala, & Frayer, 1974). Evidence suggests that students learn concept when opportunities are provided to identify and name defining attributes and when examples and nonexamples of the concept are presented and used (Klausmeier et al., 1974).

Concepts can be hierarchically organized and related to each other and are remembered best when taught in ways to explicate that organization and relationship (Klausmeier, 1984). The most overarching, all-inclusive concept may be identified as the superordinate concept. Coordinate concepts, the next level, are often represented by main ideas or categories within the superordinate concept. The lowest level of knowledge that can be categorized within a coordinate concept is identified as subordinate concepts. An author's conceptual presentation of the content in a subject matter text can be organized into these types of concepts and this organization can be recognized by readers.

Concepts, then, are the substance of schemata that are accessed and manipulated by cognitive strategies. The concept learning and development theory has certain instructional implications:

1. Instruction that explicates the attributes of a concept will affect understanding and remembering of that concept.

2. Instruction that provides examples and nonexamples of a concept will affect understanding and remembering of that concept.

3. Concepts found within content disciplines are organized in hierarchical structures that may serve as metaphors of schema(ta).

Toward the Interaction

The instructional principles derived from each of these theories has led us to an interactive model of teaching text-based concepts. The term "interactive" has been associated with this model for several reasons. First, the comprehension process is assumed to be interactive in nature. In other words, reading is not merely gaining meaning from the text and does not proceed in a strict order from perceiving the visual information in letters to the overall interpretation of the text (Anderson, 1984). Instead, reading comprehension is a constructive process in which readers combine the information presented in the text with their hypotheses about the text meaning and their current schemata.

Second, the term "interactive" has been associated with the model because it assumes that learning will be enhanced if the teacher and students utilize an interactive dialogue to discuss and organize concepts. This interactive dialogue encourages cooperative knowledge sharing in that the teacher and students share their prior knowledge concerning the key concepts. It allows the teacher to serve as a mediator for learning (Goodman, 1984; Vygotsky, 1978).

EVIDENCE TOWARD THE MODEL

An increasing amount of intervention research has focused on teaching text-based concepts and facilitating reading comprehension. Recently, Stahl and Fairbanks (1986) conducted a comprehensive review and meta-analysis of the research on vocabulary instruction as it relates to text-based comprehension. They found that instructional methods that produced the highest effect on reading comprehension were broad in instruction, deep in processing, and interactive in nature. Broad instruction refers to not only definitional information but also rich decontextualized knowledge (i.e., knowledge of the underlying concept and how that knowledge is realized in various contexts) (Beck, McKeown, & Omanson, 1987). Deep processing (Craik & Tulving, 1975) entails integrating new information with old and developing elaborated semantic networks. The interactive nature of teaching activates and instantiates students' schemata (Rumelhart, 1980), engages students in cooperative knowledge sharing (Bos & Anders, 1987), and encourages students in predicting and justifying semantic relationships (Goodman, 1984).

While the research reviewed by Stahl and Fairbanks was conducted with a variety of populations, a subset of this research has focused specifically on the learning disabled population (Bos & Anders, 1988; Bos et al., 1989; Bulgren et al., 1988). Employing an interactive model for teaching text-based concepts may have particular relevance for adolescents identified as learning/reading disabled because it compensates for some of their identified academic difficulties including limited content knowledge (Snider & Tarver, 1987), limited comprehension and comprehension monitoring strategies (Bos & Filip, 1984; Golinkoff, 1976; Wong, 1985), and deficits in elaborative memory strategies (Torgesen, 1977). Evidence toward an interactive model for teaching concepts can be drawn from this subset of research focusing specifically on the learning disabled population.

Teaching Text-Based Concepts Using Semantic Feature Analysis

In one of our first studies (Anders, Bos & Filip, 1984; Bos et al., 1989), we were interested in a question being pursued by a number of researchers in the field of reading comprehension and vocabulary learning. While a relationship between vocabulary learning and comprehension had been documented in early correlational research (e.g., Davis, 1944, 1968), a set of intervention studies with LD students failed to support a causal link. While vocabulary learning increased with vocabulary instruction, it had limited effect on the LD students' reading comprehension (Pany & Jenkins, 1978; Pany, Jenkins, & Schreck, 1982). We hypothesized that if an interactive type of instruction were employed with LD students, both vocabulary learning and reading comprehension would be affected. To test this hypothesis we utilized semantic feature analysis (SFA) (Anders & Bos, 1986; Johnson & Pearson, 1984), an instructional strategy that encourages students to predict and confirm the text-based meanings of important vocabulary and the relationships between and among the vocabulary.

Method.   To accomplish this, we selected chapters from a social studies text (Martz & Novelli, 1978) and analyzed each chapter using a content analysis to determine the superordinate, coordinate, and subordinate concepts. The key concepts or vocabulary were then placed on a relationship chart in which the superordinate concept(s) served as the title, the coordinate concepts were placed along one axis of the chart, and the subordinate concepts were listed along the other axis (see Fig. 16.1).

During instruction, the researcher/teacher used the chart prior to reading to activate students' prior knowledge and instantiate their schemata related to the topic. Using the SFA procedure (Anders & Bos, 1986), the name of the chart and each important idea (coordinate concept) were introduced by the teacher. Students were encouraged to share their knowledge by predicting meanings and

FIG. 16.1.   Relationship chart for science chapter on "Fossils."

providing examples. Next, each related vocabulary (subordinate concept) was introduced using the same procedure. Once the meaning was predicted, the teacher and students discussed, predicted, and rated the relationships between the vocabulary and each of the important ideas. When the chart was completed, students read the chapter to confirm predictions and to clarify unknown relationships. After reading, the relationship chart was reviewed and discussed.

For the contrast condition, a dictionary method adapted from Gipe (1978–79) was employed. A vocabulary list was developed by selecting the vocabulary which was judged as important for understanding and "difficult" for the students. First, the teacher and students in the contrast condition discussed the topic and practiced decoding the vocabulary. Then the students found the meanings for the vocabulary in the dictionary and wrote a definition and sentence using the word. Students read the chapter to verify and/or clarify the meanings of the words. After reading, students were encouraged to make changes in their definitions and sentences accordingly.

After instruction, students took a multiple choice test consisting of 10 vocabulary and 10 comprehension items. Whereas the vocabulary items measured students' knowledge of the context-related meanings of the vocabulary presented in the chapter, the comprehension items measured their understanding of the chapter or their ability to apply concepts presented in the chapter to novel situations. Six months later students were readministered the test.

Students who participated in the study were 50 high school students identified as learning disabled with average IQ's and reading achievement substantially below grade level.

Results and Discussion. Results indicate that immediately following instruction students participating in SFA performed significantly better on the vocabulary items ($\bar{x}$ = 7.73) and comprehension items ($\bar{x}$ = 8.33) than students using the dictionary method ($\bar{x}$ = 5.31 for vocabulary, $\bar{x}$ = 5.95 for comprehension). Students in both groups did not lose a significant amount of learned information from the time of the initial test to the follow-up test with students in the SFA group again scoring significantly higher ($\bar{x}$ = 7.61 for vocabulary, $\bar{x}$ = 7.57 for comprehension) than the dictionary group ($\bar{x}$ = 5.43 for vocabulary, $\bar{x}$ = 5.59 for comprehension). Results for this study lend initial support to the interactive model of teaching. Using the interactive principles inherent in the SFA procedure, the LD high school students demonstrated a greater understanding of the chapter both at the time of instruction and several months later.

However, this initial study has several limitations in terms of model testing. First, the dictionary method and SFA are highly contrastive. For example, while the dictionary method utilized an individual participatory structure, the SFA activity required group discussion. Second, the definitions learned by the two groups may have been different. Students in the dictionary method were expected to independently generate their own definitions whereas students in the SFA condition generated group definitions with the teacher's guidance. The relevance of these definitions to the text-based concepts may have been substantially different across the two groups. Third, only one interactive teaching strategy was tested. If the model is to serve as a generalized model for teaching concepts, then different teaching activities utilizing the interactive principles should be tested.

Teaching Text-Based Concepts Using Various Interactive Techniques

In a recently completed study (Bos & Anders, 1988), we attempted to address some of the limitations in this first study. First, we selected a different method for the contrast condition. Based on the vocabulary instruction used by Pany and her colleagues (Pany & Jenkins, 1978; Pany et al., 1982) and based on a direct instruction model (Engelmann & Carnine, 1982), we selected as a contrast method direct, definition instruction. We compared this contrast condition to three interactive teaching conditions. While we again utilized semantic feature analysis, we also employed semantic mapping (Pearson & Johnson, 1978) and semantic/syntactic feature analysis (Allen & Anders, 1984). Across the four teaching conditions, we controlled the vocabulary taught and utilized the same definitions. By switching to definition instruction, we utilized four methods that require a substantial amount of verbal interaction during instruction.

Method. Subjects for this study were 61 students identified as learning/reading disabled and attending junior high school. A measure of students' prior knowledge for the experimental topic was obtained several weeks prior to intervention. The test construction, based on a content analysis, consisted of 15 vocabulary and 15 comprehension items.

For the definition instruction condition, the vocabulary and definitions for the experimental chapter on fossils were presented and practiced both prior to and after reading the chapter. In the semantic mapping condition, the students and teachers discussed the meaning of the vocabulary and used it to construct a hierarchial relationship map (see Fig. 16.2) prior to reading the passage, verifying the map during and after reading. For the semantic feature analysis condition, a relationship chart was employed. For semantic/syntactic feature analysis students completed the relationship chart and cloze-type sentences based on the chart. Definition instruction emphasized correct and automatic pronunciation of the vocabulary and the memorization of concise, text-based definitions using high student engagement through oral recitation, teacher monitoring, and corrective feedback (Duffy & Roehler, 1982; Engelmann & Carnine, 1982). The three interactive conditions employed interactive, discussion-oriented strategies designed to assist students in activating prior knowledge, instantiating concepts, and drawing relationships among the concepts. To measure short term learning, students wrote written recalls and were given the objective test. To measure long term learning, students again completed the written recalls and the objective test 1 month later.

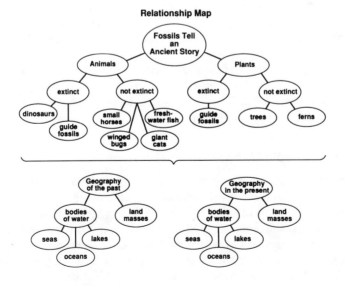

FIG. 16.2. Relationship map for the science chapter on "Fossils."

Results and Discussion.   The results of this study confirm the findings of the first study. For both the vocabulary and comprehension items on the objective test, the interactive instruction resulted in higher performance than definition instruction for short-term and long-term learning. However in this study, students did lose a significant amount of information over time. The exception was the vocabulary items for the group of students who participated in the semantic/syntactic feature analysis activities.

In contrast to the objective test, the students' written recalls showed a different outcome pattern. The recalls were analyzed for the amount of relevant vocabulary and concepts generated, a holistic score rating the overall quality of the recall, and the amount of prior knowledge represented in the recalls (Anders, Bos, & Allen, 1987; Irwin & Mitchell, 1983). In terms of the vocabulary and concepts or ideas generated and the holistic rating, no differences were evident among the groups immediately following instruction. However, a month later students in the interactive groups produced significantly more vocabulary and concepts and received higher holistic ratings than students who received the definition instruction. This would indicate that at the time of teaching the definition instruction was as facilitative as the interactive teaching in assisting students to generate relevant information about the topic. But in terms of long term learning, the teaching methodology which encouraged the LD students to tie concepts one to another and to prior knowledge resulted in greater and higher quality recall.

Students' use of prior knowledge in their recalls becomes a particularly interesting variable in terms of the interactive teaching methods. Since it is assumed interactive methods encourage students to activate relevant schemata, we hypothesized that students who received these strategies would integrate more of their prior knowledge into their written recalls. Our hypothesis did not prove correct in terms of short-term learning. Students in the definition instruction and semantic mapping groups demonstrated greater use of prior knowledge than students in the SFA or SSFA groups. However, a month later, the predicted finding was evident with the interactive groups demonstrating greater use of their prior knowledge than the definition instruction group.

Teaching Concepts Using Concept Diagrams

Although the previous studies provide support for the interactive model across short- and long-term learning, a question that still arises is the effectiveness of interactive strategies for LD students when they are implemented in mainstream secondary classes. Bulgren et al. (1988) investigated this notion using an interactive strategy that employed a concept teaching routine and concept diagram (see Fig. 16.3). Like the other interactive strategies, concept diagrams allow the teacher and students to highlight the salient aspects of a concept through the use of a visual aid. For the concept diagram, concept characteristics and examples/nonexamples are emphasized.

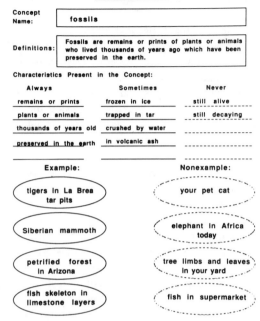

FIG. 16.3.   Concept diagram for the concept of "fossils" (Bulgren, in prep.)

Method.   In this study, nine science and social studies teachers utilized the concept diagrams and a concept teaching routine in their classrooms with 32 LD students and over 400 other students. For each student identified as learning disabled, a student who was not learning disabled (NLD) was randomly selected from students enrolled in the same course who were of the same age, sex, and grade.

During a 4-hour workshop, the participating teachers were taught to prepare concept diagrams and to use a concept teaching routine. The steps, based on the concept learning and development theory, included: (a) providing an advance organizer; (b) eliciting from the students a list of key words from the chapter and writing the words on the board; (c) reviewing the symbols on the diagram; (d) naming and defining the concept; (e) discussing the "Always," "Sometimes," and "Never" characteristics; (f) discussing one example and one nonexample of the concept; (g) linking the example and nonexample to the characteristics; (h) testing potential examples/nonexamples to determine whether they are members of the concept class; and (i) providing a post organizer. During this routine, teachers involved students in discussing the various aspects of the concepts in the decision making necessary to complete the diagram. After the concept diagram and teaching routine had been implemented several times, teachers began to conduct 5-minute concept reviews in which students studied the concept diagram, answered questions about the diagram, and filled out the diagram from memory.

Multiple baseline designs for the teacher and the LD and NLD students were used to evaluate the effectiveness of the intervention. Across the baseline and intervention conditions, teachers were measured on their performance in preparing a concept diagram and in using the teaching routine. Student performance was ascertained from concept acquisition tests and regular unit/chapter tests. While the concept acquisition tests specifically tested the definition, characteristics, and examples/nonexamples of the concept, the unit/chapter tests covered the information presented in the specific chapter or unit.

Results and Discussion.   Teacher performance in preparing and teaching the concept diagram indicates that, before training, teachers most frequently focused on naming the concept and presenting examples. This resulted in performance substantially below mastery (85% level). After training, all of the nine teachers demonstrated mastery in preparing the diagrams and six demonstrated mastery in using the teaching routine. After consultation, mastery was reached by all teachers.

Students performance on the concept acquisition tests indicates that both the LD and NLD groups increased their performance when the concept training was used by their teachers and increased again when the concept review was added. On the unit/chapter tests, the introduction of concept training did not significantly increase the LD and NLD students' performance. However, when the review was added, performance for both groups increased significantly.

This study provides an important piece of evidence toward the interactive model. It demonstrates that regular classroom teachers can select, analyze, prepare, and teach complex conceptual information in an interactive format and that both LD and NLD students can benefit when information is presented in this manner.

CONCLUSIONS

Theoretically derived intervention research should provide the field of learning disabilities with a systematic means of testing instructional models for students who have been identified as inefficient learners (Wong, 1987). This chapter presented evidence toward one such instructional model, a model for teaching text-based concepts that is theoretically grounded in schema theory, the psycholinguistic model of reading, and concept learning and development theory.

The evidence presented in this chapter provides initial support for an interactive model across several different interactive teaching strategies and content areas and in both special and regular education settings. Although the model appears powerful in its effect, many questions are still to be answered by intervention researchers focusing on the learning disabled adolescent. One logical next step in this research is the in-depth study of these interactive strategies to ascertain how such teacher and task variables as teaching style, content area, and text structure relate to learning efficiency. Another logical step for researchers is to investigate the various components of the model to determine which features are more predictive of learning. Other research might focus on the instructional and learning processes associated with mediating these interactive teaching strategies so that students can incorporate them into their cadre of learning strategies and reap greater benefits when used by content area teachers. This dovetailing of teaching and learning strategies holds particular promise for the learning disabled adolescent in secondary school settings.

REFERENCES

Allen, A. A., & Anders, P. L. (1984). *Bilingual and ESL strategies in secondary classrooms.* Unpublished manuscript. University of Arizona, Division of Language, Reading and Culture.

Anders, P. L., & Bos, C. S. (1986). Semantic feature analysis: An interactive strategy for vocabulary development and text comprehension. *Journal of Reading, 29,* 610–616.

Anders, P. L., Bos, C. S., & Allen, A. (1987). *Scoring procedures for written recalls of content area information* (Working Paper). Tucson, AZ: University of Arizona, College of Education.

Anders, P. L., Bos, C. S., & Filip, D. (1984). The effect of semantic feature analysis on the reading comprehension of learning-disabled students. In J. A. Niles (Ed.), *Changing perspectives on research in reading/language processing and instruction* (Thirty-third Yearbook, pp. 162–166). Rochester, NY: National Reading Conference.

Anderson, R. C. (1984). Role of the reader's schema in comprehension, learning and memory. In R. C. Anderson, J. Osborn, & R. J. Tierney (Eds.), *Learning to read in American schools: Basal readers and content texts* (pp. 243–258). Hillsdale, NJ: Lawrence Erlbaum Associates.

Anderson, R. C. & Freebody, P. (1981). Vocabulary knowledge. In J. T. Guthrie (Ed.), *Comprehension and teaching: Research reviews* (pp. 71–117). Newark, DE: International Reading Association.

Anderson, R. C., Reynolds, R. E., Schallert, D. L., & Goetz, E. T. (1977). Frameworks for comprehending discourse. *American Educational Research Journal, 14,* 367–382.

Anderson, R. C., Spiro, R. J., & Anderson, M. C. (1978). Schemata as scaffolding for the representation of information in connected discourse. *American Educational Research Journal, 15,* 433–440.

Beck, I. L., McKeown, M. G., & Omanson, R. C. (1987). The effects and uses of diverse vocabulary instructional techniques. In M. G. McKeown & M. E. Curtis (Eds.), *The nature of vocabulary acquisition* (pp. 147–163). Hillsdale, NJ: Lawrence Erlbaum Associates.

Bos, C. S., & Anders, P. L. (1987). Semantic feature analysis: An interactive teaching strategy for facilitating learning from text. *Learning Disabilities Focus, 3,* 55–59.

Bos, C. S., & Anders, P. L. (1988, February). *Toward an interactive model: Teaching text-based concepts to learning disabled students.* Paper presented at the meeting of the International Academy for Research in Learning Disabilities, Los Angeles, CA.

Bos, C. S., Anders, P. L., Filip, D., & Jaffe, L. E. (1989). The effects of an interactive instructional strategy for enhancing learning disabled students' reading comprehension and content area learning. *Journal of Learning Disabilities, 22,* 384–390.

Bos, C. S., & Filip, D. (1984). Comprehension monitoring in learning disabled and average students. *Journal of Learning Disabilities, 17,* 229–233.

Bulgren, J. (in preparation). *Models for concept teaching routines.* University of Kansas, Institute for Research in Learning Disabilities.

Bulgren, J., Schumaker, J. B., & Deshler, D. D. (1988). Effectiveness of a concept teaching routine in enhancing the performance of LD students in secondary-level mainstream classes. *Learning Disability Quarterly, 11,* 3–17.

Chall, J. S., & Conrad, S. S. (1984). Resources and their use for reading instruction. In A. C. Purves & O. Niles (Eds.), *Becoming readers in a complex society* (Eighty-third Yearbook, pp. 209–232). Chicago, IL: The National Society for the Study of Education.

Clark, F. L., Deshler, D. D., Schumaker, J. B., Alley, G. R., & Warner, M. M. (1984). Visual imagery and self-questioning: Strategies to improve comprehension of written material. *Journal of Learning Disabilities, 17,* 145–149.

Craik, F. I. M., & Tulving, E. (1975). Depth of processing and the retention of words in episodic memory. *Journal of Experimental Psychology: General, 104,* 268–294.

Darch, C., & Carnine, D. (1986). Teaching content area material to learning disabled students. *Exceptional Children, 53,* 240–246.

Davis, F. G. (1944). Fundamental factors of comprehension in reading. *Psychometrika, 9,* 185–197.

Davis, F. G. (1968). Research in comprehension in reading. *Reading Research Quarterly, 3,* 499–545.

Duffy, G. G., & Roehler, L. R. (1982) Direct instruction comprehension: What does it really mean. *Reading Horizons, 23,* 35–40.

Engelmann, S., & Carnine, D. W. (1982). *Theory of instruction: Principles and applications.* New York: Irvington.

Estes, T. H., & Vaughan, J. L. (1985). *Reading and learning in the content classroom: Diagnostic and instructional strategies* (2nd ed.). Boston: Allyn and Bacon.

Gipe, J. P. (1978–79). Investigating techniques for teaching word meanings. *Reading Research Quarterly, 14,* 624–644.

Golinkoff, R. (1976). A comparison of reading comprehension in good and poor comprehenders. *Reading Research Quarterly, 11,* 623–659.

Goodman, K. S. (1984). Unity in reading. In A. C. Purves & O. Niles (Eds.), *Becoming readers in a complex society* (Eighty-third Yearbook, pp. 79–114). Chicago, IL: The National Society for the Study of Education.

Graves, A. W. (1986). Effects of direct instruction and metacomprehension training on finding main ideas. *Learning Disabilities Research, 1,* 90–100.

Irwin, P. A., & Mitchell, J. N. (1983). A procedure for assessing the richness of retellings. *Journal of Reading, 26,* 391–396.

Jenkins, J. R., Heliotis, J. D., Stein, M. L., & Haynes, M. C. (1987). Improving reading comprehension by using paragraph restatements. *Exceptional Children, 54,* 54–59.

Johnson, D. D., & Pearson, P. D. (1984). *Teaching reading vocabulary* (2nd ed.). New York: Holt, Rinehart, & Winston.

Klausmeier, H. J. (1984). Conceptual learning and development. In R. Corsini (Ed.), *Encyclopedia of Psychology,* (Vol. 1, pp. 266–269). New York: Wiley.

Klausmeier, H. J., Ghatala, E. S., & Frayer, D. A. (1974). *Conceptual learning and development: A cognitive review.* New York: Academic Press.

Klausmeier, H. J., & Sipple, T. S. (1980). *Learning and teaching process concepts: A strategy for testing applications of theory.* New York: Academic Press.

Martz, C., & Novelli, R. (1978). *Criminal justice.* New York: Scholastic Inc.

McGill-Franzen, A., & Allington, R. L. (1987, December). *Influences on the design of school programs for at-risk learners.* Paper presented at the meeting of the National Reading Conference, St. Petersburg, FL.

Palincsar, A. S., & Brown, A. L. (1984). Reciprocal teaching of comprehension-fostering and comprehension-monitoring activities. *Cognition and Instruction, 1,* 117–175.

Pany, D., & Jenkins, J. J. (1978). Learning word meanings: A comparison of instructional procedures and effects on measures of reading comprehension with learning disabled students. *Learning Disability Quarterly, 1*(2), 21–32.

Pany, D., Jenkins, J. J., & Schreck, J. (1982). Vocabulary instruction: Effects on word knowledge and reading comprehension. *Learning Disability Quarterly, 5,* 202–215.

Pearson, P. D., & Johnson, D. D. (1978). *Teaching reading comprehension.* New York: Holt, Rinehart & Winston.

Richardson, V., Casanova, U., Placier, P., Guilfoyle, K. (1989). *School children at-risk.* New York: Falmer Press.

Rumelhart, D. E. (1980). Schemata: The building blocks of cognition, In R. J. Spiro, B. C. Bruce, & W. F. Brewer (Eds.), *Theoretical issues in reading comprehension* (pp. 33–58). Hillsdale, NJ: Lawrence Erlbaum Associates.

Snider, V. E., & Tarver, S. G. (1987). The effect of early reading failure on acquisition of knowledge among students with learning disabilities. *Journal of Learning Disabilities, 20,* 351–356.

Stahl, S. A., & Fairbank, M. M. (1986). The effects of vocabulary instruction: A model-based meta-analysis. *Review of Educational Research, 56,* 72–110.

Torgesen, J. K. (1987). Memorization processes in reading-disabled children. *Journal of Educational Psychology, 69,* 571–578.

Vygotsky, L. S. (1978). *Mind in society: The development of higher psychological processes.* Cambridge, MA: Harvard University Press.

Wong, B. Y. L. (1985). Issues in cognitive-behavioral interventions in academic skills areas. *Journal of Abnormal Child Psychology, 13,* 425–442.

Wong, B. Y. L. (1987). Conceptual and methodological issues in interventions with learning-disabled children and adolescents. In S. Vaughn & C. S. Bos (Eds.), *Research in learning disabilities: Issues and future trends* (pp. 185–196). San Diego: College-Hill Press.

Wong, B. Y. L., & Wong, R. (1988). Cognitive interventions for learning disabilities. In K. Kavale (Ed.), *Learning disabilities: State of the art and practice* (pp. 141–160). Boston: College-Hill Publication, Little, Brown and Company.

Wong, B. Y. L., Wong, R., Perry, N., & Sawatsky, D. (1986). The efficacy of self-questioning summarization strategy for use by underachievers and learning disabled adolescents in social studies. *Learning Disabilities Focus, 2,* 20–35.

17 Phonological Synthesis Tasks: A Developmental, Functional, and Componential Analysis

Joseph K. Torgesen
Sharon Morgan
Florida State University

One of the most important achievements of research on reading within the last 10 years has been the demonstration that facility in processing the phonological features of language is strongly related to the acquisition of beginning reading skills (Liberman, 1987). Phonological processing can be broadly defined as one's use of phonological information (the sounds of one's language) in processing oral and written language (Wagner & Torgesen, 1987). Research has focused on three major types of phonological processing: phonological awareness, phonological coding in working memory, and phonological recoding in the context of lexical access.

Although all three types of phonological abilities may be important to the attainment of early reading skills, the area studied most extensively has been phonological awareness. This aspect of phonological skill is defined as one's awareness of and access to the sound structure of language. Many different types of tasks have been used to study phonological awareness (Lewkowicz, 1980; Stanovich, Cunningham, & Cramer, 1984; Yopp, 1988), but these may be grouped into two broad categories; phonological analysis or segmentation, and phonological synthesis or blending.

Phonological analysis refers to the identification of individual phonemes in words (Elkonin, 1973; Lewkowicz, 1980). For example, a child might be asked the question "What are the different sounds in cat?" The desired response would be |k|, |a|, |t|.

Phonological synthesis refers to combining a sequence of isolated speech sounds in order to produce a recognizable word (Chall, Roswell, & Blumenthal, 1963; Helfgott, 1976). On the synthesis task the question may be asked, "What word is this: |k|, |a|, |t|?" The expected response would be "cat."

There is strong correlational evidence indicating a relationship between good performance on both types of phonological awareness tasks (synthesis and analysis) and success in early reading (Wagner & Torgesen, 1987). However, basic questions about causality remain. Some investigators argue that mastery of both tasks is fundamentally important to success in beginning reading (Lewkowicz, 1980; Williams, 1980). Others have speculated that either segmentation ability (Ball & Blachman, 1988; Bradley & Bryant, 1985) or synthesis ability (Perfetti, Beck, & Hughes, 1981) is most important in the acquisition of beginning reading skills. Some researchers (Goldstein, 1976; Alegria, Pignot, & Morais, 1982) have presented evidence supporting the reverse argument, that learning to read facilitates the growth of phonological awareness.

Although research has tended to focus more on measures of phonological analysis than synthesis, synthesis tasks are more frequently found on standardized measures of prereading skills. In spite of their wide use in assessment, many important questions remain to be answered about synthesis skills. In this paper, three basic questions are addressed: (1) What is the developmental course of sound blending skill? (2) What is the empirical evidence regarding its relationship to the attainment of reading skills? (3) What is the nature of blending ability in terms of the component skills that contribute to good performance on blending tasks?

DEVELOPMENTAL COURSE OF SOUND BLENDING SKILL

Although a full account of the development of skill in phonological synthesis would require discussion of the precursors to synthesis skills that emerge in the natural language experience of the child, the focus of this section is on formal synthesis tasks. This choice is dictated not only by space considerations, but also by the fact that it is these tasks that have the closest empirical and theoretical relationship to early reading skills. We first consider standardized test data, and then review some smaller-scale studies that support the description of the growth pattern of phonological synthesis in young children.

Standardized Test Data

The sound blending task of the Illinois Test of Psycholinguistic Ability (ITPA, Kirk, McCarthy, & Kirk, 1968) was administered to 962 children between the ages of 30 and 121 months. Each standardization subject's raw score on the blending task is available in Paraskevopoulos and Kirk (1969).

On the ITPA sound blending task, word parts or individual phonemes are presented at one-half second intervals, and the child is asked to pronounce the word as a whole. The first 7 items (more applicable to very young children) are each presented in a multiple choice format with four pictures on a card. Also, the first 5 items are not divided into phonemic components. Instead, they are segmented into two word parts—the initial consonant and the medial vowel combined with the final consonant (onset and rhyme). After item 7, the phonemes of a word are presented without pictures. At the upper end of the subtest, the last 8 items are nonsense syllables. The number of phonemes increases with successive items, beginning with item 8, and ranges between two and seven phonemes for real words. For nonsense words, starting with item 25, the number of phonemic segments ranges from three to six.

We describe the raw score data from the sound blending subtest in two ways. Table 17.1 presents the proportion of children at each level who reliably demonstrate the ability to apply synthesis skills to strings of phonemes. In order to be categorized as a synthesizer, a child had to obtain a raw score of 10 or greater. This criteria was selected because the first 7 items either do not require blending of phonemes, or involve multiple-choice responses from picture cues. By requiring three correct responses (these are two phoneme items) beyond item 7, the probability was increased that any child categorized as a "synthesizer" could reliably blend string of phonemes. Table 17.1 indicates that only 5% of children below the age of 4 were able to respond correctly to items beyond the picture cue level. After age 4, there is a steady increase in the number of children who demonstrate synthesis skills. Of particular interest is the sharp increase in numbers of children classified as synthesizers between the ages of 6 and 7.

Figure 17.1 presents the average raw scores of all children classified as "synthesizers" for each age group at 6-month intervals. Because the number of children who were able to perform the sound blending task at criterion level was negligible in the two youngest age groups, these data points were not included on the graph. Figure 17.1 clearly depicts a developmental trend in average score that is consistent with the categorical data in Table 17.1. There is gradual improvement in performance between the ages of 3 years, 9 months and 6 years, 1 month. Sounding blending skills increase very sharply between the ages of 6 and 7. After age 7, growth continues at a gradual rate once again.

Smaller Studies of Development in Synthesis Skill

Although analysis and synthesis skills do not involve identical processing operations, they are nevertheless highly correlated with one another in development

TABLE 17.1
Proportion of Children at Different Age Levels Able to
Successfully Perform the Synthesis Task

Below 3	3 to 4	4 to 5	5 to 6	6 to 7	7 to 8	8 to 9	9 to 10
2%	7%	27%	55%	86%	95%	97%	98%

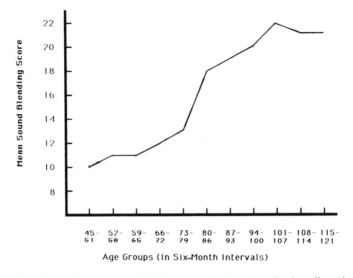

FIG. 17.1.   Mean score of children classified as "synthesizers" on the sound blending subtest of the ITPA.

(Yopp, 1988). An early study conducted by Liberman, Shankweiler, Fisher, and Carter (1974) found that the pattern of development in analytic skills was very similar to that identified in the ITPA test data. Preschool, kindergarten, and 1st grade children were instructed to tap out the number of syllabic or phonemic segments in spoken utterances. At the nursery school level, none of the children could segment phonemes. Ability to perform phoneme segmentation was exhibited by only 17% of kindergarten children, while 70% of 1st graders succeeded in phoneme segmentation. The sharp increase between kindergarten and 1st grade in the proportion of children able to successfully perform an analysis task fits with the "bump" in the growth curve (between ages 6 and 7) produced from the ITPA sound blending data.

In a recent study conducted at Florida State University (Torgesen, Wagner, Balthazar, Davis, Morgan, Simmons, Stage, & Zirps, 1989), a similar developmental trend was noted. Children in the last 2 months of kindergarten, 1st, and 2nd grades were asked to perform several different phonological synthesis tasks. The number of phonemes in the words to be blended varied from 2 to 5. The average performance of kindergarten children was very different from that of the 1st and 2nd graders, while the latter two groups performed similarly. In other words, performance on the synthesis tasks accelerated at a much greater rate between the end of kindergarten and the end of 1st grade than it did between the end of 1st and 2nd grades.

More specific analysis of the data from the Torgesen et al. study indicated that the dramatic increase in average sound blending score between kindergarten and 1st grade was the result of larger numbers of children being able to perform the task successfully, rather than a gradual increase in the scores of most subjects.

Inability to perform the sound blending activity was defined as obtaining a score of 1 or less on a sequence of 20 items. On one of the easiest tasks in this experiment (blending real words, with ½ second intervals between phonemes), 11 of 26 kindergarten subjects were unable to respond. In contrast, all of the 1st graders could respond. The average scores of kindergarten children able to respond to the task were quite similar to 1st graders. As in an earlier study of rhyming skills by Calfee, Chapman, and Venesky (1972), synthesis skills were distributed bimodally in the sample of kindergarten children.

Summary and Conclusions

Although the data on the normal development of phonological awareness skills (and particularly, synthesis skills) are limited, the data that are available are consistent. These data indicate that synthesis skills improve gradually during most periods from preschool to later elementary grades, except for the period between the end of kindergarten and mid to latter 1st grade. During this period, there is a sharp increase, or accelerated period of growth in children's proficiency on sound blending tasks.

The foregoing discussion provides a framework for posing questions that are critical in the understanding of the development of sound blending in children. For example, the abrupt improvement in performance on sound blending tasks occurring between kindergarten and 1st grade raises interesting questions about the nature of the causal relationship between blending and reading skills. These questions are addressed in the next section. The "bump" in the growth curve also raises questions about which, of the several skills involved in blending tasks, may be most responsible for the accelerated growth pattern. Thus, these data may be useful in helping us think about the relationships among the component skills that contribute to blending performance.

SYNTHESIS SKILL AND READING ACQUISITION

The acquisition of reading proficiency is a complex intellectual activity depending upon many different kinds of knowledge and cognitive skill. In thinking about the potential influence of phonological awareness on reading acquisition, it is useful to distinguish between two broad classes of reading skill. Perfetti (1984) makes this distinction in two different definitions of reading. First, reading may be defined as "thinking guided by print." It may also be defined as "decoding written to oral language."

The discussion of relationships between phonological awareness and reading skill in this chapter is concerned with the first definition of reading only indirectly, through the effects of word reading efficiency on comprehension. It is on the acquisition of word reading efficiency that individual differences in phonological awareness are likely to have their greatest impact. Thus, this chapter focuses on the relationships between phonological synthesis and reading defined as, "decoding written to oral language."

Theoretical Relationships Between Phonological Synthesis and Reading

There are several theoretical reasons to expect a causal relationship between phonological synthesis skills and reading acquisition. First, in order to make sense of both synthesis tasks and the alphabetic system of writing, a child must have an awareness that words are composed of separate, reusable phonemic segments. Second, much of beginning reading actually involves blending activities. To identify many of the words in their texts, young children must translate letters into phoneme sized units and blend these sounds together to form words. Lack of facility in blending phonological constituents together should have a direct limiting effect on the ability to apply commonly taught word decoding skills. If children have difficulty acquiring blending skill during reading instruction, their initial progress in learning to read will almost certainly be delayed.

Issues regarding the relationship between synthesis or blending ability and reading achievement are addressed by reviewing two major types of studies: (1) those involving correlational analyses; and, (2) those involving true experimental designs.

It is apparent in this review that the number of studies that focus specifically on the relationship between synthesis skills and reading acquisition is limited. For a long time, phonological awareness seems to have been linked synonymously with segmentation or word analysis skills. Only recently have investigators devoted increased effort to studying the development of synthesis skills and their relation to early reading acquisition.

Correlational Studies

Perhaps the earliest study that examined the specific relationship between blending ability and early reading skills was conducted by Chall, Roswell, and Blumenthall (1963). These investigators measured blending skill and general intelligence in 1st grade, and examined the relationship of these variables with performance on a test of silent reading comprehension measured in 3rd grade. Both blending skill and intelligence were highly correlated with later reading comprehension scores, while the two predictor variables were essentially uncorrelated ($r = .03$). Thus, blending skill remained highly predictive of subsequent reading comprehension after the effects of general ability were partialled out of the relationship ($r = .64$). This relationship is particularly impressive, given that the measure of reading did not directly assess decoding fluency or accuracy, but rather measured comprehension of written material.

In a subsequent analysis with a smaller group of subjects, these investigators showed that sound blending ability was more highly related to performance on a test of word analysis skills ($r = .57$) than it was to silent reading comprehension ($r = .41$). These results have been replicated in several other studies using a variety of synthesis and reading measures (Balmuth, 1971; Helfgott, 1976; Lundberg, Olofsson, & Wall, 1980; Skjelfjord, 1984; Yopp, 1988).

Although these studies indicate that sound blending skill and reading achievement are strongly associated in young children, they provide no information about causal relationships among the variables. Perfetti, Beck, and Hughes (1981) conducted a longitudinal study in which they examined more closely the relationship between blending ability and reading progress with a view toward elucidating causal relationships.

The subjects were 82 beginning 1st graders of whom 57 were taught by a commercial Basal program and 25 were taught by a direct code instruction program. Testing was conducted at 4 points (T/0, the pretest, first week of September; T/1, about the fourth week of October; T/2, mid-January; and T/3, the end of April) throughout their first year of school. At all 4 test points, phonemic tasks measuring both synthesis and analysis (phoneme deletion and counting), along with tests of simple sentence reading and pseudoword reading were administered. During the last testing, the Wide Range Achievement Test (WRAT) was also administered.

Initial analyses indicated that phoneme synthesis skills measured at the beginning of 1st grade were the best predictor of end of year reading scores for children in the Basal reading group. None of the phonological measures were very good predictors of performance with the direct code group, suggesting that this latter instructional approach reduced the variance in early reading skill attributable to different levels of phonological awareness prior to instruction.

In order to assess the causal direction of the relationship between awareness measures and reading skill, time lag analysis of the correlations between awareness and reading was performed. This analysis showed that the level of phonological synthesis skills measured at time T was consistently more predictive of reading at time T + 1 than was reading measured at time T predictive of synthesis skills at time T + 1. For the phoneme analysis tasks, the pattern of relationships was different. Here, the pattern was more mixed, but the correlations were predominantly higher from reading to analysis, than vice versa. These results are important, because they suggest some differentiation in the way analysis and synthesis skills may be related to reading acquisition. In fact, Perfetti et al. concluded that synthesis skills may enable reading acquisition, while skills in phonological analysis appeared to emerge primarily as a consequence of reading skill acquisition.

Experimental-Training Studies

The degree to which word reading skills are dependent on phonological synthesis skills has been investigated more completely in a variety of experimental studies. For example, Muller (1973) conducted two laboratory based learning studies that demonstrated the importance of explicit blending training as a part of reading instruction. The experiments clearly showed that knowledge of letter sounds, by itself, did not aid children learn to read words containing the letters. Only in a condition in which letter sound training was preceded by instruction on an auditory blending task did knowledge of letter sounds improve the ability to decode words composed of those sounds.

An overall pattern of results very similar to those obtained by Muller was found in two investigations by Fox and Routh (1976, 1984). In their first experiment (1976), it appeared as though blending training had an effect on reading only for children who performed well on a phoneme analysis task. This would suggest that blending training is helpful only if some minimum level of segmentation ability has already been reached. However, these results were suspect because the interaction between blending training and analysis skill may have been the result of measurement artifacts.

In their follow-up study, Fox and Routh (1984) attempted to examine more closely the relationships between analytic skills, blending skills, and reading skills. The subjects were 41 kindergartners, 31 of whom could not segment syllables into phonemes. The 31 nonsegmenters were randomly assigned to a control group, a segmenting training only group, and a segmenting plus blending group. The training groups received 5 weeks of training, for 15 min a day. All groups received pre- and posttests for analytic and synthetic skills. Following the extended training in phonological skills, the groups (including the 10 children classified as segmenters) received the same letter and word learning task that had been used in the previous study.

The most important finding was that those who received both segmenting and blending training performed much better on the word learning task than either of the other two groups. In fact, the segmenting plus blending training group did not differ significantly in word learning from those who were classified as segmenters on the pretest (and who continued to have higher blending scores on the posttest than any of the nonsegmenting groups).

These results provide an alternative interpretation to the earlier study (Fox & Routh, 1976). It is likely, for example, that the children who could segment in that study were also proficient at blending. Thus, instead of suggesting that a given level of segmentation skill is necessary before children can be trained in phonological synthesis, they may indicate simply that brief training in blending was beneficial only to children who could already perform blending tasks successfully. In the absence of a blending training only group in the later study, important questions about the relationships between synthetic and analytic skills in their influences on reading ability remain unresolved.

All of the studies considered thus far have manipulated blending skill in the context of tightly controlled laboratory studies in which the development of beginning reading skills was assessed by reading analogue tasks. There have been several more naturalistic studies investigating the impact of training in phonological awareness on the acquisition of reading skill, but none of them have manipulated synthesis skills in isolation (Ball & Blachman, 1988; Bradley & Bryant, 1985; Lundberg, Frost, & Peterson, 1988). It is also true, however, that none of the studies have provided a good test of whether training in analytic skills, by itself, has a positive effect on reading acquisition.

Perhaps the most-well known study of phonological awareness training was conducted by Bradley and Bryant (1985). These investigators trained analytic skills in young children (mean age approximately 6 years) by using a task that required them to identify similarities and differences among words on the bases of their phonemic structure. The training was administered in 40 sessions extending over a 2-year period, while the children were receiving instruction in reading. The children were divided into 4 groups. Group 1 received practice only in analytic skills using the word categorization task. Group 2 received analytic training similar to Group 1, and in addition was trained to represent the shared sounds in words with plastic letters. For example, they were shown how to create families of words that shared certain phonemes by simply substituting a single phoneme at a time. Group 3 received practice categorizing words on the basis of their conceptual relationships, and Group 4 was a no treatment control group.

When the effects of training on reading and spelling performance were examined, Group 2 showed the largest effects, followed by Group 1, Group 3, and finally Group 4. Although the group that received analytic training alone did show advantages in reading and spelling over the conceptually trained control group, these differences were not statistically reliable. Only the group that received analytic training plus practice with the plastic letters showed substantial, and reliable effects on reading and spelling achievement. This study does not provide a convincing demonstration of the effectiveness of analytic training alone for at least two reasons. First, as phonological training was offered simultaneously with reading instruction, it is possible that the children were receiving blending training and practice in the course of normal reading instruction. Second, the creation of word families with the plastic letters by Group 2 almost certainly involved some type of blending process. These children received extensive practice in combining different phonemes to form new words, which would require skill in blending. Although the enhanced performance of Group 2 may have been due to the impact of learning letter sound correspondences through the use of the plastic letters, it is also possible that part of the effect was due to the opportunity to practice skills in phonological synthesis.

Summary and Conclusions

The safest conclusion from research considered in this section is that phonological synthesis skills are strongly related to proficiency in reading acquisition, even when general intelligence levels are controlled. There is also suggestive evidence that skills in phonological synthesis, demonstrated by performance on auditory blending tasks, contribute causally to the development of reading skills. Perhaps the most important remaining theoretical questions revolve around the relative contributions of analytic and synthetic skills to reading acquisition. Other, more practical questions, revolve around appropriate methods, and timing, for training phonological skills. The analogue studies suggest that it is not sufficient to train segmentation alone, but there has also been no demonstration that it is sufficient to train synthetic skills in isolation. Is it possible to train blending skills without first training segmentation? At least a partial answer to this question might be obtained by examining the component processes involved in performance on these tasks. Consideration of the kinds of skills and knowledge that contribute to performance on synthesis tasks are considered next.

COMPONENTS OF PERFORMANCE ON BLENDING TASKS

As background to an analysis of the component skills on blending tasks, it is important to understand how performance on these tasks is related to general intellectual level, or broad verbal knowledge. The evidence on this question, in general, suggests that individual differences in phonological blending skills cannot be adequately explained by variations in level of general intelligence. For example, correlations between Stanford Binet IQ's and a standardized sound blending measure ranged from .23 at the beginning of kindergarten, to .09 in 1st and 2nd grade (Paraskevopoulos & Kirk, 1969). Of all the subtests in a general battery of language skills (ITPA, Kirk, McCarthy, & Kirk, 1968), the sound blending task had the lowest median correlation with IQ across an age span from 3 to 11 years. Slightly higher, but still weak, correlations were reported between language/vocabulary knowledge and blending performance from the standardization sample of the Woodcock-Johnson Psycho-Educational Battery (Woodcock, 1978). For example, sound blending and vocabulary knowledge correlated .35 for kindergartners, and the median correlation between blending and vocabulary for children from 1st to 8th grades was .46.

Although the data from these large standardization samples is relatively consistent, several smaller scale studies have reported correlations between sound blending skills and intelligence that are more variable. These values range from a low of .03 for 1st graders (Chall et al., 1963) to a high of .58 for a sample of 111 preschool children (Wagner et al., 1987). The latter finding raises the possibility that synthesis might be differentially related to IQ at different developmental levels. Until it is replicated, however, the best conclusion appears to be that phonological synthesis tasks measure cognitive skills that are largely independent of those assessed by broad scale measures of verbal and general intellectual ability.

According to one model (Perfetti, Beck, & Hughes, 1981), the most basic component required in responding successfully to blending tasks is some degree of awareness that words are made up of a set of speech sounds (phonemes) that can be combined in different ways to form words. Without this kind of awareness, the blending task is essentially incomprehensible. Given a level of awareness that allows understanding of the task, the model also suggests that several other processing operations are required to successfully blend phonemes into words. First, the individually presented phonemes must be represented and stored in working memory for further processing. Second, the individual phonemes must be combined to form a word-like representation. One of the skills required in this "blending" operation is the ability to separate the essential aspects of each separately pronounced phoneme from the irrelevant vowel sounds that frequently accompany consonant phonemes when spoken in isolation. After the word-like representation is formed, the child must search his or her lexicon for a real word that closely matches the constructed representation. Finally, candidates from the lexicon are compared to the blended string, and a response is selected.

Although a number of skills are required by this model, two of the obvious ones are ability to represent phonological information in working memory, and facility in searching the lexicon for words that match the blended string. Thus, individual differences in both of these skills might contribute to individual differences in performance on sound blending tasks. Wagner et al. (1987) obtained results from a confirmatory factor analysis suggesting that facility in storing items in working memory contributes importantly to performance on phonological awareness tasks in preschool children. One of their awareness tasks involved blending skills, and they concluded that "performance on the phonological awareness tasks we examined (is) determined largely, or at least in part, by efficiency of coding in working memory" (p. 369).

In contrast to these results, Torgesen et al. (1989) obtained results suggesting that neither facility in storing phonological information in working memory nor efficiency in lexical access contributes importantly to improvements on blending tasks between kindergarten and 2nd grade. These investigators manipulated working memory load and availability of a real word match in the lexicon on four different blending tasks. Although all children performed better on blending tasks that placed less stress on working memory and for which there was a real word match available in the lexicon, neither of these manipulations interacted significantly with grade level. These results provide support for a model of blending tasks that includes processing steps requiring brief storage of individual phonemes and lexical search. However, they also suggest that developmental differences on sound blending tasks are not primarily the result of differences in lexical access or working memory among children of different ages.

If changes in these latter two processing operations do not account adequately for developmental variance in performance on blending tasks, what does? At present, the best candidate appears to be attainment of a correct conceptual understanding of the phonological structure of words. The developmental data presented in the first section suggest that very rapid improvement in average performance on blending tasks occurs during 1st grade. We also indicated that these large improvements in mean performance were primarily the result of increases in the number of children who were able to understand the task, as shown by their ability to respond successfully to at least a small number of items. The bimodal distribution of blending skills in kindergarten, as well as the rapid alteration in numbers of children able to meet a minimum performance standard on the task in 1st grade suggest that development is heavily influenced by whether or not children can make sense of the task (through attaining some minimum level of phonological awareness), rather than by gradual improvements in efficiency of more continuously developing component processes.

The dependence of blending performance on attainment of phonological awareness is also suggested by strong correlations between blending and segmentation tasks. For example, one recent study (Yopp, 1988) using 104 kindergarten children reported correlations between a blending task and two tests of phonemic segmentation of .79. A factor analysis of results from 10 tests of phonological awareness showed that the blending task loaded heavily on a principle factor labeled "simple phonological awareness." The tests loading on this factor, as opposed to those loading on a factor called "compound phonemic awareness" were viewed as placing less of a demand on phonetic working memory, and requiring fewer separate processing operations.

CONCLUDING COMMENTS

If, as suggested in the last section, the principle component determining individual differences in performance on phonological synthesis tasks is phonological awareness, does the distinction between analytic and synthetic tasks remain a useful one? A positive answer to this question, at present, appears to depend on possible differences in the causal relationships between analytic and synthetic skills, and learning to read. As discussed in the second section of this paper, there is suggestive evidence that blending skills play a more enabling role in learning to decode than do strictly analytic skills. This may be because the complete set of processes involved in performing blending tasks mimics more closely than analysis tasks the operations involved in actually decoding written words. Phonological awareness may remain as relatively inert knowledge in young children until they are shown the application of this knowledge in constructing words. In addition, practice on some of the other component processes of blending tasks, such as combining phonemes when the first of them is pronounced with an irrelevant following sound, or searching the lexicon for an accurate match to a partially blended word, might have a directly facilitative effect on early reading skill.

ACKNOWLEDGMENT

Preparation of this manuscript was partially supported by Grant No. HD23340 from the National Institute of Child Health and Human Development

REFERENCES

Alegria, J., Pignot, E., & Morais, J. (1982). Phonetic analysis of speech and memory codes in beginning readers. *Memory & Cognition, 10,* 451–456.

Ball, E. W., & Blachman, B. A. (1988). *Phoneme segmentation training: Effect on reading readiness.* Unpublished manuscript, Syracuse University.

Balmuth, M. (1971). Phoneme blending and and silent reading achievement. In R. C. Aukerman (Ed.), *Some persistent questions on beginning reading* (pp. 75–106). Newark, DE: International Reading Association.

Bradley, L., & Bryant, P. (1985). *Rhyme and reason in reading and spelling.* Ann Arbor: University of Michigan Press.

Calfee, R. C., Chapman, R. S., & Venezky, R. L. (1972). How a child needs to think in order to learn to read. In L. Gregg (Ed.), *Cognition in learning and memory* (pp. 139–182), New York: Wiley.

Chall, J. S., Roswell, F. G., & Blumenthal, S. (1963). Auditory blending ability: A factor in success in beginning reading. *Reading Teacher. 17,* 113–118.

Elkonin, D. B. (1973). USSR. In J. Downing (Ed.), *Comparative reading: Cross-national studies of behavior and processes in reading and writing (pp. 137–172). New York: Macmillan.*

Fox, B., & Routh, D. K. (1976). Phonemic analysis and synthesis as word-attack skills. *Journal of Educational Psychology, 68,* 70–74.

Fox, B., & Routh, D. K. (1984). Phonemic analysis and synthesis as word attack skills: Revised. *Journal of Educational Psychology, 16,* 1059–1064.

Goldstein, D. M. (1976). Cognitive-linguistic functioning and learning to read in preschoolers. *Journal of Educational Psychology, 68,* 680–688.

Helfgott, J. A. (1976). Phonemic segmentation and blending skills of kindergarten children: implications for beginning reading acquisition. *Contemporary Educational Psychology, 1,* 157–169.

Kirk, S. A., McCarthy, J. J., & Kirk, W. D. (1968). *Illinois Test of Psycholinguistic Abilities: Revised Edition.* Urbania: University of Illinois Press.

Lewkowicz, M. K. (1980). Phonemic awareness training: What to teach and how to teach it. *Journal of Educational Psychology, 72,* 686–700.

Liberman, I. Y. (1987). Language and Literacy: The obligation of the schools of education. In R. F. Bowler (Ed.) *Intimacy with language* (pp. 1–9). Baltimore, MD: The Orton Dyslexia Society.

Liberman, I. Y., Shankweiler, D., Fisher, F. W., & Carter, B. (1974). Explicit syllable and phoneme segmentation in the young child. *Journal of Experimental Child Psychology, 18,* 201–212.

Lundberg, I., Frost, J., & Peterson, O. (1988). Effects of an extensive program for stimulating phonological awareness in preschool children. *Reading Research Quarterly, 23,* 263–284.

Lundberg, I., Olofsson, A., & Wall, S. (1980). Reading and spelling skills in the first school years predicted from phoneme awareness skills in kindergarten. *Scandinavian Journal of Psychology, 21,* 159–173.

Muller, D. (1973). Phonic blending and transfer of letter training to word reading in children. *Journal of Reading Behavior, 5,* 212–218.

Paraskevopoulos, J., & Kirk, S. A. (1969). *The development and psychometric characteristics of the revised Illinois Test of Psycholinguistic Abilities.* Urbana: University of Illinois Press.

Perfetti, C. A. (1984). Reading acquisition and beyond: Decoding includes cognition. *American Journal of Education, 33,* 40–61.

Perfetti, C. A., Beck, I., & Hughes, C. (1981, April). *Phonemic knowledge and learning to read.* Paper presented at the meeting of the Society for Research in Child Development, Boston.

Skjelfjord, V. J. (1984). *Phonemic segmentation: An important subskill in learning to read.* Institute for Educational Research, University of Oslo.

Stanovich, K. E., Cunningham, A. E., & Cramer, B. B. (1984). Assessing phonological awareness in kindergarten children: Issues of task comparability. *Journal of Experimental Child Psychology, 38,* 175–190.

Torgesen, J. K., Wagner, R. K., Balthazar, M., Davis, C., Morgan, S., Simmons, K., Stage, S., & Zirps, F. (1989). Developmental and individual differences in performance on phonological synthesis tasks. *Journal of Experimental Child Psychology, 47,* 491–505.

Wagner, R. K., Balthazar, M., Hurley, S., Morgan, S., Rashotte, C., Shaner, R., Simmons, K., & Stage, S. (1987). The nature of prereaders' phonological processing abilities. *Cognitive Development, 2,* 355–373.

Wagner, R. K., & Torgesen, J. K. (1987). The nature of phonological processing and its causal role in the acquisition of reading skills. *Psychological Bulletin, 101,* 192–212.

Williams, J. P. (1980). Teaching decoding with an emphasis on phoneme analysis and phoneme blending. *Journal of Educational Psychology, 72,* 1–15.

Woodcock, R. W. (1978). *Development and standardization of the Woodcock-Johnson Psycho-Educational Battery.* Hingham, MA: Teaching Resources.

Yopp, H. K. (1988). The validity and reliability of phonemic awareness tests. *Reading Research Quarterly, 23,* 159–177.

18 Diagnostic Assessment of Listening and Reading Comprehension

Joanne F. Carlisle
Northwestern University

Reading is perhaps the single most prevalent area of underachievement among learning-disabled students. Accurate assessment of reading difficulties is extremely important not only as a part of the process of determining whether some students are learning disabled but also as a way to determine the nature or cause of their reading problems, such information being needed to decide on the instructional program that the student will need to improve his or her reading skills. While standardized tests of reading comprehension presently available are commonly used to provide evidence of the adequacy of student's comprehension, they are not diagnostic. They tell us how well a student can perform on the given reading task in comparison to his or her peers, but they do not give insight into the sources of or nature of comprehension deficits. It is for the purpose of gathering such information that diagnosticians rely heavily on the informal reading inventory (IRI) (German, Johnson, & Schneider, 1985; Fuchs, Fuchs, & Maxwell, 1988). Whether published or created by individual school systems or teachers, the technical characteristics of these tests are not well documented, and so they may lack validity and reliability; in addition, effective use of the results depends heavily on the diagnostic skill of the examiner or teacher (Johnston, 1984; Jongsma & Jongsma, 1981).

The importance of finding better methods of diagnostic assessment of comprehension abilities has been generally acknowledged in the field (Anderson, Hiebert, Scott, & Wilkinson, 1985; Farr & Carey, 1986; Johnston, 1984; Valencia & Pearson, 1988). The project reported herein was initiated as an attempt to investigate methods of assessment of comprehension that would yield diagnostic insight into comprehension deficits. The particular purpose of this paper is to

277

explore the sentence verification technique as the basis for a diagnostic test of basic comprehension abilities.

LANGUAGE COMPREHENSION OF EXTENDED DISCOURSE

One important component of a truly diagnostic test of reading comprehension should be a means of assessing the language-processing skills that are the basis for understanding what one reads. Language comprehension can be assessed at different levels—the word, the sentence, the paragraph, and so on. For the purposes of assessing underlying skills of *reading* comprehension, paragraphs or longer passages need to be the unit of interest, since the normal reading experience involves comprehension of extended discourse. Tests of sentence comprehension are not sufficient, since researchers have found that sentence-level comprehension and text-level comprehension tasks have different processing demands (Kintsch, 1979).

Passage comprehension entails meaningful reception of language, oral language *or* written language. The comprehension of passages is based on two major components. One is the act of mentally representing the message intended by the writer/speaker. This is the application of language comprehension processes. The second is the mental manipulation (reasoning, application of strategies) of the message as it is represented in memory (Royer, 1986). The two components do not contribute equally. Language comprehension is the preliminary and primary function, as it provides the foundation on which any mental manipulation is carried out. Assessment of language comprehension, accomplished by looking at students' performances after they have listened to or read different passages, might help us understand whether the general comprehension deficits observed by classroom teachers or measured by standardized reading tests are caused by basic language-processing problems. However, such diagnostic insight can only be acquired if it is possible to measure language comprehension without requiring the reader/listener to employ reasoning skills and question-answering strategies.

Because language comprehension at the passage level is a process wherein the individual formulates a model of the meaning expressed by the writer/speaker, it can be assessed by examining performances in listening or reading. Reading comprehension and listening comprehension each constitute specialized uses of our general language comprehension capabilities. Still, while the act of reading is in many respects quite different from that of listening, the most parsimonious view is that comprehension of what is read uses the same basic mechanisms as comprehension of what is listened to. In terms of reading, linguistic competence, as Pearson and Johnson (1978) point out, constitutes ''an absolute prerequisite for reading comprehension. Such an assertion is almost tautological, since language is the medium of comprehension'' (p. 19).

COMPARISONS OF LISTENING AND READING
ABILITIES

Reading-disabled students have been found to have deficits in listening comprehension as well as reading comprehension (Berger, 1978; Curtis, 1980; Smiley, Oakley, Worthen, Campione, & Brown, 1977). To some extent, these deficits appear to be attributable to language-processing problems, including understanding of syntactic and semantic roles and morphological markers (Vogel, 1974; Wiig, Semel, & Crouse, 1973) and maintaining and integrating propositions in working memory (Perfetti, 1985). However, poor readers' comprehension deficits may also reflect deficiencies in metacognitive operations (Stanovich, 1985). It is clear that inadequate basic language processing skills can over time adversely affect the development of reasoning strategies and comprehension monitoring skills. Thus, the poor reader's basic language comprehension deficits may become more generalized and have an increasingly pervasive impact on the development of effective reading comprehension skills.

Comparisons of student's capabilities in listening and reading have yielded evidence that can help us understand the reasons for an individual's deficits in comprehension (Danks & Pezdek, 1980; Durrell, 1970; Sticht & James, 1984). Sticht (1979) uses the term "auding" to refer to reception of oral language, particularly in passages comparable to material that is read, and to differentiate auditory processing of environmental noise and language. He has argued that where auding significantly exceeds reading capabilities and is in line with general intelligence, reading comprehension is a specific comprehension deficit. In contrast, where auding and reading are both below the level expected by an estimate of general intelligence, a more general language comprehension problem is indicated. The diagnostic potential of comparisons of listening and reading skills has also received some support from a recent study of subtypes of reading disabilities, in which distinctive patterns of listening and reading comprehension deficits have been found (Aaron, 1987). One type is characterized by specific deficits in reading comprehension (without commensurate deficits in listening comprehension), and a second type by deficits in both listening and reading comprehension. These findings are in line with the position held by Sticht and others that comparisons of listening and reading disabilities can reveal the reasons for comprehension deficits.

Many studies of the reading and listening capabilities of students of different grade levels have been carried out, yielding cumulatively reliable information about the relative proficiencies of the two types of comprehension skills at different grade levels (see Stanovich, 1985; Sticht & James, 1984). In their review of over three dozen studies of auding and reading, Sticht and James (1984) demonstrate that the relationship between listening and reading has been found to be relatively weak in the early elementary years (in the order of .35 in grade 1). The young readers understand higher levels of spoken language than written language texts because of limitations in their word recognition skills (Curtis, 1980). The relationship between listening and reading is moderate in the middle school years (.60) and somewhat stronger in junior high school. Listening comprehension capabilities normally exceed reading comprehension capabilities until the 6th grade, when the two are roughly equivalent. Thereafter, it is not uncommon for reading comprehension capabilities to exceed listening comprehension capabilities, since the complexity of the processing of information appropriate for older students favors the more enduring presence of text through reading.

PROBLEMS OF ASSESSMENT OF LISTENING AND READING COMPREHENSION

Comparisons of comprehension of passages listened to or read is a method that has been used by some informal and formal reading tests in the past (e.g., Carroll, 1977; Durrell, 1970; Jongsma & Jongsma, 1981; Sticht & Beck, 1976). The general consensus is that such comparisons provide useful information, but this method of assessing language comprehension is not without its critics.

Some researchers have questioned the value of using comparisons of listening and reading to inform us about the development of children's language comprehension skills (Danks & Pezdek, 1980; Rubin, 1980). Their concern is that there are many differences in the acts of listening and reading as well as in the types of situations in which these skills are developed. Rubin (1980) dismisses experimental tasks that use similar types of passages because these violate natural differences in the "message" of normal listening and reading experiences. He also argues that differences in the "medium" of delivery (e.g., interaction and involvement of listener and speaker) are so marked that findings of different levels of performance in listening and reading may be attributable to the "medium," not to the individual being evaluated. The heart of the problem may be that while we may agree that listening and reading employ the same processing mechanisms at some level, the exact point of convergence continues to be a matter of debate (Hanson, 1981; Sinatra, 1987). Empirical evidence of a developmental relationship between the growth of listening and reading skills, however, is quite solid. Until the broader theoretical issues are investigated more thoroughly, we at least may investigate whether a given child's comprehension of passages in listening and reading does or does not follow a normal progression.

For those of us interested in the development of children's comprehension skills, differences in performance on different types of listening and reading tasks should be viewed as matters of interest and concern. Differences in what Rubin (1980) calls the "medium" are naturally occurring problems for all comprehenders. That is, it may be important to learn that a given 6th grader is significantly better at reading than listening. As suggested earlier, this may indicate that the student is taking advantage of the opportunity to process the text at his or her own speed. Normally, in listening to the reading of an article or story, the student has no control over the rate of delivery and may have trouble keeping up.

Differences in the "message" may vary in importance according to age, experience, and overall intelligence. Even though Rubin argues that what we listen to is generally different in content, structure, and nonverbal cues from what we read, it is not necessarily true that presentation of passages with similar content and structure for listening and reading is pointless. The obligations of schooling are such that children must become increasingly more skilled at understanding orally represented information that resembles the information they read—lectures, teachers' explanations, readings from texts, and so on. It seems educationally valuable to learn whether students have the ability to listen to and read content area information with adequate comprehension.

Different researchers have addressed the problem of comparability of subject matter in different ways. Durrell (1970) designed his Listening-Reading Test so that at the Intermediate and Advanced Level passages were based on comparisons. Royer, Greene, and Sinatra (1987) believe that a listening/reading test can be based on any text sample appropriate for the grade-level and educational background of the students. In their research, narratives have been used for school-age children, and curriculum-based course content passages for older students. Regardless of the choice of text structures, equating passages for content, structure, length, and density of presentation of ideas would seem to allow for reasonable inferences about students' performances, given the kinds of comprehension skills they need to acquire to be successful in school.

The selection of comparisons of listening and reading as a method of assessment involves a second consideration—namely, how best to evaluate the students' understanding of passages they listen to or read. Most listening/reading tests have relied on the answering of questions as the method of assessing comprehension, a technique that has been criticized extensively in recent years (Davey, 1987; Fuchs et al., 1988; Johnston, 1983, 1984). Answering questions as a way of demonstrating that the reader/listener has understood the meaning intended by the writer/speaker focuses on the *product* of comprehension, drawing on whatever evaluative abilities and question-answering strategies are needed to cope with the questions themselves. As such, it taps the second of the component parts of the comprehension process, as described earlier. In addition, studies have shown that many questions on comprehension tests can be answered correctly without reading the passage (Tuinman, 1973–1974) and that characteristics of the questions account for a larger proportion of the variance in reading performance than characteristics of the text itself (Drum, Calfee, & Cook, 1981). The other commonly used post-passage method of evaluation is free recall (e.g., Durrell, 1955). This method may underestimate the individual's grasp of meaning, as problems with durability of memory and expressive language skills might contribute to poor performances. A task that requires production does not ensure a clean measure of comprehension.

One alternative method of evaluation that purports to assess language comprehension is the cloze procedure, which entails filling in the blanks where, at periodic intervals, individual words have been omitted. This technique has become a popular, if problematic, method of evaluating reading comprehension. The cloze procedure has several characteristics that make it unsuitable for diagnostic assessment of language comprehension. The first and most basic reason is that it is not a viable test of listening comprehension. In reading, the test-taker can look forward as well backward in the text to select a word to fill in a blank (Kibby, 1981); this strategy is not feasible in listening, so that the tasks would not be comparable at all. In addition, cloze procedure has been found to test sentence comprehension predominantly, even when the sentences are presented in paragraphs or passages. Royer and Lynch (1982) found that students performed similarly on cloze paragraph tests when the sentences were in normal order and in random order (the latter, of course, disrupting the continuity and coherence of the text). The cloze procedure, therefore, is not sensitive to the sort of scaffolding of ideas and integration of propositions that is the essential process of formulating a mental representation of meaning of a text (Fuchs et al., 1988; Johnston, 1983; Royer, 1986). In short, cloze procedure does not appear to be an appropriate technique for assessing passage comprehension in listening *or* reading.

THE SENTENCE VERIFICATION TECHNIQUE

One recently developed method of assessing comprehension appears to offer potential for direct comparison of listening and reading without tapping question-answering abilities. This is the Sentence Verification Technique, (SVT), explored principally by Royer and his associates (Royer, 1986; Royer, Greene, & Sinatra, 1987; Royer, Hastings, & Hook, 1979; Royer, Kulhavy, Lee, & Peterson, 1986). In Royer's form of this method of assessment, the student listens to or reads passages and then is asked to label test sentences as "old" if the idea of the sentence was in the original passage and "new" if the idea was not in the original passage. Royer believes that this method taps basic language comprehension abilities without requiring the use of more sophisticated reasoning skills.

Four types of test sentences were chosen by Royer to represent alternative types of language-processing demands. "Paraphrases" are sentences that retain the idea of a sentence in the passage but present it in a different set of words and/or grammatical structures. Students who are inflexible language processors (akin to the poor "sentence coders" of Perfetti and Roth's (1981) classification system) may not see these sentences as stating an idea from the original passage. "Meaning Change" test sentences retain all of the original words of a sentence from the passage except one or two, these serving to change the meaning of the whole sentence. Students who process ideas only generally and are linguistically inattentive may identify these as sentences that were in the original passage, tricked by the superficial similarity of the test and original sentences. The third type, "Distractors," are sentences that introduce a topic related to but not discussed in the passage. Students who formulate the meaning of the text on the basis of what they think it might say or what they already know about the topic might mistakenly pick these as sentences that had been in the original passage. This sort of comprehension failure is akin to the "non-accommodating text processing strategy" described by Maria and MacGinitie (1982). The fourth sentence type is an "Original," a sentence taken directly from the passage.

One common criticism of comprehension tests is that they tend to assess details more than the central ideas of passages (Johnston, 1984). The SVT offers a particular solution to this problem, since all of the sentences of the passage are used or rewritten (as necessary) to develop the test of passage comprehension. Usually, passages of 12 sentences are selected, and the test is also made up of 12 sentences, three of each of the types already described (see Royer et al., 1987, for details and variations).

Royer and his colleagues have shown that although this method of assessment uses sentence verification as a test of passage comprehension, it is not simply a test of the capacity to remember the exact sentences; instead, to perform well on the test, the student must construct the meaning of the whole passage, using the text structure and semantic links to aid recall of the sentences themselves. As Sachs (1974) has demonstrated, forgetting of the exact words takes place within 40 syllables of interpolated text (less than 10 seconds); the sentence is encoded in an abstract representation of the meaning. Students perform significantly better on SVT tests when the sentences are in normal order than when the same sentences are in random order (Royer, 1986). This finding seems to support Royer's claim that the SVT assesses passage comprehension; and it stands in contrast to a similar test of the cloze procedure, as reported earlier.

The SVT method offers certain advantages as a test of language comprehension. The first is that the task places similar burdens on the student in terms of production requirements and memory (in the sense that the passage is not available during the listening or reading test phase). The second is that an attempt has been made to assess language comprehension, minimizing the requirements of higher-level reasoning skills or question-answering strategies. The test is always devised the same way, which ensures that equivalent demands are placed on the student across modalities and levels of difficulty of passages. The third advantage is that SVT tests can be devised to suit any text structure, any type of content material. Royer and his colleagues (1987) believe that with little training, teachers can write SVT tests based on their students' curriculum, thus having the kind of ecological validity that is presently of concern to those interested in useful evaluation of reading skills (Fuchs et al., 1988; Valencia & Pearson, 1988). A final potential advantage is the insight it might provide into the sources of and nature of different students' comprehension difficulties. Diagnostic information might be gained from comparisons of listening and reading skills, as well as from analyses of performances on the four types of test sentences. Royer has suggested that the SVT method holds such potential, but to date this use of the SVT has remained untested.

DESIGN OF THE RESEARCH PROJECT

Because of the need to devise more effective diagnostic measures of language comprehension and because of the particular advantages that appear to characterize the SVT, a research project was devised to evaluate whether it is a reasonable method of diagnostically distinguishing students with and without reading disabilities. Essentially, this meant determining whether the experimental measure was as effective as a well-respected standardized reading test in identifying students with comprehension deficits. However, it was also deemed important to begin investigating whether the comparisons of listening and reading offered more diagnostic insight than the standardized reading comprehension test.

Several initial decisions were made. First, it was necessary to pick students at a grade level where differences in performance on listening and reading passages would be interpretable. Consequently, 7th graders (normal readers and disabled readers) were selected, since Sticht and James' (1984) summary of studies indicates that students at this grade level generally perform equivalently on the two types of passage presentations. Second, an SVT test was devised using expository passages only. Topics were selected from encyclopedias found in elementary and junior high school libraries. As the students were already in junior high school, their ability to understand short explanations of phenomena or events would resemble the kinds of listening and reading obligations they encountered in their content area courses. Third, because diagnostic assessment of comprehension skills was the initial focus of this research project, a test of word recognition was added to the SVT tests of listening and reading passages. Numerous studies have shown that differences in the automaticity of word recognition account for a large portion of the variance in reading ability (Curtis, 1980; Perfetti, 1985; Stanovich, 1985). The unitary view of language comprehension processing suggests that when young readers and poor readers perform better in listening than reading tasks, the most likely reason for the discrepancy is inaccurate or slow word recognition skills.

The three subtests (listening, reading, and word recognition) were viewed as a diagnostic screening test so that expectations of students' performances could be generated. It was anticipated that good 7th-grade comprehenders would be particularly stronger than poor comprehenders in reading and word recognition. Given the fact that mild to moderately disabled readers were participating, the listening performance was expected to be a source of weakness for some poor comprehenders (suggesting an underlying language comprehension deficit) but not others (suggesting a specific reading deficit). The experimental measure was called Profiles in Listening and Reading (PILAR).

The research questions were: (1) Does performance on PILAR clearly distinguish school-identified good and poor comprehenders? (2) Do performances on PILAR discriminate good from poor comprehenders as well as the Gates MacGinitie Reading Test? and (3) Do good and poor comprehenders have different patterns of performance on the four types of test sentences of the PILAR listening and reading subtests?

Participants, Materials, and Procedures

The subjects were 60 7th-grade students attending a suburban school in western Massachusetts. They were selected to make up groups of Good and Poor Comprehenders. Forty-one students made up the Good Comprehender group. These were members of two "home room" classes who were currently taking a required developmental reading course. The Poor Comprehender group was made up of 7 students from these two "homerooms" who were receiving remedial reading training and 12 special education students who received training in reading from special education teachers. These special education students represented all 7th graders in this school whose Individualized Educational Programs specified training in reading and whose parents had given permission for participation in the research project. The special education students could be described as mildly to moderately academically handicapped. Each was classified by the prototype of 502.3, which indicates that the student will spend no more than 60% of his class day outside of his regular class (*Massachusetts Register,* 1986). (See Carlisle, in press, for details of the study reported herein.)

All of the 7th graders in the school had been given the Gates MacGinitie Reading Test, Form E (MacGinitie, 1978) by school personnel earlier in the year. Statistical analysis of the performance of the three groups (the Good Comprehenders and the two subgroups of Poor Comprehenders) on the Gates MacGinitie subtests, Vocabulary and Comprehension, indicated that the Good Comprehenders differed significantly from both groups of Poor Comprehenders as Table 18.1 shows. (Even though the remedial students had slightly higher scores on both subtests, the two groups of Poor Comprehenders did not differ significantly from each other in their Vocabulary or Comprehension scores.)

All students were given the experimental test PILAR which included the subtests Listening and Reading comprehension and Word Recognition. The Listening and Reading subtests use the general approach of the Sentence Verification Technique developed by Royer and his colleagues (Royer, 1986) described

TABLE 18.1
Performance of Good and Poor Comprehenders on the Gates MacGinitie
Reading Tests in Mean Raw Scores and Grade Equivalents (and SDs)

| | Gates MacGinitie Reading Tests | | | |
| | Vocabulary | | Comprehension | |
	Raw	GE	Raw	GE
Good Comprehenders	27.5	8.7	30.2	8.7
(n = 41)	(5.1)	(1.6)	(3.6)	(1.6)
Poor Comprehenders	17.3	5.7	18.8	5.0
(n = 19)	(3.9)	(1.1)	(4.7)	(1.4)

earlier, but are characterized by certain specific features. First, the test consists of only expository passages; each one was 12 sentences in length and was followed by 12 test sentences. Second, students responded to each test sentence by indicating whether a sentence with the same meaning had been in the original passage (a response of "yes") or had not been in the passage (a response of "no"). Royer has generally asked students to respond "old" or "new," a request that had the potential of confusing reading-disabled students. Third, specific rules were developed for the construction of several of the test sentence types. The Paraphrase sentences involved both lexical and syntactic changes. Each Meaning Change sentence was identical to an original sentence with the exception of the change of one word; this change involved one of the following: a subject-object reversal, negation or elimination of negation, or an exchange of one word for its opposite (e.g., "top" for "bottom"). Distractors were sentences discussing a topic related to but not mentioned in the paragraph. The Originals were, of course, sentences taken unchanged from the passage. The set of test sentences following each paragraph was made up of equal numbers of these four sentence types.

The topics of the passages were selected from encyclopedias available in school libraries; topics that some students would be apt to have had more personal experience with than others were avoided. Because students of different ability levels vary in their grasp of different text structures (Englert & Thomas, 1987; Richgels, McGee, Lomax, & Sheard, 1987), a type of structure seemingly accessible to all was chosen. Each paragraph is an explanation or amplification of whatever statement is made in the topic sentence. As an example, one of the 3rd-grade level passages is given in Appendix A.

The PILAR passages for the Listening and Reading subtests selected for this study were at the 3rd-, 5th-, 7th-, and 9th-grade reading levels. The comparability of passages used for Listening and Reading was determined by surface characteristics, such as sentence length and passage length, and by use of grade-level readability estimates from the Spache, Dale-Chall, and Fry systems (Minnesota Educational Computing Consortium, 1982). The passage characteristics and the grade level ratings are reported in Appendix B.

The third component of PILAR was the Word Recognition subtest, which was designed to assess accuracy and automaticity of word recognition skills for words of different levels of frequency in printed texts. The test consists of 60 words typed in 6 sets of ten (sets A through F) on a single sheet of paper. Each set was selected from words that occur within specific bands of frequencies in written materials for grades 2 through 9 (Carroll, Davies, & Richman, 1971). Set A is made of some of the most frequent words in young students' texts; in Sets B through F the words represent bands of gradually lower frequency ratings. Within each set, there is a combination of words with regular and irregular letter-sound correspondences, and there are some words of more than one morpheme.

Students were asked to read the sets aloud, starting with the Set A. If a student made more than 6 errors in a set, testing was discontinued. Scoring was done on the basis of both accuracy and automaticity, in that both have been shown to have a strong relationship to performance on reading comprehension tests (Perfetti, 1985; Stanovich, 1985).

The Listening and Reading subtests of PILAR were administered to the groups of students during normal class periods. The students completed two passages for practice, one through listening and one through reading, so that the task would be familiar to them. The answers to the questions following the practice passages were discussed. Scoring of the practice passages showed that all students understood the directions and the task. The Listening subtest was administered by a tape-recording. The Word Recognition subtest was administered to each student individually.

PILAR PERFORMANCES DISTINGUISH GOOD AND POOR COMPREHENDERS

In designing the study, the first concern was whether the Good and Poor Comprehenders, as previously identified by the school system and by performance on the Gates MacGinitie Reading Test, could be distinguished by their performances on the subtests of PILAR. As Table 18.2 shows, the Good Comprehenders' scores on all three subtests of PILAR were higher than those of the Poor Comprehenders; group differences were more pronounced for the Reading and Word Recognition subtests than the Listening subtest, but all three differences were statistically significant.

These results confirm the initial expectations that the Poor Comprehenders who took part in this study would differ from Good Comprehenders more strongly in reading than in listening. These findings are compatible with both the theoretical position and the large body of empirical evidence that suggest that

TABLE 18.2
Performance (Mean Percent Correct and SDs) of Good and Poor
Comprehenders on PILAR Subtests, Presented as Percent of Opportunity

	PILAR Subtests		
	Listening	Reading	Word Recognition
Good Comp.	79.9	83.2	89.6[a]
(n = 41)	(8.5)	(10.3)	(4.5)
Poor Comp.	70.4	70.4	66.3[b]
(n = 19)	(9.2)	(10.7)	(16.7)

Note. Difference between Good and Poor Comprehenders was significant $(p < .01)$ for all three subtests.

[a] $n = 40$
[b] $n = 16$

poor readers as an undifferentiated group are weaker than good readers not only in decoding skills (unique to reading) but also in more general language comprehension processing capabilities. Sixteen of the 19 Poor Comprehenders gave equivalently weak performances on the Listening and Reading subtests, suggesting that almost all had general comprehension deficits.

One concern at the outset of the study was whether students would perform on the PILAR Listening and Reading subtests in a manner similar to other 7th graders on other listening/reading tests. The relationship between performances on the Listening and Reading subtests for the full group was .60, in keeping with the results of other studies (see Sticht & James, 1984). The Poor Comprehenders performed equally well on the Listening and Reading subtests, whereas the Good Comprehender group performed better on the Reading than the Listening subtest. Previous studies have shown that 7th graders ordinarily perform at about the same level of competence in listening and reading passages (Sticht & James, 1984). In this case, the Good Comprehenders' superior performance in reading suggests that they are better than average readers for their grade level, an observation that is borne out by their above-grade-level mean on the Gates MacGinitie Test, Comprehension subtest (see Table 18.1).

Evidence that the SVT is sensitive to levels of proficiency in the development of language comprehension abilities comes from performance on passages of increasing difficulty. Comparison of the Good and Poor Comprehenders on the four grade-level passages of the Listening and Reading subtests (see Table 18.2) shows that the Good Comprehenders consistently earned higher scores on the individual passages of both subtests. Statistical analysis indicates that the Good Comprehenders were significantly superior on the 7th- and 9th-grade Listening passages and the 5th-, 7th-, and 9th-grade Reading passages.

BOTH READING TESTS DISTINGUISH GOOD FROM POOR COMPREHENDERS

It is possible for groups of good and poor readers to perform similarly on two measures but for individuals within the groups to vary widely in their performances. For this reason, it was important to determine the relationship between the students' performances on the two reading tests. Correlations between the performance on the subtests of the Gates MacGinitie and PILAR tests were in the moderate positive range, all significant, as can be seen in Table 18.3. On the basis of differences in approach to assessment alone, we would not expect correlations to be higher, since the two tests measure somewhat different skills. The SVT purports to assess language comprehension without the complexities of answering multiple-choice questions of both a factual and an interpretive nature. Answering multiple-choice questions following the reading of a passage has been shown to require particular metacognitive strategies (Davey, 1987).

The relationship was investigated further by examining the relative ability of the PILAR subtests and the Gates MacGinitie Reading Tests subtests to distinguish the Good from the Poor Comprehenders. To answer this question, two separate stepwise discriminant function analyses were carried out, one to show the percentage of school-diagnosed Poor Comprehenders PILAR would identify; another to record the percentage of Poor Comprehenders the Gates MacGinitie Reading Test would identify. In the first of these, all three PILAR subtests were included in one significant function, which correctly predicted the group membership of 94.6% of the students. The order of entry of the subtests, as well as the significance at each step, is given in Table 18.4.

The second stepwise discriminant function analysis resulted in one significant function that included the two subtests of the Gates MacGinitie Reading Test; the order of entry of the subtests is shown in Table 18.4. This function correctly predicted the group membership of 93.2% of the students. These analyses suggest that both tests correctly classified almost all of the students as members of the Good or Poor Comprehender groups. It may be of some interest to note that

TABLE 18.3
Correlations of PILAR Subtests and Gates MacGinitie Reading Subtests

| | Gates MacGinitie Subtests | |
	Vocabulary	Comprehension
PILAR subtests		
Listening	.42	.52
Reading	.66	.63
Word Recognition	.69	.65

Note. All correlations were significant, $p < .001$.

TABLE 18.4
Order of Entry of Subtests on Separate Discriminant Function
Analyses for the Two Reading Tests

Gates MacGinitie Reading Test:

	WILKS' LAMBDA
1. Comprehension	.354933
2. Vocabulary	.338997

PILAR:

1. Word Recognition	.442333
2. Reading	.370146
3. Listening	.353788

Note. Each of the Wilks' Lambda values was significant
$p < .0001$.

when all 5 subtests (Vocabulary and Comprehension from the Gates MacGinitie Reading Test and Listening, Reading, and Word Recognition from PILAR) were offered for potential entry into a single stepwise discriminant function analysis, the three that did enter significantly were the Gates Comprehension subtest, the PILAR Word Recognition subtest, and the PILAR Listening subtest, in that order. This function significantly predicted group membership of 96.4% of the group; not correctly classified were two of the Poor Comprehenders.

The foregoing analyses seem to indicate that both tests had the power to correctly distinguish most of the Good from the Poor Comprehenders. The ability of the Gates MacGinitie Reading Test to discriminate the groups may not be surprising, since the school personnel used this test to identify the seven of the 19 Poor Comprehenders who were taking the remedial reading class. The power of PILAR to distinguish the Poor from the Good Comprehenders, however, is a promising indicator of the diagnostic capabilities of this test, if it can offer not only an indication of who the Poor Comprehenders are but also why they are deficient in comprehension skills. We now turn to this issue.

PATTERNS OF ERRORS ON THE SENTENCE TYPES
FOLLOWING LISTENING AND READING

The final research question asked whether the groups of Good and Poor Comprehenders performed differently on the four types of sentences that make up the test on the Listening and Reading subtests of PILAR—that is, whether the Poor Comprehenders made not simply more errors but a different pattern of errors. First, it was evident that the Good Comprehenders performed quite similarly on the sentences when listening and reading, but the Poor Comprehenders did not. As Table 18.5 shows, the Good Comprehenders had generally the same pattern of errors on the Listening and Reading sentences, the only noteworthy difference

TABLE 18.5
Mean Errors Expressed as Percent of Opportunity (and SDs)
of Good and Poor Comprehenders on Sentence Types of PILAR
Listening and Reading Subtests: Originals (0),
Paraphrases (P), Meaning Changes (MC), Distractors (D)

	Listening				Reading			
	O	P	MC*	D*	O	P	MC*	D*
Good Comp.	12	27	22	22	14	25	24	6
(n=41)	(11)	(16)	(11)	(19)	(16)	(15)	(18)	(11)
Poor Comp.	19	22	33	42	16	33	41	25
(n=19)	(16)	(14)	(16)	(20)	(15)	(14)	(19)	(19)

*$p < .01$.

being fewer errors on Distractors on the Reading subtest. In contrast, the Poor Comprehenders made more errors on the sentence types in Reading than in Listening with the exception of the Originals.

Second, comparing the groups on each subtest, the Poor Comprehenders made more errors than the Good Comprehenders on all sentence types (except for the Paraphrases on the Listening subtest). More specifically, the Poor Comprehenders made significantly more errors on the Meaning Change and Distractor sentences than the Good Comprehenders on both subtests. The marked differences in the two groups' performances on the Distractors may indicate that Poor Comprehenders adopted an ineffective strategy wherein they responded on the basis of what they knew about the topic or what they thought the passage should have said, rather than what it did say (Maria & MacGinitie, 1982). Such a strategy may in turn reflect difficulties encoding or integrating propositions within and across sentences. In reading, this may mean skimming quickly over the general ideas or plodding slowly in a word-by-word fashion through the passage.

An unexpected finding was that the variability (SD) was no more pronounced for the Poor Comprehenders than for the Good Comprehenders. This may suggest either that the Poor Comprehenders were a more homogeneous group than anticipated or that the Good Comprehenders were a more heterogeneous group than anticipated.

The possibility of a response bias may seem to be suggested by the Poor Comprehenders' greater number of errors on the Meaning Change and Distractor types on the Listening subtest only (i.e., a tendency to answer "yes" when in doubt about the correct answer). However, it is noteworthy that their errors are more evenly distributed across Paraphrases, Meaning Changes, and Distractors on the Reading subtest. This evidence suggests a different reason for their large number of errors on Meaning Change and Distractor items on the Listening subtests—a general inattention to the meaning of the full text, or difficulty processing detail when the task involved listening.

The Poor Comprehenders' relatively good performance on Originals and Paraphrases seems consonant with the observation that the Poor Comprehender group is generally made up of students with relatively mild handicapping conditions (learning disabilities). Gross differences in general intellectual functioning or in language comprehension abilities would have been implicated had this group made as many errors on Originals and Paraphrases as they made on Meaning Changes and Distractors.

For the Good Comprehenders, the pattern of performance on the sentence types was similar to the pattern of normal 5th- and 6th-grade readers in an SVT study reported by Royer and his colleagues (1979). In general, the normal readers in both studies made few errors on Originals or Distractors, but made a scattering of errors on the Paraphrases and Meaning Changes, perhaps because of occasional mistakes making decisions about relatively subtle changes in the structure and meaning of the sentences or because of occasional lapses of memory or attention.

DIAGNOSTIC CONSIDERATIONS

The major value of PILAR seems to be its ability to measure the level of language comprehension and the relationship of word recognition skills to both listening and reading comprehension. Initial inferences about the source of difficulties may be made on the basis of the screening of these skills. This point can be made most clearly by comparison of two students' profiles on the subtests.

The two student profiles shown in Table 18.6 suggest different sources of comprehension difficulties. Student #1 demonstrates adequate language comprehension in Listening but not Reading, perhaps because his word recognition skills are inaccurate and/or very slow. (Seventy-five percent correct was considered a measure of basic competence reflecting understanding approximately to a 7th-grade level, since the passages were on 3rd-, 5th, 7th-, and 9th-grade levels.) The diagnostic implication is further testing of word attack and word recognition skills, given both words presented in isolation and words presented in normal passage contexts. In contrast, student #2 is experiencing global and pronounced difficulties in language comprehension. The diagnostic implication is further testing in language comprehension and evaluation of the student's intellectual capabilities.

Additional information of a diagnostic nature may be gained by scrutiny of the students' performance on the four test sentence types. Until we accumulate more information to substantiate the range of normal behavior, such analysis should be considered suggestive and not definitive. Note that student #1 has made a relatively large number of errors on Distractors in Listening but not Reading. This may suggest difficulty forming a mental model of the text in Listening. In

TABLE 18.6
Performance of Two Poor Comprehenders on PILAR Subtests
(% Correct), Including Breakdown of Errors on
Sentence Types (% of Opportunity), and on
Gates MacGinitie Reading Subtests (Grade Equivalents)

PILAR Subtests:	Student #1	Student #2
Listening	81	50
Reading	71	58
Word Recognition	47	83

	Student #1		Student #2	
PILAR	Listening	Reading	Listening	Reading
Sentence Types:				
Originals	8	8	42	58
Paraphrases	17	42	42	33
Meaning Changes	17	67	67	50
Distractors	33	0	50	25

	Student #1	Student #2
Gates MacGinitie		
Reading Subtests:		
Vocabulary	4.8	5.2
Comprehension	4.6	3.1

Reading, this student has made a very large percentage of errors on Meaning Changes (67% of all sentences of this type). This may suggest inattention to detail or difficulty retaining the meaning of sentences, since processing capacity would be largely occupied by word recognition processes (note score of 47% correct). In contrast, student #2 has made a relatively large percentage of errors (approaching 50% or more) on all of the sentence types except the Reading Paraphrases and Distractors. The relatively large proportion of errors on the Originals is striking. This pattern suggests a general comprehension failure, very unlike the more specific reading problem of student #1. Analysis of individual profiles such as these could lead to more precise diagnostic assessment of students' comprehension problems.

It should be noted that the students' scores on the Gates MacGinitie Reading subtests verify their deficits in comprehension, but give us no diagnostic information. We have no idea whether poor performance is specifically a reading problem or a more general comprehension problem.

SUMMARY

This study provides sufficient support for the use of the SVT as a diagnostic test to warrant further investigations. The combination of the three subtests of Listening, Reading, and Word Recognition provided a powerful means of discriminating the Good Comprehenders from the Poor Comprehenders in this 7th-grade student sample. It seems likely that no one of these subtests could serve as effectively to identify Poor Comprehenders. For example, the PILAR Reading subtest alone correctly classified only 76.7% of the group membership.

The usefulness of PILAR, above and beyond its capability of identifying poor comprehenders, which is essentially no different from that of the Gates Mac-Ginitie Reading Test, is its potential as a diagnostic tool. That is, if it can shed light on the source of or nature of the poor comprehenders' deficits, it may provide information that is useful for diagnosing types of disabilities and for devising effective programs of remediation. The profiles of the two students illustrate that the combination of the three subtests may give us initial indicators about the sources of individual students' comprehension difficulties. These would provide direction for further diagnostic testing. And, certainly, the diagnostic capabilities are only suggested, not clearly demonstrated, by the results of this particular study. What is needed is a study of the validity of the profiles or patterns of performances that are generated by students' performances on PILAR across grade levels and ability levels. A study of the performance of students representative of different subtypes of reading disabilities, following a model such as Lovett's (1984) that accounts for deficient and compensatory skills or Aaron's (1987) that accounts for different patterns of language comprehension abilities, might help us evaluate further the usefulness of the SVT as a means of diagnostic assessment of comprehension difficulties.

As for the use of the SVT as a method of evaluating comprehension, the results of the present study are generally in line with the results of Royer and his colleagues' investigations (Royer, 1986; Royer et al., 1979; Royer et al., 1986). That is, the particular characteristics of the SVT test used in this study (e.g., the use of expository passages, the use of ''yes/no'' responses instead of ''old/-new'' responses) have not affected the students' performances across subtests or sentence types. The 7th graders in this study are performing roughly the way they were expected to, given other students' performances on SVT tests and other listening/reading tests. Nonetheless there are problems with this method of testing that deserve attention. Most noteworthy is the potential for achieving a reasonable score by guessing alone, a common problem of true-false tests as well (Johnston, 1983). Royer recommends adjusting for guessing by using a method of statistical analysis borrowed from signal detection theory (Royer, 1986). One problem with this system is that it removes information of interest about the patterns of students' performances on the four sentence types. A second concern is the validity of the four sentence types themselves as methods of assessing language comprehension of passages. This issue too merits further study.

In sum, while the particular project reported in this paper was limited in scope and applicability, it does suggest that the SVT in the form adopted in PILAR holds promise as an effective method of identifying poor comprehenders and suggesting reasons for their comprehension deficits.

ACKNOWLEDGMENTS

I would like to thank Barbara Dautrich and Margaret Muzzey for their assistance in executing this study and Addison Stone for his suggestions on an early draft of this paper.

REFERENCES

Aaron, P. G. (1987). Developmental dyslexia: Is it different from other forms of reading disability? *Annals of Dyslexia, 37,* 109–125.

Anderson, R. C., Hiebert, E. H., Scott, J. A., & Wilkinson, I. A. G. (1985). *Becoming a nation of readers: The report of the Commission on Reading.* Washington, DC: The National Institute of Education.

Berger, N. (1978). Why can't Johnny read? Perhaps he's not a good listener. *Journal of Learning Disabilities, 11,* 633–638.

Carlisle, J. (in press). The use of the Sentence Verification Technique in diagnostic assessment of listening and reading comprehension. *Learning Disabilities Research.*

Carroll, J. B. (1977). Developing parameters of reading comprehension. In J. T. Guthrie (Ed.), *Cognition, curriculum and comprehension.* Newark, DE: International Reading Association.

Carroll, J. B., Davies, P., & Richman, B. (1971). *Word frequency book.* New York: American Heritage Publishing Co.

Curtis, M. E. (1980). Development of components of reading skill. *Journal of Educational Psychology, 72*(5), 656–669.

Danks, J., & Pezdek, K. (1980). *Reading and understanding.* Newark, DE: International Reading Association.

Davey, B. (1987). Postpassage questions: Task and reader effects on comprehension and meta-comprehension processes. *Journal of Reading Behavior, 19*(3), 261–283.

Drum, P. A., Calfee, R. C., & Cook, L. K. (1981). The effects of surface structure variables on performances in reading comprehension tests. *Reading Research Quarterly, 16,* 486–514.

Durrell, D. D. (1955). *Durrell Analysis of Reading Difficulty.* New York: Harcourt, Brace & Jovanovich.

Durrell, D. D. (1970). *Durrell Listening-Reading Series.* New York: Harcourt, Brace and World.

Englert, C. S., & Thomas, C. C. (1987). Sensitivity to text structure in reading and writing: A comparison between learning disabled and non-learning disabled students. *Learning Disability Quarterly, 10*(2), 93–105.

Farr, R., & Carey, R. F. (1986). *Reading: What can be measured?* (2nd ed.). Newark, DE: International Reading Association.

Fuchs, L. S., Fuchs, D., & Maxwell, L. (1988). The validity of informal reading comprehension measures. *Remedial and Special Education, 9*(2), 20–28.

German, D., Johnson, B., & Schneider, M. (1985). Learning disability versus reading disability: A survey of practitioners' diagnostic populations and test instruments. *Learning Disabilities Quarterly, 8,* 141–157.

Hanson, V. L. (1981). Processing of written and spoken words: Evidence for common coding. *Memory & Cognition, 9*(1), 93–100.

Johnston, P. H. (1983). *Reading comprehension assessment: A cognitive basis.* Newark, DE: International Reading Association.

Johnston, P. H. (1984). Assessment in reading, In P. D. Pearson (Ed.), *Handbook of reading research.* New York: Longman.

Jongsma, L., & Jongsma, E. (1981). Commercial informal reading inventories. *The Reading Teacher, 34*(6), 697–707.

Kibby, M. W. (1981). Test review: The degrees of reading power. *Journal of Reading, 24*(5), 416–427.

Kintsch, W. (1979). Reading comprehension as a function of text structure. In L. B. Resnick & P. A. Weaver (Eds.), *Theory and practice of early reading* (Vol. 2). Hillsdale, NJ: Lawrence Erlbaum Associates.

Lovett, M. W. (1984). The search for subtypes of specific reading disability: Reflections from a cognitive perspective. *Annals of Dyslexia, 34,* 155–178.

MacGinitie, W. H. (1978). *Gates MacGinitie Reading Tests,* Level 3 (2nd ed.). Boston: Houghton Mifflin.

Maria, K., & MacGinitie, W. H. (1982). Reading comprehension disabilities: Knowledge structures and non-accommodating text processing strategies. *Annals of Dyslexia, 32,* 33–60.

The Massachusetts Register. (August 28, 1986). Issue No. Supplemental 535. Reg. Ch. #603 CMR 28:00, Special Education.

Minnesota Educational Computing Consortium. (1982). Finding readability levels. *School Utilities* (Vol. 2).

Pearson, P. D., & Johnson, D. D. (1978). *Teaching reading comprehension.* New York: Holt, Rinehart, and Winston.

Perfetti, C. A. (1985). *Reading ability,* New York: Oxford University Press.

Perfetti, C. A., & Roth, S. (1981). Some of the interactive processes in reading and their role in reading skill. In A. M. Lesgold & C. A. Perfetti (Eds.), *Interactive processes in reading.* Hillsdale, NJ: Lawrence Erlbaum Associates.

Richgels, D. J., McGee, L. M., Lomax, R. G., & Sheard, C. (1987). Awareness of four text structures: Effects on recall of expository text. *Reading Research Quarterly, 22*(2), 177–196.

Royer, J. M. (1986). *The sentence verification technique as a measure of comprehension: Validity, reliability, and practicality.* University of Massachusetts, unpublished paper.

Royer, J. M., Greene, B. A., & Sinatra, G. M. (1987, Feb.) The sentence verification technique: A practical procedure for testing comprehension. *Journal of Reading,* 414–422.

Royer, J. M., Hastings, C. N., & Hook, C. (1979). A sentence verification technique for measuring reading comprehension. *Journal of Reading Behavior, 11*(4), 355–363.

Royer, J. M., Kulhavy, R. W., Lee, S., & Peterson, S. E. (1986). The relationship between reading and listening comprehension. *Educational and Psychological Research, 6,* 299–314.

Royer, J. M., & Lynch, D. J. (1982). The misuses and appropriate uses of norm-referenced tests of reading comprehension. *Reading Psychology, 3,* 131–142.

Rubin, A. (1980). A theoretical taxonomy of the differences between oral and written language. In R. J. Spiro, B. C. Bruce, & W. F. Brewer (Eds.), *Theoretical issues in reading comprehension.* Hillsdale, NJ: Lawrence Erlbaum Associates.

Sachs, J. S. (1974). Memory in reading and listening to discourse. *Memory & Cognition, 2*(1A), 95–100.

Sinatra, G. M. (1987). *Convergence of listening and reading processing.* University of Massachusetts, unpublished paper.

Smiley, S., Oakley, D., Worthen, D., Campione, J., & Brown, A. (1977). Recall of theoretically relevant material by adolescent good and poor readers as a function of written versus oral presentation. *Journal of Educational Psychology, 69,* 381–387.

Stanovich, K. E. (1985). Explaining the variance in reading ability in terms of psychological processes: What have we learned? *Annals of Dyslexia, 35,* 67–96.

Sticht, T. (1979). Applications of the audread model to reading evaluation and instruction. In L. B. Resnick & P. A. Weaver (Eds.), *Theory and practice of early reading* (Vol. 1). Hillsdale, NJ: Lawrence Erlbaum Associates.

Sticht, T. G., & Beck, L. J. (1976). *Experimental Literacy Assessment Battery* (LAB) (AFHRL-

TT-76-51). Lowry AFB, CA: Air Force Human Resources Laboratory/Technical Training Division.

Sticht, T. G., & James, H. J. (1984). Listening and reading. In P. D. Pearson (Ed.), *Handbook of reading research*. New York: Longman.

Tuinman, T. T. (1973–1974). Determining the passage dependence of comprehension questions in five major tests. *Reading Research Quarterly, 9,* 206–223.

Valencia, S. W., & Pearson, P. D. (1988). Principles of classroom comprehension assessment. *Remedial and Special Education, 9*(1), 26–35.

Vogel, S. (1974). Syntactic abilities in normal and dyslexic children. *Journal of Learning Disabilities, 7,* 103–109.

Wiig, E., Semel, E., & Crouse, M. (1973). The use of English morphology by high-risk and learning disabled children. *Journal of Learning Disabilities, 6,* 457–465.

APPENDIX A

Crows

Of all the birds, people believe that the crow is the biggest pest.
He is a large black bird with strong wings and a tough bill that
can be put to many uses. He eats all kinds of food, such as fruits,
seeds, grains, birds' eggs, and garbage. Being such a hardy eater,
he has no trouble finding food even in the winter. Crows rise early
in the morning to look for food. They go about in large flocks.
They talk noisily to each other. When they arrive in an area to
feed, they scare away other birds. They raid farmers' crops and
even hens' nests in the barnyard. Men have tried to scare crows away
from their fields. And they have tried to keep them from taking over
the land. But they have not been able to keep these clever birds from
causing trouble.

        Read each sentence carefully. Is the idea of the sentence found
in the passage? If it is, circle YES. If it is not, circle NO.

Crows

YES NO 1. Crows fly from place to place in big groups.

YES NO 2. Of all the birds, people believe that the crow is the
           biggest pest.

YES NO 3. Crows rise late in the morning to look for food.

YES NO 4. Being such a hardy eater, he has to search far and wide
           to find food in winter.

YES NO 5. Young crows learn to fly when they are about 4-weeks old.

YES NO 6. He eats all kinds of food, such as fruits, seeds, grains,
           birds' eggs, and garbage.

YES NO 7. Crows will pick up all sorts of objects, like rubber bands
           or paper cups, to see if they can be eaten.

YES NO 8. Men have tried to scare crows away from their fields.

YES NO 9. Crows frighten off the other birds when they come to a
           place to look for food.

YES NO 10. But men have been able to keep these clever birds from
           causing trouble.

YES NO 11. Crows steal vegetables from gardens and eggs from chicken
           nests on farms.

YES NO 12. A scarecrow, which is a dummy dressed like a person, is
           used to keep crows from raiding the crops.

APPENDIX B
Text Characteristics and Readability Levels** (Expressed as Grade Levels)
of PILAR Listening (L) and Reading (R) Passages

Level	Title	Total Words	Words of 6 or More Letters	Average Sentence Length	Dale-Chall	Fry
3L	Whales	140	21	11.8	(3.4)*	4
5L	Circus	178	38	14.8	5-6	6
7L	Gold	195	53	16.3	7-8	8
9L	Armor	221	61	18.4	9-10	9
3R	Crows	140	19	11.8	(3.2)*	3
5R	Octopus	181	37	15.1	5-6	6
7R	Lions	199	50	16.4	7-8	8
9R	Rockets	216	69	18.0	9-10	8

*Spache Word List Rating
**Minnesota Educational Computing Consortium, 1982

19

Cognition and Academic Performance in Children with Learning Disabilities, Low Academic Achievement, Diabetes Mellitus, and Seizure Disorders

John William Hagen
George Kamberelis
University of Michigan

A cognitive-social-developmental model of learning disabilities, chronic illnesses, and problems that affect children across diagnostic categories provides the rationale for the approach and the research presented here. Specifically, a dimensional approach is advocated which provides a way to take into account cognitive potential, academic performance, and behavioral and environmental information within and across diagnostic labels. The model underlying the approach is presented schematically in Fig. 19.1. For a complete discussion of it, see Hagen, Saarnio, and Laywell (1987).

The groups that have been studied using this model include children with: learning disabilities, low academic achievement attributed to motivational problems, diabetes mellitus, and seizure disorders. These labeled groups constitute the first of the three dimensions of the model. The second dimension is made up of factors that cut across these categories and includes etiology, intellectual and cognitive abilities, academic performance, motivation, self-concept, family environment, and socioeconomic status. Each of these is taken into account regardless of the diagnosed condition. The third dimension of the model is the developmental level of the child.

The core of the model is the functional, developmental characterization of strengths and weaknesses across cognitive, behavioral, and social variables. The focus is on control processes rather than structural features of the information processing system (e.g., Atkinson & Schiffrin, 1968). The cognitive-developmental approach allows investigators to concentrate on observed, potentially correctable problems in adaptive cognitive processing in various task settings. We know that in memory, for example, development progresses through stages, from mediation deficiency, to production deficiency, and then to accurate, effi-

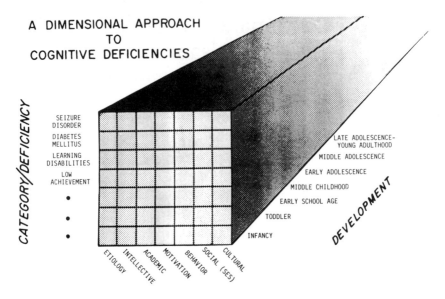

ANTECEDENT/CONSEQUENCE

FIG. 19.1. A dimensional model of cognitive deficiencies. Adapted
from Hagen, Saarnio, and Laywell (1987).

cient memorizing (Hagen & Stanovich, 1977). However, while children with
problems such as learning disabilities exhibit this pattern, it is developmentally
delayed (Newman & Hagen, 1982). Medical interventions, such as medication
taken by children with seizure disorders, have also been shown to affect the
development of memory.

The battery of instruments used in our research includes two measures of
memory from the experimental literature. Also included are selected scales of the
Wechsler Intelligence Scale for Children-Revised, (WISC-R), and reading comprehension and mathematics achievement subtests of the Peabody Individual
Achievement Test (PIAT). Additionally, measures of self-attribution and family
structure are administered. Finally, information concerning the developmental,
medical, and school histories of children participating in the research program is
obtained from extensive interviews conducted with children and parents.

The research reported here includes data from an ongoing project focusing on
groups of children with chronic physical illnesses as well as a similar project
focusing on children with learning disabilities or serious problems in academic
achievement thought to be due to motivational problems. The rationale for the
study of children with either chronic illnesses or learning problems from a
cognitive-social-developmental perspective has been presented in detail elsewhere (Hagen, Anderson, & Barclay, 1986; Hagen, Saarnio, & Laywell, 1987).

Briefly, there have been suggestions in the literature for many years that children with diabetes mellitus are "normal" in ordinary intelligence but deficient in selected areas of cognitive functioning. Moreover, many of these children have problems in school which are often related to noncognitive factors such as excessive absenteeism and low blood sugar levels.

As a group, children with seizure disorders are known to have intelligence scores that are significantly below average. However, the range of performance exhibited by these children is very wide indeed, with many falling into the mildly retarded range and others performing well above average. Problems in academic achievement are also common with these children, and, as with children with diabetes mellitus, these problems are sometimes attributed to noncognitive factors. It is illuminating to compare the patterns of intellectual, academic, and social performance demonstrated by these two groups of chronically ill children with the patterns shown by the groups of children with no chronic illnesses but who have learning and/or achievement problems.

The rationale for the study of children with learning disabilities and children who are academic underachievers from a cognitive-social-developmental perspective has been implicit in both educational and developmental psychology literature for quite a while. Much attention, for example, has been paid to understanding the different roles played by ability, information processing strategies, and motivation with respect to learning problems. In our research, children with learning disabilities and children who are academic underachievers were chosen specifically because their academic problems are usually viewed as having very different sources. Learning disabilities are commonly attributed to perceptual and informational processing deficits, while academic underachievement is usually considered to be an attributional or a motivational problem. While there is evidence to support these positions, we argue that a multidimensional explanatory framework results in a better understanding of these problems.

PROCEDURES

Subjects

Descriptive information on the subjects for each of the groups is shown in Table 19.1. Information is also included on the subjects of a normal comparison group (C). The age range for each group is wide and includes children who are quite young as well as adolescents. Table 19.2 presents a summary of pertinent diagnostic information including the mean age at diagnosis of the medical condition, learning disability, or achievement deficit, the mean duration of the illness or problem, and parents' reports about the extent to which their children's illnesses or learning problems are being controlled or remediated.

TABLE 19.1
Subject Information

	Subjects				
	SD	DB	LD	UA	C
Number	24	30	17	10	30
Sex					
Male	11	13	10	8	14
Female	13	17	7	2	16
Age in Years					
Mean	11.1	12.6	11.50	14.00	12.6
S.D.	2.3	2.7	3.5	1.9	2.7
Range	7.2-	8.0-	6.3-	10.2-	8.1-
	16.8	16.9	18.5	16.4	16.6

SD = seizure disorders
DB = diabetes mellitus
LD = learning idsabilities
UA = underachievement
C = comparison

Instruments

Most of the findings that are presented and discussed relate to the assessment instruments used in our research program. These instruments are listed in Table 19.3.

The five subscales of the WISC-R comprise the intelligence measures used. These subtests were chosen because of their high correlations with the total WISC-R battery and because previous work has suggested that they might represent problem areas for some of the groups under study. Academic achievement is

TABLE 19.2
Diagnostic Information Provided by Parents

	SD	DB	LD	UA	C
Age in Years at Diagnosis					
Mean	6.8	5.7	6.8	7.5	---
S.D.	3.7	4.2	2.4	3.9	---
Range	1.6-	0.8-	1.0-	4.0-	---
	13.8	13.5	16.1	14.5	---
Duration of Condition in Years					
Mean	4.5	6.9	4.6	4.3	---
S.D.	3.1	4.3	3.3	3.2	---
Range	1.1-	0.8-	0.3-	0.5-	---
	11.5	14.6	10.0	11.0	---
Control or Remediation of Condition					
Very Good	79%	43%	14%	00%	---
Average	21%	43%	57%	50%	---
Poor	00%	14%	29%	50%	---
Loss of Consciousness	63%	37%	00%	10%	17%
Other Learning or Medical Problems	42%	30%	41%	63%	37%

TABLE 19.3
Assessments

INTELLIGENCE	ACHIEVEMENT
Wechsler Intelligence Scale for Children-Revised	Peabody Individual Achievement Test
*Vocabulary *Information *Comprehension *Digit Span *Block Design	*Reading *Mathematics

INFORMATION PROCESSING

Central-Incidental Attention Task (Pictures)
    *Central: Recall of Task Relevant Information
    *Incidental: Recall of Task Relevant Information

Pause Time Memory Task (Words)
    *Accuracy: Percent Recalled

CHILD AND FAMILY CHARACTERISTICS

Perceived Self-Competence Scale

    *Cognitive
    *Social
    *General
    *Physical

Family Environment Scale

Developmental/Medical History Questionaire

School History and Current Academic Performance Questionaire

---

assessed with two subscales of the PIAT. Reading comprehension and mathematics subscales were chosen because high achievement in these areas is most highly correlated with successful school performance. Both the WISC-R and the PIAT have norms for chronological age. These norms (and not grade norms) are used in our research to compute all scores.

The other standardized instruments used are the Perceived Competence Scale (Harter, 1978) and the Family Environment Scale (Moos, 1974). The former is a 28-item self-report instrument that assesses the child's view of his or her competence in four domains: cognitive, social, physical, and general. The latter is a 90-item questionnaire that provides information about family structure, interactions, and activities.

The two measures of information processing used in this research come from the cognitive developmental literature and are outlined briefly next.

The Central-Incidental Serial Recall Task (Hagen, 1967) is used to measure central and incidental learning and short-term memory. It is a visual, pictorial task involving 7 trials. In each trial a series of 7 pairs of pictures mounted on separate cards are displayed individually. Each card is turned over after being shown. On each card there are two pictures, one of an animal (e.g., dog, bear, deer) and the other of a common household item (e.g., clock, book, lamp). The animal and household item pairs are always the same.

Children are instructed to remember the positions of all of the household items and not to be concerned with the animals. After all 7 cards have been individually displayed and turned over in a given trial, children are asked to recall the position of one of the cards displaying a particular household item. The total number of correct responses constitutes the measure of central recall. Trials are counterbalanced for position.

When all 7 trials are finished, children are given two new sets of cards. One set has only the animal pictures on them. The other has only the pictures of household items. The children are asked to pair the animals and the household items as they are paired on the original set of cards. The total number of correct matches constitutes the measure of incidental recall. A high incidental score usually represents a lack of attention to relevant stimuli.

In addition to obtaining central and incidental scores, primacy, medial, and recency performance is assessed using this instrument.

The second information-processing task used is the Pause-Time Serial Free Recall Task. It is based on a paradigm used by Belmont and Butterfield (1969) for investigating rehearsal activity. The Pause-Time Task involves visual presentation of words. Vocabulary words were selected from the Palermo-Jenkins word norms for children (1964). During each of 10 trials, subjects self-present lists of 9 words arranged on a computer monitor from left to right and top to bottom. Only one word can be seen at a time and it disappears after being viewed. Each new word appears in a different but predictable location on the monitor and remains visible for 0.5 seconds. The interstimulus interval is subject controlled or self-paced. This interval, from the offset of one stimulus to the onset of the next, is referred to as the rehearsal or pause time.

Before attempting the task the nature of the stimulus presentation is explained to children. Then they are instructed to try to remember as many words as they can for each trial, irrespective of order. They are also encouraged to use any strategies in their repertoires and to take as much time as they want using these strategies between word presentations. A practice trial is administered to insure the children understand the nature of the task. After the last word is viewed in each trial and children indicate that they are ready to recall the test items, they are asked to do so and their responses are recorded. In addition, interitem intervals or pause-times are recorded by the computer. The percentage of correct responses/total possible correct responses is computed as well as the percentage of correct responses per position. Thus, not only is total recall measured, but primacy, medial, and recency performance is assessed.

One important characteristic of the Pause-Time Task is that the pause patterns (i.e., the distribution of pause times over serial positions) have been related directly to age and intelligence scores (Barclay, 1979; Belmont & Butterfield,

1977; Butterfield & Belmont, 1972, 1976). Older and more intelligent children spontaneously produce more effective and systematic patterns of active-passive strategies. In addition, it has been shown that the observed pause pattern depends on the task's recall requirements (e.g., forward, backward, circular, free, or serial recall) and the type of stimuli used (e.g., single vs. multiple letters, nonsense words vs. meaningful units). The particular pause pattern of interest in our research program has been described as the "cumulative rehearsal, fast finish" strategy (Belmont & Butterfield, 1971; Pinkus & Laughery, 1970). That is, if a mature, strategic learner were placed in a free, probed, or circular recall task, the resulting response pattern typically would show a cumulative increase in pause-times followed by a decrease for the last few list items. The cumulative increase in pause times indicates that after exposure to each item, the subject actively attempts to memorize all of the previously viewed items plus the one new item. The last items in the list are not actually relevant due to recency effects.

The final set of instruments used include questionnaires and structured interviews. These are administered to the children as well as their parents and siblings. These instruments include questions about medical history, schooling and school performance, behavior, family interactions, and the parents' perceptions of their child's illness or learning problem and its impact on both the child and other family members.

Recruitment and Interviewing

Families of children with diabetes mellitus and children with seizure disorders were recruited by investigators at a research facility which is physically and administratively separate from the hospital. The children were patients seen on a regular basis for routine medical follow-up at the Pediatric Clinics at the University of Michigan. In order to be eligible for participation in the project, these children had to be generally healthy and currently attending regular school classrooms (i.e., not self-contained special education classrooms). Comparison children were recruited through local newspaper advertisements. Children with learning disabilities, and low achieving children with no discernible learning disabilities were recruited through community agencies and newspaper advertisements.

Focus children and siblings participated in a single 3-hour session of testing and interviewing. One investigator worked with each child. While the children were being tested and interviewed, a structured interview was conducted with one or both parents, and then the parents completed several questionnaires. For the convenience of families of children with chronic illnesses and to allow the concurrent collection of disease related data, testing and interviewing sessions were usually scheduled on the day of a routine clinic visit. In general, sessions were scheduled at times that were convenient for the families who participated in the project.

WISC-R

A subtest profile of performance on the WISC-R for each group is provided in Fig. 19.2. The analyses of variance for groups (5) by subscales (5) were all highly significant and ranged from $F = 6.67$, $p < 0.01$ on the digit span subscale to $F = 12.10$, $p < 0.01$ on the comprehension subscale. Pairwise comparisons revealed many interesting similarities and differences between and among groups. While all comparisons are not reported in this chapter, relevant patterns of similarities and differences are presented below. Children with seizure disorders scored well below other groups with their highest scaled score at 8.5. Children with learning disabilities were the next lowest with only one scaled score above 10. This score was on the block design which is the only subscale from the performance section of the WISC-R used in our battery. In addition, the verbal aptitude profiles of children with seizure disorders and children with learning disabilities looked remarkably similar. Overall, these two groups of children scored in the low average range, whereas the other groups scored in the average to high average range. Aptitude profiles of the children with diabetes mellitus and the underachieving children were also quite similar. Both groups performed in the average to above average range on all subscales administered. The performance of the comparison group was the highest overall, with little deviation across subscales.

PIAT

The results obtained from all groups on the PIAT are displayed in Fig. 19.3. The two scores reported for each group are percentile ranks by age for the mathematics and the reading comprehension subscales. Overall, the analyses of variance of groups (5) by subscales (2) were highly significant. (Math: $F = 10.08$, $p < 0.01$; Reading comprehension: $F = 10.99$, $p < 0.01$). Again, the comparison group's performance on both subscales was considerably higher than the other groups. Performance levels for children with diabetes mellitus and for underachieving children were almost identical. Both groups scored just above the 60th percentile on both subscales. Children with learning disabilities and children with seizure disorders received the lowest scores on both subscales, however the lower and higher scores for each group were reversed. For the seizure disorders group, reading comprehension was the higher score while for the learning disabled group, mathematics was higher. The latter finding was expected since the major presenting problems of children with learning disabilities have to do with processing and producing written language.

---

[1]Age was treated as a covariate in all analyses where age adjusted norms were not available. Socioeconomic status of the family was treated as a covariate in all analyses. However, few changes resulted from the use of these covariates.

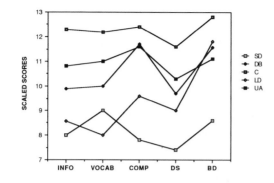

FIG. 19.2.   Wechsler Intelligence Scale for Children—Revised.

Interview information corroborated these findings about achievement. Parents reported that about one half of all children in the seizure disorders, learning disabilities and underachieving groups receive remedial services in the schools they attend. Not surprisingly, more than any other group, children in the under-achieving group were judged by their parents not to be working up to potential in school. Parents of children with chronic illnesses and learning disabilities attributed poor academic performance much less to effort. Absences from school were not found to vary much across groups, so attendance per se did not seem to account for academic performance. The differences among groups in reported ''problems making friends'' are striking and should be followed up further.

Central-Incidental Serial Recall Tasks

On the Central-Incidental Memory Task, children in the seizure disorders, learning disabilities and underachieving groups scored lower on central recall that children in the diabetic or comparison groups. Children in the seizure disorders group received particularly low scores on this task. Although there were no

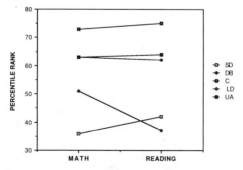

FIG. 19.3.   Peabody Individual Achievement Test.

TABLE 19.4
School History Provided by Parents

| | Percent Responding Yes | | | | |
	SD	DB	LD	UA	C
Ever repeated grade	17	13	14	00	00
Remedial educational services this year	50	27	36	38	07
Remedial educational service any year	54	40	36	25	17
Absent twice last month	08	17	07	10	07
Does not try to do best in school	42	30	50	80	55
Problems with teachers	04	07	57	38	03
Problems making friends	38	17	21	75	13

overall significant differences in incidental recall among the groups, children with diabetes mellitus, seizure disorders, and learning disabilities had considerably higher recall on the incidental task than on the central task. Thus these children demonstrated less selective attention on this task.

Of major interest were the performances of children on serial recall (see Fig. 19.4A). Children in the two groups already identified as looking similar (seizure disorders and learning disabilities groups) demonstrated virtually no primacy effects, confirming the interpretation that they did not approach serial recall tasks with any active strategies.

One other group, the underachievers, also provided evidence that effective memory strategies were not employed. This finding is difficult to interpret given the fact that these children did well on aptitude and achievement tests. One plausible explanation is that these children did not try to perform well on this task, which requires the active use of strategies to do well. Preliminary analysis of these children's latency responses along with the examiner's notes regarding their attitudes during testing support this interpretation, which is also consonant with expectations about the source of academic problems for this group. However, this finding must be considered tentative due to the small number of subjects in this cell at this time.

Caution must be exercised in interpreting the relatively low serial recall findings of children with diabetes mellitus. This group is in fact two separable groups distinguished by age of onset of the disease. Children with later onset (chronological age > 5 years) performed considerably better than children with earlier onset (chronological age < 5 years). Were we to report only the serial recall of the late onset group, results would look very much like those of the comparison group (see Hagen et al., 1985).

As expected, children in the comparison group outperformed all others, ex-

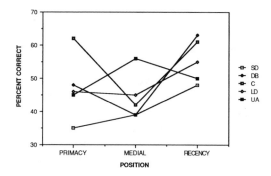

FIG. 19.4a. Central-Incidental Memory Task: Percent correct per position.

hibiting response patterns that indicated effective active-passive rehearsal strategies for encoding stimuli.

Pause Time Serial Free Recall Task

The Pause Time Serial Free Recall Task was used to infer rehearsal strategies with visually presented verbal stimuli. The 9 items that comprise each trial were collapsed into three groups to form primacy, medial, and recency scores. Analyses of variance adjusted for age yielded differences for groups, positions, and the interaction between them. For groups, $F = 6.69$, $p < 0.01$; for positions, $F = 7.08$, $p < 0.01$; for the interaction between groups and positions, $F = 2.48$, $p < 0.01$.

As shown in Fig. 19.4B, children with seizure disorders remembered fewer words on this task than children in any of the other groups, and children with learning disabilities performed only slightly better. Overall, the other three

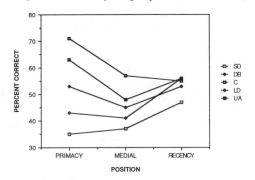

FIG. 19.4b. Pause Time Verbal Memory Task: Percent correct per position.

groups of children did much better on this task, especially in their recall of words in the primacy and medial positions. As in the Central Incidental Task, good recall of items in these positions provides evidence of the use of appropriate memory strategies.

The patterns observed indicate increasing sophistication of strategy use as a function of group membership. Children in the comparison group revealed the most effective use of strategies; children in the diabetic, learning disabilities and underachieving groups exhibited less effective strategy use; and children in the seizure disorders group demonstrated the least effective use of strategies. The primacy results of Fig. 19.4B demonstrate graphically that the information processing strategies cut across chronic illness and learning problem categories.

The other index of strategy use yielded from the pause-time task is latency of response or "pause-time." Initial analyses suggest that this index corroborates serial recall findings. Further analyses are underway.

Perceived Competence Scale

Most children scored within the normal range on the Perceived Competence Scale. As shown in Fig. 19.5, however, there were some important differences and similarities among the groups. Children with seizure disorders, diabetes mellitus, learning disabilities, and achievement deficits scored much lower on the cognitive subscale than did the comparison children. These results confirmed other findings of our research derived from interviews with both children and parents, and they were consonant with expectations. Children who performed poorly on cognitive and academic tasks were also aware of their difficulties in these areas.

Children with diabetes mellitus had exceptionally high scores on the social subscale while children with seizure disorders had scores that were quite low. Along with the low scores on the cognitive and social subscales, children with

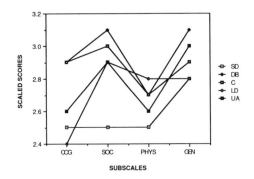

FIG. 19.5.   Perceived Self-Competence Scale.

seizure disorders also scored low on the physical subscale. Learning disabled children, children with seizure disorders, and comparison children received average scores on the general subscale, while children with diabetes mellitus and low achievers scored considerably higher.

Family Environment Scale

Most scores on the Family Environment Scale were within the normal range for both parents and children. However, some interesting results were obtained when we compared children's and parents' scores on certain subscales. Compared to their parents and to the instrument's norms, learning disabled children and academic underachievers scored quite low on the Expressiveness and Independence subscales. Similarly, on the Control subscale, learning disabled children and low academic achievers scored much higher than their parents. In other words, children in these families perceived the social environment to be controlling and to offer few opportunities for independence and expressiveness, while their parents had quite different perceptions. It would be useful to know whether these results are artifacts of the power structure of families generally or whether they are peculiar to families having children with certain kinds of problems. Because we did not have scores from this instrument for both parents and children for the other three groups, it was not possible to answer this question.

SUMMARY AND IMPLICATIONS

In this chapter we began by suggesting the usefulness of a dimensional model in trying to understand cognition and academic performance in children with chronic illnesses and children with learning problems. The dimensions of the proposed model included diagnostic categories, developmental level, and various cognitive, behavioral, and social variables. Different populations of children, each considered to be developmentally "at risk" because of the presence of disease, deficient performance, or labeling by the educational system, have been studied, compared, and contrasted. Several of the findings from our research provide support for the utility of a dimensional model.

The importance of the developmental level of the child, insofar as it is reflected by age, was apparent from the results on the information-processing tasks. Standardized measures were all adjusted for age, but, as would be expected, raw scores on these measures increased as a function of age. For some groups, (e.g., seizure disorders and learning disabilities) there is reason to believe that children follow the same developmental pattern as other children but that their development is delayed. Whether the observed delays correct themselves over time without intervention within individuals is not known. Theorists have taken various positions regarding observed delays, attributing them to deficits, deficiencies, or biological defects. It is both theoretically and practically important to distinguish developmental delay from other, more serious, deficiencies (see Hagen, Barclay, & Schwethelm, 1982, for further discussion).

Characteristics of children that cross category boundaries were found. Of particular interest were the striking number of like performances on aptitude, achievement, and information-processing tasks by children with seizure disorders and children with learning disabilities. We found that all groups of children who performed poorly on cognitive and academic tasks also reported low cognitive competence. Additionally, the low underachieving children and the comparison children were alike in many respects but were quite different in terms of academic achievement, perceived competence, and motivation. These findings corroborate recent work on the relationships among motivation, attribution, and academic achievement. Self-attributions and other motivational factors seem to distinguish underachievers as a group (Eccles & Wigfield, 1985).

Parental reports indicated that family structure and functioning changes considerably when one family member has a chronic illness or a learning problem. Although these changes were certainly not identical across groups, no doubt because of the different special needs of children in each group, the practical and psychological adjustments described by all families were surprisingly alike.

Our purpose is not to argue that children with very different illnesses, disabilities, or problems are really pretty much the same. Rather we pose a challenge to those who accept current diagnostic categories and try to prescribe interventions based on them. In the work presented here, two chronic illnesses and two conditions associated with impaired academic achievement were included. It was found that the functional patterns of performance were especially similar for children in an illness group (seizure disorders) and an academically impaired group (learning disabilities). These findings lend support for our argument that specific psychological effects are not predictable from a particular condition or type of impairment.

Another important aspect of our research is to compare carefully the patterns of performance of children with learning disabilities with the patterns of other low achieving children. Because of the heterogeneity found in both groups, there has been considerable disagreement about both labeling and treatment. Our ongoing research aims at making functional and fine-grained distinctions between these two groups of children.

In conclusion, the argument underlying our research program with both chronically ill children and children with learning problems stresses the importance of both within group and among group characteristics. Moreover, we maintain that chronic illnesses and learning problems are not isolated entities or clearly marked dysfunctions residing solely in the child. Rather, they occur and develop as a result of many related systems within and outside of the child. These include but are not restricted to biopsychological systems, social and cultural systems, and interactions among them.

From the perspective of this approach, a child's school performance must be viewed within a cognitive, developmental, functional, and social/cultural framework. The model we have proposed includes these variables within its dimensions. Thus it allows for a functional, developmental characterization of cognitive and academic deficiencies according to patterns of performance across cognitive, behavioral, and social/cultural domains. If the dimensional model is pursued and enough evidence collected, one outcome might be the replacement of diagnostic categories that form one dimension of the model with new groupings of children. Appropriate interventions based on these groupings should then be apparent (Hagen, Saarnio, & Laywell, 1987).

REFERENCES

Atkinson, R. C., & Schiffrin, R. M. (1968). Human memory: A proposed system and its control processes. In K. W. Spence & J. T. Spence (Eds.), *The psychology of learning and motivation: Advances in research and theory* (Vol. 2). New York: Academic Press.

Barclay, C. R. (1979). The executive control of mnemonic activity. *Journal of Experimental Child Psychology, 27,* 262–276.

Belmont, J. M., & Butterfield, E. C. (1969). The relations of short-term memory to development and intelligence. In L. P. Lipsitt & H. W. Reese (Eds.), *Advances in child development and behavior* (Vol. 4). New York: Academic Press.

Belmont, J. M., & Butterfield, E. C. (1971). Learning strategies as determinants of memory deficiencies. *Cognitive Psychology, 2,* 411–420.

Belmont, J. M., & Butterfield, E. C. (1977). Instructional approaches to developmental cognitive perspectives. In R. V. Kail & J. W. Hagen (Eds.), *Perspectives on the development of memory and cognition.* Hillsdale, NJ: Lawrence Erlbaum Associates.

Butterfield, E. C., & Belmont, J. M. (1972). The role of verbal processes in short-term memory. In R. L. Schiefelbusch (Ed.), *Language research with the mentally retarded.* Baltimore: University Park Press.

Butterfield, E. C., & Belmont, J. M. (1976). Assessing and improving the cognitive functions of mentally retarded people. In I. Bailer & M. Sternlicht (Eds.), *Psychological issues in mental retardation.* Chicago: Aldine.

Eccles, J., & Wigfield, A. (1985). Teacher expectations and student motivation. In J. B. Dusek (Ed.), *Teacher expectations* (pp. 185–226). Hillsdale, NJ: Lawrence Erlbaum Associates.

Hagen, J. W. (1967). The effect of distraction on selective attention. *Child Development, 38,* 685–694.

Hagen, J. W. (1972). Attention and mediation in children's memory. In W. Hartup (Ed.), *The young child* (Vol. 2, pp. 112–131). Washington, D.C.: National Association for the Education of Young Children.

Hagen, J. W., Anderson, B. J., & Barclay, C. R. (1986). Issues in research on the young chronically ill child. *Topics in Early Childhood Special Education, 5,* 49–57.

Hagen, J. W., Anderson, B., Barclay, C. R., Goldstein, G., Kandt, R., Genther, C., Freeman, D., Segal, S., & Bacon, G. (1985). *Cognitive and school performance in diabetic children.* Paper presented at the Biennial Meetings of the Society for Research in Child Development, Toronto.

Hagen, J. W., Barclay, C. R., & Schwethelm, B. (1982). Cognitive development of the learning-disabled child. In N. Ellis (Ed.), *International review of research in mental retardation: Vol II.* (pp. 1–41). New York: Academic Press.

Hagen, J. W., Saarnio, D. A., & Laywell, E. D. (1987). A dimensional approach to cognitive deficiencies. *Advances in learning and behavioral disabilities* (pp. 123–145). Greenwich, CT: Jai Press.

Hagen, J. W., & Stanovich, K. E. (1977). Memory: Strategies of acquisition. In R. V. Kail & A. W. Siegel (Eds.), *Perspectives on the development of memory and cognition* (pp. 89–111). Hillsdale, NJ: Lawrence Erlbaum Associates.

Harter, S. (1978). *The Perceived Competence Scale for Children*. Denver: University of Denver.

Moos, R. H. (1974). *Family environment scale and preliminary manual*. Palo Alto: Consulting Psychologists Press.

Newman, R. S., & Hagen, J. W. (1982). Memory strategies in children with learning disabilities. *Journal of Applied Developmental Psychology, 1,* 297–312.

Palermo, D. S., & Jenkins, J. J. (1964). *Word association norms: Grade school through college.* Minneapolis: University of Minnesota Press.

Pinkus, A. L., & Laughery, K. R. (1970). Recoding and grouping processes in short-term memory: Effects of subject-paced presentation. *Journal of Experimental Psychology, 85,* 335–341.

20 Learning Disabilities in Children with Clinical Depression

Steven R. Forness
Esther Sinclair
UCLA Neuropsychiatric Hospital

Although professionals in special education have attempted to change the Education of the Handicapped Act regarding serious emotional disturbance (SED) to criteria more relevant to school functioning (Bower 1982; Huntze, 1985), the U.S. Department of Education has not seen fit to adopt either more relevant terminology or more acceptable criteria (Tallmadge, Gamel, Munson, & Hanley, 1985). In rebuttal to proposed changes in the law, the Department repeatedly expressed grave concern that withdrawn or depressed pupils in particular might not be well served and that certain proposed modifications "might have the effect of displacing the 'quietly' emotionally disturbed children" (Tallmadge et al., 1985, p. 118).

This is in contrast to studies on behaviorally or emotionally disordered pupils' characteristics, which indicate that externalizers are by far the largest subgroup (Achenbach, 1979; Achenback & Edebrock 1978; Edelbrock & Achenbach, 1984; Epstein, Kaufman, & Cullinan, 1985; Quay, 1978) and are far more likely to be referred to special education (Algozzine, 1976; Cullinan, Epstein, & Kauffman, 1984; Mullen & Wood, 1986; Smith, Wood, & Grimes, 1987). There is considerable evidence in longitudinal studies that internalizers, such as depressed children, have been at considerably less risk for later problems in adulthood (Robins 1978, 1979).

It may well be, however, that belated recognition that depression occurs in childhood (Cantwell & Carlson, 1983; Cicchetti & Schneider Rosen, 1984) has only recently permeated the concerns of educators (Reynolds, 1984). More recent evidence also suggest that depression can nonetheless place children at risk for serious problems in subsequent adjustment (Kovacs et al., 1984a, 1984b) and that problems of an internalizing nature tend to be quite frequent in children with learning problems (Thompson, 1986). Furthermore, the only large study to date using the revised DSM III psychiatric diagnostic system with pupils in classes for the behaviorally disordered indicated that about one in five children and half of all adolescents had a primary diagnosis of depression (Mattison, Humphrey, Kales, Hernit, & Finkenbinder, 1986).

The current chapter, therefore, focuses on depression as a potentially significant area of concern in special education in order to address such questions as the nature and extent of this diagnosis in relation to school-aged children and what, if any, school characteristics are associated with its presentation. A point of clarification needs to be made at this point in that "socially withdrawn" (rather than "depressed") has long been the term of choice in special education for children with this disorder in that it perhaps more correctly addresses the task of intervention (Strain, Cooke, & Apolloni, 1976). The suggestion has been made, however, that interpretation of existing research for socially withdrawn children may suffer from lack of adequate subject description (Mastropieri & Scruggs, 1986; Mastropieri, Scruggs, & Casto, 1985; Reynolds, 1986). Depression as a subset of this term may thus prove to be more useful in differentiating among possible interventions.

DIAGNOSIS AND PHENOMENOLOGY

What educational policy makers had in mind when they adopted "a general pervasive mood of unhappiness or depression" (*Federal Register,* 1977, Section 300.5) as the fourth of five SED criteria in the Education of the Handicapped Act is not altogether clear. The term now used to denote such a condition, and one that has been predominant in the field of mental health, is that derived from the section on "Mood Disorders" in DSM III-R (American Psychiatric Association, 1987). Diagnostic criteria for a major depressive episode are quite specific and include dysphoric mood or anhedonia with selection of a combination of five symptoms from a list of nine (American Psychiatric Association, 1987). Dysthymia is likewise diagnosed by a combination of required and elective symptoms, with selection required of two of six possibilities, suggesting the somewhat more variable expression of this disorder. Bipolar affective disorders will not be discussed in detail here, since they are generally seen as less common and somewhat more difficult to diagnose in children (Carlson & Strober, 1978; Casat, 1982).

A scheme depicting the general diagnostic features of major depression and dysthymia is presented in Table 20.1. Note that symptoms generally cluster in four areas. Symptom patterns in adolescents and children have been found to differ, with a tendency in children to have more somatic complaints and depressed appearance and adolescents having more anhedonia and hopelessness (Ryan et al., 1986). It should also be pointed out that diagnosis of depression by

TABLE 20.1

Summary of Diagnostic Features for Depressive Disorders

	Major Depressive Episode	Dysthymia
Primary Features:	Dysphoric mood or loss of interest or pleasure in all, or almost all, usual activities and pastimes.	Same, but episodes are not of sufficient severity and sustained duration.
Social Symptoms:	Isolative from friends or family, seems unwilling or unable to participate in usual pastimes or activities.	Withdrawn, less likely to respond to usual pastimes or activities.
Emotional Symptoms:		
Child	Persistently sad facial expression, tearfulness, anxiety, irritability, feeling of worthlessness.	Sad, blue, down in the dumps, feeling sorry for oneself, easily annoyed, pessimistic.
Adolescent	Depressed appearance, brooding, negativistic, antisocial, inattention of physical appearance, self-depecation.	(Same as above.)
Cognitive Symptoms:	Diminished concentration, indecisiveness, slowed thinking, preoccupation with death or suicide.	Inattentive or unable to think clearly, thoughts of death or suicide.
Vegetative Symptoms:	1. Poor appetite or weight loss. 2. Sleep disorders 3. Psychomotor agitation, hypoactivity 4. Loss of energy, fatigue	Same, but usually not as many areas are affected nor to the same degree.
Symptom Duration:	Consistently for two weeks.	Most of the time for one year.

DSM III-R standards may result in a slightly more conservative diagnosis than that using criteria previously used in research on childhood depression (Carlson & Cantwell, 1982).

Clinic-based, as opposed to school-based, diagnosis of depression generally involves clinical interview, case history from parent or guardian, a confirmation of clinical impressions through objective rating scales, and, not infrequently, laboratory studies. Clinical psychiatric interview involves mental status examination of the child or adolescent, supplemented by parent interview on developmental history and present course of illness. Common objective methods used to assess depression in childhood and adolescence range from self-report measures (Beck et al., 1961; Kovacs & Beck, 1977; Reynolds, 1980, 1985b) to structured interviews (Endicott & Spitzer, 1978; Hamilton, 1967; Petti, 1978; Posnanski, Cook, & Carroll, 1979; Poznanski, Grossman, & Buchsbaum, 1984; Puig-Antich, 1982a; Puig-Antich & Chambers, 1978) to other school based measures (Lefkowitz & Tesiny 1980; Reynolds, 1981; Walker, Sevenson, & Haring, 1986). Information obtained from parents and target children, however, has been shown to differ sharply in terms of severity and duration of depressive symptomatology (Kazdin, 1981; Kazdin & Petti, 1982; Reynolds, Anderson, & Bartell, 1985; Weissman, Orvaschel, & Padian, 1980). There has also been interest in the dexamethasone suppression test (DST) as a possible diagnostic marker of endogenous depression in children and adolescents; but this test has not been as reliable as originally hoped (Klee & Garfinkel, 1984; Targum & Capodanno, 1983). This line of inquiry is nonetheless indicative of general recognition of genetic and biochemical etiology in childhood and adolescent depression (Strober & Carlson, 1982; Weissman, Prusoff, & Gammon, 1984; Puig-Antich, 1980, 1983).

Given the recency of interest in childhood depression, as well as variations in diagnostic ascertainment mentioned earlier, data on its epidemiology is still somewhat inchoate. Fifteen of the more recent studies are summarized developmentally in Table 20.2. Only recent studies are included here since these tend to be more accurate, principally because of their reliance on more objective and replicable measures; yet considerable variability is evident, often depending on choice of diagnostic criteria and instrumentation. Note that prevalence in the normal population tends to increase with increasing age, with child ascertainment around 4% or less and adolescents generally in the range of 10 to 15%. Special populations tend, of course, to have a much higher prevalence; and dysthymia is more common than major depression in both referred and nonreferred samples.

CLINICAL COURSE AND TREATMENT

Much of what is now known about the course of depression in children comes primarily from two studies described here. Kovacs and her colleagues (1984a,

TABLE 20.2
Recent Epidemiologic Findings in Childhood Depression

Study	Sample Type	Percent Depressed
Nonreferred		
Kashani & Ray (1983)	241 preschoolers	0.4
Kashani & Simonds (1979)	103 children	1.9
Kashani et al. (1983)	641 children	1.8 depressed 2.5 dysthymic
McCracken et al. (1986)	149 children	2.7 depressed 1.3 dysthymic
Kaplan et al. (1984)	330 adolescents	1.3 depressed 7.3 dysthymic
Kashani (1986)	150 adolescents	4.7 depressed 3.3 dysthymic
Kandel & Davies (1982)	4204 adolescents	13.0
Reynolds (1983)	2800 adolescents	18.0
Referred		
Kashani et al. (1984)	100 development clinic preschoolers	1.0 depressed 3.0 dysthymic
Cantwell & Baker (1982)	600 speech clinic children	4.0
Alessi (1986)	134 child psychiatric patients	37.0
Carlson & Cantwell (1980a)	102 child psychiatric patients	58.0
Petti (1978)	73 child psychiatric patients	59.0
Mattison et al. (1986)	158 special education children 128 special education adolescents	20.9
Strober et al. (1981a, 1981b)	95 adolescent psychiatric patients	17.8

1984b) studied 65 children with major depressive disorder (65%), dysthymia (43%), or adjustment disorder with depressed mood (17%). In some cases, major depression was superimposed on dysthymia, thus accounting for the overlap in the above percentages. This sample was 8- to 13-years-of-age and rather equally split between males and females. They were compared with 49 control patients referred for conduct disturbance. Conduct disorder, attention deficit, or anxiety disorder were found as associated, often preexisting, diagnoses in 79% of the depressed and in 93% of the dysthymic groups. This confirms the possibility of depression being overlooked as "masked depression," i.e., revealed if careful diagnostic ascertainment is done (Carlson & Cantwell, 1980b; Geller, Chestnut, Miller, Price, & Yates, 1985). Such associated disorders were much less typical of those having adjustment disorder with depressed mood. Age of onset was 9 years for dysthymia and 11 years for depression, with a mean episode length of nearly 3 years for the former and about 7 months for the latter. Mean length of recovery was about 3½ years for dysthymia and about 1½ years for depression. Generally, the younger the child, the more protracted was the recovery.

Control groups and adjustment disordered patients with depressed mood had only about a 5% risk of a major depressive episode over the nearly 9 years studied. However, 69% of dysthymics had such an episode within 5 years (most within 3 years); and 72% of the depressed group had a recurrent episode in that time, often occurring rather quickly (20% in the first year and 40% in the second). Those with "double depression," i.e., major depressive episode occurring during dysthymia, had higher risk and shorter periods of well-being. It is of interest to note that 32% of the depressed groups were reported to have failed a grade, 31% were in remedial or special education, and 26% had been suspended from school (these are overlapping percentages). There were, however, no directly obtained teacher or other school data available.

Puig-Antich and his colleagues (1985a, 1985b) focused on the nature of psychosocial functioning of children meeting criteria for major depressive episodes. There were 52 children (65% male), ages 6 to 12 years, matched with two control groups. One contained other nonpsychotic, nondepressed child psychiatric patients; and the others were normal children. Depressed children were less communicative and less able to maintain peer relationships than either of the control groups. Poor peer relationships in depressed children, as reported by mothers, tended to be associated with concomitant impairment in mother-child (but not father-child) relationships. Whether these psychosocial impairments were the cause or effect of depression was not clear, but they did seem to be somewhat more closely associated with depression than with other psychiatric difficulties. It is again of interest to note that, although academic testing or teacher ratings were not used, both psychiatric groups in this study were rated by mothers as significantly lower both in academic achievement and in teacher-child relationships. A small subgroup of 21 depressed children were assessed during an episode of depression and again after they had been successfully treated, most with psychopharmacology and some with therapy, and had evidenced a sustained recovery for at least 4 months. Ratings by mothers indicated that school functioning had generally normalized by that time, even when compared to the nondepressed psychiatric patients, but that there were still problems in social relationships at home.

While therapy in school settings has focused on cognitive-behavioral approaches (Butler, Miezitis, Friedman, & Cole, 1980; Reynolds, 1985a; Reynolds & Coats, 1986), there is general recognition that psychopharmacotherapy is an essential adjunct, particularly in cases with vegetative symptomatology and family history of affective disorder (Campbell, Schulman, & Rapoport, 1978; Cantwell & Carlson, 1983; Esman, 1981; Gadow, 1986; Kashani, Shekim, & Reid, 1984; Kishimoto, Ogura, Hazama, & Inoue, 1983; Klein, Gittelman, Quitkin, & Rifkin, 1980; Ogura, Petti, & Law, 1982; Preskorn, Weller, & Weller, 1982; Puig-Antich, 1982b). Such mood stabilizing drugs have potentially serious side effects, which a psychiatrist must often monitor with laboratory measures; but there are generally few long-term side effects reported thus far on cognitive functioning (Forness, Akiyama, & Campana, 1984; Forness & Kavale, 1988; Gadow, 1986; Kavale & Nye, 1984; Petti & Law, 1982).

SCHOOL-RELATED CORRELATES IN DEPRESSION

Changes in concentration and attention are relatively well established in child-hood depression (Feinstein, Blouin, Egan, & Conners, 1984) as are various difficulties in school behavior, as reviewed earlier in the Puig-Antich and Kovacs studies. It is thus disappointing to see so little systematic research in the areas of school achievement, cognition, or school-based assessment of children or ado-lescents with affective disorders. Table 20.3 summarizes selected recent studies investigating underachievement, teacher or peer assessment of social function-ing, and related school factors in childhood depression.

Of the 12 studies in Table 20.3, the first five deal with school-based samples, the next four with clinic-referred samples, and the last three with hospitalized children. Although teacher ratings and, in one case, peer ratings of school-based samples seem to suggest some difficulties in these depressed children, the diag-noses of depression are often based on screening measures alone and cannot necessarily be taken as valid. Findings on clinic samples suggest school dif-ferences specific to depression in only one instance and are characterized by generally poor choice of achievement measures. In hospital samples, there is again only one instance of a diagnosis-specific school finding. In only five studies were there samples of depressed subjects of sufficient size to be able to draw reasonably valid conclusions. Two studies suggested the possibility of cognitive gains as a result of treatment for depression (Petti & Conners, 1983; Staton, Wilson, & Brumback, 1981); but these cognitive measures could not be seen as corresponding directly to classroom progress. Second-order measures, either of school functioning or of depression, seem to characterize much of this research.

The notion of a possible link between depression and learning disabilities has been discussed elsewhere, but evidence remains merely tantalizing (Livingston, 1985). The general variability of achievement findings within samples of behav-iorally disordered children (Barnes & Forness, 1982; Forness, Bennett, & Tose, 1983; Forness, Kavale, Guthrie, Scruggs, & Mastropieri, 1987; Mastropieri, Jenkins, & Scruggs, 1985; Scruggs & Mastropieri, 1986) has not yet led to extensive investigation of achievement by specific diagnoses, such as depres-sion. As mentioned earlier, however, depressed children and adolescents have been found in significant numbers in programs for the behaviorally disordered, at

TABLE 20.3
Summary of Recent School-Related Findings in Depressed Children and Adolescents

Study	Sample	School Findings	Limitations
Leon et al. (1980)	21 screened from school, ages 8 to 12	normal IQ, low teacher ratings on attention	screened but no formal dx as depressed, used PPVT for IQ
Sacco and Graves (1984)	20 screened from school, ages 9 to 11	vocabulary and teacher ratings were lower than matched controls	screened but no formal dx as depressed, used only one WISC-R subtest
Strauss et al. (1984)	15 screened from school, ages 7 to 10	teacher ratings as under-achieving and inattentive, peers ratings as with-drawn	screened but no dx as depressed
Stevenson and Romney (1984)	103 children in LD classes ages 6 to 13	14% scored above cut-off on CDI	screened but no formal dx as depressed
Cullinan et al. (1987)	577 nonreferred and 237 in SED classes ages 6 to 18	significant correlations between brief depression "index" and several cog-nitive or social variables but mainly in nonreferred subjects only, with over-all depression index of SED pupils significantly higher than that of non-referred pupils	screened but no formal dx as depressed and only teacher estimates of achievement
Brumback et al. (1980)	59 referred to education-al diagnostic clinic, ages 5 to 12	underachieving compared to other psychiatric patients	used WRAT and PPVT as school measures
Staton et al. (1981)	11 in clinic for depres-sion, ages 6 to 13	IQ increased from 93 to 108 with tx; no achieve-ment gain	small N and used WRAT as achievement measure

(continued...)

(Table 20.3 continued)

Kovacs et al. (1984a, 1984b)	65 in clinic for depression, ages 8 to 13	26 suspended and 32% failed one or more grades but not different from other psychiatric patients	no direct measures of achievement or school behaviors
Puig-Antich et al. (1985a, 1985b)	52 in clinic for depression, ages 6 to 12	lower than normal in achievement and school behavior but not different from other psychiatric patients	used WRAT as achievement measure and no direct measure of school behavior
Kashani et al. (1982)	13 hospitalized for depression, ages 9 to 12	62% LD as compared to 22% of other psychiatric patients	small N and DSM III criteria used for LD
Colbert et al. (1982)	153 hospitalized for depression, ages 6 to 14	71% underachieving in regular class plus 7% in LD classes	LD criteria not specified
Petti and Conners (1983)	21 hospitalized for depression, ages 6 to 12	CDI measures of cognition and perception improved with drug tx	relationship of such gains to classroom not clear

least in the one large-scale study available in which careful ascertainment of depression has been made (Mattison, Humphrey, Kales, Hernit, & Finken-binder, 1986). If depression is to be seen as a critical differential diagnosis within the category of behavioral or emotional disorders, then further study must establish this fact with more specific school-based measures. A preliminary study in this area is presented in the next section.

PRELIMINARY SCHOOL FINDINGS IN DEPRESSED CHILDREN AND ADOLESCENTS

As part of a larger study of school placement of psychiatric patients (Alexson & Sinclair, 1986; Forness, Sinclair, Alexson, Seraydarian, & Garza, 1985; Sinclair, Forness, & Alexson, 1985), data was able to be gathered on a select group of depressed children seen at the UCLA Neuropsychiatric Institute (NPI). Preliminary analysis of school data on these depressed children is presented shortly. More extensive data on a smaller subsample of these children is presently being analyzed (Lucas, 1989).

Subjects for this preliminary analysis were selected from a sample of 185 inpatients and 406 outpatients. These children were from 7- to 14-years-old, and each had been diagnosed by NPI house staff (child psychiatry residents and advanced child psychology interns) according to DSM III criteria, after thorough interdisciplinary evaluation and supervision by faculty in child psychiatry, psychology, social work, speech pathology, and special education. Intellectual assessment was based on complete WISC-R or Stanford-Binet testing, and reading level was based on the PIAT reading recognition subtest. Classroom placement in community schools was obtained at admission and again at discharge, after completion of either outpatient evaluation or inpatient hospital treatment. These placements were obtained from either outpatient educational psychologists or inpatient hospital school teachers, at the time of the IEP, and were categorized as regular class without supportive services, resource room, learning-handicapped (LH) special class, or severely handicapped (SH) special class (including classrooms for seriously emotionally disturbed).

Summary of sample characteristics is depicted on Table 20.4. Of a total population of 406 outpatients and 185 inpatients gathered over a 2-year period, there were 111 children with various affective disorders in outpatient and 36 in inpatient. These are further depicted in Table 20.4 by those with only a *single* Axis 1 diagnosis of affective disorder (major depression or dysthymia), those with other Axis 1 diagnoses *in addition to* affective disorder (usually conduct or attention deficit disorders), and those with Axis 2 diagnoses of learning disorders *in addition to* affective disorder (a few of these also had some conduct or attention deficit disorders as well). Both of the latter groups were combined for the inpatient sample. Breakdown of major depression versus dysthymia for each group suggests approximately a 1 : 4 ratio for outpatient and a 2 : 5 ratio for

TABLE 20.4
Description of Sample of 147 Children with Depresssive Disorders*

Diagnosis**	N(%)	Age(SD)	% Male	% Minority
Outpatient (N = 111)				
Depressed only	47(42%)	10.2(2.3)	67	47
Depressed with other	38(34%)	10.9(2.8)	68	24
Depressed with LD	26(23%)	11.4(2.7)	62	31
Inpatient (N = 36)				
Depressed only	15(42%)	12.1(2.4)	60	40
Depressed with both	21(58%)	10.9(2.4)	57	35

* These represent 27.3% and 19.4% of the representative total populations of psychiatric outpatients and inpatients.

** Of the outpatient sample, 23% had a diagnosis of major depression with the remainder having primarily dysthymic disorder; and, of the inpatient sample, 39% had a diagnosis of major depression.

inpatient. Very few bipolar disorders or adjustment disorders with depressed mood were found in either sample, as was the case with schizoaffective disorder which is relatively rare in child samples (Freeman, Poznanski, Grossman, Buchsbaum, & Banegas, 1985).

Note that depressed children comprise about a fourth of the outpatient sample and about a fifth of the inpatient group, somewhat similar to rates in previous epidemiologic studies described above. The overall rate of learning disabilities (23%) in the outpatient sample is somewhat near the median of LD prevalence estimates, reported previously, for depressed children. The *combination,* however, of either a learning disability or a related behavioral difficulty *and* depression is characteristic of nearly 3 out of every 5 subjects in this sample, confirming certain notions, discussed earlier, that other preexisting or concurrent disorders may be routinely expected in childhood depression (Alessi, 1986).

Psychometric data are presented in Table 20.5. Note that IQ and reading achievement are largely in the normal range, except for the LD subgroup in outpatient which has a pattern of intellectual and achievement findings somewhat characteristic of the learning disabled (Kavale, Forness, & Bender, 1987). This tends to confirm the Axis 2 DSM III diagnosis of LD, thus avoiding limitations of previous studies discussed earlier. There appear to be no major differences between inpatient and outpatient samples.

Classroom placement data are reported in Table 20.6. Note that the outpatient sample tends to have been, at the time of diagnosis, mainly in regular classrooms but returned, in many cases, to special classes or resource rooms. It should be noted here that IEP meetings, as a result of outpatient evaluation, are held within a few weeks after diagnosis but while treatment for depression and related problems is still underway. The inpatient sample was less likely to have been in regular classrooms prior to treatment; but, interestingly, those patients with uncomplicated depression tended to return to regular classes in greater proportions after treatment. Caution should be exercised in interpretation here, since the

TABLE 20.5
Intellectual and Reading Achievement Data in Depressed Children

Diagnosis	IQ			VIQ-PIQ	Reading Standard Score		
	Mean	Range	SD		Mean	Range	SD
Outpatient							
Depressed only	103	69-157	17	-0.7	104	60-133	15
Depressed with other	101	71-165	22	-3.0	99	55-129	16
Depressed with LD	93	64-115	13	-9.6	84	50-113	16
Inpatient							
Depressed only	99	64-128	18	-1.8	101	81-125	14
Depressed with both	96	80-121	13	-9.9	91	73-121	15

sample size is quite small; and average length of hospital treatment was only little more than 3 months for both inpatient groups (Forness et al., 1985). Inpatients with depression complicated by learning or behavior problems, on the other hand, tended to be placed in relatively more restrictive settings even after treatment. In all, even after diagnosis and at least some psychiatric treatment, 61 of 147 (42%) of these depressed children appeared to continue to need special education. Even in those children with "pure" depression, i.e., those without accompanying learning or behavioral problems, almost a third required some form of special assistance.

Concerning the school findings reported in Tables 20.5 and 20.6, however, it should be pointed out that previous research with the same sample did not reveal statistically significant differences between these depressed children and children with other psychiatric disorders in the same treatment settings (Forness et al.,

TABLE 20.6
Type of Classroom Placements for Depressed Children

	N	% by Class at DX				% by Class After TX			
		Reg	Res	LH	SH	Reg	Res	LH	SH
Outpatient									
Depressed only	47	84	6	0	4	64	6	23	6
Depressed with other	64	86	8	5	0	58	33	8	0
Inpatient									
Depressed only	15	60	0	26	13	80	8	0	13
Depressed with other	21	52	5	38	5	33	9	29	28

1985; Sinclair et al., 1985). The exceptions were those depressed children with learning disorders, as already noted. Thus the issue of specific differential *classroom* treatments for depressed children, per se, is left in doubt.

CONCLUSION

Prior research on school characteristics of children with depression tends to support the seriousness of this disorder in reference to school functioning, but many methodological limitations were apparent. Preliminary findings presented here from a rather large sample with somewhat more systematic school data, at least relative to existing research studies in this area, suggest not only that childhood depression may indeed need to be considered a significant problem in special education but that co-morbidity with learning disabilities is also quite possible. One also cannot ignore the fact that those pupils with potential co-morbidity, i.e., depression accompanied by other behavioral disorders or learning disabilities, seemed more likely to require special education services. What is not clear, however, is the exact nature and extent of this co-morbidity, especially in the area of learning disabilities. Future study may have to unravel several possibilities such as depression as a form of demoralization resulting from learning disabilities, unrelated onset of depression and learning disabilities, learning disabilities as a result of concentration or attentional problems brought on by depression, a common etiologic pathway for both disorders, or some combination of these or other factors.

REFERENCES

Achenbach, T. M. (1979). The child behavior profile: An empirically based system for assessing children's behavioral problems and competencies. *International Journal of Mental Health, 2*, 26–40.

Achenbach, T. M., & Edelbrock, C. S. (1978). The classification of child psychopathology: A review and analysis of empirical efforts. *Psychological Bulletin, 85*, 1275–1301.

Alessi, N. E. (1986). *DSM III diagnosis associated with childhood depressive disorders.* Paper presented at American Academy of Child Psychiatry, Los Angeles, California.

Alexson, J., & Sinclair, J. (1986). Psychiatric diagnosis and school placement: A comparison between inpatients and outpatients. *Child Psychiatry and Human Development, 16*, 194–205.

Algozzine, B. (1976). The disturbing child: What you see is what you get? *Alberta Journal of Educational Research, 22*, 330–333.

American Psychiatric Association (1987). *DSM III-R: Diagnostic and statistical manual of mental disorders* (Third Edition Revised). Washington, D.C.

Barnes, T. R., & Forness, S. R. (1982). Learning characteristics of children and adolescents with various psychiatric diagnoses. *Monographs in Behavioral Disorders, 5*, 32–41.

Beck, A. T., Ward, C. H., Mendelson, M., Mock, J., & Erbaugh, J. (1961). An inventory for measuring depression. *Archives of General Psychiatry, 4*, 561–571.

Bower, E. M. (1982). Defining emotional disturbance: Public policy and research. *Psychology in the Schools, 19*, 55–60.

Brumback, R. A., Jackoway, M. K., & Weinberg, W. A. (1980). Relation of intelligence to childhood depression in children referred to an educational diagnostic center. *Perceptual and Motor Skills, 50,* 11–17.

Butler, L., Miezitis, S., Friedman, R., & Cole, E. (1980). The effect of two school-based intervention programs on depressive symptoms in preadolescents. *American Educational Research Journal, 17,* 111–119.

Campbell, M., Schulman, D., & Rapoport, J. L. (1978). The current status of lithium therapy in child and adolescent psychiatry. *Journal of Child Psychiatry, 17,* 717–720.

Cantwell, D. P., & Baker, L. (1982). Depression in children with speech, language and learning disorders. *Journal of Children in Contemporary Society, 15,* 51–59.

Cantwell, D. P., & Carlson, G. A. (1983). *Affective Disorders in childhood and adolescence: An Update.* New York: Spectrum Publications.

Carlson, G. A., & Cantwell, D. P. (1980a). A survey of depressive symptoms, syndrome and disorder in a child psychiatric population. *Journal of Child Psychology and Psychiatry, 21,* 19–25.

Carlson, G. A., & Cantwell, D. P. (1980b). Unmasking masked depression in children and adolescents. *American Journal of Psychiatry, 137,* 445–449.

Carlson, G. A., & Cantwell, D. P. (1982). Diagnosis of childhood depression: A comparison of the Weinberg and DSM III criteria. *The Journal of Child Psychiatry, 21,* 247–250.

Carlson, G. A., & Strober, M. (1978). Manic-depressive illness in early adolescence. *Journal of Child Psychiatry, 17,* 138–153.

Casat, C. D. (1982). The under- and over-diagnosis of mania in children and adolescents. *Comprehensive Psychiatry, 23,* 552–559.

Cicchetti, D., & Schneider Rosen, K. (Eds.). (1984). *Childhood depression: New directions for child development.* San Francisco: Jossey Bass.

Colbert, P., Newman, B., Ney, P., & Young, J. (1984). Learning disabilities as a symptom of depression in children. *Journal of Learning Disabilities, 15,* 333–336.

Cullinan, D., Epstein, M., & Kaufman, J. (1984). Teachers' ratings of students' behaviors: What constitutes behavior disorder in school? *Behavioral Disorders, 10,* 9–19.

Cullinan, D., Schloss, P., & Epstein, M. (1987). Relative prevalence and correlates of depressive characteristics among seriously emotionally disturbed and nonhandicapped students. *Behavioral Disorders, 12,* 90–98.

Edelbrock, C., & Achenbach, T. M. (1984). The teacher version of the child behavior profile. I: Boys aged 6–11. *Journal of Consulting and Clinical Psychology, 52,* 207–217.

Endicott, J., & Spitzer, R. L. (1978). A diagnostic interview: The Schedule for Affective Disorders and Schizophrenia. *Archives of General Psychiatry, 35,* 837–844.

Epstein, M. H., Kauffman, J. M., & Cullinan, D. (1985). Patterns of maladjustment among the behaviorally disordered. II: Boys ages 12–18, girls ages 6–11, and girls ages 12–18. *Behavioral Disorders, 10,* 125–135.

Esman, A. H. (1981). Appropriate use of psychotrophics in adolescents. *Hospital, 12,* 49–60.

Federal Register, Tuesday (August 23, 1977). Part II (Rules and regulations for amendments to Part B, Public Law 94–142, Education for All Handicapped Children Act of 1975).

Feinstein, C., Blouin, A. G., Egan, J., & Conners, C. K. (1984). Depressive symptomatology in a child psychiatric outpatient population: Correlations with diagnosis. *Comprehensive Psychiatry, 25,* 379–391.

Forness, S. R., Akiyama, K., & Campana, K. (1984). *Problems in antidepressant medication and classroom performance.* Paper presented at Annual Conference on Severe Behavioral Disorders of Children and Youth. Tempe, Arizona, November.

Forness, S. R., Bennett, L., & Tose, J. (1983). Academic deficits in emotionally disturbed children revisited. *Journal of Child Psychiatry, 22,* 140–144.

Forness, S. R., & Kavale, K. A. (1988). Psychopharmacolgic treatment: A note on classroom effects. *Journal of Learning Disabilities, 21,* 144–147.

Forness, S. R., Kavale, K., Guthrie, D., Scruggs, T., & Mastropieri, M. (1987). Analysis of academic levels and gains in behavior disordered children. *Child Psychiatry and Human Development, 18,* 71–81.

Forness, S. R., Sinclair, E., Alexson, J., Seraydarian, A., & Garza, M. (1985). Towards DRGs in child psychiatry: A preliminary study. *Journal of Child Psychiatry, 24,* 266–272.

Freeman, L. N., Poznanski, E. O., Grossman, J. A., Buchbaum, Y. Y., & Banegas, M. E. (1985). Psychotic and depressed children: A new entity. *Journal of Child Psychiatry, 24,* 95–102.

Gadow, K. D. (1986). *Children on medication. Volume 1: Hyperactivity learning disabilities and mental retardation.* San Diego: College-Hill Press.

Geller, B., Chestnut, E. C., Miller, M. D., Price, D. T., & Yates, E. (1985). Preliminary data on DSM III associated features of major depression disorder in children and adolescents. *American Journal of Psychiatry, 142,* 643–644.

Hamilton, M. (1967). Development of a rating scale for primary depressive illness. *British Journal of Social and Clinical Psychology, 6,* 278–296.

Huntze, S. L. (1985). A position paper of the Council for Children with Behavioral Disorders. *Behavioral Disorders, 10,* 167–174.

Kandel, D. B., & Davies, M. (1982). Epidemiology of depressive mood in adolescents. *Archives of General Psychiatry, 39,* 1205–1212.

Kaplan, S. L., Hong, G. K., & Weinhold, C. (1984). Epidemiology of depressive symptomatology in adolescents. *Journal of Child Psychiatry, 23,* 91–98.

Kashani, J. H. (1986). *Prevalence of depressive disorders in a community sample of adolescents.* Paper presented at the American Academy of Child and Adolescent Psychiatry Meeting, Los Angeles, California.

Kashani, J. H., Cantwell, D. P., Shekim, W. O., & Reid, J. C. (1982). Major depressive disorder in children admitted to an inpatient community mental health center. *American Journal of of Psychiatry, 139,* 671–672.

Kashani, J. H., McGee, R. O., & Clarkson, S. E. (1983). Depression in a sample of 9-year-old children. *Archives of General Psychiatry, 40,* 1217–1223.

Kashani, J. H., & Ray, J. S. (1983). Depressive related symptoms among pre-school-age children. *Child Psychiatry and Human Development, 13,* 233–238.

Kashani, J. H., Ray, J. S., & Carlson, G. A. (1984). Depression and depressive-like states in a child development unit. *American Journal of Psychiatry, 141,* 1397–1402.

Kashani, J. H., Shekim, W. O., & Reid, J. C. (1984). Amitriptyline in children with major depressive disorder: A double-blind crossover pilot study. *Journal of Child Psychiatry, 23,* 348–251.

Kashani, J. H., & Simonds, J. F. (1979). The incidence of depression in children. *American Journal of Psychiatry, 136,* 1203–1205.

Kavale, K. A., Forness, S. R., & Bender, M. (1987). *Handbook of Learning Disabilities* (Vol. 1). San Diego: College Hill Division of Little, Brown.

Kavale, K. A., & Nye, C. (1984). The effectiveness of drug treatment for severe behavior disorders: A meta-analysis. *Behavioral Disorders, 9,* 117–130.

Kazdin, A. E. (1981). Assessment techniques for childhood depression: A critical appraisal. *Journal of Child Psychiatry, 20,* 358–375.

Kazdin, A. E., & Petti, T. A. (1982). Self-report and interview measures of childhood and adolescent depression. *Journal of Child Psychology and Psychiatry, 23,* 437–457.

Kishimoto, A., Ogura, C., Hazama, H., & Inoue, H. (1983). Long-term prophylactic effects of carbamazopine in affective disorder. *British Journal of Psychiatry, 143,* 327–331.

Klee, S. H., & Garfinkel, B. D. (1984). Identification of depression in children and adolescents: The role of the dexamethasone suppression test. *Journal of Child Psychiatry, 23,* 410–415.

Klein, D. F., Gittleman, R., Quitkin, F., & Rifkin, A. (1980). *Diagnosis and drug treatment of psychiatric disorders in adults and children* (Second Edition). Baltimore: Williams & Wilkins.

Kovacs, M., & Beck, A. T. (1977). An empirical-clinical approach toward a definition of child-hood depression. In J. G. Schulterbrandt & A. Raskin (Eds.), *Depression in Childhood: Diagnosis, Treatment, and Conceptual Models*. New York: Raven Press.

Kovacs, M., Feinberg, T. L., Crouse-Novak, M. A., Paulauskas, S. L., Pollack, M., & Finkelstein, R. (1984a). Depressive disorders in childhood. I. A longitudinal prospective study of characteristics and recovery. *Archives of General Psychiatry, 41*, 229–237.

Kovacs, M., Feinberg, T. L., Crouse-Novak, M. A., Paulauskas, S. L., & Finkelstein, R. (1984b). Depressive disorders in childhood. II. A longitudinal study of the risk for a subsequent major depression. *Archives of General Psychiatry, 41*, 643–649.

Lefkowitz, M. M., & Tesiny, E. P. (1980). Assessment of childhood depression. *Journal of Consulting and Clinical Psychology, 48*, 43–50.

Leon, G. R., Kendall, P. C., & Garber, J. (1980). Depression in children: Parent, teacher, and child perspectives. *Journal of Abnormal Child Psychology, 8*(2), 221–235.

Livingston, R. (1985). Depressive illness and learning difficulties: Research needs and practical implications. *Journal of Learning Disabilities, 18*, 518–522.

Lucas, C. J. (1989). *The cognitive functioning of prepubertal children with DSM III diagnosed depressive disorders*. Doctoral Dissertation: UCLA Graduate School of Education.

Mastropieri, M. A., Jenkins, V., & Scruggs, T. (1985). Academic and intellectual characteristics of behaviorally disordered children and youth. *Monographs in Behavioral Disorders, 8*, 86–104.

Mastropieri, M. A., & Scruggs, T. (1986). Early intervention for socially withdrawn children. *Journal of Special Education, 19*, 430–441.

Mastropieri, M. A., Scruggs, T., & Casto, G. (1985). Early intervention for behaviorally disordered children and youth. *Monographs in Behavioral Disorders, 8*, 27–35.

Mattison, R. E., Humphrey, J., Kales, S., Hernit, R., & Finkenbinder, R. (1986). Psychiatric background and diagnosis of children evaluated for special class placement. *Journal of Child Psychiatry, 25*, 514–520.

McCracken, J., Shekim, W., Kashani, J., Beck, M., Martin, J., Rosenberg, J., & Costello, A. (1986). *The epidemiology of childhood depressive disorders*. Paper presented at the American Academy of Child and Adolescent Psychiatry Meeting, Los Angeles, California.

Mullen, J. A., & Wood, F. H. (1986). Teacher and student ratings of the disturbingness of common problem behaviors. *Behavioral Disorders, 11*, 168–176.

Petti, T. A. (1978). Depression in hospitalized child psychiatry patients: Approaches to measuring depression. *Journal of Child Psychiatry, 17*, 49–59.

Petti, T. A., & Conners, K. C. (1983). Changes in behavioral ratings of depressed children treated with imipramine. *Journal of Child Psychiatry, 22*(4), 355–360.

Petti, T. A., & Law, W. (1982). Imipramine treatment of depressed children: A double-blind pilot study. *Journal of Clinical Psychopharmacology, 2*, 107–110.

Poznanski, E. O., Cook, S. C., & Carroll, B. J. (1979). A depression rating scale for children. *Pediatrics, 64*, 442–450.

Poznanski, E. O., Grossman, R. N., & Buchsbaum, Y. (1984). Preliminary studies of the reliability and validity of the Children's Depression Rating Scale. *Journal of Child Psychiatry, 23*, 191–197.

Preskorn, S. H., Weller, E. B., & Weller, R. A. (1982). Depression in children: Relationship between plasma imipramine levels and response. *Journal of Clinical Psychiatry, 43*, 450–453.

Puig-Antich, J. (1980). Affective disorders in childhood. A review and perspective. *Psychiatric Clinical North American, 3*, 403–424.

Puig-Antich, J. (1982a). Editorial. The use of RDC criteria for major depressive disorder in children and adolescents. *The Journal of Child Psychiatry, 21*, 291–293.

Puig-Antich, J. (1982b). Major depression and conduct disorder in prepuberty. *The Journal of Child Psychiatry, 21*, 118–128.

Puig-Antich, J. (1983). Neuroendocrine and sleep correlates of prepubertal major depressive disorder: Current status of the evidence. In D. P. Cantwell & G. A. Carson (Eds.), *Affective disorders in childhood and adolescence: An update.* New York: Spectrum Publications.

Puig-Antich, J., & Chambers, W. (1978). *The Schedule for Affective Disorders and Schizophrenia for School-age Children (Kiddie-SADS).* New York: New York State Psychiatric Institute.

Puig-Antich, J., Lukens, E., Davies, M., Goetz, D., Brennan-Quattrock, J., & Todak, G. (1985a). Controlled studies of psychosocial functioning in prepubertal major depressive disorders. I: Interpersonal relationships during the depressive episode. *Archives of General Psychiatry, 42,* 500–507.

Puig-Antich, J., Lukens, E., Davies, M., Goetz, D., Brennan-Quattrock, J., & Todak, G. (1985b). Psychosocial functioning in prepubertal major depressive disorders. II: Interpersonal relationships after sustained recovery from affective episode. *Archives of General Psychiatry, 42,* 511–517.

Quay, H. C. (1978). Behavior disorders in the classroom. *Journal of Research and Development in Education, 11,* 8–17.

Reynolds, W. M. (1980). *Child Depression Scale.* (Available from William M. Reynolds, Department of Educational Psychology, University of Wisconsin, Madison, Wisconsin 53706.)

Reynolds, W. M. (1981). *Reynolds Adolescent Depression Scale.* (Available from William M. Reynolds, Department of Educational Psychology, University of Wisconsin, Madison, Wisconsin 53706.)

Reynolds, W. M. (1983, March). *Depression in adolescents: Measurement, epidemiology and correlates.* Paper presented at annual meeting of the National Association of School Psychologists, Detroit.

Reynolds, W. M. (1984). Depression in children and adolescents: Phenomenology, evaluation and treatment. *School Psychology Review, 13,* 171–182.

Reynolds, W. M. (1985a). Depression in childhood and adolescence: diagnosis, assessment, intervention strategies and research. *Advances in School Psychology, 4,* 133–189.

Reynolds, W. M. (1985b). *Development and validation of a scale to measure depression in adolescents.* Paper presented at the Annual Meeting Society for Personality Assessment, Berkeley, California.

Reynolds, W. M. (1986). A model for the screening and identification of depressed children and adolescents in school settings. *Professional School Psychology, 1*(2), 117–129.

Reynolds, W. M., Anderson, G., & Bartell, N. (1985). Measuring depression in children: A multimethod assessment investigation. *Journal of Abnormal Child Psychology, 13,* 513–526.

Reynolds, W. M., & Coats, K. I. (1986). A comparison of cognitive-behavioral therapy and relaxation training for the treatment of depression in adolescents. *Journal of Consulting and Clinical Psychology, 54,* 001–008.

Robins, L. N. (1978). Sturdy childhood predictors of adult antisocial behavior: Replications from longitudinal studies. *Psychological Medicine, 8,* 611–622.

Robins, L. N. (1979). Follow-up studies. In H. C. Quay & J. S. Werry (Eds.), *Psychopathological disorders of childhood.* New York: Wiley.

Ryan, N. D., Puig-Antich, J., Ambrosini, P., Rabinovich, H., Robinson, D., Nelson, B., Iyengar, S., & Twomey, J. (1986). *The clinical picture of major depression in children and adolescents.* Paper presented at the American Academy of Child and Adolescent Psychiatry Meeting, Los Angeles, California.

Sacco, W. P., & Graves, D. J. (1984). Childhood depression, interpersonal problem-solving, and self-ratings of performance. *Journal of Clinical Child Psychology, 13,* 10–15.

Scruggs, T. E., & Mastropieri, M. (1986). Academic characteristics of behaviorally disordered and learning disabled students. *Behavioral Disorders, 11,* 184–190.

Sinclair, E., Forness, S. R., & Alexson, J. (1985). Psychiatric diagnosis: A study of its relationship to school needs. *Journal of Special Education, 19,* 334–344.

Smith, C. R., Wood, F., & Grimes, J. (1987). Issues in education of behaviorally disordered students. In M. Wang, M. Reynolds and H. Walberg (Eds.), *Handbook of special education (Volume 2)*. Oxford, England: Pergamon.

Staton, R. D., Wilson, H., & Brumback, R. A. (1981). Cognitive improvement associated with tricyclic antidepressant treatment of childhood major depressive illness. *Perceptual and Motor Skills, 51,* 219–234.

Stevenson, O. T., & Romney, D. M. (1984). Depression in learning disabled children. *Journal of Learning Disabilities, 17,* 579–582.

Strain, P., Cooke, T., & Appolloni, T. (1976). *Teaching exceptional children: Assessing and modifying social behavior.* New York: Academic Press.

Strauss, C. C., Forehand, R., Frame, C., & Smith, D. (1984). Characteristics of children with extreme scores on the Children's Depression Inventory. *Journal of Clinical Child Psychology, 13,* 227–231.

Strober, M., & Carlson, G. (1982). Bipolar illness in adolescents with major depression: Clinical, genetic, and psychopharmacologic predictors in a three- to four-year prospective follow-up investigation. *Archives of General Psychiatry, 39,* 549–555.

Strober, M., Green, J., & Carlson, G. (1981a). Phenomenology and subtypes of major depressive disorder in adolescence. *Journal of Affective Disorders, 3,* 281–290.

Strober, M., Green, J., & Carlson, G. (1981b). Reliability of psychiatric diagnosis in hospitalized adolescents. *Archives of General Psychiatry, 38,* 141–145.

Tallmadge, C. K., Gamel, M. N., Munson, R. G., & Hanley, T. (1985). *Special Study on Terminology.* (Report submitted under contract No. 300-84-0144 to U.S. Department of Education). Mountainview, CA: SRA Technologies.

Targum, S. D., & Capodanno, A. (1983). The dexamethasone suppression test in adolescent psychiatric inpatients. *American Journal of Psychiatry, 140,* 589–591.

Thompson, R. J. (1986). Behavior problems in children with developmental and learning disabilities. *International Academy of Research in Learning Disabilities Monograph Series, 3,* 1–125.

Walker, H. M., Severson, H., & Haring, G. (1986). *Standardized screening and identification of behavior disordered pupils in the elementary age range: Rationale, procedures and guidelines.* Eugene: Oregon Research Institute.

Weissman, M. M., Orvaschel, H., & Padian, N. (1980). Children's symptom and social functioning self-report scales: Comparison of mother's and children's reports. *Journal of Nervous and Mental Disease, 168,* 736–740.

Weissman, M. M., Prusoff, B. A., & Gammon, G. D. (1984). Psychopathology in the children (ages 6–18) of depressed and normal parents. *Journal of Child Psychiatry, 23,* 78–84.

21

Children with Learning Disabilities: The Role of Achievement in Their Social, Personal, and Behavioral Functioning

Annette M. La Greca
University of Miami

Wendy L. Stone
Vanderbilt University School of Medicine

In recent years, much attention has been devoted to the study of interpersonal skills among youngsters with learning disabilities. Beginning with seminal studies by Bryan in the 70s (Bryan, 1974, 1976), many students with learning disabilities were found to encounter difficulties in their peer relationships (see reviews by La Greca, 1981, 1987; Wiener, 1987). Concerns about these youngsters' social relationships led to the development of intervention programs to teach learning disabled (LD) students more effective interpersonal skills, in order to improve their peer relations (La Greca & Mesibov, 1979, 1981; Madden & Slavin, 1983; Schumaker & Hazel, 1984; Vaughn, Lancelotta, & Minnis, 1988). While such intervention programs appear to be important and helpful, a closer examination of the research on the peer relations of learning disabled students may be critical to furthering our understanding of the types of peer problems LD students encounter and to improving our intervention strategies. Consequently, one goal of this chapter is to describe recent research on the types of peer status difficulties that affect children with learning disabilities.

Aside from social concerns, a greater prevalence of personal and behavioral adjustment difficulties also have been observed among children with identified learning disabilities relative to their nondisabled (NLD) peers. In particular, researchers have found LD students to display lower self-esteem (Rogers & Saklofske, 1985) and more internalizing and externalizing behavior problems (McConaughy, 1986; McConaughy & Ritter, 1986) than normal comparison groups. In this chapter, we briefly review recent literature on these commonly reported personal and behavioral difficulties among LD children.

Throughout our review, we highlight several conceptual issues and methodological concerns that have affected our understanding of LD students, and suggest avenues for further research. In particular, we discuss the tendency of investigators to confound LD status and academic achievement, and raise the issue of whether the social, personal, and behavioral difficulties that are reportedly so common among LD students can be primarily explained by the low academic achievement that is the hallmark of this group.

STUDIES OF SOCIAL STATUS AMONG CHILDREN WITH LEARNING DISABILITIES

Numerous studies have found children with learning disabilities to experience social difficulties with peers. Using different definitions of learning disabilities and diverse methodologies for assessing social status, LD children in mainstreamed classrooms consistently have been found to be less accepted and more rejected than their NLD peers (Bruininks, 1978; Bryan, 1974, 1976; Garrett & Crump, 1980; Gresham & Reschly, 1986; Horowitz, 1981; Hutton & Polo, 1976; Perlmutter, Crocker, Cordray, & Garstecki, 1983; Scranton & Ryckman, 1979; Siperstein, Bopp, & Bak, 1978; Siperstein & Goding, 1983). Especially noteworthy was Bryan's (1976) study of LD children's peer acceptance over a 12-month period. Over this period, the composition of the children's peer group changed substantially, yet the LD youngsters retained their poor social status. Although a handful of studies have failed to detect social status difficulties in LD students as compared to their NLD classmates (e.g., Bursuck, 1983; Prillaman, 1981; Sabornie & Kauffman, 1986), none have found students with learning disabilities to have higher social status.

Although it appears that children with learning disabilities are at risk for developing peer relationship problems, not all LD students are rejected or less accepted by their peers. In fact, some LD students have been found to be among those who are well liked (e.g., Perlmutter et al., 1983; Siperstein et al., 1978; Stone & La Greca, in press). What we do not clearly understand are the reasons for the low peer status that some LD children encounter. What factors contribute to the development of low peer status experienced by some, but not all, students with learning disabilities? What are the strengths and skills displayed by LD youngsters with positive and successful peer interactions? And, how can we use this information to design effective interventions for children who encounter difficulties with peers?

Investigators have begun to address some of these important questions. However, at least two major issues that have been neglected in research on children's social competence may have confused and confounded findings in this area. These issues pertain to the *types* of peer relationship problems LD children experience, and to the presence of gender differences in LD youngsters' peer status. These two issues are discussed at length here.

Types of Peer Status Problems Encountered by LD Students

In order to appreciate and conceptualize the factors that contribute to LD children's difficulties with peers, we first must gain a clearer understanding of the *types* of social status problems LD children encounter. Does the lower peer status of LD students reflect disproportionate numbers of youngsters who are actively rejected by their peers, or are such students more typically neglected and ignored by their peer group? Surprisingly little attention has been devoted to this issue, despite the fact that developmental research has documented the importance of distinguishing between youngsters who are rejected and those who are neglected by their peers (e.g., Coie & Dodge, 1988; Coie, Dodge, & Coppotelli, 1982; Dodge, Coie & Brakke, 1982). Rejected and neglected children differ markedly in their patterns of social interactions with peers and, consequently, may require very different social intervention strategies.

Rejected children, for example, have been described by peers as highly disruptive, aggressive, and less cooperative; their classroom behavior has been observed to be more off-task and disruptive compared with their more well-accepted classmates (Coie et al., 1982). In general, accumulating evidence on the correlates of peer rejection in children suggests that these youngsters are the ones who are at most risk for negative future outcomes (Coie, 1985). Social intervention strategies with rejected children appear to be most effective when prohibitions for negative behaviors are instituted concurrently with efforts to promote more positive peer interactions (Bierman, Miller, & Stabb, 1987).

In contrast, children who are neglected or ignored by peers have been described by others as shy and withdrawn, and not offensive (Coie et al., 1982). Neglected children also report more social anxiety than their peers, especially social avoidance, distress, and discomfort during peer interactions (La Greca, Dandes, Wick, Shaw, & Stone, 1988; La Greca & Stone, 1988). However, at this point, it is not clear whether neglected children are at risk for later adjustment problems (Rubin, 1985). Some studies have suggested that neglected children are likely to improve their peer status spontaneously over time (Coie & Dodge, 1983), so that this peer status problem may not be as devastating or pervasive as active peer rejection.

In a recent review of the peer status literature for LD children and adolescents, Wiener (1987) noted that existing research has not determined whether the negative peer ratings common to LD groups predominantly reflect an isolated or rejected peer status. To address this issue, we examined the sociometric classifications of LD youngsters in the 4th through 6th grades (Stone & La Greca, in press).

The LD group consisted of 38 boys and 19 girls who were attending regular classrooms for their academic instruction, but who also received up to 12 hours per week of LD resource help for one or more academic subjects. The comparison sample included 490 NLD students (233 boys, 257 girls) who were classmates of the LD youngsters, and who did not display any educational exceptionalities (e.g., gifted, speech delayed).

All children were administered a series of measures that included same-sex peer ratings of acceptance and positive nominations (see Stone & La Greca, in press, for details). Using the procedure described by Asher and Dodge (1986), 72% of the LD and 65% of the NLD youngsters were classified into one of the following groups: popular, rejected, neglected, average, and controversial. This latter group includes children who receive many positive and negative nominations from peers; that is, peers' reactions to them are very mixed.

When the sociometric classifications were compared, significant differences were evident between those in the LD and NLD groups (see Fig. 21.1). In particular, LD students were overrepresented in *both* the rejected and neglected groups, and underrepresented in the popular and average groups. In fact, nearly 75% of the LD children who could be classified were assigned to one of the low peer status groups.

Overall, this data indicated that low status LD students may fall into either the rejected or neglected groups, and are not characterized by one type of peer relationship problem. Given the different implications of these two peer status categories for children's social functioning and later emotional adjustment, further attention to these subgroups of LD children is essential.

Until now, studies of LD children's interpersonal skills and social behavior have not systematically differentiated between rejected and neglected youngsters. In fact, most studies have not even attempted to link LD children's interpersonal skills to their level of peer acceptance or rejection (see Vaughn & La Greca, 1988, and Vaughn & Hogan, this volume, for reviews). Our finding that both neglected and rejected subgroups likely exist within the LD population means that very different types of social status problems have been combined and

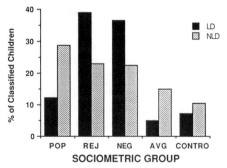

FIG. 21.1. Peer status in LD versus NLD students.

confused in our existing research base on LD children. Given that the correlates of peer rejection and social neglect are so markedly different for nondisabled populations, it is imperative that we also distinguish these subgroups in future investigations of interpersonal skills and social behavior among LD students. Failure to do so will limit our understanding of the processes that underlie LD students' peer relationship difficulties, and undermine efforts to design effective social intervention programs.

Social Status of LD Girls

Another issue that has arisen in the context of understanding the peer relations of LD students is the social status of LD girls. LD girls fare more poorly socially than LD boys (Bryan, 1974; Hutton & Polo, 1976; Scranton & Ryckman, 1979). Although gender differences in social status have not been obtained uniformly, when differences have been reported, they have consistently indicated greater peer relationship problems for LD girls. No studies have found LD girls to be more socially adept with peers than LD boys or NLD girls. At the present time, however, information is lacking on the types of social status problems LD girls encounter.

In the previously described study of peer status among LD and NLD students (Stone & La Greca, in press), we additionally examined sociometric patterns separately for boys and girls, to determine whether the same pattern was evident for children of each sex. (Given the very small numbers of LD children in the average ($n = 2$) and controversial ($n = 3$) groups, these two categories were collapsed and labeled "other" in these later analyses.) As can be seen from the data in Fig. 21.2, the sociometric patterns were fairly comparable for LD boys and girls, except that the LD girls appeared to be even more disproportionately represented in the rejected sociometric group than either the LD boys or the NLD students. In fact, nearly half (47%) of the LD girls who could be classified were rejected by their peers, as compared with only 22% of the classified NLD girls.

These findings are consistent with previous reports of greater peer relationship difficulties for girls with learning disabilities, and underscore two very important issues. The first is that we need to systematically investigate gender differences in the *factors that contribute to the social status* of boys and girls with learning disabilities. It is quite likely that different factors underlie the low peer status of LD girls and boys. Hops (1988), for example, found that elementary school girls' perceptions of their peers as preferred playmates were more strongly related to their academic achievement and classroom behavior than was the case for boys. To the extent that achievement plays a bigger role in determining girls' peer status, LD girls will be at greater risk than LD boys for peer relationship difficulties.

The second issue of concern pertains to the high degree of peer rejection found among the LD girls. These findings are alarming, given the stability of

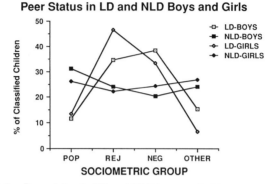

FIG. 21.2.   Peer status in LD and NLD boys and girls.

peer rejection over time, and the negative adjustment outcomes associated with this peer status. Peer rejection among LD girls is a problem that may require intensive social intervention efforts.

Currently, little is known about the social and behavioral characteristics of girls with learning disabilities. Undoubtedly, the relatively low number of girls who are identified as having learning disabilities represents a major obstacle to research in this area. The infrequency of learning disabilities among girls also may contribute to the peer relation problems that LD girls encounter, as these girls may appear more obvious and different to their classmates. Additional efforts to understand the parameters that affect peer status among LD girls will be essential. Collaborative research that brings together the resources of several school districts or multiple investigators may be needed to establish an adequate data base for understanding the social difficulties encountered by many girls with learning disabilities.

SELF PERCEPTIONS OF CHILDREN WITH LEARNING DISABILITIES

Our second major area of investigation concerns the self-perceptions of children with learning disabilities. Evidence suggests that children with learning disabilities have more negative self-concepts than their nondisabled classmates (e.g., Bruininks, 1978; Bryan & Pearl, 1979; Hoyle & Serafica, 1987; Rogers & Saklofske, 1985; Sheare, 1978), although a few studies have not found LD students to differ from NLD youngsters in this regard (e.g., Silverman & Zigmond, 1983).

The advent of self-concept measures that assess domain-specific areas of self-perceptions (e.g., Harter, 1982, 1985) has enabled us to obtain a more precise understanding of the areas in which LD youngsters display negative self-perceptions. In particular, recent findings have noted that LD youngsters perceive their social, academic, and/or general self-esteem to be lower than nondisabled comparison youth (Gregory, Shanahan, & Walberg, 1985; Hoyle & Serafica, 1987; Morrison, 1985; Rogers & Saklofske, 1985; Sobol, Earn, Bennett, & Humphries, 1983). Given that children with learning disabilities, by definition, display problems with academic achievement, their lowered self-concepts in this domain are not surprising. Most likely, LD students' academic self-concepts accurately reflect their appraisal of their achievement skills. In support of this position, Renick (1985) found that mainstreamed LD students reported lower cognitive competence in the regular classroom as compared with an LD classroom.

The lower general self-esteem often noted among LD students also may be related to their poor academic achievement. Renick (1985) examined the factor structure of the Perceived Competence Scale for Children (Harter, 1982) for LD children, and found that items reflecting cognitive competence *and* general self-worth both loaded on the same factor. This was not the case for normal achieving students. Based on this distinction, Renick suggested that LD students perceive their personal worth as being closely tied to their perceptions of academic competence in the regular classroom.

Of particular relevance to the present review are LD students' social self-concepts. A parallel may exist between LD children's poor social self-perceptions and their generally lower peer status (as reviewed in the previous chapter section). Many LD youngsters are aware of peers' impressions of them. In fact, the findings of Garrett and Crump (1980) suggested that LD youngsters were more accurate than their NLD peers in estimating their social acceptance, which was significantly lower for the LD students. However, the question remains as to whether LD children's poor social self-esteem is related to their low peer acceptance or can be explained by other factors associated with their LD status.

To address this question in part, Sobol and colleagues (Sobol et al., 1983) examined LD youngsters perceptions of their peer self-esteem, as part of a larger investigation of the social attributions of children with learning disabilities. Three groups of youngsters, ranging in age from approximately 7 to 13 years, were compared on: attributions for success and failure in a variety of social situations, expectations for social success, and peer-related self-esteem. The groups consisted of: youngsters with learning disabilities (LD); a group of non-disabled youngsters who were matched to the LD students with respect to their age, sex, and low levels of social acceptance (LA); and nondisabled youngsters, matched to the LD group on age and sex, but who received high social acceptance ratings (HA). None of the LA and HA students had been identified as having learning problems; however, achievement levels were not reported for these two groups.

Sobol et al., found that children in the LD group used luck more frequently as an explanation for social outcomes and personality interaction less, than did those in the LA or HA groups. The LD students also had the lowest expectations for social success. In contrast, both LD and LA youngsters reported a poorer social self-image than HA youngsters. These findings are intriguing, in that they suggest that the low peer-related self-esteem of LD youth may be related to their low social status, rather than to their LD status per se; the LD students did not differ from the LA children on the measure of peer self-esteem.

On the other hand, the LD children reported more dysfunctional social attributions and lower expectations for social success than the LA and HA youngsters. Given these attributions, LD children may be more susceptible to perceiving their social world and peer relationships as beyond their control. Such negative social expectations might further undermine LD students' efforts to improve their social standing with peers.

In summary, data from the Sobol et al., (1983) study suggest that LD children's low social self-esteem is related, at least in part, to their low peer status, but that other dysfunctional social perceptions may be a function of their LD status or other correlates of learning disabilities. Of interest to consider further, is whether or not LD students' generally negative social perceptions might interfere with their peer relations and motivation to participate in peer activities. Additional research assessing LD children's social perceptions in conjunction with their actual social behavior would be helpful to evaluate this premise. In this manner, the implications of LD students' negative social perceptions could be better ascertained.

BEHAVIORAL FUNCTIONING OF LD YOUTH

In addition to concerns regarding peer relations and self-perceptions, LD students have been noted to exhibit more behavior problems than normal achieving youngsters. Both parent and teacher reports on standardized behavior checklists reveal LD children to have more behavior problems than nondisabled children, although the specific patterns of behavioral dysfunction are less clear.

For instance, a series of recent studies (McConaughy, 1986; McConaughy & Ritter, 1986) found that parents of LD boys reported significantly more behavior problems in their sons, on the Child Behavior Checklist, than parents in normative samples. Across these two studies, the LD boys (aged 6 through 16 years) were rated as having more "externalizing" and "internalizing" types of behavior problems than nondisabled youth; no specific pattern of behavioral difficulties distinguished the LD boys from those in the normal comparison group. Compared to a sample of "clinically-referred" boys, LD boys (aged 6 to 11 years) were more likely to display a hyperactive profile pattern (McConaughy & Ritter, 1986), but other profile differences were observed for the 12 to 16 year old LD students (McConaughy, 1986). These results suggest that LD youth experience a wide variety of behavioral problems, in addition to their academic difficulties.

When teachers' ratings of behavior problems are considered, some studies find learning disabled students to display more anxiety-withdrawal (Cullinan & Epstein, 1985; Cullinan, Epstein, & Dembinski, 1979; Cullinan, Epstein, & Lloyd, 1981; Stone & La Greca, 1984) than nondisabled youth. Other investigators have found evidence for more externalizing types of behavior problems, such as acting-out behavior and distractibility (Bender, 1985). At this point, the most parsimonious interpretation of the data is that LD youth display more behavior problems than nondisabled youth, although there does not appear to be a specific behavioral pattern associated with learning disability status.

One issue that may have muddled the research on the behavioral concomitants of learning disabilities is the substantial overlap between children who are identified as learning disabled and those who display attention deficits with hyperactivity (ADHD). Lambert and Sandoval (1980), for example, found that approximately 40% of the ADHD children in a large elementary school sample also met stringent criteria for the presence of a learning disability.

This diagnostic overlap between learning disabilities and attention deficits is a point of concern for the study of behavioral functioning in LD students, as youngsters with ADHD also have been found to exhibit more behavior problems than normal comparison youth. In this regard, Flicek and Landau (1985) found that boys who were *both* hyperactive and learning disabled were rated as more aggressive than (nonhyperactive) LD boys or normal controls; these latter two groups did not differ in behavioral functioning. Findings such as these raise the question of whether or not some of the behavior problems attributed to LD students may, in fact, be predominantly characteristic of the subgroup of LD students who are also hyperactive.

Given the tremendous heterogeneity of youngsters with learning disabilities, future investigations of the behavioral concomitants of this condition must begin to examine relevant subgroups within the LD population. Some of the work by McKinney and associates (e.g., Speece, McKinney, & Applebaum, 1985) has begun to address this question of behavioral subgroups. Certainly, identifying and evaluating the behavioral characteristics of LD/ADHD subgroups, in particular, may serve to further our understanding of behavioral difficulties displayed by LD children.

Another major issue that has been neglected in this research area is the contribution of youngsters' achievement level to their behavioral adjustment. It is quite possible that LD children's behavior problems are a function of their poor academic achievement. A discussion of this issue follows.

ROLE OF ACHIEVEMENT IN THE SOCIAL-BEHAVIORAL FUNCTIONING OF STUDENTS WITH LEARNING DISABILITIES

Up to this point, we have reviewed investigations of children's social, personal, and behavioral functioning that differentiate LD students from their NLD peers.

The predominant research strategy has been to compare LD students to class-mates who have not been identified as having learning problems. However, these classmates differ from LD students in myriad ways including, but certainly not limited to: the way they are perceived by teachers and peers; the amount of time they spend in a normal classroom; their degree of on-task classroom behavior; and their level of academic achievement. Consequently, multiple factors, that might contribute to differences in LD and NLD youngsters' social and behavioral functioning, are confounded or masked by this group comparison strategy.

Perhaps the most serious problem with this research approach has been the confounding of LD status and academic achievement. The one unifying charac-teristic of children with learning disabilities, which clearly differentiates these children from their classmates, is their relatively poor academic achievement. Yet, LD children typically are compared to youngsters who differ in academic achievement, as well as LD identification. This confound is especially troubling in that, as we describe later, academic achievement is a significant correlate of social and emotional functioning among elementary school students! We must ask ourselves whether we are really studying LD/NLD differences, or actually investigating the correlates of low academic achievement.

As we have emphasized (La Greca, Stone & Halpern, 1988), to avoid this problem youngsters' achievement levels must be evaluated and controlled for, if we are to begin to understand the factors (other than, or in addition to, academic skills) that put LD children at risk for social, personal, and behavioral adjustment problems. For example, academic achievement has been demonstrated to be a significant correlate of children's peer acceptance (Dodge et al., 1982; Gottman, Gonso, & Rasmussen, 1975; Green, Forehand, Beck, & Vosk, 1980). Despite this, the overwhelming majority of investigations of children's social functioning have neglected to control for achievement differences between LD students and their NLD classmates. To date, only one study could be found that compared the peer acceptance ratings and friendship nominations of LD boys to those of NLD boys who were matched on reading achievement (Bursuck, 1983). The LD and NLD boys in the Bursuck study did not differ on the peer rating measures, suggesting that low achievement, rather than LD status per se, may determine a child's peer status. However, the very small sample size (12 LD boys), and the fact that additional groups of average and high achievers also were found to perform comparably to the LD students and the low achievers on the peer measures, limit the conclusions that can be drawn from these findings. This leaves the question open as to whether or not the low achievement that typifies LD students can account for their problems with peer acceptance.

Similarly, children with poor academic achievement have been found to have lower self-concepts and more behavior problems, especially attention problems (see Campbell & Werry, 1986; Ledingham & Schwartzman, 1984; Quay & Peterson, 1987). Thus, poor achievement might also account for the personal and behavioral difficulties observed among LD students. Additional research is necessary to rule in or rule out academic achievement as a primary explanation for LD students' difficulties.

DESCRIPTION OF THE PRESENT STUDY

Given these concerns regarding the role of achievement in the adjustment difficulties that often characterize children with learning disabilities, we compared LD children to their classmates, using an NLD group with a restricted range of academic achievement (La Greca et al., 1988). Specifically, the goals of the study were: (1) to determine whether LD/NLD differences in social functioning, as indexed by peer and self report, were largely accounted for by achievement differences between the groups, and (2) to examine whether LD/NLD differences in self-esteem and behavioral functioning were primarily a function of group differences in achievement.

Subjects

The sample consisted of 57 mainstreamed LD students (38 male, 19 female) from the 4th through 6th grades. All LD students evidenced at least normal intellectual functioning, as assessed by WISC-R Full Scale IQ scores of 80 or higher.

NLD students who did not evidence any educational exceptionality were considered for participation. Only classmates of LD children whose average reading and math achievement scores, on the Stanford Achievement Test, were in the same range as for the LD students were included. The NLD group consisted of 181 boys and 187 girls.

Measures

Peer Ratings and Peer Nominations.   Two widely used sociometric measures were employed. The first consisted of a *peer rating scale,* on which children indicated how much they would like to "play with" each of their classmates (Oden & Asher, 1977; Singleton & Asher, 1977). Each same-sex classmate was rated on a 5-point scale. An average score was computed for each child, and these scores were then standardized by sex within each classroom, so that cross-class comparisons could be made.

Standardized liking scores were obtained by administering a positive nomination measure. Children circled the names of the three classmates they liked most (Coie et al., 1982). *Standardized disliking* scores were obtained using the procedure recommended by Asher and Dodge (1986). The ratings of "1" (do not like at all) on the peer rating scale were tabulated for each child, and used to index peer rejection. Both scores were standardized by sex within each classroom.

Self Perception Profile for Children.   The Self Perception Profile for Children (Harter, 1985) assesses children's self-perceptions in the following areas: athletic competence, scholastic competence, physical appearance, behavioral conduct, social acceptance, and global self-worth. For the present study, only the *social acceptance* and *global self-worth* scales were used.

Revised Behavior Problem Checklist (RBPC).   A modified form of the RBPC (Quay & Peterson, 1987) was completed by classroom teachers on each student. The RBPC contains 89 problem behaviors; children are rated by teachers on these items on a scale ranging from "0" (not at all present) to "2" (often). Four major subscale scores can be derived: conduct problems, anxiety-withdrawal, attention-problems, and socialized aggression.

Only the scores from the *conduct disorder, attention problems,* and *anxiety-withdrawal* subscales were of interest in the present study. Given the difficulty of having teachers complete the full RBPC on all students in their class, a shortened form of the instrument was used (see La Greca & Stone, 1988). Teacher ratings were standardized within each classroom, so that cross-class comparisons could be made.

Comparison of LD and NLD Students

LD and NLD students were compared on the peer, self, and teacher ratings. The group means for these measures appear in Table 21.1.

Analyses revealed that the LD children were (a) rated less positively by peers, (b) accepted less by peers, and (c) rejected more. With respect to self-ratings, LD children perceived themselves as lower in social acceptance and global self-worth. Teacher ratings indicated that the LD and NLD children did not differ with respect to ratings of conduct problems; however, the LD students were rated as having more attention problems and more anxious-withdrawn behavior.

Given the importance of considering gender issues in social and behavioral functioning, and the disproportionate numbers of girls and boys in the LD versus the NLD group, LD/NLD comparisons were repeated separately for boys and girls. Table 21.2 contains the means for the dependent measures, broken down by LD status and gender.

In general, the findings for boys and girls paralleled those for the total sample. Boys and girls in the LD groups received lower peer ratings of acceptance, and fewer positive nomination from peers than their same-sex NLD counterparts. The self-perceptions of LD boys and girls were more negative than those of NLD students. Finally, teacher ratings indicated higher levels of attention problems and anxiety-withdrawal for LD boys and girls, as compared with their NLD classmates.

Therefore, even when attempts are made to restrict the NLD sample to students whose achievement is within the same range as that for the LD students, the NLD group appears more competent on a variety of social and behavioral

Table 21.1
Peer, Self and Teacher Ratings for LD and NLD Students

	LD	NLD
Peer Ratings[a]		
Peer Rating Scale	-.50	.00***
Standardized Liking	-.53	.06***
Standardized Disliking	.27	.00*
Self Ratings		
Social Acceptance	2.71	3.00**
Global Self Worth	2.83	3.20**
Teacher Ratings[a]		
Conduct Disorder	.21	.07
Attention Problems	.74	.09***
Anxiety Withdrawal	.55	.01***

*Raw scores for these measures have been converted to standard scores with a mean = 0, and standard deviation = 1. Asterisks indicate LD/NLD differences. $*p < .05$, $**p < .01$, $***p < .001$.

measures. These group differences appear to be relevant for boys as well as for girls.

Role of Achievement

To further explore the role of achievement in the social, personal, and behavioral functioning of LD students, the LD and NLD groups were divided according to achievement levels. Two subgroups were formed: those who were low achievers (average scores in reading and math below the 40th percentile) and average achievers (average scores in reading and math between the 40th and 70th percen-

TABLE 21.2
Peer, Self, and Teacher Ratings for LD and NLD Students by Gender

	Boys		Girls	
Measure	LD	NLD	LD	NLD
Peer Ratings[a]				
Peer Rating Scale	-.38	.01*	-.73	.00***
Standardized Liking	-.44	.06*	-.69	.06***
Standardized Disliking	.22	-.01	.35	.02*
Self Ratings				
Social Acceptance	2.68	3.03**	2.77	2.98
Global Self Worth	2.91	3.24**	2.68	3.15***
Teacher Ratings[a]				
Conduct Disorder	.48	.40	-.33	-.25
Attention Problems	1.02	.39***	.18	-.20*
Anxiety Withdrawal	.35	-.05*	.94	.02***

*Scores for those variables have been converted to standard scores, with a mean of 0 and a standard deviation of 1.
Note: Asterisks indicate LD/NLD differences.
$*p < .05$, $**p < .01$, $***p < .001$.

tiles). Two factor (LD Status X Achievement Level) analysis of variance procedures were used to evaluate these subgroups.

With respect to two of the three peer ratings, significant effects for LD Status, but not for Achievement Level, were obtained. (See Table 21.3.) On the peer ratings of acceptance and standardized liking scores, LD students fared more poorly than the NLD children. However, the low achieving LD and NLD students did not differ from their average achieving counterparts. Similarly, a main effect for LD status revealed that LD students (accurately) perceived their social acceptance to be lower than their NLD peers; perceptions of social acceptance were not related to achievement levels.

When the youngsters' global perceptions of self-worth were examined, there was a main effect for LD Status, and a significant LD Status by Achievement interaction. The LD students perceived themselves as lower in self-worth than the NLD students, and this effect was most pronounced for the *average* achievers. More specifically, the *average* achieving LD students perceived themselves more negatively than any other group.

For the teacher ratings of attention problems, main effects for LD status and for Achievement were obtained. *Both* the LD students and the low achievers displayed greater evidence of attention problems. In fact, the low achieving NLD students were rated on a par with low and average achieving LD students. In contrast, teacher ratings of anxiety-withdrawal revealed a main effect for Achievement, and an LD Status by Achievement interaction. Low achievers, *but not LD students per se,* were reported to have higher levels of anxious-withdrawn behavior. In addition, the magnitude of the difference between the low and high achieving groups was greater for the LD versus the NLD students. Teachers' ratings of conduct disorder did not reveal LD status or achievement effects.

TABLE 21.3
Peer, Self, and Teacher Ratings for LD and NLD Students with Low and Average Academic Achievement

Measure	LD		NLD	
	Low	Average	Low	Average
Peer Ratings[a]				
Peer Rating Scale	-.53	-.52	-.20	.02
Standardized Liking	-.49	-.50	-.27	.08
Standardized Disliking	.31	.29	.13	.00
Self Ratings				
General Acceptance	2.75	2.65	2.82	3.02
Global Self Worth	2.98	2.63	3.08	3.20
Teacher Ratings[a]				
Conduct Disorder	.17	.25	.24	.06
Attention Problems	.82	.69	.66	.05
Anxiety Withdrawal	.76	-.12	.26	-.03

[a]Scores for these variables have been converted to standrad scores, with a mean of 0 and a standard deviation of 1.

General Discussion

What can we conclude from this data? Basically, that the poor social status of children with learning disabilities does not appear to be merely a function of their lower academic achievement. The average achieving LD students fared as poorly as the low achieving LD students, and both LD subgroups were rated more negatively by peers than the low achieving NLD students. Although poor academic achievement undoubtedly contributes to the social problems of LD youngsters, achievement alone cannot account for their lower social status.

Furthermore, the data on children's perceptions of their social acceptance parallel the findings from the peer ratings. They too suggest that LD youngsters' perceptions of poor social acceptance are not merely a function of their lower achievement. Rather, these perceptions most likely reflect the poor social status of these children.

A different picture emerged for children's perceptions of their global self-worth. Although children with learning disabilities fared more poorly than their NLD peers in this area, the most deviant subgroup was the average achieving LD students, who reported *lower* levels of global self-worth than even the low achieving LD students. This latter group did not differ from low achieving NLD students. These findings are intriguing, as they suggest that the brighter and better achieving LD students may be more prone to feeling negatively about themselves. Perhaps these children are more aware of their "deficits" relative to their NLD peers, and consequently internalize some of these differences. Further research of this issue would be desirable.

Teacher ratings of children's behavior problems were of interest, in that they suggested that the frequently reported findings of greater attention problems in LD students, as compared to their nondisabled classmates, may be related both to their LD status and poor achievement. Attention problems were evident both for the LD children (low and average achievers), and low achievers who were in the NLD group. Thus, behaviors that LD students and low achievers share in common, relative to average achieving NLD students, are a higher degree of distractibility and lower levels of attention in the classroom. These teacher ratings are consistent with behavioral observations that highlight the greater off-task behavior and distractibility of LD students in classroom settings (McKinney & Feagans, 1984).

In contrast with the findings for attention problems, anxious-withdrawn behavior appeared to be more characteristic of the low achieving students in this sample, rather than LD students, per se. Average achieving LD and NLD students were not reported to have difficulty with anxious withdrawn behavior.

SUMMARY AND CONCLUSIONS

This chapter had provided an overview to the current status of research on the peer relations, self-esteem, and behavioral functioning of students with learning disabilities. In each area, research suggests that youngsters with learning disabilities fare more poorly than their nondisabled peers. However, very little attention has been paid to the role of low achievement as a factor that contributes to these LD/NLD differences.

With respect to peer relations, the findings presented indicated that LD boys and girls receive lower peer ratings than NLD children with comparable achievement levels. Thus, *poor academic achievement alone* does not appear to be an adequate explanation of the peer relationship problems that characterize many LD students. On the other hand, it is not clear what factors do underlie these LD/NLD differences. Although research on the social perceptions and interpersonal skills of LD students, for example, may help to explain their low peer status, serious methodological and conceptual problems limit the conclusions that can be drawn from this data. In particular, existing research on the correlates of LD children's low peer acceptance has failed to differentiate youngsters who are rejected and those who are neglected by peers. As we have highlighted in this paper, significant proportions of LD students are either neglected or rejected, and there is very good reason to believe that the correlates of these two peer status problems are quite different. Until researchers begin examining these subgroups of LD students, our progress in understanding and remediating peer relationship problems in LD students will be severely compromised. Furthermore, the peer status of LD girls appears to warrant special attention, as the factors that contribute to the peer status of LD boys and girls may be very different.

The review of studies on self-esteem, and the data presented herein, both suggest that LD students' perceptions of poor social status likely are a function of their low peer status, rather than their academic achievement. With respect to global self-esteem, however, the picture is less clear. Overall, the LD students reported lower self-esteem than their low- to average-achieving NLD classmates. Yet, within the LD group, those with higher achievement reported lower overall self-worth. Although the reason for this pattern is not clear, it is possible that the average achieving LD students were more acutely aware of their social and academic deficiencies than the other LD students, and therefore were more likely to evaluate themselves negatively. Further research that looks *within* the LD population, to examine factors contributing to self-esteem, would help to elucidate this issue.

Finally, the literature on behavioral dysfunction of LD students suggested that no one behavior pattern can be linked to LD status, although the incidence of behavior problems typically has been found to be higher in LD versus NLD groups. The failure of previous studies to account for LD/Hyperactive subgroups, or to consider achievement differences between LD and NLD students, was noted. These issues were further highlighted by the data presented near the end of the chapter. When NLD children with low to average achievement levels were compared with LD students, attention problems were found to be elevated in both the LD and low achieving NLD groups. Given the high rate of attention problems among the LD students, the behavioral subgroup of LD/Hyperactive students appears to be an important one for future investigation. Moreover, efforts to distinguish low and average achievers in the LD and NLD groups, revealed that anxiety-withdrawal may not be specific to LD youngsters, and may be more related to children's academic achievement than to their LD status per se.

In conclusion, academic achievement appears to be a critical variable to examine in future research on the social, personal, and behavioral functioning of LD students. Research efforts that consider the mediating effects of academic achievement, and that examine relevant subgroups within the LD population, will be essential to the advancement of the field.

ACKNOWLEDGMENTS

The preparation of this paper was supported in part by the Dade County Public Schools through the University of Miami, Florida Diagnostic Learning and Resources System. Special thanks are extended to Dr. Eleanor Levine, and to the principals and teachers of the following elementary schools: Blue Lakes, David Fairchild, Kendall Lakes, and the West Laboratory School.

REFERENCES

Asher, S., & Dodge, K. (1986). Identifying children who are rejected by their peers. *Developmental Psychology, 22*, 444–449.

Bender, W. N. (1985). Differences between learning disabled and nonlearning disabled children in temperament and behavior. *Learning Disabled Quarterly, 8*, 11–18.

Bierman, K. L., Miller, C. L., & Stabb, S. D. (1987). Improving the social training with instructions and prohibitions. *Journal of Consulting and Clinical Psychology, 55*, 194–200.

Bruininks, V. (1978). Peer status and personality characteristics of LD and nondisabled students. *Journal of Learning Disabilities 11*, 29–34.

Bryan, T. (1974). Peer popularity of LD children. *Journal of Learning Disabilities, 7*, 31–35.

Bryan, T. (1976). Peer popularity of LD children: A replication. *Journal of Learning Disabilities, 9*, 307–311.

Bryan, T., & Pearl, R. (1979). Self-concepts and locus of control of learning disabled children. *Journal of Clinical Child Psychology, 8*, 223–226.

Bursuck, W. (1983). Sociometric status, behavior ratings, and social knowledge of LD and low achieving students. *Learning Disability Quarterly, 6*, 329–338.

Campbell, S. B., & Werry, J. S. (1986). Attention Deficit Disorder (Hyperactivity). In H. C. Quay & J. S. Werry (Eds.), *Psychopathological disorders of children* (pp. 111–155). New York: Wiley.

Coie, J. D. (1985). Fitting social skills intervention to the target group. In B. H. Schneider, K. H. Rubin, & J. E. Ledingham (Eds.), *Children's peer relations: Issues in assessment and intervention* (pp. 141–156). New York: Springer-Verlag.

Coie, J. D., & Dodge, K. A. (1983). Continuities and changes in children's social status: A five-year longitudinal study. *Merrill-Palmer Quarterly, 29*, 261–281.

Coie, J. D., & Dodge, K. A. (1988). Multiple sources of data on social behavior and social status in the school: A cross-age comparison. *Child Development, 59,* 815–829.

Coie, J., Dodge, K., & Coppotelli, H. (1982). Dimensions and types of social status: A cross-age perspective. *Developmental Psychology, 18,* 557–570.

Cullinan, D., & Epstein, M. H. (1985). Adjustment problems of mildly handicapped students. *Remedial and Special Education, 6,* 5–11.

Cullinan, D., Epstein, M., & Dembinski, R. J. (1979). Behavior problems of educationally handicapped and normal pupils. *Journal of Abnormal Child Psychology, 7,* 495–502.

Cullinan, D., Epstein, M. H., & Lloyd, J. (1981). School behavior problems of learning disabled and normal girls and boys. *Learning Disability Quarterly, 4,* 163–169.

Dodge, K. A., Coie, J. D., & Brakke, N. P. (1982). Behavior patterns of socially rejected and neglected preadolescents: The roles of social approach and aggression. *Journal of Abnormal Child Psychology, 10,* 389–410.

Flicek, M., & Landau, S. (1985). Social status problems of learning disabled and hyperactive/learning disabled boys. *Journal of Clinical Child Psychology, 14,* 340–344.

Garrett, M. K., & Crump, W. D. (1980). Peer acceptance, teacher preference, and self-appraisal of social status among learning disabled students. *Learning Disability Quarterly, 3,* 42–48.

Gottman, J. M., Gonso, J., & Rasmussen, B. (1975). Social interaction, social competence, and friendship in children. *Child Development, 46,* 709–718.

Green, K. D., Forehand, R., Beck, S. J., & Vosk, B. (1980). An assessment of the relationship among measures of children's social competence and children's academic achievement. *Child Development, 51,* 1149–1156.

Gregory, J. F., Shanahan, T., & Walberg, H. (1985). Learning disabled 10th graders in mainstreamed settings: A descriptive analysis. *Remedial and Special Education, 6,* 25–33.

Gresham, F., & Reschly, D. (1986). Social skill deficits and low peer acceptance of mainstreamed learning disabled children. *Learning Disability Quarterly, 9,* 23–32.

Harter, S. (1982). The Perceived Competence Scale for Children. *Child Development, 53,* 87–97.

Harter, S. (1985). *Manual for the Self Perception Profile for Children.* Denver, CO: Author.

Hops, H. (1988). February. *Impact of classroom setting on social interactions.* Presented at the International Academy for Research in Learning Disabilities. Los Angeles.

Horowitz, E. (1981). Popularity, decentering ability, and role-taking skills in LD and normal children. *Learning Disability Quarterly, 4,* 23–30.

Hoyle, S. G., & Serafica, F. C. (1987, April). *Social stereotyping in children with learning disabilities: Myth or reality?* Poster presented at the Biennial Meeting of the Society for Research in Child Development, Baltimore, MD.

Hutton, J. B., & Polo, L. (1976). A sociometric study of learning disability children and type of teaching strategy. *Group Psychotherapy, Psychodrama, and Sociometry, 29,* 113–120.

La Greca, A. M. (1981). Social behavior and social perception in learning disabled children: A review with implications for social skills training. *Journal of Pediatric Psychology, 6,* 395–416.

La Greca, A. M. (1987). Children with learning disabilities: Interpersonal skills and social competence. *Journal of Reading, Writing, and Learning Disabilities International, 3,* 167–185.

La Greca, A. M., Dandes, S. K., Wick, P., Shaw, K., & Stone, W. L. (1988). Development of the Social Anxiety Scale for Children: Reliability and concurrent validity. *Journal of Clinical Child Psychology, 17,* 84–91.

La Greca, A. M., & Mesibov, G. B. (1979). Social skills intervention with learning disabled children: Selecting skills and implementing training. *Journal of Clinical Child Psychology, 8,* 234–241.

La Greca, A. M., & Mesibov, G. B. (1981). Facilitating interpersonal functioning with peers in learning disabled children. *Journal of Learning Disabilities, 14,* 197–199, 238.

La Greca, A. M., & Stone, W. L. (1988). *Social Anxiety Scale for Children - Revised: Relationship with peer, self, and teacher ratings.* Manuscript submitted for publication.

La Greca, A. M., Stone, W. L., & Halpern, D. (1988, February). *LD status and achievement:*

Confounding variables in the study of children's social and behavioral functioning? Presented at the International Academy for Research in Learning Disabilities, Los Angeles.

Lambert, N. M., & Sandoval, J. (1980). The prevalence of learning disabilities in a sample of children considered hyperactive. *Journal of Abnormal Child Psychology, 8,* 33–50.

Ledingham, J. E., & Schwartzman, A. E. (1984). A 3-year follow-up of aggressive and withdrawn behavior in childhood: Preliminary findings. *Journal of Abnormal Child Psychology, 12,* 157–168.

Madden, N. A., & Slavin, R. E. (1983). Mainstreaming students with mild handicaps: Academic and social outcomes. *Review of Educational Research, 53,* 519–569.

McConaughy, S. H. (1986). Social competence and behavioral problems of learning disabled boys aged 12–16. *Journal of Learning Disabilities, 19,* 101–106.

McConaughy, S. H., & Ritter, D. R. (1986). Social competence and behavioral problems of learning disabled boys aged 6–11. *Journal of Learning Disabilities, 19,* 39–45.

McKinney, J. D., & Feagans, L. (1984). Academic and behavioral characteristics of learning disabled children and average achievers: Longitudinal studies. *Learning Disability Quarterly, 7,* 251–265.

Morrison, G. M. (1985). Differences in teacher perceptions and student self-perceptions for learning disabled and nonhandicapped learners in regular and special education settings. *Learning Disabilities Research, 1,* 32–41.

Oden, S., & Asher, S. (1977). Coaching children in social skills for friendship making. *Child Development, 48,* 495–506.

Perlmutter, B. F., Crocker, J., Cordray, D., & Garstecki, D. (1983). Sociometric status and related personality characteristics of mainstreamed learning disabled adolescents. *Learning Disability Quarterly, 6,* 20–30.

Prillaman, D. (1981). Acceptance of learning disabled students in a mainstream environment: A failure to replicate. *Journal of Learning Disabilities, 14,* 344–352.

Quay, H. C., & Peterson, D. R. (1987). *Manual for the Revised Behavior Problem Checklist.* Miami, FL: Authors.

Renick, M. J. (1985). *The development of learning disabled children's self perceptions.* Unpublished master's thesis, University of Denver.

Rogers, H., & Saklofske, D. H. (1985). Self-concepts, locus of control and performance expectations of learning disabled children. *Journal of Learning Disabilities, 18,* 273–278.

Rubin, K. H. (1985). Socially withdrawn children: An "at risk" population? In B. H. Schneider, K. H. Rubin, & J. E. Ledingham (Eds.), *Children's peer relations: Issues in assessment and intervention* (pp. 125–140). New York: Springer-Verlag.

Sabornie, E. J., & Kauffman, J. M. (1986). Social acceptance of learning disabled adolescents. *Learning Disability Quarterly, 9,* 55–60.

Schumaker, J. B., & Hazel, J. S. (1984). Social skills assessment and training for the learning disabled: Who's on first and what's on second? Part I. *Journal of Learning Disabilities, 17,* 442–431.

Scranton, T., & Ryckman, D. (1979). Sociometric status of LD children in an integrative program. *Journal of Learning Disabilities, 12,* 49–54.

Sheare, J. B. (1978). The impact of resource programs upon the self-concept and peer acceptance of learning disabled children. *Psychology in the Schools, 15,* 406–412.

Silverman, R., & Zigmond, N. (1983). Self-concept in learning disabled adolescents. *Journal of Learning Disabilities, 16,* 478–482.

Singleton, L. C., & Asher, S. R. (1977). Peer preferences and social interaction among third-grade children in an integrated school district. *Journal of Educational Research, 69,* 330–336.

Siperstein, G., Bopp, M., & Bak, J. (1978). Social status of LD children. *Journal of Learning Disabilities, 11,* 49–51.

Siperstein, G., & Goding, M. J. (1983). Social integration of learning disabled children in regular classrooms. *Advances in Learning and Behavioral Disabilities. 2,* 227–263.

Sobol, M. P., Earn, B. M., Bennett, D., & Humphries, T. (1983). A categorical analysis of social attributions of learning-disabled children. *Journal of Abnormal Child Psychology, 11,* 217–228.

Speece, D. L., McKinney, J. D. & Appelbaum, M. I. (1985). Classification and validation of behavioral subtypes of learning-disabled children. *Journal of Educational Psychology, 77,* 67–77.

Stone, W. L., & La Greca, A. M. (1984). Comprehension of nonverbal communication: A reexamination of the social competencies of learning disabled children. *Journal of Abnormal Child Psychology, 12,* 205.

Stone, W. L., & La Greca, A. M. (in press). The social status of children with learning disabilities: A reexamination. *Journal of Learning Disabilities.*

Vaughn, S. R., & La Greca, A. M. (1988). Social interventions for learning disabilities. In K. A. Kavale (Ed.), *Learning disabilities: State of the art and practice* (pp. 123–140). Boston, MA: College-Hill Press.

Vaughn, S., Lancelotta, G. X., & Minnis, S. (1988). Social strategy training and peer involvement: Increasing peer acceptance of a female LD student. *Learning Disabilities Focus, 4,* 32–37.

Wiener, J. (1987). Peer status of learning disabled children and adolescents: A review of the literature. *Learning Disabilities Research, 2,* 62–79.

Author Index

Numbers in *italics* denote pages with complete bibliographic information.

A

Aaron, P. G., 279, 294, *295*
Abelson, R. P., 144, *152*
Achenbach, T. M., 155, 156, 166, *172*, 178, *188*, 205, *211*, 216, 217, *227*, 315, *327*, *328*
Ackerman, P. L., 55, *56*
Adams, K. M., 202, 205, *211*
Adelman, H. S., 195, *198*, *199*, 215, *227*
Akiyama, K., 321, *328*
Aldenderfer, M. S., 208, 209, *211*, 221, *227*
Alegria, J., 264, *275*
Alessi, N. E., 325, *327*
Alexson, J., 324, *327*, *329*, *331*
Algozzine, B., 15, *19*, 25, *39*, 197, *200*, 236, *243*, *245*, 315, *327*
Allen, A. A., 254, 256, *259*
Alley, G. R. 27, *36*, *38*, 140, *152*, 248, *260*
Allington, R. L., 81, 85, 89, *90*, 247, *260*
Ambrosini, P., *331*
Anderberg, M. R., 208, *211* , 221, *227*
Anders, P. L., 9, 248, 251, 252, 254, 256, *259*
Anderson, B. J., 300, *313*
Anderson, G., 318, *331*

Anderson, J. R., *35*, 47, 48, 55, *56*, 233, *243*
Anderson, L. M., 27, *36*
Anderson, M. C., 249, *259*
Anderson, R. C., 81, *91*, 248, 249, 251, *259*, 277, *295*
Andrist, C. G., 95, 106, *109*
Anthony, H., 27, *36*
Appelbaum, M., 93, 105, *109*, 196, *199*, *200*, 204, 205, 206, 208, 210, *211*, *213*, 341, *352*
Appolloni, T., 316, *332*
Arnold, L. E., 115, 123, *126*
Ashcraft, M. H., 49, *56*
Asher, S. R., 133, *138*, 177, 182, 185, *188*, *191*, 336, 343, *349*, *351*
Atkinson, R. C., 299, *313*
Ayers, R. R., 177, *189*

B

Bacon, G., *313*
Bailey, D. E., 221, *230*
Bak, J., 334, *350*
Baker, J. G., 27, *35*, 60, 67, 72
Bakker, D. J., 15, *19*
Ball, E. W., 264, 271, *275*

353

Subject Index